New Zealand

"When it comes to information on regional history, what to see and do, and shopping, these guides are exhaustive."

—*USAir Magazine*

"Usable, sophisticated restaurant coverage, with an emphasis on good value."

—Andy Birsh, *Gourmet Magazine* columnist

"Valuable because of their comprehensiveness."

—*Minneapolis Star-Tribune*

"Fodor's always delivers high quality...thoughtfully presented...thorough."

—*Houston Post*

"An excellent choice for those who want everything under one cover."

—*Washington Post*

Fodor's Travel Publications, Inc.
New York • Toronto • London • Sydney • Auckland
http://www.fodors.com/

Fodor's New Zealand

Editor: Stephen Wolf

Contributors: Steven Amsterdam, Robert Andrews, Bob Blake, Barbara Blechman, David Brown, Audra Epstein, Stu Freeman, Nick Lund, Helayne Schiff, Mary Ellen Schultz, Linda K. Schmidt, M. T. Schwartzman (Gold Guide editor), Dinah Spritzer

Creative Director: Fabrizio LaRocca

Cartographers: David Lindroth; Mapping Specialists

Cover Photograph: Tony Stone Images

Text Design: Between the Covers

Copyright

Fourth Edition

ISBN 0-679-03264-9

Special Sales

Fodor's Travel Publications are available at special discounts for bulk purchases for sales promotions or premiums. Special editions, including personalized covers, excerpts of existing guides, and corporate imprints, can be created in large quantities for special needs. For more information, contact your local bookseller or write to Special Markets, Fodor's Travel Publications, 201 East 50th Street, New York, NY 10022. Inquiries from Canada should be directed to your local Canadian bookseller or sent to Random House of Canada, Ltd., Marketing Department, 1265 Aerowood Drive, Mississauga, Ontario L4W 1B9. Inquiries from the United Kingdom should be sent to Fodor's Travel Publications, 20 Vauxhall Bridge Road, London, England SW1V 2SA.

PRINTED IN THE UNITED STATES OF AMERICA

10 9 8 7 6 5 4 3 2 1

CONTENTS

ON THE ROAD WITH FODOR'S

WE'RE ALWAYS THRILLED to get letters from readers, especially one like this:

It took us an hour to decide what book to buy and we now know we picked the best one. Your book was wonderful, easy to follow, very accurate, and good on pointing out eating places, informal as well as formal. When we saw other people using your book, we would look at each other and smile.

Our editors and writers are deeply committed to making every Fodor's guide "the best one"—not only accurate but always charming, brimming with sound recommendations and solid ideas, right on the mark in describing restaurants and hotels, and full of fascinating facts that make you view what you've traveled to see in a rich new light.

About Our Writers

Our success in achieving our goals—and in helping to make your trip the best of all possible vacations—is a credit to the hard work of our extraordinary writers and editors.

Michael Gebicki wrote the first edition of this book. British by birth, American by education, and Australian since 1979—after a stint living in New Zealand in his youth—he now works as a freelance travel writer and photographer based in Sydney. Dashing articles about his global wanderings appear regularly in travel publications in North America, Europe, and Asia.

This year's man on the islands, **Stu Freeman,** like most Kiwis, loves to get out into the bush on a regular basis, watch rugby, toss back a pint every now and then. He escaped the life of a daily newspaper journalist in the early 80s, threw a pack on his back, and tramped through Asia and Europe. Since then he's been freelance writing about New Zealand and the South Pacific.

Painter, garden designer, and passionate traveler **Barbara Blechman** took her expertise halfway around the world on reports that New Zealand is one of the finest places for growing just about anything. She found it to be a gardener's paradise, which accounts for the horticultural shock she experienced on returning to the island of Manhattan, where she lives, plants, and dreams of antipodean flora.

By a timely turn of fate, **Stephen Wolf** was assigned to edit Fodor's *New Zealand '96,* which led to a trip to the country last November to do first-hand research—a tremendous editorial boon—for this year's guide. So began three weeks of strenuous bushwalking, the sampling of a necessary variety of New Zealand wine (solely for the purpose of research), driving on the wrong side of impossibly narrow and precipitous roads, tasting as much local seafood as was reasonably possible (more research), and—just read this book and you'll find out what else.

The breath of new life into this year's guide, part of which comes out of an editorial reconnaissance trip to glorious New Zealand, owes a debt of gratitude to a number of people and organizations. First and foremost, thanks go to James Boyd of Air New Zealand, Kim Wong of the New Zealand Tourism Board, and Allen and Cait Falck of Mt. Cook Airlines for their generous support. A slew of Kiwis also deserve mention and thanks for their help and hospitality: Doug Johansen and Jan Poole, Jan and Paul Preston-Campbell, Pam Gwynne, Keith and Bertha Anderson, Elaine Gill, Gwynneth Masters, Jo and Bob Munro, David Brown, Sara Darby, Bridget Molyneux, Deborah and Grant Baxter, Shelley and Neil Johnston, Michelle Kinney, Ernst and Sabine Wipperfuerth, Birgit and Monty Claxton, Mr. Anne Bastiaans, Rachel and Dr. Gerry McSweeney, Louisa and Cliff Hobson-Corry, Carol and Bruce Hyland, Ross Morley, and on the home turf Caroline Haberfeld and Karen Cure.

New This Year

This year we've reformatted our guides to make them easier to use. Each chapter of *Fodor's New Zealand* begins with brand-new recommended itineraries to help you decide what to see in the time you have; a section called When to Tour points out the optimal time of day, day of the week, and season for your journey. You may also notice our fresh graphics, new in 1996. More readable and more helpful than ever? We think so—and we hope you do, too.

We have a great edition this year: adding 64 pages of new regional coverage, gardens to tour, fantastic hikes, and the very best in New Zealand wineries. Based on his local expertise, Stu Freeman has written brand-new material on Gisborne and the East Cape, Taranaki, the Wairarapa, Marlborough, Wanaka, and a number of sites and activities around the country. Barbara Blechman turned her energies toward the glorious gardens of New Zealand, writing for professionals and weekend gardeners alike. (Kiwi gardens are spectacular, and more and more people are visiting the country to see them.) And Stephen Wolf has added a crop of restaurants, lodges, wineries, occasional advice, and whatever else happened to wow him on his recent trip from Auckland down to Queenstown.

On the Web

Also check out Fodor's Web site (http://www.fodors.com/), where you'll find travel information on major destinations around the world and an ever-changing array of travel-savvy interactive features.

How to Use This Book

Organization

Up front is the **Gold Guide.** Its first section, **Important Contacts A to Z,** gives addresses and telephone numbers of organizations and companies that offer destination-related services and detailed information and publications. **Smart Travel Tips A to Z,** the Gold Guide's second section, gives specific information on how to accomplish what you need to in New Zealand as well as tips on savvy traveling. Both sections are in alphabetical order by topic.

Chapters in *Fodor's New Zealand* are arranged two-per-island. There happens to be more to cover in the lower parts of both North and South islands, so chapters 3 and 5 are the longest. All chapters are broken into geographical areas; within each area, towns are covered in logical geographical

order, and attractive stretches of road and minor points of interest between them are indicated by the designation *En Route*. Throughout, Off the Beaten Path sights appear after the places from which they are most easily accessible. And within town sections, all restaurants and lodgings are grouped together.

To help you decide what to visit in the time you have, all chapters begin with recommended itineraries; you can mix and match those from several chapters to create a complete vacation. The A to Z sections at the end of each region covers getting there, getting around, and helpful contacts and resources.

We also have a chapter called Adventure Vacations, which covers a number of outdoor activities and tour guides that can help you get the most out of them while you're in New Zealand. The advantage of using local guides is that they know the territory very well, and they will educate you about animals and plants you're seeing, which can be very exotic. They can also be quite entertaining. So don't pass up Chapter 6.

At the end of the book you'll find Portraits—a chronology of New Zealand history and a shortlist of local flora and fauna—followed by suggestions for pretrip reading, both fiction and nonfiction, and movies on tape with New Zealand as a backdrop.

Icons and Symbols

★ Our special recommendations
✕ Restaurant
🏨 Lodging establishment
✕🏨 Lodging establishment whose restaurant warrants a detour
⚠ Campgrounds
☺ Good for kids (rubber duckie)
☞ Sends you to another section of the guide for more information
✉ Address
☎ Telephone number
☉ Opening and closing times
💰 Admission prices (those we give apply only to adults; substantially reduced fees are almost always available for children, students, and senior citizens)

Numbers in white and black circles—② and ❷, for example—that appear on the maps, in the margins, and within the tours correspond to one another.

Dining and Lodging

The restaurants and lodgings we list are the cream of the crop in each price range. Price categories are as follows:

For restaurants:

CATEGORY	COST*
$$$$	over $45
$$$	$35–$45
$$	$25–$35
$	under $25

*per person, excluding drinks, service, and general sales tax (GST, 12.5%)

For hotels:

CATEGORY	COST*
$$$$	over $200
$$$	$125–$200
$$	$80–$125
$	under $80

*All prices are for a standard double room, excluding general sales tax (GST, 12.5%).

Hotel Facilities

We always list the facilities that are available—but we don't specify whether they cost extra: When pricing accommodations, always ask what's included.

Restaurant Reservations and Dress Codes

Reservations are always a good idea; we note only when they're essential or when they are not accepted. Book as far ahead as you can, and reconfirm when you get to town. Unless otherwise noted, the restaurants listed are open daily for lunch and dinner. We mention dress only when men are required to wear a jacket or a jacket and tie. Look for an overview of local habits in the Pleasures and Pastimes section that follows each chapter introduction.

Credit Cards

The following abbreviations are used: **AE**, American Express; **DC**, Diners Club; **MC**, MasterCard; and **V**, Visa.

Don't Forget to Write

You can use this book in the confidence that all prices and opening times are based on information supplied to us at press time; Fodor's cannot accept responsibility for any errors. Time inevitably brings changes, so always confirm information when it matters—especially if you're making a detour to visit a specific place. In addition, when making reservations be sure to mention if you have a disability or are traveling with children, if you prefer a private bath or a certain type of bed, or if you have specific dietary needs or any other concerns.

Were the restaurants we recommended as described? Did our hotel picks exceed your expectations? Did you find a museum we recommended a waste of time? If you have complaints, we'll look into them and revise our entries when the facts warrant it. If you've discovered a special place that we haven't included, we'll pass the information along to our correspondents and have them check it out. So send your feedback, positive *and* negative, to the New Zealand editor at 201 East 50th Street, New York, New York 10022—and have a wonderful trip!

Karen Cure
Editorial Director

New Zealand

Cape Reinga — North Cape
Te Kao
Bay of Islands
NORTHLAND
Whangarei — Hauraki Gulf — Great Barrier Island
Dargaville — (1)
Coromandel Peninsula
Auckland — Tairua
Thames — Whangamata
Port Waikato — (1) Tauranga — Bay of Plenty — Cape Runaway
Hamilton — Tikitiki
WAIKATO — EASTLAND
(3) Rotorua — Urewera N.P. — (2)
NORTH ISLAND — Gisborne
North Taranaki Bight — Lake Taupo
Taupo
New Plymouth — HAWKE'S
TAKANAKI — Tongariro N.P. — BAY — Hawke Bay
Cape Egmont — Stratford
(3) Wanganui — Napier
Hastings
Palmerston North — (1) (2)
Tasman Sea
ABEL TASMAN N.P.
Cape Farewell
Tasman Bay
N.W. Nelson Forest Park — Picton — Tararua Forest Park — Upper Hutt — Masterton
NELSON — Nelson
BAYS — WAIRARAPA
Blenheim — Wellington
Cape Foulwind — MARLBOROUGH
(6)
Lake Summer Forest Park — (1) Kaikoura
Greymouth
Hokitika — Arthur's Pass N.P.
WEST — CANTERBURY
COAST — Christchurch
WESTLAND N.P. — Franz Josef
Fox Glacier — Mt. COOK N.P. — Akaroa — Banks Peninsula
Haast — (6) — Ashburton
Haast River — Southern Alps — (8) — Timaru
Mt. Aspiring — AORANGI — Waitaki R.
Milford Sound — Wanaka — SOUTH ISLAND
Lake Te Anau — Queenstown — Oamaru
Lake Wakatipu
Te Anau — (8) — SOUTH PACIFIC OCEAN
Lake Manapouri — OTAGO — Dunedin
SOUTHLAND
FIORDLAND N.P. — (6) (1)
Foveaux Strait — Invercargill
Halfmoon Bay
Stewart Island

N

KEY
— Rail Lines

0 — 200 miles
0 — 300 km

x

NORTH ISLAND

Cape Reinga
Kerr Point
Te Kao
Ninety Mile Beach
Bay of Islands
Kaitaia
Russell
NORTHLAND
Whangarei
Dargaville
Matakohe
Port Jackson
Coromandel
Great Barrier Island
Hauraki Gulf
Coromandel Peninsula
Whitianga
Coroglen
Auckland
Tapu
Tairua
Firth of Thames
Thames
Whangamata
Waiuku
Paeroa
Tauranga
Cape Runaway
Te Araroa
Port Waikato
Te Puke
Bay of Plenty
Hamilton
Whakatone
Opotiki
Cambridge
Raglan
Rotorua
EAST CAPE
Waitomo Caves
Tokomaru Bay
Marakopa
UREWERA N.P.
Gisborne
Tasman Sea
North Taranaki Bight
Awakino
Lake Taupo
Taupo
TONGARIRO
New Plymouth
HAWKE'S BAY
Hawke Bay
MT. Egmont
Inglewood
TONGARIRO N.P.
Cape Egmont
Stratford
Mt. Ruapehu
Napier
Taihape
Hastings
WANGANUI
Wanganui
Bulls
Palmerston North
MANAWATU
ABEL TASMAN NATIONAL PARK
TARARUA FOREST PARK
WAIRARAPA
Cape Farewell
Farewell Spit
Golden Bay
Waikane
Masterton
N.W. NELSON FOREST PARK
Tasman Bay
Upper Hutt
Martinborough
Motueka
Lower Hutt
Cook Strait
Wellington
NELSON BAYS
Nelson
Blenheim
Seddon
MARLBOROUGH
Cape Foulwind
Murchison
NELSON LAKES FOREST PARK
Kekerengu
Punakaiki
Grey R.
Greymouth
Hanmer Springs
Kaikoura
LAKE SUMNER FOREST PARK
ARTHURS PASS N.P.
MT. COOK N.P.
Christchurch
Dunedin
SOUTH PACIFIC OCEAN

KEY
Rail Lines
N
0   100 miles
0   150 km

South Island

Inglewood
Cape Egmont
Mt. Egmont
Stratford
③
Wanganui

ABEL TASMAN NATIONAL PARK
Cape Farewell
Farewell Spit
Golden Bay
N.W. NELSON FOREST PARK
Tasman Bay
Waikane
Upper Hutt
Wellington
Cook Strait

SOUTH ISLAND

Motueka
NELSON BAYS
Nelson
Blenheim
⑥
MARLBOROUGH
Seddon
Kekerengu
①

Cape Foulwind
Murchison
NELSON LAKES FOREST PARK
Kaikoura

Punakaiki
Greg R.
LAKE SUMMER FOREST PARK
Hanmer Springs

Greymouth
WEST COAST
Hokitika
ARTHURS PASS N. P.
Hawarden

CANTERBURY
Christchurch

Franz Josef
Fox Glacier
MT. COOK N. P.
Mt. Cook Village
Lake Tekapo
Ashburton
Okains Bay
Akaroa

Lake Moeraki
⑥
Lake Pukaki
⑧
Fairlee
AORANGI
Timaru

Haast
Haast River
Southern Alps
Mt. Aspiring
Lake Wanaka

Milford Sound
Wanaka
Arrowtown
Lake Wakatipu
Queenstown
OTAGO
Oamaru

Doubtful Sound
Lake Te Anau
COASTAL NORTH OTAGO
⑧

Lake Manapouri
Te Anau
Lumsden
OTAGO
Dunedin

SOUTHLAND
⑥
①
Balclutha

SOUTH PACIFIC OCEAN

FIORDLAND N. P.
Invercargill

Foveaux St.

Halfmoon Bay
Stewart Island

Muttonbird Islands

N

KEY
— Rail Lines
0   100 miles
0   150 km

World Time Zones

Numbers below vertical bands relate each zone to Greenwich Mean Time (0 hrs.).
Local times frequently differ from these general indications,
as indicated by light-face numbers on map.

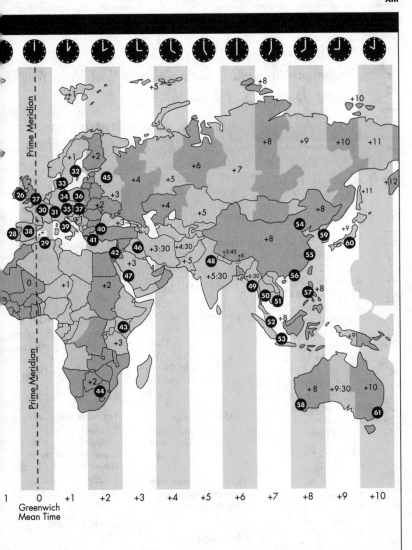

Prime Meridian

0
Greenwich
Mean Time

+1 +2 +3 +4 +5 +6 +7 +8 +9 +10

Mecca, **47**
Mexico City, **12**
Miami, **18**
Montréal, **15**
Moscow, **45**
Nairobi, **43**
New Orleans, **11**
New York City, **16**

Ottawa, **14**
Paris, **30**
Perth, **58**
Reykjavík, **25**
Rio de Janeiro, **23**
Rome, **39**
Saigon (Ho Chi Minh City), **51**

San Francisco, **5**
Santiago, **21**
Seoul, **59**
Shanghai, **55**
Singapore, **52**
Stockholm, **32**
Sydney, **61**
Tokyo, **60**

Toronto, **13**
Vancouver, **4**
Vienna, **35**
Warsaw, **36**
Washington, D.C., **17**
Yangon, **49**
Zürich, **31**

IMPORTANT CONTACTS A TO Z

An Alphabetical Listing of Publications, Organizations, and Companies that Will Help You Before, During, and After Your Trip

A

AIR TRAVEL

The major gateway to **New Zealand** is Auckland International Airport (☎ 09/275–0789).

FLYING TIMES

From New York to Auckland (via Los Angeles) it takes about 19 hours; from Chicago, about 17 hours; from Los Angeles to Auckland (nonstop), about 12 hours. Flights from London to Auckland take about 24 hours, either via the U.S. or via Southeast Asia. These are all actual air hours and do not include ground time.

CARRIERS

IN THE U.S. AND CANADA➤ **Air New Zealand** (☎ 800/262–1234 and 310/615–1111 in the U.S., 800/663–5494 in Canada) and **Qantas** (☎ 800/227–4500 in the U.S. and Canada) fly from Los Angeles to New Zealand, nonstop and direct. **United** (☎ 800/538–2929 in the U.S.) and **Air Canada** connect from points in North America with flights of their own out of L.A. Air New Zealand is the only carrier with direct flights from North America to Christchurch as well as Auckland.

IN THE U.K.➤ **British Airways, Cathay Pacific,**

Japan Airlines, Qantas, and **Singapore Airlines** (☎ 0171/439–8111) operate between London and Auckland, with a stopover in Asia. **Air New Zealand** (☎ 0181/741–2299) and **United** (☎ 0181/990–9900) operate between London and Auckland by way of the United States.

COMPLAINTS

To register complaints about charter and scheduled airlines, contact the U.S. Department of Transportation's **Aviation Consumer Protection Division** (☒ C-75, Washington, DC 20590, ☎ 202/366–2220). Complaints about lost baggage or ticketing problems and safety concerns may also be logged with the **Federal Aviation Administration (FAA) Consumer Hotline** (☎ 800/322–7873).

CONSOLIDATORS

For the names of reputable air-ticket consolidators, contact the **United States Air Consolidators Association** (☒ 925 L St., Suite 220, Sacramento, CA 95814, ☎ 916/441–4166, FAX 916/441–3520). For discount air-ticketing agencies, call 800/FLY–4–LESS in the U.S.

DISCOUNT PASSES

☞ Travel Passes *in* Smart Travel Tips A to Z.

PUBLICATIONS

For general information about charter carriers, ask for the Department of Transportation's free brochure **"Plane Talk: Public Charter Flights"** (☒ Aviation Consumer Protection Division, C-75, Washington, DC 20590, ☎ 202/366–2220). The Department of Transportation also publishes a 58-page booklet, **"Fly Rights,"** available from the Consumer Information Center (☒ Supt. of Documents, Dept. 136C, Pueblo, CO 81009; $1.75).

For other tips and hints, consult the Consumers Union's monthly **"Consumer Reports Travel Letter"** (☒ Box 53629, Boulder, CO 80322, ☎ 800/234–1970; $39 1st year).

WITHIN NEW ZEALAND

The major domestic airlines are **Air New Zealand** (☎ 09/357–3000) and **Ansett New Zealand** (☎ 09/302–2146). The two compete on intercity trunk routes. **Mount Cook Airline** (☎ toll-free in N.Z. 0800/800–737) is an Air New Zealand affiliate that flies between a few North Island and a number of South Island cities, including resort and adventure activity areas.

B

For local contacts in the hometown of a tour operator you may be considering, consult the **Council of Better Business Bureaus** (✉ 4200 Wilson Blvd., Suite 800, Arlington, VA 22203, ☎ 703/276–0100, FAX 703/525–8277).

BUS TRAVEL

InterCity (☎ 09/357–8400) is a major bus line, and also operates the railroad system. The other major operators in North Island are **Newmans** (☎ 09/309–9738) and **Mount Cook Landline–Gray Line** (☎ toll-free in the U.S.: 800/468–2665, or 310/640–2823 in L.A.; in Canada: 800/999–9306; in the U.K. 081/741–5652; and toll-free in N.Z.: 0800/800–287).

C

CAR RENTAL

The major car-rental companies represented in New Zealand are **Avis** (☎ 800/331–1084; in Canada, 800/879–2847), **Budget** (☎ 800/527–0700; in the U.K., 0800/181181), and **Hertz** (☎ 800/654–3001; in Canada, 800/263–0600; in the U.K., 0345/555888). Rates in New Zealand begin at $48 a day and $298 a week for an economy car with unlimited mileage. This does not include tax on car rentals, which is 12.5%.

The New Zealand company **Mauitours** (☎ 800/351–2323; in Canada, 800/663–2002; in the U.K., 1737/843242; in New Zealand, 09/275–3013) rents cars as well as the popular campervans.

CHILDREN & TRAVEL

FLYING

Look into **"Flying with Baby"** (✉ Third Street Press, Box 261250, Littleton, CO 80163, ☎ 303/595–5959; $4.95 includes shipping), cowritten by a flight attendant. **"Kids and Teens in Flight,"** free from the U.S. Department of Transportation's Aviation Consumer Protection Division (✉ C-75, Washington, DC 20590, ☎ 202/366–2220), offers tips on children flying alone. Every two years the February issue of *Family Travel Times* (☞ Know-How, *below*) details children's services on three dozen airlines. **"Flying Alone, Handy Advice for Kids Traveling Solo"** is available free from the American Automobile Association (AAA) (✉ send stamped, self-addressed, legal-size envelope: Flying Alone, Mail Stop 800, 1000 AAA Dr., Heathrow, FL 32746).

KNOW-HOW

Family Travel Times, published quarterly by Travel with Your Children (✉ TWYCH, 40 5th Ave., New York, NY 10011, ☎ 212/477–5524; $40 per year), covers destinations, types of vacations, and modes of travel.

STROLLER AND BASSINET RENTAL

Strollers and bassinets can be rented from the **Royal New Zealand Plunket Society** (✉ 10 Halver St., Manurewa, Auckland, ☎ 09/267–5082).

CUSTOMS

IN THE U.S.

The **U.S. Customs Service** (✉ Box 7407, Washington, DC 20044, ☎ 202/927–6724) can answer questions on duty-free limits and publishes a helpful brochure, "Know Before You Go." For information on registering foreign-made articles, call 202/927–0540 or write U.S. Customs Service, Resource Management, 1301 Constitution Ave. NW, Washington DC, 20229.

COMPLAINTS➤ Note the inspector's badge number and write to the commissioner's office (✉ 1301 Constitution Ave. NW, Washington, DC 20229).

CANADIANS

Contact **Revenue Canada** (✉ 2265 St. Laurent Blvd. S, Ottawa, Ontario K1G 4K3, ☎ 613/993–0534) for a copy of the free brochure **"I Declare/Je Déclare"** and for details on duty-free limits. For recorded information (within Canada only), call 800/461–9999.

U.K. CITIZENS

HM Customs and Excise (✉ Dorset House, Stamford St., London SE1 9NG, ☎ 0171/202–4227) can answer questions about U.K. customs regulations and publishes a free pamphlet, **"A Guide for Travellers,"** detailing standard procedures and import rules.

D
DISABILITIES & ACCESSIBILITY

CAR RENTAL

Only **Budget** (☎ 800/527–0700 in the U.S. and Canada) offers cars fitted with hand controls, but these are limited. **Hertz** (☎ 800/654–3131 in the U.S., 800/263–0600 in Canada) will fit hand-held controls onto standard cars in some cities.

COMPLAINTS

To register complaints under the provisions of the Americans with Disabilities Act, contact the U.S. Department of Justice's **Disability Rights Section** (✉ Box 66738, Washington, DC 20035, ☎ 202/514–0301 or 800/514–0301, FAX 202/307–1198, TTY 202/514–0383 or 800/514–0383). For airline-related problems, contact the U.S. Department of Transportation's **Aviation Consumer Protection Division** (☞ Air Travel, *above*). For complaints about surface transportation, contact the Department of Transportation's **Civil Rights Office** (✉ 400 7th St., SW, Room 10215, Washington, DC 20590, ☎ 202/366–4648).

LODGING

The **New Zealand Tourism Board** (☎ 04/472–8860) publishes *Access: A Guide for the Less Mobile Traveller*, listing accommodations, attractions, restaurants, and thermal pools with special facilities. In New Zealand, all accommodations are required by law to provide at least one room with facilities for guests with disabilities.

ORGANIZATIONS

TRAVELERS WITH HEARING IMPAIRMENTS➤ The **American Academy of Otolaryngology** (✉ 1 Prince St., Alexandria, VA 22314, ☎ 703/836–4444, FAX 703/683–5100, TTY 703/519–1585) publishes a brochure, "Travel Tips for Hearing Impaired People."

TRAVELERS WITH MOBILITY PROBLEMS➤ Contact the **Information Center for Individuals with Disabilities** (✉ Box 256, Boston, MA 02117, ☎ 617/450–9888; in MA, 800/462–5015; TTY 617/424–6855); **Mobility International USA** (✉ Box 10767, Eugene, OR 97440, ☎ and TTY 541/343–1284, FAX 541/343–6812), the U.S. branch of a Belgium-based organization (☞ *below*) with affiliates in 30 countries; **MossRehab Hospital Travel Information Service** (☎ 215/456–9600, TTY 215/456–9602), a telephone information resource for travelers with physical disabilities; the **Society for the Advancement of Travel for the Handicapped** (✉ 347 5th Ave., Suite 610, New York, NY 10016, ☎ 212/447–7284, FAX 212/725–8253; membership $45); and **Travelin' Talk** (✉ Box 3534, Clarksville, TN 37043, ☎ 615/552–6670, FAX 615/552–1182), which provides local contacts worldwide for travelers with disabilities.

TRAVELERS WITH VISION IMPAIRMENTS➤ Contact the **American Council of the Blind** (✉ 1155 15th St. NW, Suite 720, Washington, DC 20005, ☎ 202/467–5081, FAX 202/467–5085) for a list of travelers' resources or the **American Foundation for the Blind** (✉ 11 Penn Plaza, Suite 300, New York, NY 10001, ☎ 212/502–7600 or 800/232–5463, TTY 212/502–7662), which provides general advice and publishes "Access to Art" ($19.95), a directory of museums that accommodate travelers with vision impairments.

IN THE U.K.

Contact the **Royal Association for Disability and Rehabilitation** (✉ RADAR, 12 City Forum, 250 City Rd., London EC1V 8AF, ☎ 0171/250–3222) or **Mobility International** (✉ rue de Manchester 25, B-1080 Brussels, Belgium, ☎ 00–322–410–6297, FAX 00–322–410–6874), an international travel-information clearinghouse for people with disabilities.

PUBLICATIONS

Several publications for travelers with disabilities are available from the **Consumer Information Center** (✉ Box 100, Pueblo, CO 81009, ☎ 719/948–3334). Call or write for its free catalog of current titles. The Society for the Advancement of Travel for the Handicapped (☞ Organizations, *above*) publishes the quarterly magazine **"Access to Travel"** ($13 for 1-year subscription).

The 500-page **Travelin' Talk Directory** (✉ Box 3534, Clarksville, TN 37043, ☎ 615/552–6670, FAX 615/552–

1182; $35) lists people and organizations who help travelers with disabilities. For travel agents worldwide, consult the *Directory of Travel Agencies for the Disabled* (⊠ Twin Peaks Press, Box 129, Vancouver, WA 98666, ☎ 360/694–2462 or 800/637–2256, FAX 360/696–3210; $19.95 plus $3 shipping).

TRAVEL AGENCIES & TOUR OPERATORS

The Americans with Disabilities Act requires that all travel firms serve the needs of all travelers. That said, you should note that some agencies and operators specialize in making travel arrangements for individuals and groups with disabilities, among them **Access Adventures** (⊠ 206 Chestnut Ridge Rd., Rochester, NY 14624, ☎ 716/889–9096).

TRAVELERS WITH MOBILITY PROBLEMS➤ Contact **Hinsdale Travel Service** (⊠ 201 E. Ogden Ave., Suite 100, Hinsdale, IL 60521, ☎ 708/325–1335), a travel agency that benefits from the advice of wheelchair traveler Janice Perkins; and **Wheelchair Journeys** (⊠ 16979 Redmond Way, Redmond, WA 98052, ☎ 206/885–2210 or 800/313–4751), which can handle arrangements worldwide.

TRAVELERS WITH DEVELOPMENTAL DISABILITIES➤ Contact the nonprofit **New Directions** (⊠ 5276 Hollister Ave., Suite 207, Santa Barbara, CA 93111, ☎ 805/967–2841).

TRAVEL GEAR

The **Magellan's** catalog (☎ 800/962–4943, FAX 805/568–5406) includes a section devoted to products designed for travelers with disabilities.

DISCOUNTS & DEALS

AIRFARES

For the lowest airfares to New Zealand, call 800/FLY–4–LESS.

CLUBS

Contact **Entertainment Travel Editions** (⊠ Box 1068, Trumbull, CT 06611, ☎ 800/445–4137; $28–$53, depending on destination), **Great American Traveler** (⊠ Box 27965, Salt Lake City, UT 84127, ☎ 800/548–2812; $49.95 per year), **Moment's Notice Discount Travel Club** (⊠ 7301 New Utrecht Ave., Brooklyn, NY 11204, ☎ 718/234–6295; $25 per year, single or family), **Privilege Card** (⊠ 3391 Peachtree Rd. NE, Suite 110, Atlanta, GA 30326, ☎ 404/262–0222 or 800/236–9732; $74.95 per year), **Travelers Advantage** (⊠ CUC Travel Service, 49 Music Sq. W, Nashville, TN 37203, ☎ 800/548–1116 or 800/648–4037; $49 per year, single or family), or **Worldwide Discount Travel Club** (⊠ 1674 Meridian Ave., Miami Beach, FL 33139, ☎ 305/534–2082; $50 per year for family, $40 single).

PASSES

☞ Bus Travel, Train Travel, *and* Air Travel *in* Smart Travel Tips A to Z.

STUDENTS

Members of Hostelling International–American Youth Hostels (☞ Students, *below*) are eligible for discounts on car rentals, admissions to attractions, and other selected travel expenses.

PUBLICATIONS

Consult *The Frugal Globetrotter,* by Bruce Northam (⊠ Fulcrum Publishing, 350 Indiana St., Suite 350, Golden, CO 80401, ☎ 800/992–2908; $16.95 plus $4 shipping). For publications that tell how to find the lowest prices on plane tickets, *see* Air Travel, *above.*

G
GAY & LESBIAN TRAVEL

ORGANIZATIONS

The **International Gay Travel Association** (⊠ Box 4974, Key West, FL 33041, ☎ 800/448–8550, FAX 305/296–6633), a consortium of more than 1,000 travel companies, can supply names of gay-friendly travel agents, tour operators, and accommodations.

PUBLICATIONS

The premier international travel magazine for gays and lesbians is *Our World* (⊠ 1104 N. Nova Rd., Suite 251, Daytona Beach, FL 32117, ☎ 904/441–5367, FAX 904/441–5604; $35 for 10 issues). The 16-page monthly **"Out & About"** (☎ 212/645–6922 or 800/929–2268, FAX 800/929–2215; $49 for 10 issues and quarterly calendar) covers gay-friendly resorts, hotels, cruise lines, and airlines.

TOUR OPERATORS

Toto Tours (⊠ 1326 W. Albion Ave., Suite 3W, Chicago, IL 60626, ☎ 312/274–8686 or 800/565–1241, FAX 312/274–8695) offers group tours to worldwide destinations.

TRAVEL AGENCIES

The largest agencies serving gay travelers are **Advance Travel** (⊠ 10700 Northwest Fwy., Suite 160, Houston, TX 77092, ☎ 713/682–2002 or 800/292–0500), **Islanders/Kennedy Travel** (⊠ 183 W. 10th St., New York, NY 10014, ☎ 212/242–3222 or 800/988–1181), **Now Voyager** (⊠ 4406 18th St., San Francisco, CA 94114, ☎ 415/626–1169 or 800/255–6951), and **Yellowbrick Road** (⊠ 1500 W. Balmoral Ave., Chicago, IL 60640, ☎ 312/561–1800 or 800/642–2488). **Skylink Women's Travel** (⊠ 2460 W. 3rd St., Suite 215, Santa Rosa, CA 95401, ☎ 707/570–0105 or 800/225–5759) serves lesbian travelers.

H
HEALTH

MEDICAL ASSISTANCE COMPANIES

The following companies are concerned primarily with emergency medical assistance, although they may provide some insurance as part of their coverage. For a list of full-service travel insurance companies, *see* Insurance, *below*.

Contact **International SOS Assistance** (⊠ Box 11568, Philadelphia, PA 19116, ☎ 215/244–1500 or 800/523–8930; Box 466, Pl. Bonaventure, Montréal, Québec H5A 1C1, ☎ 514/874–7674 or 800/363–0263; 7 Old Lodge Pl., St. Margarets, Twickenham TW1 1RQ, England, ☎ 0181/744–0033), **Medex Assistance Corporation** (⊠ Box 5375, Timonium, MD 21094-5375, ☎ 410/453–6300 or 800/537–2029), **Traveler's Emergency Network** (⊠ 3100 Tower Blvd., Suite 3100A, Durham, NC 27702, ☎ 919/490–6065 or 800/275–4836, FAX 919/493–8262), **TravMed** (⊠ Box 5375, Timonium, MD 21094, ☎ 410/453–6380 or 800/732–5309), or **Worldwide Assistance Services** (⊠ 1133 15th St. NW, Suite 400, Washington, DC 20005, ☎ 202/331–1609 or 800/821–2828, FAX 202/828–5896).

I
INSURANCE

IN CANADA

Contact **Mutual of Omaha** (⊠ Travel Division, 500 University Ave., Toronto, Ontario M5G 1V8, ☎ 800/465–0267 in Canada, or 416/598-4083).

IN THE U.S.

Travel insurance covering baggage, health, and trip cancellation or interruptions is available from **Access America** (⊠ 6600 W. Broad St., Richmond, VA 23230, ☎ 804/285–3300 or 800/334–7525), **Carefree Travel Insurance** (⊠ Box 9366, 100 Garden City Plaza, Garden City, NY 11530, ☎ 516/294–0220 or 800/323–3149), **Near Travel Services** (⊠ Box 1339, Calumet City, IL 60409, ☎ 708/868–6700 or 800/654–6700), **Tele-Trip** (⊠ Mutual of Omaha Plaza, Box 31716, Omaha, NE 68131, ☎ 800/228–9792), **Travel Guard International** (⊠ 1145 Clark St., Stevens Point, WI 54481, ☎ 715/345–0505 or 800/826–1300), **Travel Insured International** (⊠ Box 280568, East Hartford, CT 06128, ☎ 203/528–7663 or 800/243–3174), and **Wallach & Company** (⊠ 107 W. Federal St., Box 480, Middleburg, VA 22117, ☎ 540/687–3166 or 800/237–6615).

IN THE U.K.

The **Association of British Insurers** (⊠ 51 Gresham St., London EC2V 7HQ, ☎ 0171/600–3333) gives advice by phone and publishes the free pamphlet **"Holiday Insurance and Motoring Abroad,"** which sets out typical policy provisions and costs.

L
LODGING

B&B AGENCY

Heritage Inns of New Zealand (⊠ 47 Hallenstein St., Queenstown, ☎ FAX 03/442–4424) is a group of 28 historic houses-turned-B&B on North and South islands. All meet a consistent international standard and provide a great opportunity to meet interesting, friendly New Zealanders. Write, call, or fax for a brochure and/or reservations for any of the member B&Bs,

eleven of which are included in this guide.

HOME AND FARM STAYS

For a list of available home and farm stays, contact **New Zealand Farm Holidays Ltd.** (✉ Box 256, Silverdale, Auckland, ☎ 09/307–2024) or **Homestay Ltd. Farmstay Ltd.** (✉ Box 25–115, Auckland, ☎ 09/575–9977). *Baches and Holiday Homes to Rent,* by Mark and Elizabeth Greening ($14.95; ✉ Box 3017, Richmond, Nelson, New Zealand, ☎ and FAX 03/544–5799), lists 430 self-contained holiday homes.

HOME EXCHANGE

Some of the principal clearinghouses are **HomeLink International/ Vacation Exchange Club** (✉ Box 650, Key West, FL 33041, ☎ 305/294–1448 or 800/638–3841, FAX 305/294–1148; $78 per year), which sends members five annual directories, with a listing in one, plus updates; and **Intervac International** (✉ Box 590504, San Francisco, CA 94159, ☎ 415/435–3497, FAX 415/435–7440; $65 per year), which publishes four annual directories.

M
MONEY

ATMS

For specific foreign **Cirrus** locations, call 800/424–7787; for foreign **Plus** locations, consult the Plus directory at your local bank.

CURRENCY EXCHANGE

If your bank doesn't exchange currency, contact **Thomas Cook Currency Services** (☎ 800/287–7362 for locations). **Ruesch International** (☎ 800/424–2923 for locations) can also provide you with foreign banknotes before you leave home and publishes a number of useful brochures, including a "Foreign Currency Guide" and "Foreign Exchange Tips."

WIRING FUNDS

Funds can be wired via **MoneyGram**^{SM} (for locations and information in the U.S. and Canada, ☎ 800/926–9400) or **Western Union** (for agent locations or to send money using MasterCard or Visa, ☎ 800/325–6000; in Canada, 800/321–2923; in the U.K., 0800/833833; or visit the Western Union office at the nearest major post office).

P
PACKING

For strategies on packing light, get a copy of *The Packing Book,* by Judith Gilford (✉ Ten Speed Press, Box 7123, Berkeley, CA 94707, ☎ 510/559–1600 or 800/841–2665, FAX 510/524–4588; $7.95 plus $3.50 shipping).

PASSPORTS & VISAS

IN THE U.S.

For fees, documentation requirements, and other information, call the State Department's **Office of Passport Services** information line (☎ 202/647–0518).

CANADIANS

For fees, documentation requirements, and other information, call the Ministry of Foreign Affairs and International Trade's **Passport Office** (☎ 819/994–3500 or 800/567–6868).

U.K. CITIZENS

For fees, documentation requirements, and to request an emergency passport, call the **London Passport Office** (☎ 0990/210410).

PHOTO HELP

The **Kodak Information Center** (☎ 800/242–2424) answers consumer questions about film and photography. The *Kodak Guide to Shooting Great Travel Pictures* (available in bookstores; or contact Fodor's Travel Publications, ☎ 800/533–6478; $16.50 plus $4 shipping) explains how to take expert travel photographs.

S
SAFETY

"Trouble-Free Travel," from the AAA, is a booklet of tips for protecting yourself and your belongings when away from home. Send a stamped, self-addressed, legal-size envelope to Trouble-Free Travel (✉ Mail Stop 75, 1000 AAA Dr., Heathrow, FL 32746).

SENIOR CITIZENS

EDUCATIONAL TRAVEL

The nonprofit **Elderhostel** (✉ 75 Federal St., 3rd Floor, Boston, MA 02110, ☎ 617/426–7788), for people 55 and older, has offered inexpensive study programs since 1975.

THE GOLD GUIDE / IMPORTANT CONTACTS

Courses cover everything from marine science to Greek mythology and cowboy poetry. Costs for two- to three-week international trips—including room, board, and transportation from the United States—range from $1,800 to $4,500.

ORGANIZATIONS

Contact the **American Association of Retired Persons** (⊠ AARP, 601 E St. NW, Washington, DC 20049, ☎ 202/434–2277; annual dues $8 per person or couple). Its Purchase Privilege Program secures discounts for members on lodging, car rentals, and sightseeing.

Additional sources for discounts on lodgings, car rentals, and other travel expenses, as well as helpful magazines and newsletters, are the **National Council of Senior Citizens** (⊠ 1331 F St. NW, Washington, DC 20004, ☎ 202/347–8800; annual membership $12) and Sears's **Mature Outlook** (⊠ Box 10448, Des Moines, IA 50306, ☎ 800/336–6330; annual membership $14.95).

SPORTS

For information on guided bicycling, canoeing and sea-kayaking, cross-country skiing, diving, fishing, hiking, horseback riding, rafting, and sailing tours and tour operators, *see* Chapter 6.

GOLF

For more information, contact the Executive Director, **NZ Golf Association,** Box 11–842, Wellington.

STUDENTS

BACKPACKING

To find out about backpacker hostels, contact **Budget Backpackers Hostels NZ, Ltd.** (⊠ Rainbow Lodge, 99 Titiraupenga St., Taupo, ☎ 07/378–5754 or Foley Towers, 208 Kilgore St., Christchurch, ☎ 03/366–9720).

DISCOUNTS

Backpackers Discounts is a bus pass for young budget travelers. Contact SO/PAC (☎ 800/551–2012) for information and reservations.

GROUPS

A major tour operator specializing in student travel is **Contiki Holidays** (⊠ 300 Plaza Alicante, Suite 900, Garden Grove, CA 92640, ☎ 714/740–0808 or 800/266–8454).

HOSTELING

In the United States, contact **Hostelling International–American Youth Hostels** (⊠ 733 15th St. NW, Suite 840, Washington, DC 20005, ☎ 202/783–6161, FAX 202/783–6171); in Canada, **Hostelling International–Canada** (⊠ 205 Catherine St., Suite 400, Ottawa, Ontario K2P 1C3, ☎ 613/237–7884); and in the United Kingdom, the **Youth Hostel Association of England and Wales** (⊠ Trevelyan House, 8 St. Stephen's Hill, St. Albans, Hertfordshire AL1 2DY, ☎ 01727/855215 or 01727/845047). Membership (in the U.S., $25; in Canada, C$26.75; in the U.K., £9.30) gives you access to 5,000 hostels in 77 countries that charge $5–$40 per person per night.

In addition to the International Youth Hostels, a network of low-cost, independent backpacker hostels operates in New Zealand. They can be found in nearly every city and tourist spot, and they offer clean, twin- and small-dormitory–style accommodations and self-catering kitchens, similar to those of the Youth Hostel Association (or YHA, the Australian version of IYH), with no membership required.

Hostelling information and registration are available at **YHA Travel Centres** (⊠ 36 Customs St. East or Box 1687, Auckland, ☎ 09/379–4224 and corner of Gloucester and Manchester Sts., Christchurch, ☎ 03379–8046).

ORGANIZATIONS

A major contact is the **Council on International Educational Exchange** (⊠ mail orders only: CIEE, 205 E. 42nd St., 16th Floor, New York, NY 10017, ☎ 212/822–2600, info@ciee.org). The **Educational Travel Centre** (⊠ 438 N. Frances St., Madison, WI 53703, ☎ 608/256–5551 or 800/747–5551, FAX 608/256–2042) offers rail passes and low-cost airline tickets, mostly for flights that depart from Chicago.

For air travel only, contact **TMI Student Travel** (⊠ 3617 DuPont

Ave. S., Minneapolis, MN 55409, ☎ 800/ 245–3672).

In Canada, also contact **Travel Cuts** (✉ 187 College St., Toronto, Ontario M5T 1P7, ☎ 416/979–2406 or 800/ 667–2887).

T
TELEPHONES

The country code for New Zealand is 64. For local access numbers abroad, contact **AT&T** USADirect (☎ 800/ 874–4000), **MCI** Call USA (☎ 800/444– 4444), or **Sprint** Express (☎ 800/793–1153).

TOUR OPERATORS

Among the companies that sell tours and packages to New Zealand, the following are nationally known, have a proven reputation, and offer plenty of options.

GROUP TOURS

SUPER-DELUXE➤ **Aber-crombie & Kent** (✉ 1520 Kensington Rd., Oak Brook, IL 60521-2141, ☎ 708/954– 2944 or 800/323–7308, FAX 708/954–3324) and **Travcoa** (✉ Box 2630, 2350 S.E. Bristol St., Newport Beach, CA 92660, ☎ 714/476– 2800 or 800/992–2003, FAX 714/476–2538).

DELUXE➤ **Globus** (✉ 5301 S. Federal Circle, Littleton, CO 80123, ☎ 303/797–2800 or 800/221–0090, FAX 303/ 795–0962), **Maupintour** (✉ Box 807, 1515 St. Andrews Dr., Lawrence, KS 66047, ☎ 913/843– 1211 or 800/255–4266, FAX 913/843–8351), and **Tauck Tours** (✉ Box 5027, 276 Post Rd. W,

Westport, CT 06881, ☎ 203/226–6911 or 800/468–2825, FAX 203/ 221–6828).

FIRST-CLASS➤ **Brendan Tours** (✉ 15137 Califa St., Van Nuys, CA 91411, ☎ 818/785– 9696 or 800/421–8446, FAX 818/902–9876), **Collette Tours** (✉ 162 Middle St., Pawtucket, RI 02860, ☎ 401/728– 3805 or 800/832–4656, FAX 401/728–1380), and **Gadabout Tours** (✉ 700 E. Tahquitz Canyon Way, Palm Springs, CA 92262, ☎ 619/325– 5556 or 800/952– 5068).

BUDGET➤ **Cosmos** (☞ Globus, *above*).

Several other operators specialize in tours to New Zealand. Contact **AAT King's Australian Tours** (✉ 9430 Topanga Canyon Blvd., #207, Chatsworth, CA 91311, ☎ 800/353–4525, FAX 818/700–2647), **ATS Tours** (✉ 2381 Rosencrans Ave., #325, El Segundo, CA 90245, ☎ 310/643–0044 or 800/ 423–2880), **Newmans South Pacific Vacations** (✉ 6033 W. Century Blvd., #1270, Los Angeles, CA 90045, ☎ 310/ 348–8282 or 800/421– 3326, FAX 310/215– 9705), **South Pacific Your Way** (✉ 2819 1st Ave., #280, Seattle, WA 98121-1113, ☎ 206 /441–8682 or 800/426– 3615, FAX 206/441– 8862, worldtra£nwlink. com), or **Swain Australia Tours** (✉ 6 W. Lancaster Ave., Ardmore, PA 19003, ☎ 610/896– 9595 or 800/227–9246, FAX 610/896–9592). **Gogo Tours** in Ramsey, New Jersey, sells packages only through travel agents.

PACKAGES

All of the operators that specialize in group tours to New Zealand also offer independent vacation packages. For more choices, try **Down Under Connections** (✉ 4653 Olde Towne Pkwy., #100, Marietta, GA 30068, ☎ 404/565– 8600 or 800/937–7878, FAX 404/565–5085), **Islands in the Sun** (✉ 2381 Rosencrans Ave., #325, El Segundo, CA 90245, ☎ 310/536– 0051 or 800/828–6877, FAX 310/536–6266), **Qantas Vacations** (✉ 300 Continental Blvd., #610, El Segundo, CA 90245, ☎ 800/641– 8772, FAX 310/535– 1057), and **United Vacations** (☎ 800/328– 6877).

FROM THE U.K.

For holiday packages contact **British Airways Holidays** (✉ Astral Towers, Betts Way, London Rd., Crawley, West Sussex RH10 2XA, ☎ 01293/723– 191), **Kuoni Travel** (✉ Kuoni House, Dorking, Surrey RH5 4AZ, ☎ 01306/741–111), or **Jetabout Holidays** (✉ Sovereign House, 361 King St., Hammersmith, London W6 9NJ, ☎ 0181/741– 3111).

THEME TRIPS

Customized tours of New Zealand, tailored to your interests, are available from **Australia/New Zealand Down Under Travel** (✉ 4962 El Camino Real, #107, Los Altos, CA 94022, ☎ 415/969– 2153 or 800/886–2153, FAX 415/969–3215, http://ANZTRAVEL.co m) and **Pacific Experi-**

ence (⊠ 366 Madison Ave., #1203, New York, NY 10017, ☎ 212/661–2604 or 800/279–3639, FAX 212/661–2587), which arranges deluxe tours.

ADVENTURE➤ Action-packed tours are sold by **Adventure Center** (⊠ 1311 63rd St., #200, Emeryville, CA 94608, ☎ 510/654–1879 or 800/227–8747, FAX 510/654–4200, Info£MT-Sobek.com, http://www.MTSobek.com), **Backroads** (⊠ 1516 5th St., Berkeley, CA 94710-1740, ☎ 510/527–1555 or 800/462–2848, FAX 510/527–1444, goactive@Backroads.com), **Safaricentre** (⊠ 3201 N. Sepulveda Blvd., Manhattan Beach, CA 90266, ☎ 310/546–4411 or 800/223–6046), and **Wilderness Travel** (⊠ 801 Allston Way, Berkeley, CA 94710, ☎ 510/548–0420 or 800/368–2794, FAX 510/548–0347, info£wildernesstravel.com).

BICYCLING➤ For easy or challenging rides in Kiwi country, try **Backroads** (☞ Adventure, *above*) and **Down Under Answers** (⊠ 12115 100th Ave. NE, Kirkland, WA 98034, ☎ 206/814–0777 or 800/788–6685, FAX 206/820–5571, dua£accessone.com).

FISHING➤ Land-based and live-aboard packages can be arranged by **Anglers Travel** (⊠ 3100 Mill St., #206, Reno, NV 89502, ☎ 702/324–0580 or 800/624–8429, FAX 702/324–0583), **Fishing International** (⊠ Box 2132, Santa Rosa,

CA 95405, ☎ 800/950–4242), and **Rod & Reel Adventures** (⊠ 3507 Tully Rd., Unit B6, Modesto, CA 95356-1052, ☎ 209/524–7775 or 800/356–6982, FAX 209/524–1220).

GOLF➤ For golf vacations including accommodations, greens fees, and guaranteed tee-off times, try **Australia/New Zealand Down Under Travel** (☞ Theme Trips, *above*) or **ITC Golf Tours** (⊠ 4134 Atlantic Ave., #205, Long Beach, CA 90807, ☎ 310/595–6905 or 800/257–4981).

HIKING➤ Try **Backroads** (☞ Adventure, *above*).

HORSEBACK RIDING➤ Contact **FITS Equestrian** (⊠ 685 Lateen Rd., Solvang, CA 93463, ☎ 805/688–9494 or 800/666–3487, FAX 805/688–2943).

LEARNING➤ To learn more about the wildlife and environment of New Zealand, contact **Earthwatch** (⊠ Box 403, 680 Mt. Auburn St., Watertown, MA 02272, ☎ 617/926–8200 or 800/776–0188, FAX 617/926–8532, info£earthwatch.org, http://www.earthwatch.org), **Nature Expeditions International** (⊠ Box 11496, Eugene, OR 97440, ☎ 503/484–6529 or 800/869–0639, FAX 503/484–6531), **Questers** (⊠ 381 Park Ave. S, New York, NY 10016, ☎ 212/251–0444 or 800/468–8668, FAX 212/251–0890), and **Smithsonian Study Tours and Seminars** (⊠ 1100 Jefferson Dr., SW, Room 3045, Room 3045,

MRC 702, Washington, DC 20560, ☎ 202/357–4700, FAX 202/633–9250).

MOTORCYCLING➤ **Beach's Motorcycle Adventures** (⊠ 2763 W. River Pkwy., Grand Island, NY 14072-2053, ☎ 716/773–4960, FAX 716/773–5227, robbeach£buffnet.net) explores New Zealand.

SINGLES AND YOUNG ADULTS➤ **Contiki Holidays** (⊠ 300 Plaza Alicante, #900, Garden Grove, CA 92640, ☎ 714/740–0808 or 800/266–8454, FAX 714/740–0818) specializes in tours for travelers 18–35.

WALKING➤ **Country Walkers** (⊠ Box 180, Waterbury, VT 05676-0180, ☎ 802/244–1387 or 800/464–9255, FAX 802/244–5661).

YACHT CHARTERS➤ Contact **Huntley Yacht Vacations** (⊠ 210 Preston Rd., Wernersville, PA 19565, ☎ 610/678–2628 or 800/322–9224, FAX 610/670–1767, yachts4u@enter.net) and **The Moorings** (⊠ 19345 U.S. Hwy. 19 N, 4th floor, Clearwater, FL 34624-3193, ☎ 813/530–5424 or 800/535–7289, FAX 813/530–9474).

ORGANIZATIONS

The **National Tour Association** (⊠ NTA, 546 E. Main St., Lexington, KY 40508, ☎ 606/226–4444 or 800/755–8687) and the **United States Tour Operators Association** (⊠ USTOA, 211 E. 51st St., Suite 12B, New York, NY 10022, ☎ 212/750–7371) can provide lists of members and information on booking tours.

PUBLICATIONS

Contact the USTOA (☞ Organizations, *above*) for its **"Smart Traveler's Planning Kit."** Pamphlets in the kit include the "Worldwide Tour and Vacation Package Finder," "How to Select a Tour or Vacation Package," and information on the organization's consumer protection plan. Also get a copy of the Better Business Bureau's **"Tips on Travel Packages"** (✉ Publication 24-195, 4200 Wilson Blvd., Arlington, VA 22203; $2).

New Zealand's railroad system operates under the **InterCity** (☎ 09/357–8400) banner.

DISCOUNT PASSES

Travelers can purchase an **InterCity Travelpass** for unlimited travel by train, bus, and Inter-Island ferry. The pass allows 8 days of travel within a 21-day period ($425), 15 days of travel within 36 days ($530), or 22 days of travel within 56 days ($650). Children ages 4 to 14 pay 67% of the adult fare. The 4-in-1 **New Zealand Travelpass**, available for purchase outside New Zealand only, includes one flight sector on Ansett New Zealand between assigned city pairs. The flight may be at any time after the date of issue of the Travelpass and up to seven days after expiration of the Travelpass. The pass entitles the visitor to 8 days of travel in 21 days ($616),

15 days of travel in 35 days ($721), or 22 days of travel in 56 days ($841). Children ages 4 to 14 pay 67% of the adult fare. Two additional flight sectors may be purchased at $191 per sector. For Youth Hostel Association members, the **InterCity Youth Hostel Travel Card** ($75 for 14 days, $99 for 28 days) gives a 50% discount on most train service, all Inter-City coach service, and on InterIsland ferries. Students with an **International Student Identity Card** (ISIC) get a 20% discount.

Contact **InterCity Travel Centres** (☎ 09/357–8400 in Auckland, 03/379–9020 in Christchurch, 04/472–5111 in Wellington) for ticket information. In the United States, contact ATS Tours (☎ 818/841–1030) or Austravel Inc. (☎ 800/633–3404).

For travel apparel, appliances, personal-care items, and other travel necessities, get a free catalog from **Magellan's** (☎ 800/962–4943, FAX 805/568–5406), **Orvis Travel** (☎ 800/541–3541, FAX 703/343–7053), or **TravelSmith** (☎ 800/950–1600, FAX 415/455–0554).

ELECTRICAL CONVERTERS

Send a self-addressed, stamped envelope to the **Franzus Company** (✉ Customer Service, Dept. B50, Murtha Industrial Park, Box 142, Beacon Falls, CT 06403, ☎ 203/723–6664) for a copy of the

free brochure "Foreign Electricity Is No Deep, Dark Secret."

For names of reputable agencies in your area, contact the **American Society of Travel Agents** (✉ ASTA, 1101 King St., Suite 200, Alexandria, VA 22314, ☎ 703/739–2782), the **Association of Canadian Travel Agents** (✉ Suite 201, 1729 Bank St., Ottawa, Ontario K1V 7Z5, ☎ 613/521–0474, FAX 613/521–0805), or the **Association of British Travel Agents** (✉ 55-57 Newman St., London W1P 4AH, ☎ 0171/637–2444, FAX 0171/637–0713).

U

The U.S. Department of State's American Citizens Services office (✉ Room 4811, Washington, DC 20520; enclose SASE) issues **Consular Information Sheets** on all foreign countries. These cover issues such as crime, security, political climate, and health risks as well as listing embassy locations, entry requirements, currency regulations, and providing other useful information. For the latest information, stop in at any U.S. passport office, consulate, or embassy; call the interactive hot line (☎ 202/647–5225, FAX 202/647–3000); or, with your PC's modem, tap into the department's computer bulletin board (☎ 202/647–9225).

V

VISITOR

INFORMATION

For information about travel to and within New Zealand, contact the nearest **New Zealand Tourism Board.**

In the U.S.: ⊠ 501 Santa Monica Blvd., Los Angeles, CA 90401, ☎ 310/395–7480 or 800/388–5494, FAX 310/395–5454.

In Canada: ⊠ 888 Dunsmuir St., Suite 1200, Vancouver, BC V6C 3K4, ☎ 800/888–5494, FAX 604/684–1265.

In the U.K.: ⊠ New Zealand House, Haymarket, London, SW1Y 4TQ, ☎ 0171/930–1662, FAX 0171/839–8929.

W

WEATHER

For current conditions and forecasts, plus the local time and helpful travel tips, call the **Weather Channel Connection** (☎ 900/932–8437; 95¢ per minute) from a Touch-Tone phone.

The *International Traveler's Weather Guide* (⊠ Weather Press, Box 660606, Sacramento, CA 95866, ☎ 916/974–0201 or 800/972–0201; $10.95 includes shipping), written by two meteorologists, provides month-by-month information on temperature, humidity, and precipitation in more than 175 cities worldwide.

SMART TRAVEL TIPS A TO Z

Basic Information on Traveling in New Zealand and Savvy Tips to Make Your Trip a Breeze

A
AIR TRAVEL

Always look for non-stop flights, which require no change of plane. The flight to New Zealand from Los Angeles takes about 12 hours, which you probably won't want to lengthen by adding a stopover. From the U.S. and Canada, you will have to connect to a New Zealand bound flight in L.A.

When flying to New Zealand, the national carrier, **Air New Zealand,** has high passenger satisfaction ratings. Service is professional and courteous, two meals are served en route, and food is better than what you'll find on most airlines. There are also informative progress reports charting your course over the Pacific shown on movie screens when films are not running. The carrier introduced a fleet of renovated planes late in 1995.

CUTTING COSTS

The Sunday travel section of most newspapers is a good place to look for deals (☞ Travel Passes, *below*).

MAJOR AIRLINES➢ The least-expensive airfares from the major airlines are priced for round-trip travel and are subject to restrictions. Usually, you must **book in advance and buy the ticket within 24 hours** to

get cheaper fares, and you may have to **stay over a Saturday night.** The lowest fare is subject to availability, and only a small percentage of the plane's total seats is sold at that price. It's smart to **call a number of airlines, and when you are quoted a good price, book it on the spot**—the same fare may not be available on the same flight the next day. Airlines generally allow you to change your return date for a $25 to $50 fee. If you don't use your ticket, you can apply the cost toward the purchase of a new ticket, again for a small charge. However, most low-fare tickets are nonrefundable. To get the lowest airfare, **check different routings.** If your destination has more than one gateway, **compare prices to different airports.**

FROM THE U.K.➢ To save money on flights, **look into an APEX or Super-Pex ticket.** APEX tickets must be booked in advance and have certain restrictions. Super-PEX tickets can be purchased right at the airport.

CONSOLIDATORS➢ Consolidators buy tickets for scheduled flights at reduced rates from the airlines, then sell them at prices below the lowest available from the airlines directly—usually without advance restrictions. Sometimes you can even get your

money back if you need to return the ticket. Carefully read the fine print detailing penalties for changes and cancellations. If you doubt the reliability of a consolidator, **confirm your reservation with the airline.**

ALOFT

AIRLINE FOOD➢ If you hate airline food, **ask for special meals when booking.** These can be vegetarian, low-cholesterol, or kosher, for example; commonly prepared to order in smaller quantities than standard fare, they can be tastier.

JET LAG➢ To avoid this syndrome, which occurs when travel disrupts your body's natural cycles, try to maintain a normal routine. At night, **get some sleep.** By day, move about the cabin to **stretch your legs, eat light meals, and drink water—not alcohol.**

SMOKING➢ Smoking is not allowed on flights of six hours or less within the continental United States. Smoking is also prohibited on flights within Canada. For U.S. flights longer than six hours or international flights, **contact your carrier regarding their smoking policy.** Some carriers have prohibited smoking throughout their system; others allow smoking only on certain routes or even certain

THE GOLD GUIDE / SMART TRAVEL TIPS

THE GOLD GUIDE / SMART TRAVEL TIPS

departures of that route.

TRAVEL PASSES

Airlines offer international visitors various reductions in adult fares. Prices quoted were effective at press time; check with a travel agent or the airline to see if there have been any changes.

Economy-price air travel is expensive compared with the cost of bus or train travel, but you can save a substantial amount of money if you **buy multi-trip tickets.** Ansett New Zealand has a **New Zealand Airpass** entitling you to fly between three and eight sectors (i.e., point-to-point flights) starting from $450 for a three-sector pass and costing $150 for each additional sector. The pass is valid for the duration of your stay in New Zealand and should be purchased prior to arrival to avoid New Zealand sales tax. Also inquire about Ansett's 4-in-1 **InterCity New Zealand Travelpass.** Air New Zealand and Mount Cook offer similar discount tickets, available through travel agents.

B

BUS TRAVEL

New Zealand is served by an extensive bus network and for many travelers, buses offer the optimal combination of cost and convenience.

DISCOUNT PASSES

The **InterCity Travelpass** allows unlimited travel on all InterCity buses and trains and on the InterIslander ferries that link the North and South Islands (☞ Train Travel, *below*).

BUSINESS HOURS

Banks are open weekdays 9–4:30, but trading in foreign currencies ceases at 3. **Shops** are generally open Monday–Thursday 9–5:30, Friday 9–9, and Saturday 9–noon. Sunday trading is becoming more common but still varies greatly from place to place.

C

CAMERAS, CAMCORDERS, & COMPUTERS

IN TRANSIT

Always **keep your film, tape, or disks out of the sun;** never put these on the dashboard of a car. Carry an extra supply of batteries, and **be prepared to turn on your camera, camcorder, or laptop computer for security personnel** to prove that it's real.

X-RAYS

Always ask for hand inspection at security. Such requests are virtually always honored at U.S. airports, and are usually accommodated abroad. Photographic film becomes clouded after successive exposure to airport x-ray machines. Videotape and computer disks are not harmed by X-rays, but **keep your tapes and disks away from metal detectors.**

CUSTOMS

Before departing, register your foreign-made camera or laptop with U.S. Customs. If your equipment is U.S.-made, call the consulate of the country you'll be visiting to find out whether it should be registered with local customs upon arrival.

CAR RENTAL

CROSS-ISLAND RENTALS

Most major international companies have a convenient service if you are taking the ferry between North and South islands and want to continue your rental contract. You simply drop off the car in Wellington and on the same contract pick up a new car in Picton, or vice-versa. It saves you from paying the considerable fare for taking a car across on the ferry (and it's easier for the company to keep track of its rental fleet). Your rental contract is terminated only at the far end of your trip, wherever you end up. In this system, there is no drop-off charge for one-way rentals, making an Auckland–Queenstown rental as easy as it could be.

CUTTING COSTS

To get the best deal, book through a travel agent who is willing to shop around. Ask your agent to **look for fly-drive packages,** which also save you money, and **ask if local taxes are included** in the rental or fly-drive price. These can be as high as 20% in some destinations. Don't forget to find out about required deposits, cancellation penalties, drop-off charges, and the cost of any required insurance coverage.

Always find out what equipment is standard

at your destination before specifying what you want; automatic transmission and air-conditioning are usually optional—and very expensive. You may, however, consider paying extra for an automatic if you are unfamiliar with manual transmissions. Driving on the "wrong" side of the road will probably be enough to worry about.

INSURANCE

When driving a rented car, you are generally responsible for any damage to or loss of the rental vehicle, as well as any property damage or personal injury that you cause. Before you rent, see what coverage you already have under the terms of your personal auto insurance policy and credit cards.

In New Zealand, deductibles are very high with the most basic coverage, so you may want to opt for total coverage. Be sure to get all of the details from the rental agent before you decide.

LICENSE REQUIREMENTS

In New Zealand your own driver's license is acceptable at most rental companies. An International Driver's Permit is a good idea; it's available from the American or Canadian automobile associations, or, in the United Kingdom, from the AA or RAC.

SURCHARGES

To avoid a hefty refueling fee, fill the tank just before you turn in the car—but be aware that gas stations near the rental outlet may overcharge.

CHILDREN & TRAVEL

When traveling with children, plan ahead and involve your youngsters as you outline your trip. When packing, include a supply of things to keep them busy en route (☞ Children & Travel *in* Important Contacts A to Z). On sightseeing days, try to schedule activities of special interest to your children, like a trip to a zoo or a playground. If you plan your itinerary around seasonal festivals, you'll never lack for things to do. In addition, check local newspapers for special events mounted by public libraries, museums, and parks.

BABY-SITTING

For recommended local sitters, check with your hotel desk. In New Zealand, most hotels and resorts have baby-sitters available at a charge of around $10 to $15 per hour. Baby-sitting services are also listed in the yellow pages of city telephone directories.

BABY SUPPLIES

Baby products such as disposable diapers (ask for napkins or nappies), formula, and baby food can be found in chemists' shops. They are less expensive in supermarkets, but these are scarce outside major cities.

DINING

New Zealanders are genuinely fond of and considerate toward children, and their own children are included in most of their parents' social activities. Children are welcome in all restaurants throughout the country. However, they are rarely seen in those restaurants that appear in Fodor's very expensive ($$$$) and expensive ($$$) price categories. These restaurants may not have high chairs or be prepared to make special children's meals.

DRIVING

If you are renting a car, don't forget to arrange for a car seat when you reserve. Most car-rental agencies in New Zealand provide "cocoons" for newborns as well as child safety seats. Sometimes they're free.

FLYING

As a general rule, infants under two not occupying a seat fly at greatly reduced fares and occasionally for free. If your children are two or older ask about special children's fares. Age limits for these fares vary among carriers. Rules also vary regarding unaccompanied minors, so again, check with your airline.

BAGGAGE➤ In general, the adult baggage allowance applies to children paying half or more of the adult fare. If you are traveling with an infant, ask about carry-on allowances before departure. In general, for infants charged 10% of the adult fare you are allowed one carry-on bag and a collapsible stroller, which may have to be checked; you may be limited to less if the flight is full.

SAFETY SEATS➤ **According to the FAA, it's a good idea to use safety seats aloft** for children weighing less than 40 pounds. Airline policies vary. U.S. carriers allow FAA-approved models but usually require that you buy a ticket, even if your child would otherwise ride free, since the seats must be strapped into regular seats. However, some U.S. and foreign-flag airlines may require you to hold your baby during takeoff and landing—defeating the seat's purpose. New Zealand carriers do not allow infant seats.

FACILITIES➤ **When making your reservation, request children's meals or freestanding bassinets** if you need them; the latter are available only to those seated at the bulkhead, where there's enough legroom. If you don't need a bassinet, **think twice before requesting bulkhead seats**—the only storage space for in-flight necessities is in inconveniently distant overhead bins.

LODGING

Most hotels allow children under a certain age to stay in their parents' room at no extra charge; others charge them as extra adults. Be sure to **ask about the cutoff age.**

In hotels in New Zealand, roll-away beds are usually free, and children under 12 sharing a hotel room with adults either stay free or receive a discount rate. Few hotels have separate facilities for children.

Home hosting provides an ideal opportunity for visitors to stay with a local family, either in town or on a working farm. For information on home and farm stays, home exchange, and apartment rentals, *see* Lodging *in* Important Contacts A to Z.

CUSTOMS & DUTIES

To speed your clearance through customs, **keep receipts for all your purchases abroad** and **be ready to show the inspector what you've bought.** If you feel that you've been incorrectly or unfairly charged a duty, you can **appeal assessments in dispute.** First ask to see a supervisor. If you are still unsatisfied, **write to the port director** your point of entry, sending your customs receipt and any other appropriate documentation. The address will be listed on your receipt. If you still don't get satisfaction, you can take your case to customs headquarters in Washington.

IN NEW ZEALAND

New Zealand has stringent regulations governing the import of weapons, foodstuffs, and certain plant and animal material. Anti-drug laws are strict and penalties severe. In addition to personal effects, nonresidents over 17 years of age may bring in, duty-free, 200 cigarettes or 250 grams of tobacco or 50 cigars, 4.5 liters of wine, one bottle containing not more than 1,125 milliliters of spirits or liqueur, and personal purchases and

gifts up to the value of US $440 (NZ$700).

Don't stash any fruit in your carry-on to take into the country. The agricutural quarantine is serious business. So if you've been hiking recently and are bringing your boots with you, clean them before you pack. The authorities for very good reason don't want any non-native seeds haplessly transported into the country. It's a small and fragile ecosystem, and Kiwis rightfully want to protect it.

IN THE U.S.

You may bring home $400 worth of foreign goods duty-free if you've been out of the country for at least 48 hours and haven't already used the $400 allowance, or any part of it, in the past 30 days.

Travelers 21 or older may bring back 1 liter of alcohol duty-free, provided the beverage laws of the state through which they reenter the United States allow it. In addition, regardless of their age, they are allowed 100 non-Cuban cigars and 200 cigarettes. Antiques, which the U.S. Customs Service defines as objects more than 100 years old, are duty-free. Original works of art done entirely by hand are also duty-free. These include, but are not limited to, paintings, drawings, and sculptures.

Duty-free, travelers may mail packages valued at up to $200 to themselves and up to $100 to others, with a limit of one parcel per addressee per day (and no alcohol or tobacco products or perfume valued at more than $5); on the outside, the package must be labeled as being either for personal use or an unsolicited gift, and a list of its contents and their retail value must be attached. Mailed items do not affect your duty-free allowance on your return.

IN CANADA

If you've been out of Canada for at least seven days, you may bring in C$500 worth of goods duty-free. If you've been away for fewer than seven days but for more than 48 hours, the duty-free allowance drops to C$200; if your trip lasts between 24 and 48 hours, the allowance is C$50. You cannot pool allowances with family members. Goods claimed under the C$500 exemption may follow you by mail; those claimed under the lesser exemptions must accompany you.

Alcohol and tobacco products may be included in the seven-day and 48-hour exemptions but not in the 24-hour exemption. If you meet the age requirements of the province or territory through which you reenter Canada, you may bring in, duty-free, 1.14 liters (40 imperial ounces) of wine or liquor *or* 24 12-ounce cans or bottles of beer or ale. If you are 16 or older, you may bring in, duty-free, 200 cigarettes, 50 cigars or cigarillos, and 400

tobacco sticks or 400 grams of manufactured tobacco. Alcohol and tobacco must accompany you on your return.

An unlimited number of gifts with a value of up to C$60 each may be mailed to Canada duty-free. These do not affect your duty-free allowance on your return. Label the package "Unsolicited Gift— Value Under $60." Alcohol and tobacco are excluded.

IN THE U.K.

From countries outside the EU, including New Zealand, you may import, duty-free, 200 cigarettes, 100 cigarillos, 50 cigars, or 250 grams of tobacco; 1 liter of spirits or 2 liters of fortified or sparkling wine or liqueurs; 2 liters of still table wine; 60 milliliters of perfume; 250 milliliters of toilet water; plus £136 worth of other goods, including gifts and souvenirs.

DINING

Some restaurants offer a fixed-price dinner, but the majority are à la carte. **It's wise to make a reservation** and **inquire if the restaurant has a liquor license** or is "BYOB" or "BYO" (Bring Your Own Bottle). Attire country-wide is pretty casual; unless you're planning to dine at the finest of places, men won't need to bring a jacket and tie. At the same time, the most common dinner attire is usually one level above jeans and sports shirts.

TIPPING

Tipping is not widely practiced in New Zealand. Only in the better city restaurants will you be expected to show your appreciation for good service with a 10% tip.

DISABILITIES & ACCESSIBILITY

New Zealand is at the forefront in providing facilities for people with disabilities. Still, **when discussing accessibility with an operator or reservationist, ask hard questions.** Are there any stairs, inside *or* out? Are there grab bars next to the toilet *and* in the shower/tub? How wide is the doorway to the room? To the bathroom? For the most extensive facilities, meeting the latest legal specifications, **opt for newer accommodations,** which more often have been designed with access in mind. Older properties or ships must usually be retrofitted and may offer more limited facilities as a result. Be sure to **discuss your needs before booking.**

AIR TRAVEL

In addition to making arrangements for wheelchair-using passengers, both Qantas and Ansett Airlines accommodate trained dogs accompanying passengers with sight- and hearing-impairments. On Air New Zealand, wheelchairs for in-flight mobility are standard equipment; seat-belt extensions, quadriplegic harnesses, and padded leg rests are also available. Ask for the com-

SMART TRAVEL TIPS / THE GOLD GUIDE

pany's brochure "Air Travel for People with Disabilities."

LODGING

The major hotel chains (such as Parkroyal) provide three or four rooms with facilities for guests with disabilities in most of their properties.

TAXIS

Companies have recently introduced vans equipped with hoists and floor clamps, but these should be booked several hours in advance if possible; contact the Plunket Society (☞ Children & Travel *in* Important Contacts A to Z) for more information.

TRAIN TRAVEL

Passengers on mainline passenger trains in New Zealand can request collapsible wheelchairs to negotiate narrow interior corridors. However, compact toilet areas and platform access problems make long-distance train travel difficult.

DISCOUNTS & DEALS

You shouldn't have to pay for a discount. In fact, you may already be eligible for all kinds of savings. Here are some time-honored strategies for getting the best deal.

LOOK IN YOUR WALLET

When you use your credit card to make travel purchases, you may get free travel-accident insurance, collision damage insurance, medical or legal assistance, depending on the card and bank

that issued it. Visa and MasterCard provide one or more of these services, so **get a copy of your card's travel benefits.** If you are a member of the AAA or an oil-company-sponsored road-assistance plan, always **ask hotel or car-rental reservationists for auto-club discounts.** Some clubs offer additional discounts on tours, cruises, or admission to attractions. And don't forget that auto-club membership entitles you to free maps and trip-planning services.

SENIOR CITIZENS & STUDENTS

As a senior-citizen traveler, you may be eligible for special rates, but you should mention your senior-citizen status up front. If you're a student or under 26 you can also get discounts, especially if you have an official ID card (☞ Senior-Citizen Discounts *and* Students on the Road, *below*).

DIAL FOR DOLLARS

When booking a room, always call the hotel's local toll-free number (if one is available) rather than the central reservations number—you'll often get a better price. Ask the reservationist about special packages or corporate rates, which are usually available even if you're not traveling on business.

JOIN A CLUB?

Discount clubs can be a legitimate source of savings, but you must use the participating hotels and visit the participating attractions

in order to realize any benefits. Remember, too, that you have to pay a fee to join, so **determine if you'll save enough to warrant your membership fee.** Before booking with a club, **make sure the hotel or other supplier isn't offering a better deal.**

GET A GUARANTEE

When shopping for the best deal on hotels and car rentals, **look for guaranteed exchange rates,** which protect you against a falling dollar. With your rate locked in, you won't pay more even if the price goes up in the local currency.

DRIVING

Nothing beats the freedom and mobility of a car for exploring. Even for those nervous about driving on the "wrong" side of the road, motoring here is relatively easy. Roads are well maintained and generally uncrowded, though signposting, even on major highways, is often poor. The speed limit is 100 kilometers per hour (62 mph) on the open road and 50 kph (31 mph) in towns and cities. A circular sign with the letters LSZ (Limited Speed Zone) means there is no speed limit—speed should be governed by prevailing road conditions.

When driving in rural New Zealand, cross one-lane bridges with caution—there are plenty of them. A yellow sign on the left will usually warn that you are approaching a one-lane bridge, and another sign will tell you whether you have the right-of-way. A rectangular blue sign means you have the right-of-way, and a circular sign with a red border means you must pull over to the left and wait to cross until oncoming traffic has passed. Even when you have the right-of-way, slow down and take care. Some one-lane bridges in South Island are used by trains as well as cars. Trains always have the right-of-way.

Two more points: because traffic in New Zealand is relatively light, there has been little need to create major highways, and there are few places where you get straight stretches for very long. So don't plan on averaging 100 km per hour in too many areas. Most of the roads pass through beautiful scenery—so much in fact that you may be constantly agog at what you're seeing. **The temptation is strong to look at everything, but keep your eyes on the road.** Some are incredibly windy; others, like the road from Wanaka to Arrowtown outside of Queenstown, are off limits for rental cars. Ask your rental company in advance where you can and cannot drive if you plan to go off the beaten path.

Finally, remember this simple axiom: drive left, look right. That means keep to the left lane, and when turning right or left from a stop sign, the closest lane of traffic will be coming from the right, so look in that direction first.

By the same token, **pedestrians should look right before crossing the street.** Americans and Canadians, you can blindly step into the path of an oncoming car by looking left as you do when crossing streets at home. So repeat this several times: drive left, look right.

You'll find yourself in a constant comedy of errors when you go to use directional signals and windshield wipers—in Kiwi cars it's the reverse of what you're used to. You won't be able to count how many times those wipers start flapping back and forth when you go to signal a turn (it'll happen in reverse when you get back home). You can be sure it's time to call it a day when you reach over your left shoulder for the seat belt and grab a handful of air.

H
HEALTH

Nutrition and general health standards in New Zealand are high, and it would be hard to find a more pristine natural environment. There are no venomous snakes, and the only poisonous spider, the katipo, is a rarity. There is one surprising health hazard: **don't drink the water in New Zealand's outdoors.** While the country's alpine lakes might look like backdrops for mineral-water ads, some in South Island harbor a tiny organism that can cause "duck itch," a temporary but intense skin irritation. The organism

is found only on the shallow lake margins, so the chances of infection are greatly reduced if you stick to deeper water. Streams can be infected by giardia, a water-borne protozoal parasite that can cause gastrointestinal disorders, including acute diarrhea (though some Kiwis say this is just a load of crap). Giardia is most likely contracted when drinking from streams that pass through an area inhabited by mammals (such as cattle or possums). There is no risk of infection if you drink from streams above the tree line.

The major health hazard in New Zealand is sunburn or sunstroke. Even people who are not normally bothered by strong sun should cover up with a long-sleeve shirt, a hat, and long pants or a beach wrap. Keep in mind that at higher altitudes you will burn more easily. **Apply sunscreen liberally before you go out**—even for a half-hour—and wear a visored cap or sunglasses.

Dehydration is another serious danger that can be easily avoided, so be sure to carry water and drink often. Above all, **limit the amount of time you spend in the sun** for the first few days until you are acclimatized, and always avoid sunbathing in the middle of the day.

One New Zealander you will come to loathe is the tiny black sandfly, common to the western half of South Island, which inflicts a painful bite that can itch for several days (some call it the state bird). **Be sure to use insect repellent,** readily available throughout the country.

DIVERS' ALERT

Scuba divers take note: Do not fly within 24 hours of scuba diving.

INSURANCE

Travel insurance can protect your monetary investment, replace your luggage and its contents, or provide for medical coverage should you fall ill during your trip. Most tour operators, travel agents, and insurance agents sell specialized health-and-accident, flight, trip-cancellation, and luggage insurance as well as comprehensive policies with some or all of these coverages. Comprehensive policies may also reimburse you for delays due to weather—an important consideration if you're traveling during the winter months. Some health-insurance policies do not cover preexisting conditions, but waivers may be available in specific cases. Coverage is sold by the companies listed in Important Contacts A to Z; these companies act as the policy's administrators. The actual insurance is usually underwritten by a well-known name, such as The Travelers or Continental Insurance.

Before you make any purchase, **review your existing health and homeowner's policies** to find out whether they cover expenses incurred while traveling.

BAGGAGE

Airline liability for baggage is limited to $1,250 per person on domestic flights. On international flights, it amounts to $9.07 per pound or $20 per kilogram for checked baggage (roughly $640 per 70-pound bag) and $400 per passenger for unchecked baggage. Insurance for losses exceeding the terms of your airline ticket can be bought directly from the airline at check-in for about $10 per $1,000 of coverage; note that it excludes a rather extensive list of items, shown on your airline ticket.

COMPREHENSIVE

Comprehensive insurance policies include all the coverages described above plus some that may not be available in more specific policies. If you have purchased an expensive vacation, especially one that involves travel abroad, comprehensive insurance is a must; **look for policies that include trip delay insurance,** which will protect you in the event that weather problems cause you to miss your flight, tour, or cruise. A few insurers will also sell you a waiver for preexisting medical conditions. Some of the companies that offer both these features are Access America, Carefree Travel, Travel Insured International, and Travel Guard International. (☞ Insurance *in* Important Contacts A to Z).

FLIGHT

You should **think twice before buying flight insurance.** Often purchased as a last-minute impulse at the airport, it pays a lump sum when a plane crashes, either to a beneficiary if the insured dies or sometimes to a surviving passenger who loses his or her eyesight or a limb. Supplementing the airlines' coverage described in the limits-of-liability paragraphs on your ticket, it's expensive and basically unnecessary. Charging an airline ticket to a major credit card often automatically provides you with coverage that may also extend to travel by bus, train, and ship.

HEALTH

Medicare generally does not cover health care costs outside the United States; nor do many privately issued policies. If your own health insurance policy does not cover you outside the United States, **consider buying supplemental medical coverage.** It can reimburse you for $1,000–$150,000 worth of medical and/or dental expenses incurred as a result of an accident or illness during a trip. These policies also may include a personal-accident, or death-and-dismemberment, provision, which pays a lump sum ranging from $15,000 to $500,000 to your beneficiaries if you die or to you if you lose one or more limbs or your eyesight, and a medical-assistance provision, which may either reimburse you for the cost of referrals, evacuation, or repatriation and other services, or automatically enroll you as a member of a particular medical-assistance company. (☞ Health *in* Important Contacts A to Z.)

U.K. TRAVELERS

You can buy an annual travel insurance policy valid for most vacations during the year in which it's purchased. If you are pregnant or have a preexisting medical condition make sure you're covered before buying such a policy.

TRIP

Without insurance, you will lose all or most of your money if you cancel your trip regardless of the reason. Especially if your airline ticket, cruise, or package tour is nonrefundable and cannot be changed, it's essential that you **buy trip-cancellation-and-interruption insurance.** When considering how much coverage you need, look for a policy that will cover the cost of your trip plus the nondiscounted price of a one-way airline ticket should you need to return home early. Read the fine print carefully, especially sections that define "family member" and "preexisting medical conditions." Also **consider default or bankruptcy insurance,** which protects you against a supplier's failure to deliver. Be aware, however, that if you buy such a policy from a travel agency, tour operator, airline, or cruise line, it may not cover default by the firm in question.

L

LANGUAGE

To an outsider's ear, Kiwi English can be mystifying. Even more so, the Maori (pronounced *mo-*rie) language has added to the New Zealand lexicon words that can seem utterly unpronounceable. It is still spoken by many New Zealanders of Polynesian descent, but English is the everyday language for all people. A number of Maori words have found their way into common usage, most noticeably in place names, which often refer to peculiar features of the local geography or food supply. The Maori word for New Zealand, *Aotearoa,* means "land of the long white cloud." The South Island town of Kaikoura is famous for its crayfish—the word means "to eat crayfish." *Whangapiro* (fang-ah-pee-ro), the Maori name for the Government Gardens in Rotorua, means "an evil-smelling place," and if you visit the town you'll find out why. A Polynesian noun you'll sometimes come across in Maori churches is *tapu*—"sacred"—which has entered the English language as the word taboo. Another Maori word you will frequently encounter is *pakeha,* which means you, the non-Maori. The Maori greeting is *kia ora,* which can also mean "goodbye," "good health," or "good luck."

A Personal Kiwi-Yankee Dictionary, by Louis S. Leland, Jr., is an amusing and informative guide to New Zealand idioms.

LODGING

The New Zealand Tourism Board (☞ Visitor Information *in* Important Contacts A to Z) publishes an annual *Where to Stay* directory listing more than 1,000 properties.

CAMPING

There are almost 900 backcountry huts in New Zealand. They provide basic shelter but few frills. Huts are usually placed about four hours apart, although in isolated areas it can take a full day to get from one hut to the next. They are graded 1 to 4, and cost varies from nothing to $14 per person per night. Category 1 huts (the $14 ones) have cooking equipment and fuel, bunks or sleeping platforms with mattresses, toilets, washing facilities, and a supply of water. At the other end of the scale, Category 4 huts (the free ones) are simple shelters without bunks or other facilities. Pay for huts with coupons, available in books from Department of Conservation offices. If you plan to make extensive use of huts, an annual pass giving access to all Category 2 and 3 huts for one year is available for $58.

HOME AND FARM STAYS

Home and farm stays, which are very popular with visitors to New Zealand, offer not only comfortable accommodations but a chance to get to know the lands and their people—a great thing to do because Kiwis are so naturally friendly. Most

T H E   G O L D   G U I D E   /   S M A R T   T R A V E L   T I P S operate on a bed-and-breakfast basis, though some also offer an evening meal. Farm accommodations vary from modest shearers' cabins to elegant homesteads. Guests can join in farm activities or explore the countryside. Some hosts offer day trips, as well as horseback riding, hiking, and fishing. For two people, the average cost is $90–$150 per night, including all meals. Home stays, the urban equivalent of farm stays, are less expensive. Most New Zealanders seem to have vacation homes, called baches on North Island, cribs on South Island, and these are frequently available for rent (☞ Lodging *in* Important Contacts A to Z).

HOME EXCHANGE

If you would like to find a house, an apartment, or some other type of vacation property to exchange for your own while on holiday, **become a member of a home-exchange organization,** which will send you its updated listings of available exchanges for a year, and will include your own listing in at least one of them. Arrangements for the actual exchange are made by the two parties involved, not by the organization.

MOTELS

Motels are by far the most common accommodations, and most offer comfortable rooms for $60–$90 per night. Some motels have two-bedroom suites for families. All motel rooms come equipped

with tea- and coffee-making equipment, many have toasters or electric frying pans, and full kitchen facilities are not uncommon.

SPORTING LODGES

At the high end of the price scale, a number of luxury sporting lodges offer the best of country life, fine dining, and superb accommodations. Fishing is a specialty at many of them, but there is usually a range of outdoor activities for nonanglers. Tariffs run about $350–$800 per day for two people; meals are generally included.

TOURIST CABINS AND FLATS

The least expensive accommodations in the country are the tourist cabins and flats in most of the country's 400 motor camps. Tourist cabins offer basic accommodation and shared cooking, laundry, and bathroom facilities. Bedding and towels are not provided. A notch higher up the comfort scale, tourist flats usually provide bedding, fully equipped kitchens, and private bathrooms. Overnight rates run about $6–$20 for cabins and $25–$70 for flats.

M

MAIL

Post offices are open weekdays 9–5. The cost of mailing a letter within New Zealand is 40¢ standard post, 80¢ fast post. Sending a standard size letter by air mail costs $1.50 to North America, $1.80 to Europe, and $1 to

Australia. Aerogrammes and postcards are $1 to any overseas destination.

RECEIVING MAIL

If you wish to receive correspondence, **have mail sent to New Zealand held for you** for up to one month at the central post office in any town or city if it is addressed to you "c/o Poste Restante, CPO," followed by the name of the town. This service is free.

MONEY

All prices quoted in this guide are in New Zealand dollars.

New Zealand's unit of currency is the dollar, divided into 100 cents. Bills are in $100, $50, $10, and $5 denominations. Coins are $2, $1, 50¢, 20¢, 10¢, and 5¢. At press time the rate of exchange was NZ$1.60 to the U.S. dollar, NZ$1.25 to the Canadian dollar, NZ$2.45 to the pound sterling, and NZ$1.25 to the Australian dollar. Exchange rates change on a daily basis.

ATMS

CASH ADVANCES➤ Before leaving home, **make sure that your card has been programmed for ATM use** in New Zealand. Your bank card may not work overseas; **ask your bank about a Visa debit card,** which works like a bank card but can be used at any ATM displaying a Visa logo.

TRANSACTION FEES➤ Although fees charged for ATM transactions may be higher abroad than at home, Cirrus and Plus exchange rates are excellent, because they are based on wholesale rates offered only by major banks.

COSTS

For most travelers, New Zealand is not an expensive destination. The cost of meals, accommodation, and travel is slightly higher than in the United States but considerably less than in Western Europe. At about $1 per liter—equal to about US$2.10 per gallon—premium-grade gasoline is expensive by North American standards, but not by European ones.

Inflation, which reached a peak of almost 20% in the late 1980s, has now been reduced to less than 5%.

The following are sample costs in New Zealand at press time:

Cup of coffee $2.50; glass of beer in a bar $2.50–$4; take-out ham sandwich or meat pie $2.50; hamburger in a café $5–$8; room-service sandwich in a hotel $12; a 2-kilometer (1¼-mile) taxi ride $5.

EXCHANGING CURRENCY

For the most favorable rates, **change money at banks.** You won't do as well at exchange booths in airports or rail and bus stations, in hotels, in restaurants, or in stores, although you may find their hours more convenient. To avoid lines at airport exchange booths, **get a small amount of the local currency before you leave home.**

TAXES

A goods and services tax (GST) of 12.5% is levied throughout New Zealand. It's usually incorporated into the cost of an item, but in hotels and some restaurants it is added to the bill.

AIRPORT➤ Visitors exiting New Zealand must pay a departure tax of $20.

TRAVELER'S CHECKS

Whether or not to buy traveler's checks depends on where you are headed; **take cash to rural areas and small towns, traveler's checks to cities.** The most widely recognized checks are issued by American Express, Citicorp, Thomas Cook, and Visa. These are sold by major commercial banks for 1%–3% of the checks' face value— it pays to **shop around.** Both American Express and Thomas Cook issue checks that can be countersigned and used by either you or your traveling companion. So you won't be left with excess foreign currency, **buy a few checks in small denominations** to cash toward the end of your trip. Before leaving home, **contact your issuer for information on where to cash your checks** without incurring a transaction fee. Record the numbers of all your checks, and keep this listing in a separate place, crossing off the numbers of checks you have cashed.

WIRING MONEY

For a fee of 3%–10%, depending on the amount of the transaction, you can have

money sent to you from home through Money-Gram^{SM} or Western Union (☞ Money *in* Important Contacts A to Z). The transferred funds and the service fee can be charged to a MasterCard or Visa account.

P

PACKING FOR NEW ZEALAND

In New Zealand, be prepared for temperatures varying from day to night and weather that can turn suddenly, particularly at the change of seasons. The wisest approach to dressing is to **wear layered outfits.** You'll appreciate being able to remove or put on a jacket. **Take along a light raincoat and umbrella,** but remember that plastic raincoats and nonbreathing polyester are uncomfortable in the tropics. **Don't wear lotions or perfume** in the tropics either, since they attract mosquitoes and other bugs; **carry insect repellent. Bring a hat with a brim** to provide protection from the strong sunlight (☞ Health, *above*). You'll need warm clothing for South Island.

Dress is casual in most cities, though top resorts and restaurants may require a jacket and tie. In autumn, a light wool sweater and/or a jacket will suffice for evenings in coastal cities, but winter demands a heavier coat—a raincoat with a zip-out wool lining is ideal. **Comfortable walking shoes are a must.** You should have a pair of running shoes or the equivalent if you're planning to trek, and rubber-sole sandals or canvas shoes are needed for walking on reef coral.

Bring an extra pair of eyeglasses or contact lenses in your carry-on luggage, and if you have a health problem, **pack enough medication** to last the trip or have your doctor write you a prescription using the drug's generic name, because brand names vary from country to country (you'll then need a duplicate prescription from a local doctor). It's important that you **don't put prescription drugs or valuables in luggage to be checked,** for it could go astray. To avoid problems with customs officials, carry medications in the original packaging. Also, don't forget the addresses of offices that handle refunds of lost traveler's checks.

ELECTRICITY

To use your U.S.-purchased electric-powered equipment, **bring a converter and an adapter.** The electrical current in New Zealand is 240 volts, 50 cycles alternating current (AC); wall outlets take slanted three-prong plugs (but not the U.K. three-prong) and plugs with two flat prongs set at a "V" angle.

If your appliances are dual-voltage, you'll need only an adapter. Hotels sometimes have 110-volt outlets for low-wattage appliances near the sink, marked FOR SHAVERS ONLY; don't use them for high-wattage appliances like blow-dryers. If your laptop computer is older, carry a converter; new laptops operate equally well on 110 and 220 volts, so you need only an adapter.

LUGGAGE

Airline baggage allowances depend on the airline, the route, and the class of your ticket; ask in advance. In general, on domestic flights and on international flights between the United States and foreign destinations, you are entitled to check two bags. A third piece may be brought on board, but it must fit easily under the seat in front of you or in the overhead compartment. In the United States, the FAA gives airlines broad latitude regarding carry-on allowances, and they tend to tailor them to different aircraft and operational conditions. Charges for excess, oversize, or overweight pieces vary.

If you are flying between two foreign destinations, note that baggage allowances may be determined not by piece but by weight—generally 88 pounds (40 kilograms) in first class, 66 pounds (30 kilograms) in business class, and 44 pounds (20 kilograms) in economy. If your flight between two cities abroad *connects* with your transatlantic or transpacific flight, the piece method still applies.

SAFEGUARDING YOUR LUGGAGE➤ Before leaving home, **itemize your bags' contents** and their worth, and label them with your name, address, and phone number. (If you use your home address, cover it so that potential thieves can't see it readily.) Inside each bag, **pack a copy of your itinerary.** At check-in, **make sure that each bag is correctly tagged** with the destination airport's three-letter code. If your bags arrive damaged—or fail to arrive at all—file a written report with the airline before leaving the airport.

PASSPORTS & VISAS

If you don't already have one, **get a passport.** It is advisable that you **leave one photocopy of your passport's data page** with someone at home and keep another with you, separated from your passport, while traveling. If you lose your passport, promptly call the nearest embassy or consulate and the local police; having the data page information can speed replacement.

IN THE U.S.

All U.S. citizens, even infants, need only a valid passport to enter New Zealand for stays of up to 90 days. Application forms for both first-time and renewal passports are available at any of the 13 U.S. Passport Agency offices and at some post offices and courthouses. Passports are usually mailed within four weeks; allow five weeks or more in spring and summer.

CANADIANS

You need only a valid passport to enter New Zealand for stays of up to 90 days. Passport application forms are available at 28 regional passport offices, as well as post offices and travel agencies. Whether for a first or a renewal passport, you must apply in person. Children under 16 may be included on a parent's passport but must have their own to travel alone. Passports are valid for five years and are usually mailed within two to three weeks of application.

U.K. CITIZENS

Citizens of the United Kingdom need only a valid passport to enter New Zealand for stays of up to 90 days. Applications for new and renewal passports are available from main post offices and at the passport offices in Belfast, Glasgow, Liverpool, London, Newport, and Peterborough. You may apply in person at all passport offices, or by mail to all except the London office. Children under 16 may travel on an accompanying parent's passport. All passports are valid for 10 years. Allow a month for processing.

S
SENIOR-CITIZEN DISCOUNTS

To qualify for age-related discounts, **mention your senior-citizen status up front** when booking hotel reservations, not when checking out, and before you're seated in restaurants, not when paying the bill. Note that discounts may be limited to certain menus, days, or hours.

When renting a car, **ask about promotional car-rental discounts**—they can net even lower costs than your senior-citizen discount.

SPORTS AND THE OUTDOORS

FISHING

Wherever you fish, and whatever you fish for, you will profit immensely from the services of a local guide. On Lake Taupo or Rotorua, a boat with a guide plus all equipment will cost around $130 for two hours. In South Island, a top fishing guide who can supply all equipment and a four-wheel-drive vehicle will charge about $400 per day for two people. In the Bay of Islands region, an evening fishing trip aboard a small boat can cost as little as $35. For a big-game fishing boat, expect to pay between $600 and $1,000 per day. There are also several specialist lodges that provide guides and transport to wilderness streams sometimes accessible only by helicopter.

Fishing licenses are available from fishing-tackle and sports shops for daily, weekly, monthly, or seasonal periods. Costs range from $10.50 for a single day to $53 for the season, and licenses are valid for the entire country, with the exception of Lake Taupo, for which a separate permit is required. For anyone who plans to fish extensively, the best buy is a tourist fishing license—available from Visitor Information Centres in all major cities—which, for $56.26, permits

fishing anywhere in New Zealand for one month.

GOLF

Generally speaking, clubs can be rented, but you'll need your own shoes. Greens fees range from $5 at country courses to $40 at exclusive city courses. The better urban courses also offer resident professionals and golf carts for hire.

HIKING

The traditional way to hike in New Zealand is freedom walking. Freedom walkers carry their own provisions, sleeping bags, food, and cooking gear, and sleep in basic huts. A more refined alternative—usually available only on more popular trails—is the guided walk, on which you trek with just a light day pack, guides do the cooking, and you sleep in heated lodges. If you prefer your wilderness served with hot showers and an eiderdown on your bed, the guided walk is for you.

If you plan to walk the spectacular Milford or Routeburn Tracks in December or January, book at least six months in advance. At other times, three months is usually sufficient. (If you arrive without a booking, there may be last-minute cancellations, and parties of one or two can often be accommodated.) The Milford Track is closed due to snowfall from the end of April to early September.

Plan your clothing and footwear carefully. Even at the height of summer weather can change quickly, and hikers must be prepared—especially for the rainstorms that regularly drench the Southern Alps. (The Milford Sound region, with its average annual rainfall of 160 inches, is one of the wettest places on earth.) The most cost-effective rain gear you can buy is the U.S. Army poncho.

Wear a hat and sunglasses and put on sun block to protect your skin against the sun. Keep in mind that at higher altitudes, where the air is thinner, you will burn more easily. Sun reflected off of snow, sand, or water can be especially strong. Apply sunscreen liberally before you go out—even if only for a half-hour—and wear a visored cap or sunglasses.

Also, **be careful about heatstroke.** Symptoms include headache, dizziness, and fatigue, which can turn into convulsions, unconsciousness, and can lead to death. If someone in your party develops any of these conditions, have one person seek emergency help while others move the victim into the shade, wrap him or her in wet clothing (is a stream or lake nearby?) to cool him or her down.

Temperatures can vary widely from day to night. Be sure to **bring enough warm clothing for hiking and camping, along with wet weather gear.** Exposure to the degree that body temperature dips below 95°F (35°C) produces

the following symptoms: chills, tiredness, then uncontrollable shivering and irrational behavior, with the victim not always recognizing that he or she is cold. If someone in your party is suffering from any of this, wrap him or her in blankets and/or a warm sleeping bag immediately and try to keep him or her awake. The fastest way to raise body temperature is through skin-to-skin contact in a sleeping bag. Drinking warm liquids also helps.

Avoid drinking from streams or lakes, no matter how clear they may be. Giardia organisms can turn your stomach inside out. And in South Island a tiny organism found on the shallow margins of lakes can cause "duck itch," a temporary but intense skin irritation. The easiest way to purify water is to dissolve a water purification tablet in it. Camping equipment stores also carry purification pumps. Boiling water for 15 minutes is always a reliable method, if time- and fuel-consuming.

For information on camping, *see* Lodging, *above.*

STUDENTS ON THE ROAD

To save money, **look into deals available through student-oriented travel agencies.** To qualify, you'll need to have a bona fide student ID card. Members of international student groups are also eligible (☞ Students *in*

Important Contacts A to Z).

Hostels and backcountry hikers' huts are very popular in New Zealand. For more information, *see* Lodging, *above.*

T

TELEPHONES

Most pay phones now accept PhoneCards rather than coins. These plastic cards, available in denominations of $5, $10, $20, or $50, are sold at shops displaying the green PhoneCard symbol. To use a PhoneCard, lift the receiver, put the card in the slot in the front of the phone, and dial. The cost of the call is automatically deducted from your card; the display on the telephone tells you how much credit you have left at the end of the call. A local call from a public phone costs 20¢ per minute. **Don't forget to take your PhoneCard with you** when you finish your call. You may end up making some very expensive calls by leaving it behind.

CALLING HOME

The long-distance services of AT&T, MCI, and Sprint make calling home relatively convenient, but in many hotels you may find it impossible to dial the access number. The hotel operator may also refuse to make the connection. Instead, the hotel will charge you a premium rate—as much as 400% more than a calling card—for calls placed from your hotel room. To avoid such price gouging, travel with more than one company's long-distance calling card—a hotel may block Sprint but not MCI. If the hotel operator claims that you cannot use any phone card, ask to be connected to an international operator, who will help you to access your Phonecard. You can also dial the international operator yourself. If none of this works, try calling your phone company collect in the United States. If collect calls are also blocked, call from a pay phone in the hotel lobby. Before you go, **find out the local access codes** for your destinations.

TIPPING

Tipping is not widely practiced in New Zealand. Only in the better city restaurants will you be expected to show your appreciation for good service with a 10% tip.

TOUR OPERATORS

A package or tour to New Zealand can make your vacation less expensive and more hassle-free. Firms that sell tours and packages reserve airline seats, hotel rooms, and rental cars in bulk and pass some of the savings on to you. In addition, the best operators have local representatives available to help you at your destination.

A GOOD DEAL?

The more your package or tour includes, the better you can predict the ultimate cost of your vacation. Make sure you know exactly what is covered, and **beware of hidden costs.** Are taxes, tips, and service charges included? Transfers and baggage handling? Entertainment and excursions? These can add up.

Most packages and tours are rated deluxe, first-class superior, first class, tourist, or budget. The key difference is usually accommodations. If the package or tour you are considering is priced lower than in your wildest dreams, **be skeptical.** Also, **make sure your travel agent knows the accommodations** and other services. Ask about the hotel's location, room size, beds, and whether it has a pool, room service, or programs for children, if you care about these. Has your agent been there in person or sent others you can contact?

BUYER BEWARE

Each year a number of consumers are stranded or lose their money when operators—even very large ones with excellent reputations—go out of business. To avoid becoming one of them, take the time to **check out the operator**—find out how long the company has been in business and ask several agents about its reputation. Next, **don't book unless the firm has a consumer-protection program.** Members of the USTOA and the NTA are required to set aside funds for the sole purpose of covering your payments and travel arrangements in case of default. Non-member operators may instead carry insurance; look for the details in the operator's brochure—and for the name of an underwriter with a solid reputation. Note: When it comes to tour operators, **don't trust escrow accounts.** Although there are laws governing those of charter-flight operators, no governmental body prevents tour operators from raiding the till.

Next, **contact your local Better Business Bureau and the attorney general's offices** in both your own state and the operator's; have any complaints been filed? Finally, **pay with a major credit card.** Then you can cancel payment, provided that you can document your complaint. Always **consider trip-cancellation insurance** (☞ Insurance, *above*).

BIG VS. SMALL➤ Operators that handle several hundred thousand travelers per year can use their purchasing power to give you a good price. Their high volume may also indicate financial stability. But some small companies provide more personalized service; because they tend to specialize, they may also be more knowledgeable about a given area.

USING AN AGENT

Travel agents are excellent resources. In fact, large operators accept bookings made only through travel agents. But it's good to **collect brochures from several agencies** because some agents' suggestions may be skewed by promotional relationships with tour and package firms that reward them for volume sales. If you have a special interest, **find an agent with expertise in that area;** ASTA can provide leads in the United States. (Don't rely solely on your agent, though; agents may be unaware of small-niche operators, and some special-interest travel companies only sell direct.)

SINGLE TRAVELERS

Prices are usually quoted per person, based on two sharing a room. If traveling solo, you may be required to pay the full double-occupancy rate. Some operators eliminate this surcharge if you agree to be matched up with a roommate of the same sex, even if one is not found by departure time.

TRAIN TRAVEL

Trains in New Zealand's InterCity network usually cost the same as buses and are marginally quicker, but they run far less frequently. The country's most notable rail journey is the **Tranz-Alpine Express,** a spectacular scenic ride across Arthur's Pass and the mountainous spine of South Island between Greymouth and Christchurch.

To save money, **look into rail passes (☞ Train Travel in Important Contacts A to Z).** But be aware that if you don't plan to cover many miles, you may come out ahead by buying individual tickets.

Many travelers assume that rail passes guarantee them seats on the trains they wish to ride.

Not so. You need to **book seats ahead even if you are using a rail pass;** seat reservations are required on some European trains, particularly high-speed trains, and are a good idea on trains that may be crowded—particularly in summer on popular routes. You will also need a reservation if you purchase sleeping accommodations.

TRAVEL GEAR

Travel catalogs specialize in useful items that can **save space when packing** and make life on the road more convenient. Compact alarm clocks, travel irons, travel wallets, and personal-care kits are among the most common items you'll find. They also carry dual-voltage appliances, currency converters, and foreign-language phrase books. Some catalogs even carry miniature coffeemakers and water purifiers.

TRIP PLANNING

The difficulty with planning a trip to New Zealand is exquisite agony—nearly every square kilometer of the country is spectacular. Yet if you try to see too much, you may end up feeling like you haven't seen anything at all. So give yourself time to really savor two or three areas and get to know them and meet a few locals. **Four days to a week per locale will leave you feeling that you have actually been somewhere.** It's no exaggeration that time in New Zealand will feel like paradise.

U
U.S. GOVERNMENT

The U.S. government can be an excellent source of travel information. Some of this is free and some is available for a nominal charge. When planning your trip, **find out what government materials are available.** For just a couple of dollars, you can get a variety of publications from the Consumer Information Center in Pueblo, Colorado. Free consumer information also is available from individual government agencies, such as the Department of Transportation or the U.S. Customs Service. For specific titles, see the appropriate publications entry in Important Contacts A to Z, *above*.

W
WHEN TO GO

New Zealand is in the Southern Hemisphere, which means that **seasons are reversed**—it's winter down under during the American and European summer. The ideal months for comfortable all-round travel are October–April, especially if you want to participate in adventure activities. Avoid school holidays, when highways may be congested and accommodation is likely to be scarce and more expensive. Summer school holidays (the busiest) fall between mid-December and the end of January; other holiday periods are mid-May to the end of May, early July to mid-July, and late August to mid-September.

CLIMATE

Climate in New Zealand varies from subtropical in the north to temperate in the south. Summer (December–March) is generally warm, with an average of seven to eight hours of sunshine per day throughout the country. Winter (June–September) is mild at lower altitudes in South Island, but heavy snowfalls are common in South Island, particularly on the peaks of the Southern Alps. Rain can pour at any time of the year. (Some areas on the west coast of South Island receive an annual rainfall of more than 100 inches.)

The following are average daily maximum and minimum temperatures for some major cities in New Zealand.

AUCKLAND

Month	°F	°C	Month	°F	°C	Month	°F	°C
Jan.	74F	23C	May	63F	17C	Sept.	61F	16C
	61	16		52	11		49	9
Feb.	74F	23C	June	58F	14C	Oct.	63F	17C
	61	16		49	9		52	11
Mar.	72F	22C	July	56F	13C	Nov.	67F	19C
	59	15		47	8		54	12
Apr.	67F	19C	Aug.	58F	14C	Dec.	70F	21C
	56	13		47	8		58	14

CHRISTCHURCH

Month	°F	°C	Month	°F	°C	Month	°F	°C
Jan.	70F	21C	May	56F	13C	Sept.	58F	14C
	54	12		40	4		40	4
Feb.	70F	21C	June	52F	11C	Oct.	63F	17C
	54	12		36	2		45	7
Mar.	67F	19C	July	50F	10C	Nov.	67F	19C
	50	10		36	2		47	8
Apr.	63F	17C	Aug.	52F	11C	Dec.	70F	21C
	45	7		36	2		52	11

QUEENSTOWN

Month	°F	°C	Month	°F	°C	Month	°F	°C
Jan.	72F	22C	May	52F	11C	Sept.	56F	13C
	49	9		36	2		38	3
Feb.	70F	21C	June	47F	8C	Oct.	61F	16C
	50	10		34	1		41	5
Mar.	67F	19C	July	46F	8C	Nov.	65F	18C
	47	8		34	− 1		45	7
Apr.	61F	16C	Aug.	50F	10C	Dec.	70F	21C
	43	6		34	1		49	9

1 Destination: New Zealand

THE EDEN DOWN UNDER

IFIRST LAID EYES on New Zealand in 1967, near the end of an ocean voyage from Los Angeles to Australia. For a long morning, we skirted the New Zealand coastline north of Auckland, slipping past a land of impossibly green hills that seemed to be populated entirely by sheep. When the ship berthed in Auckland, I saw parked along the quay a museum-quality collection of vintage British automobiles, the newest of which was probably 15 years old. The explanation was simple enough: The alternative would be new imports, and imports were taxed at an enormous rate. But to a teenager fresh from the U.S.A., it seemed as though we had entered a time warp. When we took a day tour into the hills, the bus driver kept stopping for chats with other drivers; in those days it seemed possible to know everyone in New Zealand.

Since then, Auckland has caught up with the rest of the world. Its cars, its cellular-phone-toting execs, its waterfront restaurants with sushi and French mineral water all exist, unmistakably, in the 1990s. Yet the countryside still belongs to a greener, cleaner, friendlier time. Nostalgia is a strong suit in New Zealand's deck—second, of course, to its incomparable scenery. You'll still find people clinging sentimentally to their Morris Minors, Wolseley 1300s, VW Beetles, or Austin Cambridges—even though inexpensive used Japanese imports have flooded the market in recent years. So if you travel in search of glamorous shopping, sophisticated nightlife, and gourmet pleasures, this may not be the place for you. For some of New Zealand's most notable cultural achievements have been made in conjunction with nature—in the spectacular displays of its gardens, the growing reputation of its wineries, the fascinating lives and artifacts of the Maori, even the respect for nature shown in its current ecotourism boom. Auckland, Christchurch, and Wellington may never rival New York, Paris, or Rome, but that's probably not why you're considering a trip to New Zealand. And when you are in the cities, you're likely to find just as much warmth, calm, and graciousness as you will in rural areas.

Humanity was a late arrival to New Zealand. Its first settlers were Polynesians who reached its shores about AD 850, followed by a second wave of Polynesian migrants in the 14th century. These were not carefree, grass-skirted islanders living in a palmy utopia, but a fierce, martial people who made their homes in hilltop fortresses, where they existed in an almost continual state of warfare with neighboring tribes. That fierceness turned out to insure them more respect from Pakeha—the Maori word for Europeans—than many other native groups around the world ended up with in their encounters with colonial powers. The first Europeans to come across New Zealand were on board the Dutch ships of explorer Abel Tasman, which anchored in Golden Bay atop South Island on December 16, 1642. Miscommunication with a local Maori group the next day resulted in the death of four Europeans. The famous Captain James Cook was the next to explore New Zealand in the 18th century, but it wasn't until the 1840s that European settlers, primarily from England, arrived in numbers.

Compared with other modern immigrant societies such as the United States and Australia, New Zealand is overwhelmingly British—in its love of gardens, its architecture, its political system, and its food. Even so, changes are afoot. Momentum is gathering toward New Zealand becoming a republic, though it would undoubtedly remain within the British Commonwealth. In 1993, the country held a referendum which threw out the "first past the post" electoral system inherited from Westminster, adopting instead a mixed-member proportional election, the first of which was held in 1996. This means that each voter now casts two votes, one for a local representative and the other for the party of their choice. To govern, a party (or combination of parties) must have at least 50% of the actual vote—not just 50% of parliamentary seats. So rather than being dominated by just two strong parties, with various minor political entities filling out the numbers, New Zealand is now likely to be governed by party coalitions.

The Maori remain an assertive minority of 9%, a dignified, robust people whose oral tradition and art bears witness to a rich culture of legends and dreams. That culture comes dramatically to life in performances of songs and dances, including the *haka,* or war dance, which was calculated to intimidate and demoralize the enemy. It's little wonder that the national rugby team performs a haka as a prelude to its games. It would be a mistake, however, to feel that the Maori people's place in New Zealand is confined to history and cultural performances for tourists. They are having considerable impact in a modern political sense, reclaiming lost rights to land, fisheries, and other resources. You'll see Maori as prominent television newscasters, literary figures, and major athletes, at the same time keeping their cultural traditions alive.

The New Zealand land mass consists of two principle islands, with other outlying islands as well. Most of the country's 3.42 million people live on North Island, while South Island has the lion's share of the national parks. (More than one-tenth of the total area has been set aside as park land.) In a country about the size of Colorado—or just slightly larger than Great Britain—nature has assembled active volcanoes, subtropical rain forests, geysers, streams now filled with some of the finest trout on earth, fjords, beaches, glaciers, and some two dozen peaks that soar to more than 3,000 meters (10,000 feet). The country has scenic spectaculars from top to bottom, but while North Island often resembles a pristine, if radically hilly, golf course, South Island is wild, majestic, and exhilarating.

Experiencing these wonders is painless. New Zealand has a well-developed infrastructure of hotels, motels, and tour operators—but the best the country has to offer can't be seen through the windows of a tour bus. A trip here is a hands-on experience: hike, boat, fish, hunt, cycle, raft, and breathe some of the freshest air on earth. If these adventures sound a little too intrepid for you, the sheer beauty of the landscape and the clarity of the air will give you muscles you never knew you had.

—Michael Gebicki

WHAT'S WHERE

Geography and Population

New Zealand consists of three main islands: North Island (44,197 square miles), South Island (58,170 square miles), and Stewart Island (676 square miles). There are also Antarctic islands and the Chatham Islands some 500 miles east of Christchurch in the South Pacific. If New Zealand were stretched out along the west coast of the United States, the country would extend from Los Angeles to Seattle. No point is more than 70 miles from the sea, and owing to the narrow, hilly nature of the country, rivers tend to be short, swift, and broad.

About 3,550,000 people live on the islands of New Zealand, and population density is very low. It is less than half that of the United States (with all of its open land in the West), and about 1/20th that of the United Kingdom. New Zealanders are very friendly people—they seem to go out of their way to be hospitable. Some would argue that the low population takes away many of the stresses that people in more densely occupied areas experience. True or not, you're likely to be charmed by Kiwi hospitality.

More than 70% of the total population lives on North Island, where industry and government are concentrated. South Island is dominated by the Southern Alps, a spine of mountains running almost two-thirds the length of the island close to the west coast.

North Island

The mighty 1,200-year-old kauri trees, ferny subtropical forests, and miles of island-strewn coastline of Northland and the Coromandel Peninsula are the perfect complements to Auckland, New Zealand's largest city, and its neighborhood bustle and sprawl. Mid-island, Sulphuric Rotorua bubbles and oozes with surreal volcanic activity. It is one of the population centers of New Zealand's pre-European inhabitants, the Maori—try dining at a traditional hangi feast. Great hiking abounds in a variety of national parks, glorious gardens grow in the rich soil of the Taranaki province, and charming, Art Deco Napier and the nation's capital in Wellington are friendly counterpoints to the countryside.

South Island

Natural wonders never cease—not on South Island. Nor do the opportunities for adventure: sea kayaking, glacier hiking, trekking, fishing, mountain biking, rafting, and rock climbing. If you'd rather have an easier feast for your senses, fly over brilliant glaciers and snowy peaks, watch whales from on deck, and taste some of Marlborough's delicious wine. South of urbane Christchurch you'll head straight into picture-postcard New Zealand, where the country's tallest mountains are reflected in crystal clear lakes and sheer rock faces tower above the fjords. The choice of activity is yours. You can enjoy some of the world's most dramatic views in complete peace and quiet, or leap—literally, if you'd like—from one adrenaline rush to the next. Take the four-day Milford Track walk, or opt for the remote isolation of pristine Stewart Island. Add New Zealand hospitality to all of that and you can't go wrong.

PLEASURES AND PASTIMES

As much as or more than any other countries, New Zealanders love sports—professional, amateur, and any variety of weekend sports. You'll see a number of them listed below. If you are interested in a particular adventure activity, be sure to consult Adventure Vacations, Chapter 6, for specific guided trips. If you want to do it yourself, Adventure Vacations can also point out desirable regions where you can strike out on your own.

Other pleasures and pastimes described below include dining, lodging, shopping, and wine. Be sure to look in the Gold Guide, *above,* for travel tips on categories listed in this section.

Beaches

The list of unique and outstanding New Zealand beaches is almost endless—including the dramatic Karekare beach in West Auckland shown in Jane Campion's film, *The Piano.* There are no private beaches and no risks from pollution. The greatest danger is sunburn. Most New Zealanders prefer beaches along the east coast of North Island, where the combination of gentle seas and balmy summers is a powerful attraction during January holidays. Sand on the west coast of North Island is black as a result of volcanic activity. South Island beaches are no less spectacular, particularly those in the northwest in Abel Tasman National Park and down the West Coast. In summer, popular beaches close to cities and in major holiday areas are patrolled by lifeguards. Swim with caution on unpatrolled beaches.

Bicycling

Despite its often precipitous topography, New Zealand is great for biking. A temperate climate, excellent roads with relatively little traffic, and scenic variety make it a delight for anyone who is reasonably fit and has time to travel slowly. The most common problem for cyclists is buckled wheel rims: Narrow, lightweight alloy rims won't stand up long to the rigors of the road. A wide-rimmed hybrid or mountain bike with road tires is a better bet for extensive touring.

If two-wheel touring sounds appealing but pedaling a heavily laden bicycle doesn't, consider a guided cycle tour. Tours last from 2 to 18 days; bikes are supplied, and your gear is loaded on a bus or trailer that follows the riders. And you have the option of busing in the "sag wagon" when your legs give out.

Boating: Sailing, Rafting, and Sea-Kayaking

The country's premier cruising regions are the Bay of Islands, Marlborough Sounds, and the coast around Abel Tasman National Park, near the northern tips of North and South Islands respectively. Both areas offer sheltered waters, marvelous scenery, and secluded beaches. The Bay of Islands enjoys warmer summer temperatures, while Marlborough Sounds has a wild, untamed quality.

The Wanganui River, flowing from the western slopes of Mount Tongariro on North Island to meet the sea at the west coast town of Wanganui, is New Zealand's premier canoeing river. The longest navigable waterway in the country, this captivating river winds through native bushland with occasional rapids, cascades, and gorges. The most popular canoe trip begins at Taumarunui, taking four to five days to get downstream to Pipriki. Do this in warmer months, between November and March.

For thrills and spills, white-water rafting on the Shotover River near Queenstown is hard to beat. Don't try it unless you have some experience in the sport—there are gentler rivers in both the South and North islands for beginners. Again, *see* Chapter 6 for information on these activities.

Country Life

In New Zealand, rural settings are never far away from even the largest cities. To really get a taste of Kiwi life, don't confine your stay to tourist spots, towns, and cities. Many farms are open to visitors, either for a day visit or an overnight stay. You are usually welcome to try your hand at milking a cow or taking part in other activities. ☞ The Gold Guide for information on farmstays.

Another way to get insight into the rural scene is to attend an agricultural and pastoral (A and P) fair. These are held at various times of the year by communities large and small, but the best time to see them is during summer. Check at information centers to find out where the nearest show is being held during your stay. These events are an opportunity for farmers to bring their chickens, cattle, goats, sheep, and other stock into town and compete for ribbons. The farmers are only too happy to chat about their live exhibits to anyone who will ask. A and P Shows are great for kids, who are usually welcome to pat and stroke the animals. Other favorites include wood chopping contests, sheep shearing, and crafts displays. One tip: Many of these shows go on for two or three days, but have one public day, which is declared a local holiday so that families in the area can attend. If possible, avoid such times and go on quieter days.

Dining

Old New Zealand, new New Zealand— what you'll find culinarily on your trip spans the 20th century, from farmers fare of yore to very contemporary preparations. Auckland, Wellington, and Christchurch offer cosmopolitan dining, but, apart from the odd enlightened restaurateur and a few expensive sporting lodges, much country cooking still follows the meat-and-two-veg school of English cuisine.

The waters around New Zealand are some of the cleanest in the world, and their produce is sensational. The New Zealand crayfish, essentially a clawless lobster, is delicious, and succulent white-shelled Bluff oysters, available from March to about July, are rated highly by aficionados. Watch for orange roughy, a delicate white-fleshed fish best served with light sauce. And don't miss pipis (clams), scallops (with delicious roe in spring), green-lipped mussels, paua (abalone) with their iridescent shells, the small seasonal fish called whitebait usually served in fritters, and very fine freshwater eel.

Back on land, lamb and venison are widely available, and many chefs are preparing exciting dishes using cervena, a leaner, lighter deer raised on farms. Other foods: Capsicum is red or green bell pepper; courgettes are zucchini. The kumara (*koo-mer-ah*) is a tasty, white-fleshed sweet potato that the Maori brought with them from Polynesia. It grows in warmer North Island soil. Don't confuse entrées with main courses, it is the appetizer course following hors d'oeuvres. Pudding generally speaking is dessert, and one New Zealand favorite is pavlova, also called pav, a white meringue pie named after ballerina Anna Pavlova.

A native specialty is the *hangi,* a Maori feast of steamed meat and vegetables. Tour operators can take you to a hangi at a Maori *marae* (meeting house). Several hotels in Rotorua offer a hangi, usually combined with an evening of Maori song and dance. Unfortunately, these days it's often unlikely that food will be cooked by steaming it in the traditional earthen oven.

For inexpensive lunches, the standard take-aways are meat pies and fish and chips. But keep in mind that there are more and more contemporary cafés opening up in unexpected places. Occasionally, you'll also find good vegetarian restaurants. Most country pubs serve reasonable cooked lunches and sometimes a selection of salads. In season, stock up on fruit from roadside stalls that are scattered throughout the country's fruit-growing areas.

Fishing

Considering that trout were introduced from California little more than a hundred years ago, today's population of these fish in New Zealand's lakes and rivers is phenomenal. One reason for this is that commercial trout fishing is illegal, which means that you won't find trout on restaurant menus. You can, however, bring your own catch for a chef to prepare.

Getting back to fishing, the average summer rainbow trout taken from Lake Tarawera, near Rotorua, weighs 5 pounds, and 8- to 10-pound fish are not unusual. In the lakes of North Island, fingerlings often reach a weight of 4 pounds nine months after they are released. Trout do not reach maturity until they grow to 14 inches, and all trout below that length must be returned to the water.

Trout fishing has a distinctly different character on the two islands. In the Rotorua-Taupo region of North Island, the main quarry is rainbow trout, which are usually taken from the lakes with wet flies or spinners. Trolling is also popular and productive. On South Island, where brown trout predominate, there is outstanding dry-fly fishing. It's best in the Nelson region and in the Southern Lakes district, at the top and bottom ends of South Island respectively. Trout season lasts from October through April in most areas, though Lakes Taupo and Rotorua are open all year.

Salmon are found in rivers that drain the eastern slopes of the Southern Alps, especially those that reach the sea between Christchurch and Dunedin. Salmon season runs from October to April, reaching its peak from January to March.

The seas off the east coast of North Island are among the world's finest big-game fishing waters. The quarry is mako, hammerhead, tiger shark, and marlin—especially striped marlin, which average around 250 pounds. For light tackle fishing, bonito and skipjack tuna and kahawai (sea trout) offer excellent sport. Many anglers maintain that kahawai are better fighters, pound for pound, than freshwater trout. Bases for big-game fishing are the towns of Paihia and Russell, which have a number of established charter operators. The season runs from January to April, although smaller game fishing is good all year.

Glorious Gardens

New Zealand is rapidly becoming a major destination for garden lovers on vacation. Since the first British settlers arrived with seeds from their homeland, Kiwis have looked toward Great Britain for horticultural inspiration. However, as elsewhere in the world, gardeners here are discovering the unique beauty of their native plants and are gradually welcoming them into their gardens, successfully mixing them with exotics and creating a look that couldn't be achieved anywhere else.

So when northern hemisphere gardens lie fast asleep for the winter, head to New Zealand to see nature in full bloom. The climate couldn't be more accommodating, with cool summers, mild winters, and abundant rainfall. The rich, spongey soil readily absorbs the rain, courtesy of countless volcanic eruptions over time. With few stresses, plants respond by growing to enormous proportions. Trees are taller, flowers more abundant, perfumes stronger.

Equally delightful are the gardeners themselves—a large part of the population that appears to include all economic and social groups. Being New Zealanders, they are enthusiastic, hospitable, and only too glad to show off their hearts' delights. As a result, enormous numbers of private gardens, in addition to public gardens, are open to visitors. With the foresight of a phone call, not only can a beautiful garden be visited, but a passion can be shared—an exchange that makes the world feel like a smaller, friendlier place.

Golf

You will find courses of an extremely high standard, such as Titirangi and Millbrook. However, keen golfers should also take the time to enjoy a country course, where the main hazards include sheep droppings and friendly locals who will keep you chatting until the sun goes down if you let them. You can play year-round; winter is the major season. Most of New Zealand's 400 courses welcome visitors.

Hiking

If you want to see the best of what New Zealand has to offer, put on a pair of hiking boots and head for the hills. Range upon range of mountains, deep, ice-carved valleys, wilderness areas that have never been farmed, logged, or grazed, and a first-class network of marked trails and tramping huts are just some of the reasons that hiking is a national addiction.

The traditional way to hike in New Zealand is freedom walking. Freedom walkers carry their own provisions, sleeping bags, food, and cooking gear, and sleep in basic huts. A more refined alternative—usually available only on more popular trails—is the guided walk, on which you trek with just a light day pack, guides do the cooking, and you sleep in heated lodges. If you prefer your wilderness served with hot showers and an eiderdown on your bed, the guided walk is for you.

The most popular walks are in the Southern Alps, where South Island's postcard views of mountains, wild rivers, mossy beech forests, and fjords issue a challenge to the legs that is hard to resist. Trekking season in the mountains usually lasts from October to mid-April. The best-known of all New Zealand's trails is the Milford Track, a four-day walk through breathtaking scenery to the edge of Milford Sound. Its main drawback is its popularity. This is the only track in New Zealand on which numbers are controlled: You are required to obtain a permit and to begin walking on the day specified (to ensure that the overnight huts along the track don't become impossibly crowded).

While the Milford gets the lion's share of publicity, many other walks offer a similar—some would say better—combination of scenery and exercise. The Routeburn Track is a three-day walk that rises through beech forests, traverses a mountain face across a high pass, and descends through a glacial valley. The Kepler and the Hollyford are both exceptional, and the Abel Tasman, at the northern end of South Island, is a spectacular three- to four-day coastal track that can be walked year-round.

By all means don't rule out tramping on North Island, which has plenty of wonders of its own. The Coromandel Peninsula has tremendous forests of gigantic, 1,200-year-old kauri trees, 80-foot-tall tree ferns, and a gorgeous coastline, and a Coromandel Track scheduled to open soon. You can hike among active volcanic peaks in Tongariro National Park. And on a nub of the west coast formed by volcanic activity hundreds of years ago, the majestic, Fuji-like Mount Taranaki, also known as Mount Egmont, is positively mystifying as it alternately dons cloaks of mist and its brilliant, sunlit, snowy cap. In fact, there are few areas in North or South islands that don't have their own intriguing geological eccentricities worth exploring on foot.

Kiwi English

Somebody should really teach those Kiwis how to speak the English language—just kidding, Doug! In fact, there are a few Kiwi expressions that you should know about to avoid eliciting puzzled looks or embarrassment from time to time. In a restaurant, don't ask for a napkin unless your baby needs a diaper, as in nappies—ask for a **serviette.** A bathroom is where you actually bathe, so ask for a **toilet** (or **loo**) if you have to go—in fact, New Zealand may be the easiest country in the world to find a public toilet, especially on the road; they're signposted in even the smallest of hamlets that have them.

Keep in mind that **tea** isn't just the beverage, it also generally means dinner. **Devonshire tea** is served morning and afternoon: cream tea with scones. If someone offers you a **cuppa,** say whether you'd like a cuppa tea or a cuppa coffee; the word refers to both. If you've stopped at a pub to **sink a few** and the local you start talking with offers to **shout,** say **ta** (thanks a lot), tell him what you're drinking, and consider shouting a round later to return the favor.

There are two terms for vacation houses: In North Island it's **bach** (baches plural); in South Island it's **crib. En suites** are bathrooms attached to your hotel or B&B room. The great outdoors is called the **bush,** through which you **tramp** (hike). When you go tramping, be sure not to call your waist pack a fanny pack—if you do you'll shock Kiwis, for whom fanny refers to women's privates. And use insect repellent for the **mozzies** (mosquitos) and biting sandflies.

And when you're driving on the left, **sealed** (paved) road, **metal** (gravel), or dirt, for God's sake don't get yourself into a **prang** (accident).

Maori Language

Even if you have a natural facility for picking up languages, the Maori words that you'll find all over New Zealand can be baffling. The West Coast town of Punakaiki, pronounced "poon-ah-kie-kee," is relatively straightforward, but when you get to places like Whangamata, the going gets tricky—the opening "wh" is pronounced like an "f," and the accent is placed on the last syllable: "fahng-ah-ma-*ta*." Sometimes it is the mere length of words that makes them difficult, as in the case of Waitakaruru (why-ta-ka-ru-ru) or Whakarewarewa (fa-ka-*re*-wa-*re*-wa). You'll notice in both of those words that the last syllables are repeated, which is something to look out for to make longer words more manageable. Town names like Waikanea (*why*-can-eye) you'll just have to repeat to yourself a few times before saying them without pause.

A few more points: the Maori "r" is rolled so that it sounds a little like a "d." Thus the Northland town of Whangarei is pronounced "fang-ah-day," and the word Maori is pronounced "mo-dee," with the "o" sounding like it does in the word mould, and a rolled "r." All of this is a little too complicated for some Pakeha (pahk-ey-ha), the Maori word for descendents of European settlers, who choose not to bother with Maori pronunciations. So in some places, if you say you've just driven over from "fahng-ah-ma-*ta*," the reply might be: "You mean 'wang-ah-*ma*-tuh.' " You can pronounce these words either way, but more and more Kiwis are saying Maori words as the Maori do.

There are some key Maori words that you should know. *Kia ora* (kee-ah oar-ah) means hello or good luck. *Haere mai* (ha-air-ay my) means welcome, *haere ra* means good-bye if you are the one staying, and *e noho ra* if you are leaving. Thank you is *ka pai* (kah pie). And a *hoa* is a friend.

The Maori word *tapu* is the origin of the Western word taboo, which has its roots in sacredness. Other words you'll encounter are *hangi* (hahng-ee), both the traditional feast and the oven in which the feast is cooked. *Manu* means bird, *ika* is fish. *Moku* is the Maori facial tatoo. *Motu* means island, *puke* is hill, *rangi* is the sky, and *whanga* means harbor. A *pa* is a fortified Maori villiage, often atop a hill, and a *whare* (fah-ray) is a house. Some of these words occur in place names.

Shopping

New Zealand produces several unique souvenirs, but don't expect to find many bargains. Sheepskins and quality woolens are widely available. Bowls hewn from native timber and polished to a lustrous finish are distinctive souvenirs, but a fine example will cost several hundred dollars. Greenstone, a type of jade once prized by the Maori, is now used for ornaments and jewelry—especially the figurines known as *tiki*, often worn as pendants. The two major areas for crafts are the Coromandel Peninsula close to Auckland and the environs of Nelson at the northern tip of South Island; those areas also have local potters. The Parnell area of Auckland and the Galleria in Christchurch Arts Centre are the places to shop for souvenirs. In Nelson, Craft Habitat brings together some of the finest local arts and crafts under one roof.

Skiing

New Zealand has 27 peaks that top the 10,000-foot mark, and the June–October ski season is the reason many skiers head "down under" when the snow melts in the northern hemisphere. On South Island, the site of most of the country's 13 commercial ski areas, the outstanding ones being Treble Cone and Cardrona, served by the town of Wanaka, and Coronet Peak and the Remarkables, close to Queenstown. North Island has only two commercial ski areas, Whakapapa and Turoa, both near Lake Taupo on the slopes of Mount Ruapehu.

What New Zealand ski fields lack is sophistication. By international standards they are comparatively small, and slopes lack the extensive interlocking lift systems that are a feature of European skiing. There is no such thing as liftside accommodations: Skiers must stay in nearby subalpine towns.

Heli-skiing is very popular. Harris Mountains Heliski, the second largest heli-ski operation in the world, gives access from the town of Wanaka to more than 200 runs on more than 100 peaks accessible to skiers by no other means. The ultimate heli-ski adventure is the 13-kilometer (8½-mile) run down Tasman Glacier.

Wine

New Zealand is one of the wine world's latest upstarts: connoisseurs might complain about this or that quality, but Kiwi grapes and vingerons are producing first-class wine. Sauvignon blanc was the first New Zealand varietal to win an international award—that was Hunter's 1985 vintage, from the Marlborough region. Dry rieslings and rich chardonnays are also excellent, and some méthode champagnoise sparkling wines are coming into their own as well. As for reds, pinot noir tends to be the most refined. Cabernets, merlots, and blends are perhaps best appreciated with food.

New Zealand winemakers more often than not have food in mind when they create their wine, and you should plan to try sauvignon blanc alongside scallops or crayfish, chardonnay with salmon, or some of the bold reds with lamb or venison. You'll discover just how well those audacious flavors work with local cuisine.

You won't have to go out of your way to try New Zealand wine—licensed restaurants are extremely loyal to Kiwi wineries—but you might want to nonetheless. Much of the country's wine is exported to the U.K. and Australia, so if you're coming from there you might know what to expect. But in the States, California has acted as a barrier to the importation of New Zealand wine, as has the volume required for mass distribution, which the industry simply can't provide for the U.S. market.

Of the major Kiwi wine routes, we cover four: Hawke's Bay, one of the best known regions, growing excellent chardonnay, cabernet sauvignon, cabernet franc, and merlot grapes; Gisborne–East Cape, which is often overshadowed by nearby Hawke's Bay but may make better chardonnay itself; Wairarapa-Martinborough, which specializes in pinot noir; and Marlborough, where sauvignon blanc reigns supreme, but there are also very good sparkling whites, rieslings, chardonnays, even muller-thurgau, and a host of reds.

If you aren't familiar with New Zealand wine, you might find special pleasure in tasting—and in bringing home—wine that isn't available at your local vintner. Bring back as much as you can, sauvignon blanc to drink soon, chardonnay to let stand for a year or two, and the red of choice to age longer.

FODOR'S CHOICE

Special Moments

North Island

★Digging out your own thermal bath at Hot Water Beach, Coromandel Peninsula

★Listening to the Maori choir, St. Faith's Church, Rotorua

★Biting into a crisp, juicy apple just picked from an orchard in Hawke's Bay

★Your first glimpse of Mount Taranaki (Mount Egmont), be it in sunshine or cloud, Taranaki

★Taking a horse and carriage tour around Wairarapa vineyards, Martinborough

South Island

★Kayaking with dolphins off of Abel Tasman National Park

★Sampling smoked snapper at Nature Smoke, Mapua, Nelson Lakes

★Watching the sun climb up Franz Josef or Fox glacier, West Coast

★Punting on the Avon River with someone special, Christchurch

★Sailing on a fjord, just taking in the wonder of it all, Fiordland National Park

★Hurtling along Shotover River in a jetboat, Queenstown

National Parks and Natural Wonders

North Island

★*The Piano*'s Karekare Beach, West Auckland

★Taking one of Kiwi Dundee's wilderness hikes on the Coromandel Peninsula

★Stands of giant native kauri and tree ferns, Coromandel Peninsula

★Gurgling, slopping, bubbling volcanic activity in Rotorua

★Fishing in the lakes and rivers around Rotorua and Taupo

★The wild landscapes of volcanic Tongariro National Park

★Remote landscapes of the East Cape

★Lake Waikaremoana, Urewera National Park

★The Pinnacles, Wairarapa

South Island

★The seascapes of Abel Tasman National Park and Golden Bay, Nelson Lakes

★Dipping a line into a backcountry river in Nelson Lakes National Park

★Glaciers grinding down 12,000-foot peaks into the rain forests of the West Coast

★Mount Cook and Tasman Glacier in Mount Cook National Park

★The Remarkables viewed as a backdrop to lake Wakatipu, Queenstown

★Fiordland National Park's Milford Track, Mitre Peak, and Milford Sound

★The isolation and night skies of southernmost Stewart Island

Wildlife Viewing

North Island

★Diving in the Bay of Islands

★Birding in Tongariro National Park

★The gannet colony at Cape Kidnapper, south of Napier

South Island

★Dolphins off of Abel Tasman National Park

★Cruising with sperm whales off Kaikoura

★Fiordland crested penguins and fur seals at Wilderness Lodge Lake Moeraki, West Coast

★The royal albatrosses, Taiaroa Head, Otago Peninsula

★Nightwatch for kiwis on Stewart Island

Dining

North Island

★Virtu, Auckland ($$$)

★Cin Cin on Quay, Auckland ($$)

★The Steps Restaurant, New Plymouth, Taranaki ($)

★The Mountain House, Stratford, Taranaki ($$$)

★Le Petit Lyon, Wellington ($$$$)

★Brasserie Flipp, Wellington ($$$)

South Island

★Crayfish shacks around Kaikoura ($$)

★Canterbury Tales, Christchurch ($$$$)

★Espresso 124, Christchurch ($$)

★Main Street Café and Bar, Christchurch ($)

City Lodging

North Island

★Stamford Plaza, Auckland ($$$$)

★Peace and Plenty Inn, Devonport, Auckland ($$$$)

★Sedgwick-Kent Lodge, Remuera, Auckland ($$–$$$$)

★Devonport Villa, Devonport, Auckland ($$)

★Parkroyal, Wellington ($$$$)

South Island

★Timara Lodge, Blenheim ($$$$)

★Cashmere House, Christchurch ($$$)

★Riverview Lodge, Christchurch ($$)

Country Lodging

North Island

★Brenton Lodge, Whangamata, Coromandel Peninsula ($$$)

★Huka Lodge, Lake Taupo ($$$$)

★Martinborough Hotel, Wairarapa ($$$)

South Island

★Lake Brunner Sporting Lodge, near Greymouth ($$$$)

★Millbrook Resort, near Queenstown ($$$$)

★Timara Lodge, Blenheim, Marlborough ($$$$)

★Wilderness Lodge Lake Moeraki, West Coast ($$$)

★Willow Cottage, near Wanaka ($$$)

FESTIVALS AND SEASONAL EVENTS

Sport features heavily in New Zealand's festival calendar. Horse and boat races, triathlons, and fishing competitions are far more prominent than celebrations of the arts. Just about every town holds a yearly agricultural and pastoral ("A & P") show, and these proud displays of local crafts, produce, livestock, and wood-chopping and sheep-shearing prowess provide a memorable look at rural New Zealand. An annual calendar, *New Zealand Special Events,* is available from government tourist offices.

DEC. 25–26➣ On **Christmas Day** and **Boxing Day** the country virtually closes down.

JAN. 1➣ **New Year's Day** is a nationwide holiday.

JAN. 28➣ For the **Auckland Anniversary Day Regatta,** Auckland's birthday party, the "City of Sails" takes to the water.

FEB. 6➣ **Waitangi Day,** New Zealand's national day, commemorates the signing of the Treaty of Waitangi between Europeans and Maori in 1840. The focus of the celebration is, naturally enough, the town of Waitangi in the Bay of Islands.

FEB. 11–12➣ **Speights Coast to Coast** is the ultimate iron-man challenge—a two-day, 238-kilometer (148-mile)

marathon of cycling, running, and kayaking that crosses South Island from west to east. Information: Robin Judkins, ☎ 03/326–5493.

FEB. 3–14➣ **The Festival of Romance** is held in Christchurch—the city where lovers can stroll through an old English garden and enjoy a punt ride on the Avon River. ☎ 03/379–9629.

FEB. 14–22➣ Christchurch's **Garden City Festival of Flowers,** the country's largest flower show, finds the city bursting with blossoms and activity, with plenty of related events, displays, and exhibitions.

FEB. 22–24➣ **The Devonport Food and Wine Festival** showcases some of the country's best restaurants and is easily reached by a ferry trip from Auckland city.

1ST THURS.–SAT. OF MAR.➣ **Golden Shears International Shearing Championship** is a three-day event that pits men armed with shears against the fleecy sheep in Masterton, just north of Wellington. Information: Masterton Visitor Information Centre, 5 Dixon St., ☎ 06/378–7373.

MAR. 31–APR. 3➣ The **Easter** holiday weekend lasts from Good Friday through Easter Monday. The Royal Easter Show is

held in Auckland over the holiday.

APR. 25➣ **Anzac Day** honors the soldiers, sailors, and airmen and women who fought and died for the country.

EARLY MAY➣ **The Fletcher Marathon** around Lake Rotorua is New Zealand's premier long-distance event.

1ST MON. IN JUNE➣ **The Queen's Birthday** is celebrated nationwide.

EARLY TO MID-JULY➣ At the **Queenstown Winter Festival,** the winter sports capital hits the slopes for a week of competition by day and entertainment by night.

LATE JULY➣ **Mad, Mad Mid-Winter Festival** is a mixture of sporting events held in Rotorua, from outrigger canoeing to nighttime mountain biking to a mountain rafting championship contest.

OCT. 18–25➣ **Dunedin Rhododendron Festival** opens the city's gardens for tours and offers lectures and plant sales. ☎ 03/474–3300.

OCT. 23➣ **Labour Day** is observed throughout the country.

Nov. 1–10➤ **Taranaki Rhododendron Festival** in and around New Plymouth is a major event. One hundreds–plus of private gardens open to the public, there are lectures, and the vast Pukeiti Rhododendron Trust holds a series of cultural events and festivities. ☎ 06/752–4141.

Mid- to late Nov.➤ **Ellerslie Flower Show** in Auckland is one of the headline events on New Zealand's gardening calendar. It is modeled on London's Chelsea Flower Show.

2nd Week in Nov.➤ **Canterbury Agricultural and Pastoral Show** spotlights the farmers and graziers of the rich countryside surrounding Christchurch. Information: Canterbury Visitor Information Centre, Worcester St. and Oxford Terr., Christchurch, ☎ 03/379–9629.

2nd Weekend in Nov.➤ **Garden Marlborough** has local garden tours and a fête with products for sale. The festival follows the Ellerslie Flower Show, which allows its organizers to include international experts who attended the Auckland event; they give excellent lectures and workshops. Blenheim, ☎ 03/572–8707.

2 Auckland and the North

The mighty 1,200-year-old kauri trees, ferny subtropical forests, and miles of island-strewn coastline of Northland and the Coromandel Peninsula are the perfect counterpoint to Auckland, New Zealand's largest city, and its neighborhood bustle and sprawl.

By Michael
Gebicki and
Stu Freeman

AS YOU FLY INTO AUCKLAND, New Zealand's gateway city, you may wonder where the city is. Most people arriving for the first time, and even New Zealanders coming home, are impressed by the sea views and the green forest that dominates the view on the approach to the airport.

The drive from the airport—with scenery commanded by some of the city's 46 volcanic hills, their grass kept closely cropped by those four-legged lawnmowers known as sheep—does little to dispel the "clean green" image so many people have of the country. And reading the highway signs will begin to give you a taste of the unusual and sometimes baffling Maori place names around the country.

Yet a couple of days in this city of about 1 million will reveal a level of development and sophistication that belies first impressions. In the past 10 years Auckland has grown up in more ways than one. Many shops are open seven days, central bars and nightclubs welcome patrons well into the night and early morning, and a cosmopolitan mix of Polynesians, Asians, and Europeans all contribute to the cultural milieu. Literally topping things off is the newly opened 1,082-foot Sky Tower, dwarfing everything around it and acting as a beacon for the casino, hotel, and restaurant complex that opened early in 1996. This is the newest, if least pervasive, face of modern New Zealand.

In the midst of the city's activity, you'll see knots of cyclists and joggers. Like all other New Zealanders, Aucklanders are addicted to the outdoors—especially the water. There are some 70,000 powerboats and sailing craft in the Greater Auckland area—about one for every four households. And a total of 102 beaches lie within an hour's drive of the city center. The city is currently working to enhance its greatest asset, Waitemata Harbour—a Maori name meaning "Sea of Sparkling Waters." The city will stage its first defense of the America's Cup in 2,000, and the regatta has been acting as a catalyst for major redevelopment of the waterfront.

Auckland is not easy to explore. Made up of a sprawling array of neighborhoods, locally called suburbs, the city spreads out on both shores of Stanley Bay and Waitemata Harbour. It's best to have a car for getting around between neighborhoods, and even between some city center sights. One good introduction to the city, particularly if you arrive at the end of a long flight and time is limited, is the commuter ferry that crosses the harbor to the village of Devonport, where you can soak up the charming enclave's atmosphere in a leisurely stroll, at a local café or bookstore, or munching on fish and chips on the town green.

As you put Auckland behind you, and with it the signs of overdevelopment, you'll find yourself in the midst of some of the open space that is so pervasive in New Zealand. North of the city, the Bay of Islands is both beautiful—for its lush forests, spendid beaches, and shimmering harbors—and historic—as the place where Westernized New Zealand came into being with the signing of the Treaty of Waitangi in 1840. South and east of the city is the rugged and exhilarating Coromandel Peninsula, with mountains stretching the length of its middle and its Pacific coastline afloat with picturesque islands.

Note: For more information on bicycling, diving, deep-sea fishing, hiking, and sailing in Auckland and the north, *see* Chapter 6.

Pleasures and Pastimes

Beaches

When the sun comes out, Aucklanders head to the beach. With seas both to the west and the east, few people in the city live more than a 15-minute drive from the coast. Generally speaking the best surfing is at the black sand beaches on the west coast, and the safest swimming is found on the east. Beaches that do have a reputation for large waves and rips are patrolled in the summer, so play it safe and swim between the flags. The only other danger is from the sun itself. The ozone layer is weak above New Zealand, so slap on the sunscreen and resist the temptation to sunbake. ☞ Beaches, *below.*

Boating

Auckland is dubbed "City of Sails" for good reason. The population is crazy about boating and any other recreation associated with the sea. A variety of ferries and high speed catamarans operate on Waitemata Harbor. Just go down to the ferry building on Princes Wharf and take your pick at the Fullers Cruise Centre. Even better, go for a sail on the *Pride of Auckland.* Northland and the ravishing Bay of Islands also has a diverse choice of boat and sailing trips.

Dining

International influences have transformed Auckland's dining scene from a "roast of the day" mentality to a cosmopolitan mix of cafés, European and eastern fare, food halls, and top class seafood restaurants. Many places on the harbor and elsewhere in Auckland have daily seafood specials—don't miss such delicacies as Bluff oysters, New Zealand mussels, scallops, and crayfish (clawless lobster).

Parnell Village has an eclectic mix of Indian, Chinese, and Southeast Asian eateries sitting comfortably alongside taverns and fine restaurants. For lunch at Victoria Park or in the city center, a few dollars will buy you anything from fish and chips, to nachos, noodles, or naan bread. South of the city center, the suburb of Ponsonby claims the city's "café mile" in Ponsonby Road just off Karangahape Road. During the summer this is the place to go for streetside dining. Pull up a chair at a place that looks good to you, choose your fancy from the blackboard or menu, and watch this small corner of the world go by.

As you put Auckland behind you the choice of fare reduces sharply, though you'll occasionally find enlightened cooks in countryside nooks. But keep in mind that New Zealand's non-trendiness is one of its most refreshing qualities. At least once, give roast lamb and vegetables a try. If you don't enjoy New Zealand lamb, chances are you won't like it anywhere.

Lodging

Around Auckland and the north, a great variety of accommodation is available, from flashy downtown hotels to comfortable B&Bs to mom-and-pop motels. Because Kiwis are so naturally hospitable, it's hard not to recommend lodgings where you have a chance to talk with your hosts—unless you prefer anonymity.

Volcanoes and Vistas

Auckland is built on and around 48 volcanoes, and the tops of many of them provide sweeping views of the city. Mt. Eden is probably the most popular, and several bus tours include this central site. Rangitoto Island has an even better vista. This volcano emerged from the sea just 600 years ago, no doubt much to the wonder of the Maori people living right next door on Motutapu Island. You need to take a ferry to the island, then either a short ride or a one-hour walk to the top will give you a 360° sweep of the city and the Hauraki Gulf islands—and a chance to peer into the volcano's crater.

Walking and Hiking

New Zealand's most famous tracks are in South Island, but don't pass up the superb bushwalking around Auckland, Northland, and the Coromandel Peninsula. New Zealand's largest city is fringed by bush to the west, and the Waitakere Ranges are an ideal way for you to experience the country's flora if you have limited time. Trails often start or finish at a beach where you can cool off. The Coromandel and Northland bush is full of impressive ancient kauri trees and interesting birds, such as tuis, fantails, and wood pigeons.

Exploring Auckland and the North

Northland and the Coromandel Peninsula have beautiful countryside, coasts, and mountains—some of the finest in North Island. Auckland is a thoroughly modern, car-oriented metropolis, with interesting restaurants and a handful of suburbs to poke around. But it isn't the easiest place to get a handle on in a couple of days, the way you can in other New Zealand cities. Auckland has built out, rather than up, and the sprawl makes the city close to impossible to explore on foot. What may look like reasonable walking distances on maps can turn out to be 20- to 30-minute treks, and stringing a few of those together can get frustrating. If you only want to see the city center close to the harbor, Devonport, and Parnell, you can get around by busing and ferrying between places.

Interestingly enough, Aucklanders seem to talk as much about what surrounds the city as what's in it: beaches, the Waitakere Ranges, Waiheke Island and its vineyards. To get to most of these and to happening suburbs like Ponsonby, you will need a car, which you can then use to go farther afield to Northland and the Coromandel Peninsula. The Auckland area's compact and diverse landscape means that having a car will allow you to go from the middle of Auckland city to a beach 10 minutes later and the middle of subtropical bush 20 minutes after that.

Great Itineraries

Numbers in the text correspond to numbers in the margin and on the Auckland, Northland and the Bay of Islands, and Coromandel Peninsula maps.

IF YOU HAVE 2 DAYS

Explore central Auckland by starting at the **Civic Theatre** ① and walking down to the **Ferry Building** ⑩. Then spend the best part of the day on the harbor. Take a boat to **Devonport** for some shopping and a streetside lunch. On returning to the city side, visit **Kelly Tarlton's Underwater World and Antarctic Encounter** ⑫ and follow that with some seafood in a nearby restaurant. The next day, visit the **Auckland Domain** ④ for a peaceful stroll and the **Auckland Institute Museum** ⑤ for a look into Maori history and culture. Then head to **Parnell Village** ⑧ for some of Auckland's best shopping and dining and the **Parnell Rose Garden.** Any spare time in the afternoon could be spent back in the city at the **National Maritime Museum** ⑪, which houses historical and current exhibits with plenty of "hands-on" opportunities.

If you're not in an urban mood, spend a day on Auckland's beaches, the **Waitakere Ranges,** or just chuck it all and go to the **Coromandel Peninsula** for two glorious days in the bush and on the beach. Just two hours from Auckland by car, the Coromandel is a great, unspoiled getaway.

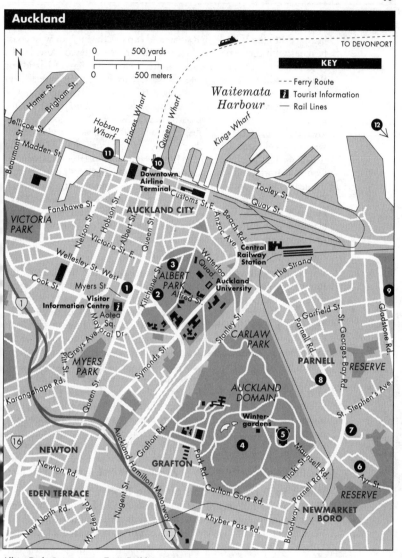

Auckland

Albert Park, **3**
Auckland City Art Gallery, **2**
Auckland Domain, **4**
Auckland Institute Museum, **5**
Cathedral Church of St. Mary, **7**
Civic Theatre, **1**
Ewelme Cottage, **6**

Ferry Building, **10**
Kelly Tarlton's Underwater World and Antarctic Encounter, **12**
National Maritime Museum, **11**
Parnell Rose Gardens, **9**
Parnell Village, **8**

Spend the first day or two looking around metropolitan Auckland, then head west to the Waitakere Ranges and explore the bush or west coast beaches with their volcanic black sand. Or visit a few of Auckland's vineyards instead. Then head either to the popular Bay of Islands or the less-trodden Coromandel Peninsula. With more than a week, you could see both, but the drive connecting the two is more than six hours, making it more sensible to choose one of the two places. Heading north to the Bay of Islands, stop in **Warkworth** ⑭ for a look at some great old kauri trees or a hillside garden. **Whangarei** ⑮ is also on the way—a good place for lunch, perhaps a picnic by the harbor or at the waterfall. This area is steeped in history and has superb coastal scenery. Continue north and spend a couple of days exploring **Paihia** ⑯, with the nearby **Waitangi Treaty House,** and the charming town of **Russell** ⑰. When you return south, take the western route to **Waipoua State Forest** ⑲, and stop farther down at the **Matakohe Kauri Museum** ⑳ to learn about the area's incredible native trees. If you want to stay off of the main road dropping back into Auckland, go past the scenic Kaipara Harbour then through Helensville.

To get to the Coromandel Peninsula, go south from Auckland over the Bombay Hills, which serve as both a physical and mental barrier between the big city and the more rural lifetsyle to the south. Turn off at Highway 2 to travel around the southern reaches of the Firth of Thames, then take Highway 25 to **Thames** ㉑ itself, a logical first stop on a tour around the Coromandel Peninsula. Follow the coast on 25 to the town of **Coromandel** ㉒, a good base for exploring the upper peninsula. Then turn to the east coast, where you'll find some of the best Coromandel beaches. **Hot Water Beach** ㉔ is a delicious combination of thermal activity and surf—dig a hole in the sand and you've got a hot bath!—and you can overnight in nearby **Tairua** ㉕. A range of mountains runs in a line up the Coromandel, and from just about any point you can head into the hills for great hiking through lush ferny forests. To the south are the popular surf beaches of **Whangamata** ㉖ and Wahi. If you have extra time you could linger here, or even head toward coastal Bay of Plenty or Rotorua, covered in the next chapter.

When to Tour Auckland and the North

Snow doesn't fall on this part of New Zealand, and the weather doesn't exactly get frigid. Still, to see these areas at their finest, mid-November through mid-April are the beautiful months, with December through March being the highest season for tourism. If you plan to come around the Christmas holidays, reserve well in advance, especially in seaside places. The Bay of Islands is a summertime hot spot for vacationing Kiwis, and the Coromandel town of Whangamata for example gets overrun by surfer dudes around the new year.

AUCKLAND

City Center

❸ **Albert Park.** These 15 acres of formal gardens, fountains, and statue-studded lawns are a favorite for Aucklanders who pour out of nearby office blocks and the university and polytechnic to eat lunch on a sunny day. The park is built on the site of a garrison from the 1840s and 1850s that was used to protect settlers from neighboring Maori tribes. There are still remnants of its stone walls (with rifle slits) behind university buildings on the eastern side of the park. On the university side is a floral clock. ⊠ *Wellesley St. West, Kitchener St., Waterloo Quad.*

❷ Auckland City Art Gallery. The country's finest collection of contemporary art as well as paintings of New Zealand dating back to the time of Captain Cook hang here. Look for works by Frances Hodgkins, New Zealand's best-known artist. The gallery expanded with the opening of what is known as the **New Art Gallery** in 1995; historic items of interest are to be found in the older **Heritage Art Gallery.** In winter the museum presents jazz and classical music concerts some Sunday afternoons. ⊠ *Kitchener St. and Wellesley St. E,* ☎ *09/307–7700,* ☎ *09/302–1096.* ☒ *Free.* ☉ *Daily 10–4:30.*

❹ Auckland Domain. Sunday picnickers and morning runners are two types of Aucklanders who take advantage of the rolling, 340-acre Domain. Watch the local paper for free weekend evening concerts, which usually include opera and fireworks displays. They can attract up to 300,000 people and are held five or six times each summer. Take a bottle of wine and a basketful of something tasty and join in with the locals. Within the Domain near the **Auckland Institute Museum,** the domed **Wintergardens** house a collection of tropical plants and palms and seasonally display hothouse plants. The gardens may not be worth going out of your way for, unless you're missing your house plants. ⊠ *Entrances at Stanley St., Park Rd., Carlton Gore Rd., and Maunsell Rd.* ☉ *Wintergardens daily 10–4.*

❺ Auckland Institute Museum. Dominating the Domain atop a hill, the Greek-Revival Institute is known especially for its Maori artifacts, the largest and finest collection of its kind. Portraits of Maori chiefs by C.F. Goldie are splendid character studies of a fiercely martial people. Other exhibits in the museum are dedicated to natural history, geology, military history, and a reconstructed streetscape of early Auckland. While entrance remains free the museum is combating a local image of becoming tired and dusty by putting on special exhibits and charging a nominal fee for these. The best of the lot is **Weird and Wonderful,** an interactive display for kids of all ages. ⊠ *Auckland Domain,* ☎ *09/309–0443.* ☒ *Free.* ☉ *Daily 10–5.*

❼ Cathedral Church of St. Mary. Gothic Revival wooden churches don't get much finer than this one, which was built in 1886. It is one of a number of churches commissioned by the early Anglican missionary Bishop Selwyn. The craftsmanship inside the church is remarkable, as is the story of its relocation. St. Mary's originally stood on the other side of Parnell Road, and in 1982 the entire structure was moved across the street. Photographs inside show the progress of the work. The church now forms part of the Cathedral of the Holy Trinity. ⊠ *Parnell Rd. and St. Stephen's Ave.* ☉ *Daily 8–6.*

❶ Civic Theatre. This extravagant art nouveau movie theater was the talk of the town when it opened in 1929, but just nine months later the owner, Thomas O'Brien, went bust and fled, taking with him the week's revenues and an usherette. During World War II a cabaret show in the basement was popular with Allied servicemen in transit to the battlefields of the Pacific. One of the entertainers, Freda Stark, is said to have appeared regularly wearing nothing more than a coat of gold paint. To see the best of the building, don't restrict your visit to standing outside. Sit down to a movie, look up to the ceiling and you will see a simulated night sky. The theater is close to the Visitor Information Centre. ⊠ *Queen and Wellesley Sts.,* ☎ *09/377–3315.*

❻ Ewelme Cottage. Built by the Reverend Vicesimus Lush and inhabited by his descendants for more than a century, the cottage stands behind a picket fence. The house was constructed of kauri, a resilient timber highly prized by the Maori for their war canoes, and later by Europeans for ship masts. Kauri became the basic building material for Western settlers, and most of the great old trees were cut down. All kauri are now protected by law, but only a few majestic examples of mature trees remain in forests. Ewelme Cottage contains much of the original furniture and personal effects of the Lush family. ⊠ *14 Ayr St.,* ☎ *09/379–0202.* 🖅 *$3.* ⊙ *Daily 10:30–noon and 1–4:30.*

⑩ Ferry Building. Boats leave here for Devonport weekdays on the hour between 10 and 3, and at half-hour intervals during the morning and evening commuter periods; on Saturday they leave every hour from 6:15 AM until 1 AM, on Sunday from 7 AM to 11 PM. On Friday and Saturday after 7 PM, the regular Devonport boat is replaced by the MV *Kestrel,* a turn-of-the-century ferry with its wood and brass restored and fitted out with a bar and a jazz band. This is also the place to catch ferries to the Hauraki Gulf Islands: Waiheke, Rangitoto, and Motutapu. ⊠ *Quay St.* 🖅 *Round-trip $7.*

🕑 ⑫ Kelly Tarlton's Underwater World and Antarctic Encounter. The creation of New Zealand's most celebrated undersea explorer and treasure hunter, this harborside marine park offers a fish-eye view of the sea. A submerged transparent tunnel, 120 yards long, makes a circuit past moray eels, lobsters, sharks, and stingrays. In Antarctic Encounter, you enter a replica of Scott's Hut at McMurdo Sound, then circle around a deep-freeze environment aboard a heated snow cat that winds through a penguin colony and an aquarium exhibiting marine life of the polar sea, emerging at Scott Base 2000 for a glimpse of the next century's Antarctic research and exploration. ⊠ *Orakei Wharf, Tamaki Dr.,* ☎ *09/528–0603.* 🖅 *$16.* ⊙ *Daily 9–9, last admission 8 PM.*

🕑 ⑪ National Maritime Museum. New Zealand's rich seafaring history is on display in a marina complex on Auckland Harbour. You can experience what it was like to travel "steerage class" in the 1800s, right down to the creaking boards, the cramped quarters, and the undulation of the sea. There are detailed exhibits on early whaling, a collection of outboard motors, yachts, ship models, Polynesian outriggers, the replica of a shipping office from the turn of the century, and a scow which conducts short trips on the harbor are among other exhibits. The museum also hosts workshops, where traditional boatbuilding, sailmaking, and rigging skills are kept alive. The pride of the museum is the *KZ1,* the 133-foot racing sloop built for the America's Cup challenge in 1988. ⊠ *Eastern Viaduct, Quay St.,* ☎ *09/358–3010.* 🖅 *$9.* ⊙ *Oct.–Easter, Mon.–Thurs. 10–6, Fri.–Sun. 10–9; Easter–Sept., daily 10–5.*

⑨ Parnell Rose Gardens. When you tire of boutiques and cafés, take a 10-minute stroll to gaze upon and whiff this collection of some 5,000 rose bushes. The main beds contain mostly modern hybrids, with new introductions being planted regularly. The adjacent **Nancy Steen Garden** is the place to admire the antique varieties. And don't miss the garden's incredible trees. There is a 200-year-old pohutukawa (puh-hoo-too-ka-wa) whose weighty branches touch the ground and rise up again, and a kanuka (*leptospermum pricoides*) that is one of Auckland's oldest trees, dating from when the area was called Maryland. The Rose Garden Restaurant serves lunch (open Sunday–Friday and public holidays noon–2). ⊠ *Gladstone and Judges Bay Rds.,* ☎ *09/302–1252.* ⊙ *Daily dawn–dusk.*

⑧ Parnell Village. The pretty Victorian timber villas along the slope of Parnell Road have been transformed into antiques shops, designer boutiques, street cafés, and restaurants. Parnell Village is the creation of Les Harvey, who saw the potential of the quaint but run-down shops and houses and almost single-handedly snatched them from the jaws of the developers' bulldozers by buying them, renovating them, and leasing them out. Harvey's vision has paid handsome dividends, and today this village of trim pink-and-white timber facades is a delightful part of the city. At night its restaurants, pubs, and discos attract Auckland's smart set. Parnell's shops are open Sunday. ⊠ *Parnell Rd. between St. Stephen's Ave. and Augustus Rd.*

NEED A BREAK?

At the heart of Parnell Village, **Konditorei Boss** is a pleasant and inexpensive sidewalk café selling open sandwiches, soups, salads, and an irresistible collection of cakes. There is no table service; walk inside and make your selection from the counter. ⊠ *305 Parnell Rd., Parnell,* ☎ *09/377-8953.* ⊙ *Daily 8-5.*

Devonport

The 20-minute ferry to Devonport across **Waitemata Harbour** provides one of the finest views of Auckland. The first harbor ferry service began with whaleboats in 1854. Later in the century the Devonport Steam Ferry Co. began operations, and ferries scuttled back and forth across the harbor until the Harbour Bridge opened in 1959. The bridge now carries the bulk of the commuter traffic, but the ferry still has a small, devoted clientele.

Originally known as Flagstaff after the signal station on the summit of Mount Victoria, Devonport was the first settlement on the north side of the harbor. Later the area drew some of the city's wealthiest traders, who built their homes where they could watch their sailing ships arriving with cargoes from Europe. These days, Aucklanders have fixed up and repopulated its great old houses, laying claim to the suburb's relaxed, seaside atmosphere.

The **Esplanade Hotel** is one of the first things you'll see as you leave the ferry terminal. It stands at the harbor end of **Victoria Road,** a pleasant street for taking a stroll, stopping at a shop, a bookstore, or a café, or for picking up some fish and chips to bite into next to the giant Moreton Bay fig tree across the street on the green.

Long before the era of European settlement, the ancient volcano now called **Mount Victoria** was the site of a Maori *pa,* a fortified village, of the local Kawerau tribe. On the northern and eastern flanks of the hill you can still see traces of the terraces once protected by palisades of sharpened stakes. Don't be put off by its name—this is more molehill than mountain, and the climb isn't much. ⊠ *Kerr St. off Victoria Rd.*

While New Zealand's navy is hardly a threatening force on a global scale, the small **Naval Museum** has interesting exhibits on the early exploration of the country, as well as information on its involvement in various conflicts. The museum is five blocks west of Victoria Wharf along Queens Parade. ⊠ *Queens Parade.* ⊙ *Daily 10–4.*

North Head is an ancient Maori defense site, and its position jutting out from Devonport into Auckland's harbor was enough to convince the European settlers that they, too, should use the head for strategic purposes. Rumor has it that veteran aircraft are still stored in the dark, twisting tunnels under North Head, but plenty of willing explorers have not found any. You can still get into most tunnels, climb all over the abandoned antiaircraft guns, and get great views of Auckland and the islands to the east. North Head is a 20-minute walk east of the ferry terminal on King Edward Parade, then Cheltenham Street, then out Takarunga Road. ⊠ *Takarunga Rd.*

Around Auckland

★ **Beaches.** Auckland's beaches are commonly categorized by area—East, West, or North. The ones closest to the city are the east coast beaches along Tamaki Drive on the south side of the harbor, which are well protected and safe for children. **Judge's Bay** and **Mission Bay** are particularly recommended for their settings. The best swimming is at high tide.

Black-sand west coast beaches are popular in summer, but the sea is often rough, and sudden rips and holes can trap the unwary. The most visited of these is **Piha,** some 40 kilometers (25 miles) from Auckland, which has pounding surf as well as a sheltered lagoon dominated by the reclining mass of Lion Rock. **Whatipu,** south of Piha, is a broad sweep of sand offering safe bathing behind the sand bar that guards Manukau Harbour.

Bethells, to the north, is exposed and often subject to heavy surf. In the vicinity, **Karekare** is the beach where the dramatic opening scenes of Jane Campion's *The Piano* were shot. Across Waitemata Harbour from the city, a chain of magnificent beaches stretches north as far as the Whangaparaoa Peninsula, 40 kilometers (25 miles) from Auckland. In the Hauraki Gulf, the island of **Waiheke** is ringed by a number of splendid small beaches.

🛱 **Museum of Transport and Technology.** This fascinating collection of aircraft, telephones, cameras, locomotives, steam engines, and farming equipment is a tribute to Kiwi ingenuity. One of the most intriguing exhibits is the remains of an aircraft built by Robert Pearse, who made a successful powered flight barely three months after the Wright brothers first took to the skies. The flight ended inauspiciously when his plane crashed into a hedge, but Pearse, considered a wild eccentric by his farming neighbors, is recognized today as a mechanical genius. ⊠ *Great North Rd. (off North-Western Motorway, Rte. 16), Western Springs,* ☎ *09/846–0199.* 🎟 *$8.50.* ☉ *Weekdays 9–5, weekends 10–5.*

Waitakere Ranges. This scenic mountain range west of Auckland is a favorite walking and picnic spot for locals that is all too often left out of visitors' itineraries. The 20-minute **Arataki Nature Trail** is a great introduction to kauri, a species of pine, and other native trees. If you have more time, take the **Auckland City Walk,** the highlight of which is Cascade Falls. The **Arataki Visitors Centre** displays modern Maori carvings and has information on the Waitakeres and other Auckland Parks. To get to the Waitakeres, head along the northwestern motorway, route 16, from central Auckland, take the Waterview turnoff, and keep heading west to the small village of Titirangi, the gateway to the Waitakere. A sculpture depicting fungal growths tells you you're heading in the right direction. From here the best route to follow is the Scenic Drive, with spectacular views of Auckland and its two harbors. The visitors center is 5 kilometers (3 miles) along the drive.

Dining

City Center

$$$ ✕ **The Brasserie.** This breezy, not-too-formal dining room in Auckland's Stamford Plaza hotel is right for all seasons. The menu is a showcase for all that New Zealand does best—seafood, lamb, and cervena (lean New Zealand) venison in particular—handled with imagination in dishes such as crayfish (clawless lobster) tempura with mustard-seed sauce and potato cake, barbecued salmon steak with red caviar, and grilled lamb loin with *rösti* potatoes (hash browns) and spinach. ⊠ *Albert St.,* ☎ *03/309–8888. AE, DC, MC, V.*

Auckland Dining and Lodging

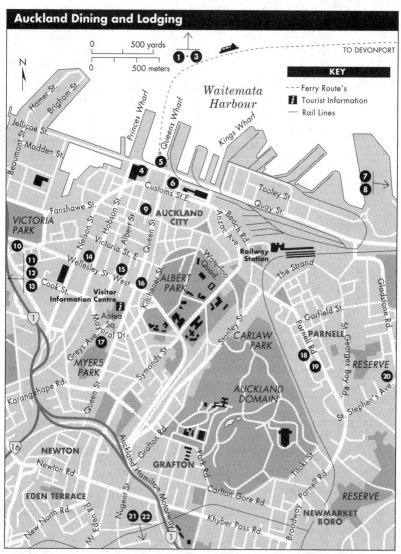

0 — 500 yards
0 — 500 meters

N

Waitemata Harbour

KEY
- - - Ferry Route's
i Tourist Information
— Rail Lines

TO DEVONPORT

Hamer St.
Brigham St.
Jellicoe St.
Beaumont St.
Madden St.
Fanshawe St.
Princes Wharf
Queens Wharf
Kings Wharf
Customs St. E.
Tooley St.
Quay St.
Beach Rd.
Anzac Ave.

VICTORIA PARK

Nelson St.
Hobson St.
Albert St.
Queen St.
Victoria St. E.
Wellesley St. West
Cook St.

AUCKLAND CITY

Waterloo Quad
Railway Station
The Strand
Gladstone Rd.

Visitor Information Centre *i*

ALBERT PARK

Kitchener St.
Stanley St.

CARLAW PARK

Aotea Sq.
Mayoral Dr.
Greys Ave.

MYERS PARK

Queen St.
Symonds St.

Garfield St.
Parnell Rd.
St. Georges Bay Rd.
PARNELL

RESERVE

St. Stephen's Ave.

Karangahape Rd.

AUCKLAND DOMAIN

NEWTON
Newton Rd.
Grafton Rd.
Park Rd.
GRAFTON

EDEN TERRACE
New North Rd.
Mt. Eden Rd.
Nugent St.
Auckland Hamilton Motorway
Carlton Gore Rd.
Khyber Pass Rd.

Titoki St.
Broadway
Parnell Rd.

RESERVE

NEWMARKET BORO

Dining
Alligator Pear, **18**
The Brasserie, **9**
Cin Cin on Quay, **5**
Death by Chocolate, **11**
Harbourside Seafood Bar and Grill, **5**
Iguacu, **19**
Kermadec Ocean Fresh Restaurant, **4**

Rick's Café Americain, **10**
Saint's Waterfront Brasserie, **7**
Torpedo Bay Bar and Brasserie, **1**
Tuatara, **13**
Vinnie's, **12**
Virtu, **16**

Lodging
Albion Hotel, **14**
Ascot Parnell, **20**
Carlton, **17**
Centra, **15**
Devonport Villa, **2**
Florida Motel, **8**
Hotel du Vin, **22**
Novotel, **6**
Peace and Plenty Inn, **3**

Sedgwick-Kent Lodge, **21**
Stamford Plaza, **9**

$$$ ✕ **Cin Cin on Quay.** With aqua-and-amber decor and music that's any-
★ thing but subtle—and fare that varies from pizza made in the wood-
fired oven, to bar snacks such as sweet-potato fries with chili-spiced
sour cream, to exotic main courses such as Thai-style seafood cooked
in a clay pot—this busy, bold, waterfront oyster bar and brasserie is
an appealing combination to Auckland's twenty- to thirty-somethings,
who come as much to let their hair down as to sample the menu. New
Zealand wines are well represented, and a wide range of domestic and
imported beer is available. The site right next to the Devonport ferry
terminal is enough to pull in anyone with time to kill before the next
ferry. If you happen to be in town on the weekend, come for break-
fast at an outside table overlooking the harbor. ⊠ *Auckland Ferry Bldg.,
99 Quay St.,* ☎ *09/307–6966. AE, DC, MC, V.*

$$$ ✕ **Kermadec Ocean Fresh Restaurant.** On the Viaduct Quay near the
National Maritime Museum, Kermadec has harborside views and suit-
able Pacific-theme decor. And its loyal following, not surprisingly,
comes for the seafood. Start with a salad of crab and feta cheese with
a gooseberry dressing, then move to a main course of panfried South
Island salmon with a melon and saffron salsa—and leave room for
dessert. ⊠ *Quay and Lower Hobson Sts., 1st floor, Viaduct Quay,* ☎
09/309–0412. AE, DC, MC, V.

$$$ ✕ **Harbourside Seafood Bar and Grill.** Overlooking the water from the
upper level of the restored ferry building, this vast, modish seafood restau-
rant is the perfect choice for warm-weather dining. Some of the finest
New Zealand fish and shellfish, including orange roughy, salmon, and
snapper, appear on a menu with a fashionably Mediterranean accent.
Lobster fresh from the tank is a house specialty, and the reason the restau-
rant is a favorite with Japanese tourists. Non-fish eaters have their choice
of venison, lamb, and poultry. On warm nights, book ahead and re-
quest a table outside on the deck. ⊠ *Auckland Ferry Bldg., 99 Quay
St.,* ☎ *09/307–0486. AE, DC, MC, V.*

$$$ ✕ **Virtu.** Relatively new on Auckland's dining scene, this central city
★ restaurant is popular with the local business community both for its lo-
cation and food. For that reason, many diners will be dressed in suit
and tie, but the atmosphere remains friendly and casual. Cold dishes
include char-grilled lamb, marinated and served on a tasty salad with
tapenade vinaigrette and flatbread. You'll also find a hot lamb dish, along
with braised rabbit, crispy roast duckling, and prime aged sirloin. The
fish of the day is consistently worth considering, too. ⊠ *New Gallery
Bldg., Lorne and Wellesley Sts.,* ☎ *09/377–9973. AE, DC, MC, V.*

$$ ✕ **Alligator Pear Restaurant.** This trendy, downstairs Parnell haunt serves
imaginative, well-seasoned dishes. Calamari is lightly sautéed and
served with black olives, garlic, and tomato salsa over pasta. Artichoke
gnocci with cheese and leek sauce is baked with ricotta cheese. And
Moorish chicken kebab, lightly spiced chicken grilled and basted with
a jalapeno, honey, and mustard glaze, makes for a pleasant world-beat
diversion. ⊠ *211 Parnell Rd.,* ☎ *09/307–2223. AE, DC, MC, V. Din-
ner only. Closed Mon.*

$$ ✕ **Iguacu.** With flares blazing near the entrance, dappled red ocher
walls, enormous mirrors in Mexican metalwork frames, a glass ceiling,
and a pair of chandeliers made from copper tubing festooning the interior—the decor strives as much for cultural cacophany as do dishes such
as Cajun-blackened kingfish with jambalaya rice, chicken curry with dhal
(puréed lentils) and fried rice, teriyaki roast venison, and Polish sausage
with sauerkraut. Befitting its fashionable status, the restaurant is generally full of patrons who come to see and be seen as much as to enjoy the
food. ⊠ *269 Parnell Rd., Parnell,* ☎ *09/309–4124. AE, DC, MC, V.*

$$ ✕ **Rick's Café Americain.** Once owned by an American named Rick, but now by a New Zealand rugby league player, this casual bistro in the Victoria Park Market is aimed at a young crowd, but the chrome-and-neon decor, spirited service, reasonable prices, and subdued rock and funky jazz give it a wide appeal. Burgers, spareribs, steaks, and pasta are staples on the menu, and there are several exotic surprises, such as tandoori lamb satay, rack of lamb with fruit stuffing, and a vegetarian pie with spinach and feta cheese. Service is fast and friendly, and Rick's is open daily for breakfast. ⊠ *Victoria Park Market,* ☎ *09/309–9074. AE, DC, MC, V. Rick's Blue Falcon, ⊠ 27 Falcon St., Parnell,* ☎ *09/309–0854.*

Devonshire and Ponsonby

$$ ✕ **Torpedo Bay Bar and Brasserie.** Overlooking the harbor from the new Devonport ferry terminal, Auckland's breeziest restaurant has exceptional views. The two dozen dishes on the summer menu include pizzas, pasta, salads, and main courses such as baked salmon, chicken breast with scallops, roast lamb, and baked venison. The art deco–inspired interior is pleasant but a long second to the deck; it's essential to book ahead to ensure an outside table. ⊠ *Devonport Wharf, Devonport,* ☎ *09/445–9770. AE, DC, MC, V.*

$$ ✕ **Tuatara.** Although it takes its name from a local reptile, there is nothing sluggish about one of Auckland's hippest bistros. The menu is a capable but unambitious roundup of current crowd pleasers, with a choice of salads, focaccia, an antipasto plate, pasta, fish and shellfish, and main courses such as grilled chicken breast with sweet peppers, sun-dried tomatoes, and baby potatoes. Ambience is consciously understated: bare wooden floors, cream-color walls, chunky tables, a big wooden bar in the middle, medium-volume reggae music, and folding glass doors that allow the inevitably crowded tables to spill out onto Ponsonby Road. ⊠ *198 Ponsonby Rd., Ponsonby,* ☎ *09/360–0098. AE, DC, MC, V.*

$ ✕ **Death by Chocolate.** This dessert-only restaurant is strictly for chocoholics. Butterscotch pecan ice cream with fresh cream and chocolate flakes in a chocolate-covered waffle cone, chocolate scallop shells with melon and summer berries dusted with caster sugar, and ice cream studded with caramel balls and served with hot fudge sauce are typical of the gooey delights. ⊠ *42 Jervois Rd., Ponsonby,* ☎ *09/360–2828. AE, DC, MC, V. No lunch.*

Other Suburbs

$$$ ✕ **Saint's Waterfront Brasserie.** On any warm weekend, this stylish brasserie, a 15-minute drive east of the city, is the perfect place to enjoy the city of sails sunny side up. The extensive lunch menu is mostly derived from French and Italian cooking and includes soups, salads, open sandwiches, pasta, fish, beef, lamb, and sweetbreads. The dinner menu is a more substantial variation on the same theme. The weekend brunch menu offers healthy combinations of fresh fruit plates with yogurt, bagels, croissants, fruit whips, and muesli. The gray carpet and white tablecloths under glass create a smart, clean atmosphere, accented by Art Deco motifs. Big concertina doors frame an impressive sea view dominated by the cone of Rangitoto Island. ⊠ *425 Tamaki Dr., St. Heliers,* ☎ *09/575–5210. AE, DC, MC, V.*

$$$ ✕ **Vinnie's.** The decor—white tablecloths, black chairs, and a gunmetal-★ gray carpet—borders on austere, but there is nothing restrained about the gutsy French–Italian-provincial cooking at this shopfront restaurant in suburban Herne Bay west of the city center. Carpaccio of salmon with vanilla and olive oil, figs wrapped in prosciutto and flavored with melted mascarpone, lamb shanks cooked with rosemary and red wine with roasted garlic, and duck and beetroot ravioli are typical selections from a menu that also includes imaginative game dishes. ⊠ *166 Jervois Rd., Herne Bay,* ☎ *09/376–5597. AE, DC, MC, V. Closed Sun. No lunch.*

Lodging

City Center

$$$$ 🏨 **Carlton.** Its proximity to the Aotea Centre and downtown make the Carlton a favorite with business travelers. Guest rooms are spacious and elegantly furnished, and the bathrooms are particularly well equipped. The best views are from the rooms that overlook the parklands and the harbor to the east. Polished granite and warm, earthy tones have been used liberally throughout the building. Under new management, the hotel's restaurants and bars have been improved and fitted with activities such as food festivals and cooking classes. ⊠ *Mayoral Dr.,* ☎ *09/366–3000,* 𝔽𝔸𝕏 *09/366–0121. 286 rooms with bath. 2 restaurants, 2 bars, coffee shop, tennis court. AE, DC, MC, V.*

$$$$ 🏨 **Novotel.** This was Auckland's premier hotel for almost two decades after it was built in the late 1960s, but although it has been scrupulously maintained and constantly upgraded, no amount of tender loving care can overcome the slightly cramped rooms and, by today's standards, limited natural light. On the positive side, it has a comforting clublike atmosphere, and its location at the lower end of Queen Street, close to the ferry terminal, is one of the best of any city hotel. ⊠ *8 Customs St.,* ☎ *09/377–8920,* 𝔽𝔸𝕏 *09/307–3739. 188 rooms with bath. 2 restaurants, 4 bars. AE, DC, MC, V.*

$$$$ 🏨 **Stamford Plaza.** This mid-city hotel brought a dash of style to
★   Auckland when it opened as a Regent in the mid-'80s, and despite some energetic competitors, its service, sophistication, and attention to detail keep it on top. Standard rooms are large and furnished extensively with natural fabrics and native timbers in an updated Art Deco style. The marble bathrooms are luxuriously appointed. The best rooms are on the harbor side—the higher the better. ⊠ *Albert St.,* ☎ *09/309–8888,* 𝔽𝔸𝕏 *09/379–6445. 332 rooms with bath. 3 restaurants, bar, pool. AE, DC, MC, V.*

$$$ 🏨 **Centra.** Rooms at this city landmark are equal to those in just about any of Auckland's leading hotels, but cutting down on facilities and glossy public areas has made the price substantially lower. Rooms have a standard, functional layout, and each has its own iron and ironing board. Accommodations begin on the 16th floor, and every room has a view. The suites on the 28th floor have great views and bigger bathrooms for just a slightly higher price. The hotel opened in 1991 and is aimed primarily at business travelers. Service is keen and professional. ⊠ *128 Albert St.,* ☎ *09/302–1111,* 𝔽𝔸𝕏 *09/302–3111. 252 rooms with bath. Restaurant, bar, exercise room. AE, DC, MC, V.*

$$ 🏨 **Ascot Parnell.** Accommodations and facilities in this sprawling guest house are comfortable and functional, but space and character have been sacrificed to provide rooms with en-suite facilities or private bathrooms at a reasonable price. The room with the attached sun room at the back of the house is small but pleasant. The house stands on a relatively busy street, within easy walking distance of the shops and nightlife of Parnell Village. Smoking is not permitted inside. Rates include full breakfast. ⊠ *36 St. Stephens Ave., Parnell,* ☎ *09/309–9012,* 𝔽𝔸𝕏 *09/309–3729. 9 rooms with bath. AE, MC, V.*

$ 🏨 **Albion Hotel.** If you're looking for comfortable, modern accommodations in the heart of the city and outstanding value, look no further. Rooms are modest in size and have no views, but all are neat and well kept. The best room in the house, the Hobson Suite, is equipped with a water bed and Jacuzzi and costs only slightly more than a standard room. Despite the busy corner location, the area is quiet after 6 PM. However, rooms on the lower floor can be affected by noise from the ground floor pub, which is especially busy on Friday nights. The Aotea Centre and the shops of Queen Street are only a few blocks away. ⊠ *Hobson and Wellesley Sts.,* ☎ *09/379–4900,* FAX *09/379–4901. 20 rooms with bath. Brasserie, pub. AE, DC, MC, V.*

Devonport and Other Suburbs

$$$$ ★ 🏨 **Hotel du Vin.** There can be no finer introduction to New Zealand than to head south from the Auckland International Airport to this smart, luxurious hotel, set on the floor of a valley and surrounded by native forests and the grapevines of the de Redcliffe Estate. Standard rooms are palatial, and the rooms built in 1987 were upgraded in 1994, but the newer rooms at the far end of the resort are superior. The decor is crisp and modern, and the central restaurant and reception areas glow with honey-color wood and rough stone fireplaces. The restaurant has an excellent reputation, though prices are high. The hotel is 64 kilometers (40 miles) from Auckland, a 45-minute drive from both Auckland airport and the city via the motorway. ⊠ *Lyons Rd., Mangatawhiri Valley,* ☎ *09/233–6314,* FAX *09/233–6215. 46 rooms with bath. Restaurant, bar, indoor pool, spa, tennis courts, exercise room, bicycles. AE, DC, MC, V.*

$$$$ ★ 🏨 **Peace and Plenty Inn.** Devonport's neighborhoody atmosphere makes for a pleasant alternative to staying in central Auckland, and Carol and Bruce Hyland's beautiful Victorian B&B is one of the treats of the town. In guest rooms, milk-painted walls, country antiques, thoughtfully combined decorative objects, cushy duvets, and abundant flowers create a feeling of earthy sophistication. Two rooms have small private verandas, and one garden-level room has its own entrance. On the main floor, there is a spacious lounge where you can make coffee, tea, or pour yourself a glass of sherry or port. Breakfasts are an all-out display of culinary finesse and Kiwi hospitality. Rates include breakfast. ⊠ *6 Flagstaff Terr., Devonport,* ☎ *09/445–2925,* FAX *09/445–2901. 4 rooms with bath. AE, MC, V.*

$$–$$$$ ★ 🏨 **Sedgwick-Kent Lodge.** On a quiet street in the suburb of Remuera, between the airport and downtown, the single-story Edwardian villa where Louisa and Cliff Hobson-Corry care so well for their guests is a wonderful retreat from the city. Entering through a garden courtyard, you immediately sense the lodge's graceful style. Inside, native timber trims intriguing doorways—appropriate transitions to rooms fitted with writing desks and luxuriously appointed antique bedsteads. Some rooms open onto elevated verandas. Decorative touches everywhere indicate excellent taste. The hosts' elegant breakfasts are delightful, whether you give in and ask for a sumptuous hot dish or restrain yourself and stick with freshly squeezed orange juice, muffins, fruit, and homemade muesli and yogurt. Rates include breakfast. ⊠ *65 Lucerne Rd., Remuera,* ☎ *09/524–5219,* FAX *09/520–4825. 4 rooms with TV and bath, 1 apartment with kitchen. AE, MC, V.*

$$ ★ 🏨 **Devonport Villa.** This gracious timber villa combines tranquil, historic surroundings and fresh sea air, a 20-minute ferry ride from the city. Rooms are individually decorated and have handmade quilts, queen-size beds with Edwardian-style headboards, lace curtains, and colonial furniture. Cheltenham Beach, which offers safe swimming, is a two-minute walk away, and the picture-book village of Devonport is a short walk. Arriving guests can be collected from the Devonport ferry terminal. Rates include breakfast. ⊠ *46 Tainui Rd., Devonport,* ☎ *09/445–8397,* FAX *09/445–9766. 4 rooms with bath. Lounge. AE, V.*

$$ 🏨 **Florida Motel.** In a harborside suburb a 15-minute drive east of the city center (and close to a major bus route into the city), this motel of-

fers exceptional value. Rooms come in three versions: studios or one- or two-bedroom units. The units have a lounge room separate from the bedroom, and the two-bedroom units are particularly good for families. All rooms have separate, fully equipped kitchens and a few nice touches, such as wall-mounted hair dryers, French-press coffee makers, and ironing boards with irons. As the motel is immaculately maintained and extremely popular, rooms must be booked several months in advance. ⊠ *11 Speight Rd., Kohimarama,* ☎ *09/521–4660,* FAX *09/ 521–4662. 8 rooms with bath. AE, DC, MC, V.*

Nightlife and the Arts

The Arts

For a current listing of plays, opera, dance, and musical events in Auckland, a brochure called *Auckland Alive* is available from the Visitor Information Centre (⊠ 299 Queen St., at Aotea Sq.) and the Aotea Centre. For current films, check the entertainment pages of the daily newspapers.

For tickets, **Ticketek** (☎ 09/307–5000) is the central agency for all theater, music, and dance performances, as well as major sporting events.

MUSIC AND OPERA

Aotea Centre. Auckland's main venue for music and the performing arts hosts musical and dramatic performances throughout the year. For general inquiries there is an Information Desk in the Owens Foyer, level 2 of the complex. The **Auckland Philharmonia Orchestra** performs regularly at the center, and the **New Zealand Symphony Orchestra** performs both at the Town Hall and at the Aotea Centre. ⊠ *Aotea Sq., Queen and Myers Sts.,* ☎ *09/309–2678 or 09/307–5050.*

Dame Kiri Te Kanawa often performs at the Aotea Centre on return visits to her homeland, but tickets are usually sold out months in advance.

THEATER

The **Watershed Theatre** stages a mix of drama, comedy, musicals, and dance. It seats 220 and has a bar with harbor views. ⊠ *Customs St. West and Market Pl., Viaduct Basin,* ☎ *09/358–4028.*

Nightlife

After sunset, the liveliest area of the city is Parnell, which has several restaurants, bars, and nightclubs.

BARS AND LOUNGES

Civic Tavern. At the heart of the city center, this unremarkable building houses the **London Bar**, which has a vast selection of beer, **Murphy's Irish Bar**, with jazz every night from Wednesday through Saturday, and **Younger's Tartan Bar**, "Auckland's only Scottish bar," with an impressive variety of Scotch whiskey. ⊠ *1 Wellesley St.,* ☎ *09/373–3684.* ☉ *Mon.–Sat. 11 AM–midnight.*

Loaded Hog. This popular brewery and bistro with indoor or outdoor dining and drinking can become crowded late in the week, so try to arrive early. Part of the new Hobson's Wharf development, the tavern has a vaguely nautical feel. Jazz musicians perform most evenings. ⊠ *104 Quay St.,* ☎ *09/366–6491.* ☉ *Daily about 11 AM–1 AM.*

Shakespeare Tavern. The beer in this atmospheric city-center brew-pub goes by colorful names like Willpower Stout and Falstaff's Real Ale. There are several bars inside and live rock or jazz most evenings. ⊠ *Albert and Wyndham Sts.,* ☎ *09/373–5396.* ☉ *Mon.–Sat. 11–11.*

DISCOS

Staircase. This gay nightclub draws all orientations to its site in the city's nefarious "K Road," the nucleus of Auckland's sex trade. Drinks are moderately priced. ⊠ *340 Karangahape Rd.,* ☎ *09/379–9320.* 🖃 *$5.* ⊙ *Wed.–Sun. 9 PM–5 AM.*

NIGHTCLUBS

Number 7. At this long-standing favorite with Auckland sophisticates, you'll have to dress up to get through the door. Most evenings the club has live jazz as well as disco music. ⊠ *7 Windsor St., Parnell,* ☎ *09/379–4341.* 🖃 *$6–$10.* ⊙ *Wed.–Sat. 9 PM–3 AM.*

Rick's Blue Falcon. Auckland's version of the Hard Rock Café has a voguish interior decorated with car parts, rainbow-color cocktails, and a steak and burger menu. Here, as elsewhere, this well-tested recipe attracts a varied clientele. Prices are moderate. The Attic Bar has live jazz or restrained rock every night from about 9. ⊠ *27 Falcon St., Parnell,* ☎ *09/309–0854.* ⊙ *Daily noon–midnight.*

Studebaker Diner and Bar. Picture a cross between a '50s-style diner and a stage set for *Phantom of the Opera.* The loud bar, disco, and café appeal to Auckland's early-twenties set. Theme nights vary from rock on Tuesday to psychedelic on Sunday. ⊠ *3 Lower Albert St.,* ☎ *09/377–1950.* ⊙ *Sun.–Tues. 5 PM–midnight, Wed. and Thurs. 5 PM–2 AM, Fri. and Sat. 5 PM–3 AM.*

Outdoor Activities and Sports

Biking

Auckland is a pleasant and relaxed city for two-wheel exploring, especially around the waterfront. **Penny Farthing Cycle Shop** hires out mountain bikes for $30 per day or $165 per week. ⊠ *Symonds St. and Khyber Pass Rd.,* ☎ *09/379–2524.* ⊙ *Mon.–Thurs. 8:30–5:30, Fri. 8:30 AM–9 PM, weekends 10–4.*

Golf

Chamberlain Park Golf Course is an 18-hole public course in a parkland setting a five-minute drive from the city. The club shop rents clubs and carts. Greens fees are $14. ⊠ *Linwood Ave. (off North-Western Motorway, Rte. 16), Western Springs,* ☎ *09/846–6758.*

Titirangi Golf Course, a 15-minute drive south of the city, is one of the country's finest 18-hole courses. Nonmembers are welcome to play provided they contact the professional in advance and show evidence of membership at an overseas club. Clubs and golf carts can be rented; the greens fee is $60. ⊠ *Links Rd., New Lynn,* ☎ *09/827–5749.*

Running

Auckland's favorite running track is **Tamaki Drive,** a 10-kilometer (6-mile) route that heads east from the city along the south shore of Waitemata Harbour and ends at St. Heliers Bay. Close to the city, the **Auckland Domain** (☞ City Center, *above*) is popular with executive lunchtime runners.

Tennis

ASB Tennis Centre has 12 hard courts indoors and outdoors, 1 kilometer (½ mile) east of the city center. ⊠ *72 Stanley St.,* ☎ *09/373–3623.* 🖃 *Outdoor court $24 per hr, indoor court $36 per hr.* ⊙ *Weekdays 7–11, weekends 8–8.*

Spectator Sports

Eden Park is the city's major stadium for sporting events. This is the best place to see New Zealand's sporting icon, the rugby team All Blacks, consistently among the world's top three teams, in winter. Cricket is played in summer. For information on sporting events, **Auckland Alive** is a quarterly guide available from the Visitor Information Centre. Tickets can be booked through Ticketek (☎ 09/307–5000).

Swimming

The Tepid Baths, near the heart of Auckland, has a large indoor swimming pool, a whirlpool, saunas, and a steam room. ⊠ *102 Customs St. W,* ☎ *09/379–4794.* ⌷ *$5.50; pool only, $3.50.* ⊙ *Weekdays 6 AM–10 PM, weekends 7–7.*

Shopping

Department Store

Smith and Caughey Ltd. ⊠ *253–261 Queen St.,* ☎ *09/377–4770.* ⊙ *Mon.–Thurs. 9–5, Fri. 9–9, Sat. 9–1.*

Shopping Districts

Auckland's main shopping precinct for clothes, outdoor gear, duty-free goods, greenstone jewelry, and souvenirs is **Queen Street. Ponsonby,** about 1½ kilometers (1 mile) west of the city center, is known for its antiques shops and fashion boutiques.

Street Markets

Victoria Park Market. Auckland's main bazaar consists of 2½ acres of clothing, footwear, sportswear, furniture, souvenirs, and crafts at knockdown prices. It's housed in the city's former garbage incinerator. The International Foodhall has a range of inexpensive dishes from Thai to Texan. ⊠ *Victoria and Wellesley Sts.,* ☎ *09/309–6911.* ⊙ *Mon.–Sat. 9–7, Sun. 10–7.*

Specialty Stores

BOOKS

Legendary Hard to Find (but worth the effort) Quality Second-hand Books, Ltd. With a name like that, what's more to say—except that it's probably the biggest for second-hand in the country and a local favorite. Its smaller sister in Devonport, **Baxter & Mansfield** (⊠ 81A Victoria St., ☎ 09/446–0300) is a great spot to stop into for a browse. ⊠ *171–175 The Mall, Onehunga,* ☎ *09/634–4340.* ⊙ *Mon.–Thurs. 9:30–5, Fri. 9:30–7:30, Sat. 9:30–4:30, Sun. 10–4:30.*

Stratford Books. Second-hand books, rare, and out of print New Zealand titles of all stripes fill the shelves at Stratford. ⊠ *Downtown Shopping Center, Queen and Custom Sts.,* ☎ *09/379–3661.* ⊙ *Mon.–Thurs. 9:30–5:30, Fri.–Sun. 10–8.*

Unity Books. This general bookstore specializes in travel, fiction, science, biography, and New Zealand–related books. ⊠ *10 High St.,* ☎ *09/307–0731.* ⊙ *Mon.–Thurs. 8:30–6, Fri. 8:30 AM–9 PM, Sat. 9–9, Sun. 11–4.*

CLOTHES

Action Downunder. This nationwide chain of stores sells high-quality outdoor clothing for men and women. ⊠ *75 Queen St.,* ☎ *09/309–6571.* ⊙ *Mon.–Thurs. 10–6:30, Fri. 10–8, weekends 10–5.*

Wool 'n' Trends. The selection of knitted woolen garments and woven hangings here is of very good quality. ⊠ *85 Victoria Rd., Devonport,* ☎ *09/445–2226.* ⊙ *Oct.–Mar., daily 9–6; Apr.–Sept., Mon.–Sat. 9–6.*

SPORTS AND HIKING

Infomaps. Published by the Department of Survey and Land Information, these maps are essential equipment for wilderness walkers. The complete range is available from the department's office. ⊠ *AA Cen-*

tre, Albert and Victoria Sts., 6th floor, ☎ *09/377–1899.* ☉ *Weekdays 8–4.*

Kathmandu. If you haven't brought your own, Kathmandu sells quality New Zealand–made clothing and equipment for the outdoor enthusiast. ⊠ *350 Queen St.,* ☎ *09/309–4615.* ☉ *Mon.–Thurs. 9–5:30, Fri. 9–9, Sat. 9–2.*

Tisdall's Sports. The extensive range of outdoor gear, especially boots and clothing, is made especially for New Zealand conditions. ⊠ *176 Queen St.,* ☎ *09/379–0254,* ⛶ *09/303–4321.* ☉ *Mon.–Thurs. 9–5:30, Fri. 9–9, Sat. 9:30–4.*

Elephant House. Follow elephant footprints down an alley in Parnell Village for an extensive collection of souvenirs, many unavailable elsewhere. ⊠ *237 Parnell Rd.,* ☎ *09/309–8740.* ☉ *Weekdays 9:30–5:30, weekends 9:30–5.*

Wild Places. Proceeds from posters, T-shirts, books, and cards on the themes of whales, rain forests, and native birds all go to conservation projects in New Zealand and the Pacific. ⊠ *28 Lorne St.,* ☎ *09/358–0795.* ☉ *Mon.–Thurs. 9–5:30, Fri. 9–7, Sat. 10–4.*

Accent on Wine. If you've circled New Zealand without picking up a few bottles of wine to take home with you, stop in Parnell to stock up. At the very least bring home some sauvignon blanc—Cloudy Bay if you can get it. ⊠ *347 Parnell Rd., Parnell,* ☎ *09/358–2552.*

Auckland A to Z

Arriving and Departing

BY BUS

The terminal for **InterCity Coaches** (☎ 0800/802–802) is the Auckland Central Railway Station (☞ *above*). **Newmans Coaches** (☎ 09/309–9738) arrive and depart from the Downtown Airline Terminal (⊠ Quay and Albert Sts.).

BY CAR

By the standards of most cities, Auckland traffic is light, parking space is inexpensive and readily available, and motorways pass close to the heart of the city.

BY PLANE

Auckland International Airport lies 21 kilometers (13 miles) southwest of the city center. The **Visitor Information Centre** (open daily 5 AM–2 AM) in the terminal provides free maps and brochures as well as a booking service for tours and accommodations. And there are two currency exchange booths: one in the gate area, and one near rental car booths outside of the customs area.

A free **Interterminal Bus** links the international and domestic terminals, with frequent departures in each direction 6 AM–10 PM. Otherwise, the walk between the two terminals takes about 10 minutes along a signposted walkway. Luggage for flights aboard the two major domestic airlines, Air New Zealand and Ansett New Zealand, can be checked in at the international terminal.

Major international carriers serving Auckland include **Air New Zealand** (☎ 09/357–3000), **Cathay Pacific** (☎ 09/379–0861), **Canadian Airlines International** (☎ 09/309–0735), **Qantas** (☎ 09/357–8900), **Singapore Airlines** (☎ 09/379–3209), and **United Airlines** (☎ 09/379–3800).

Domestic carriers with services to Auckland are **Air New Zealand** (☎ 09/357–3000), **Air Nelson** (☎ 09/379–3510), **Ansett New Zealand** (☎ 09/302–2146), and **Mount Cook Airlines** (☎ 800/80–0737).

Airport to City Center. The journey between the airport and the city center takes about 30 minutes.

The **Airbus** (☎ 09/275–9396) leaves the international terminal every 20 minutes between 6:20 AM and 8:20 PM. The fixed route between the airport and the Downtown Airline Terminal, on the corner of Quay Street and Albert Road, includes a stop at the railway station and, on request, at any bus stop, hotel, or motel along the way. Returning from the city, the bus leaves the Downtown Airline Terminal at 20-minute intervals between 6:20 AM and 9 PM. 🖅 *$9.*

Hallmark Limousines and Tours (☎ 09/629–0940) operates Ford LTD limousines between the airport and the city. The cost is approximately $65.

Johnston's Shuttle Link (☎ 09/275–1234) operates a minibus service between the airport and any address in the city center. The cost is $14 for a single traveler, $10 per person for two traveling together. The service meets all incoming flights.

Taxi fare to the city is approximately $35.

BY TRAIN

The terminal for all InterCity train services is **Auckland Central Railway Station** (☎ 0800/802–802) on Beach Road, about 1½ kilometers (1 mile) east of the city center. A booking office is inside the Auckland Visitor Information Centre (⊠ Aotea Sq., Queen and Meyer Sts.).

Getting Around

BY BUS

Auckland's public bus system, the **Yellow Bus Company,** operates Monday–Saturday 6 AM–11:30 PM, Sunday 9 AM–5 PM. The main terminal for public buses is the **Municipal Transport Station,** between Commerce Street and Britomart Place near the Central Post Office. The bus network is divided into zones; fares are calculated according to the number of zones traveled. For travel within the inner city, the fare is 50¢ for adults. **BusAbout passes,** which allow unlimited travel on all buses after 9 AM daily, are available from bus drivers for $8.40 adults. For timetables, bus routes, fares, and lost property, stop by the **Bus Place** (⊠ Hobson and Victoria Sts.), which is open weekdays 8:15–5, or call **Buz A Bus** (☎ 09/366–6400), open Monday–Saturday 7–7.

BY FERRY

Various companies serve Waitemata Harbor; one of the best and least expensive is the **Devonport commuter ferry.** The ferry terminal is on the harbor side of the Ferry Building on Quay Street, near the corner of Albert Street. Ferries depart Monday–Thursday 6:15 AM–11 PM, Friday and Saturday 6:15 AM–1 AM, and Sunday 7 AM–11 PM. ☎ *09/367–9118.* 🖅 *Round-trip $7.*

BY TAXI

Taxis can be hailed in the street but are more readily available from taxi ranks throughout the city. Auckland taxi rates vary with the company, but the fare and flag fall are listed on the driver's door. Most taxis will accept major credit cards. **Alert Taxis** (☎ 09/309–2000), **Auckland Cooperative Taxi Service** (☎ 09/300–3000), and **Eastern Taxis** (☎ 09/527–7077) are reliable operators with radio-controlled fleets.

Contacts and Resources

CAR RENTAL

Avis, Budget, and **Hertz** have offices inside the Auckland International Airport (☞ Car Rental *in* the Gold Guide).

CONSULATES

U.S. Consulate. ✉ *General Assurance Bldg., Shortland and O'Connell Sts.,* ☎ *09/303–2724.* ◷ *Weekdays 9:30–12:30.*

British Consulate. ✉ *Fay Richwhite Bldg., 151 Queen St.,* ☎ *09/303– 2971.* ◷ *Weekdays 9:30–12:20.*

Canadian Consulate. ✉ *Jetset Centre, 48 Emily Pl.,* ☎ *09/309–3690.* ◷ *Weekdays 8:30–4:30.*

Australian Consulate. ✉ *Union House, 32–38 Quay St.,* ☎ *09/303– 2429.* ◷ *Weekdays 8:30–4:45.*

CURRENCY EXCHANGE

Two Bank of New Zealand branches inside the international terminal of Auckland International Airport are open for all arriving and departing flights. In the city, there are several currency-exchange agencies on Queen Street between Victoria and Customs streets, offering the same rate as banks (open weekdays 9–5 and Saturday 9–1). Foreign currency may also be exchanged daily 8–4 at the cashier's office above Celebrity Walk at the Drake Street entrance of Victoria Park Market (☎ 09/309– 6911). A 24-hour exchange machine outside the Downtown Airline Terminal on Quay Street will change notes of any major currency into New Zealand dollars, but the rate is significantly less than that offered by banks.

EMERGENCIES

Dial 111 for **fire, police,** or **ambulance** services.

Auckland Hospital. ✉ *Park Rd., Grafton,* ☎ *09/379–7440.*

Southern Cross Central. ✉ *122 Remuera Rd., Remuera,* ☎ *09/524– 5943 or 09/524–7906.*

St. John's Ambulance. St. John's can refer you to the nearest dentist on duty. ☎ *09/579–9099.*

GUIDED TOURS

The **Antipodean Explorer** (☎ 09/302–2400) offers a minibus tour of the wineries, coast, and native forests of the Waitakere Ranges west of Auckland, including a visit to a gannet colony. It costs $65 and departs daily at 9:30 AM with pick-ups from your accommodation. The company also offers specialist tours from one to four weeks duration.

Fullers Cruise Centre (☎ 09/367–9111) has a variety of cruises around the harbor and to the islands of Hauraki Gulf. The two-hour coffee cruise ($22) departs daily at 9:30, 11:30, and 2:30, with an extra afternoon cruise from late December to April. The Jetraider cruise ($50) to Great Barrier Island, the most distant of the Hauraki Gulf Islands, is a popular day trip for Aucklanders; however, the voyage can be cancelled due to rough seas. You may want to take a guided bus tour of the island ($17). The cruise departs Tuesday, Thursday, Friday, and weekends at 9, returning to Auckland at about 6. Reservations are essential.

The **Pride of Auckland Company** sails for lunch and dinner on the inner harbor. The 1½-hour lunch cruise departs at 11 and 1, and the 3-hour dinner cruise departs at 6. An "experience sailing" trip departs at 3. Boats leave from the wharf opposite the Downtown Airline Terminal on the corner of Quay and Albert streets. ☎ 09/373–4557. ✑ *Experience sailing $30, lunch cruise $39, dinner cruise $75.*

Scenic Tours (☎ 09/634–0189) operates a three-hour City Highlights guided bus tour, which takes in the main attractions in the city and Parnell and the view from the lookout on Mount Eden. Tours leave at 9:30 and 2, and tickets are $35. The **Gray Line** (☎ 09/377–0904) runs a Morning Highlights tour, which includes admission to Kelly Tarlton's Underwater World. This tour departs daily from the Downtown Airline Terminal on Quay Street at 9 AM and costs $51.

United Airlines Explorer Bus (☎ 09/360–0033) is a convenient introduction to Auckland. The blue-and-gray double-decker bus travels in a circuit, stopping at eight of the city's major attractions; you can leave at any stop and reboard any following Explorer bus. The loop begins at the Downtown Airline Terminal every hour between 9 and 4 daily; tickets are available from the driver. ☞ *1-day pass $15, 2-day pass $25.*

LATE-NIGHT PHARMACY
The Late-night Pharmacy. ⊠ *60 Broadway,* ☎ *09/520–6634.* ☺ *Weekdays 5:30 PM–7 AM, weekends 9 AM–7 AM.*

TRAVEL AGENCIES
American Express Travel Service. ⊠ *101 Queen St.,* ☎ *09/379–8243.*

Thomas Cook. ⊠ *107 Queen St.,* ☎ *09/379–3924.*

VISITOR INFORMATION
Published every Thursday, **Auckland Tourist Times** is a free newspaper with the latest information on tours, exhibitions, and shopping. The paper is available from hotels and from the Visitor Information Centre.

Auckland Visitor Information Centre. ⊠ *Aotea Sq., Queen and Meyer Sts.,* ☎ *09/366–6888.*

NORTHLAND AND THE BAY OF ISLANDS

Beyond Auckland, North Island stretches a long arm into the South Pacific. This is Northland, an undulating region of farms, forests, and marvelous beaches. The Bay of Islands is the main attraction, an island-littered seascape with a mild, subtropical climate and some of the finest game-fishing waters in the country—witness its record catches of marlin and mako shark. Big-game fishing is expensive, but many small fishing boats will take you out for an evening of trawling for under $50.

It was on the Bay of Islands that the first European settlement was established, and here that modern New Zealand became a nation with the signing of the Treaty of Waitangi in 1840. The main town is Paihia, a strip of motels and restaurants along the waterfront. If you plan to spend more than a day in the area, the town of Russell, just a short ferry trip away, makes for a more atmospheric and attractive base.

You can explore Northland in an easy loop from Auckland, driving up Highway 1 and returning on Highway 12 with little revisiting of sights on the way back. Bay of Islands is a favorite vacation spot for Kiwis, particularly from mid-December to the end of January, when accommodations are often filled months in advance.

Albany

⓭ *12 km (7 mi) north of Auckland.*

Albany is a small village north of Auckland, the first town north after the northern motorway narrows. In December, the pohutukawa trees along the roadside blossom out for the Kiwi Christmas by erupting in

Northland and the Bay of Islands

NEW ZEALAND

SOUTH
PACIFIC
OCEAN

Doubtless Bay
Mangonui
10
Kaeo
Takou Bay
1 Mangamuka
Kerikeri
Mount Bledisloe
Bay of Islands
Paihia and Waitangi 16 17 **Russell**
Rawene
Opua
Moerewa
Kawakawa
12
18 **Opononi**
Kaikohe
1
Towai
Waiotu
Poor Knights Islands
19 **Waipoua State Forest**
Awarua
Otonga
Matapouri
NORTHLAND
12
Titoki
Whangarei
15 ■ **Clapham's Clock Museum**
Maungatapere
Whangarei Harbour
14
Portland
Bream Bay
Parry Channel
Hen and Chickens Group
Kaihu River
Waiotira
Dargaville
Taipuga
Little Barrier Island
Te Kopuru
12
Paparoa
Waipu Cove
■ **Bellvue**
20
Maungaturoto
Jellicoe Channel
Matakohe Kauri Museum
Kaipara
Wellsford
Harbour
Poutu
Tapora
14 **Warkworth**
Ahuroa
Kawau Island
1
Tasman Sea
16
Shelly Beach
Orewa
Hauraki Gulf
Helensville
Coatesville
Waiheke Island
Albany 13
Rangitoto Island
Waimauku
Takapuna
Waitakere
Auckland
Papatoetoe
Manukau
Manukau Harbour
Papakura
Pukekohe
2
Waiuku
1

N

KEY
— Rail Lines

0 ———————— 40 miles
0 ———————— 60 km

a blaze of scarlet, hence their Pakeha (European) name—the New Zealand Christmas tree. To the Maori (*moe*-rie), the flowers had another meaning: the beginning of shellfish season. The spiky-leaved plants that grow in clumps by the roadside are New Zealand flax. The fibers of this plant, the raw material for linen, were woven into clothing by the Maori. The huge tree ferns—common throughout the forests of North Island, where they can grow as high as 30 feet—are known locally as pungas.

Warkworth

⓮ *47 km (29 mi) north of Albany.*

One of the great natural features of the north half of North Island is one native pine species, the kauri (*cow*-rie) tree. Two giants stand near the **Warkworth Museum.** The larger one, the **McKinney Kauri,** measures almost 25 feet around its base, yet this 800-year-old colossus is a mere adolescent by kauri standards. Kauri trees, once prolific in this part of the North Island, were highly prized by Maori canoe builders, because a canoe capable of carrying a hundred warriors could be made from a single trunk. Unfortunately these same characteristics—strength, size, and durability—made kauri timber ideal for ships, furniture, and housing, and the kauri forests were rapidly depleted by early European settlers. Today the trees are protected by law, and infant kauris are appearing in the forests of North Island, although their growth rate is painfully slow. The museum contains a collection of Maori artifacts and farming and domestic implements from the pioneering days of the Warkworth district. The museum also has a souvenir shop with kauri bowls and other wooden items. ⊠ *Tudor Collins Dr.,* ☎ *09/425–7093.* ⌸ *$3.* ⊙ *Daily 9–4.*

En Route   Even if you aren't a hortomaniac, come to Daniel and Vivian Papich's **Bellvue** for its spectacular views of the Pacific Ocean. The Hen and Chickens Islands lie right off the coast, and on clear days you can see the Poor Knights Islands as well a good 70 kilometers (45 miles) away. This hillside garden has been designed on several levels to take advantage of these aspects. The bold foliage of agave, bromeliads, succulants, and puka trees is abundant, setting off the more delicate exotics and adding year-round interest. Vivian's container plantings—300 at last count—are everywhere, even hanging from the trees. Conceived as a way to keep more demanding plants from struggling in the hard clay soil here, the containers have evolved into an art form. They are often composed of unconventional materials and used in inventive seasonal displays. Birders keep your eyes and ears open for the fantails, whiteyes, and tuis (*too*-ees) that frequent the garden. ⊠ *Coastal Hwy., Langs Beach, southeast of Waipu,* ☎ *09/432–0465.* ⌸ *Small entry fee.* ⊙ *By appointment.*

Whangarei

⓯ *127 km (79 mi) north of Warkworth, 196 km (123 mi) north of Auckland.*

Many people on the way to the Bay of Islands bypass Whangarei (*fahng*-ar-ay), but it is well worth taking the turnoff from the main highway, especially since the area known as the **Whangarei Town Basin** has recently been improved. Here you will find a **Museum of Fishes,** which in New Zealand means looking at exhibits of species that you wouldn't see back home. Also at the basin is **Ahipupu Maori and Pacific Arts and Crafts,** where you will find both traditional and contemporary works.

Claphams Clock Museum is another Town Basin site. Just about every conceivable method of telling time is represented in this collection of more than 1,400 clocks, from primitive water clocks to ships' chronometers to ornate masterworks from Paris and Vienna. Some of the most intriguing examples were made by the late Mr. Clapham himself, like his World War II air force clock that automatically changed the position of aircraft over a map. Ironically, the one thing you won't find here is the correct time. If all the bells, chimes, gongs, and cuckoos went off together the noise would be deafening, so the clocks are set to different times. ⊠ *Quayside Whangarei,* ☎ *09/438–3993.* ☞ *$3.50.* ☉ *Daily 10–4.*

The oldest kauri villa in Whangarei, **Historical Reyburn House** contains the Northland Society of Arts exhibition gallery, which hosts a free exhibition each month. It is separated from the new Town Basin by a playground. ⊠ *Lower Quay St.,* ☎ *09/438–3074.* ☉ *Tues.–Sun. 10–4.*

The town also has a lovely picnic spot at **Whangarei Falls.** There are viewing platforms atop the falls, and a short trail through the local bush. ⊠ *Ngunguru Rd., 5 km (3 mi) northeast of town.*

Early settlers anxious to farm the rich volcanic land around Whangarei found their efforts constantly thwarted by an abundance of rock in the soil. To make use of the stuff they dug up, they built walls—miles of walls. The current settlers at **Greagh,** Kathleen and Clark Abbot, have carried on this tradition, giving their gardens the Celtic name for "land among the stone." It comes as no surprise then that the hardscape here first catches the eye, forming a handsome framework for perennials and roses. Plantings emphasize the beauty and strength of the stone on terraces and in five separate walled gardens. ⊠ *Three Mile Bush Rd., Whangarei,* ☎ *09/435–1980.* ☞ *Small entry fee.* ☉ *Oct.–mid-Dec., daily 10–4; mid-Dec.–Apr. by appointment.*

Paihia and Waitangi

🔟 *69 km (43 mi) north of Whangarei.*

As the main holiday base for the Bay of Islands, Paihia is an unremarkable stretch of motels at odds with the quiet beauty of the island-studded seascape and the rounded green hills that form a backdrop to the town, yet nearby Waitangi is one of the country's most important historic sites. It was near here that the Treaty of Waitangi, the founding document for modern New Zealand, was signed.

Waitangi National Reserve is at the northern end of Paihia. Inside the visitor center, a 23-minute video, shown every hour on the hour, sketches the events that led to the Treaty of Waitangi. The center also displays Maori artifacts and weapons, including a musket that belonged to Hone Heke Pokai, the first Maori chief to sign the treaty. After his initial display of enthusiasm for British rule, Hone Heke was quickly disillusioned, and less than five years later he attacked the British in their stronghold at Russell. From the visitor center, follow a short track through the forest to **Nga Toki Matawhaorua** (ng-ga to-ki ma-ta-fa-oh-roo-ah), a Maori war canoe. This huge kauri canoe, capable of carrying 150 warriors, is named after the vessel in which Kupe, the Polynesian navigator, is said to have discovered New Zealand.

Treaty House in Waitangi National Reserve is a simple white timber cottage, which has a remarkable air of dignity despite its size. The interior is fascinating, especially at back, where exposed walls demonstrate the difficulties that early administrators faced—such as an acute shortage of bricks (since an insufficient number had been shipped from New South Wales) with which to finish the walls.

The Treaty House was prefabricated in New South Wales for the British Resident, James Busby, who arrived in New Zealand in 1832. Busby had been appointed to protect British commerce and put an end to the brutalities of the whaling captains against the Maori, but Busby lacked either the judicial authority or the force of arms necessary to impose peace. On one occasion, unable to resolve a dispute between Maori tribes, Busby was forced to shelter the wounded of one side in his house. While tattooed head hunters screamed war chants outside the windows, one of the warriors sheltered Busby's infant daughter, Sarah, in his cape.

The real significance of the Treaty House lies in the events that took place here on February 6, 1840, the day that the **Treaty of Waitangi** was signed by Maori chiefs and Captain William Hobson, representing the British crown. Under the treaty, the chiefs agreed to accept the authority of the crown; in return, the British recognized the Maori as the legitimate landowners and granted them all the rights and privileges of British subjects. The treaty also confirmed the status of New Zealand as a British colony, forestalling French overtures in the area, and legitimized—at least according to European law—the transfer of land from Maori to European hands. In recent years the Maori have used the treaty successfully to reclaim land that, they maintain, was misappropriated by white settlers.

The Treaty House has not always received the care its significance merits. When Lord Bledisloe bought the house and presented it to the nation in 1932, it was being used as a shelter for sheep.

Whare Runanga (fah-ray roo-nang-ah) is a Maori meeting house with an elaborately carved interior. Inside, an audio show briefly outlines traditional Maori society. The house is on the northern boundary of Waitangi National Reserve. ⊠ *Waitangi Rd., Waitangi,* ☎ *09/402–7437.* ⊡ *$5.* ⊙ *Daily 9–5.*

☾ ***The Tui***, high and dry on the banks of the Waitangi River, is a historic kauri sailing vessel that was built to carry sugar to a refinery in Auckland. Below decks is an exhibition of artifacts recovered from shipwrecks by the famous New Zealand salvage diver Kelly Tarlton. In addition to the brass telescopes, sextants, and diving helmets that you can try on for size, there is an exquisite collection of jewelry that belonged to Isidore Jonah Rothschild (of the famous banking family), which was lost when the SS *Tasmania* sank in 1897. Rothschild was on a sales trip to New Zealand at the time. ⊠ *Waitangi Bridge, Paihia,* ☎ *09/402–7018.* ⊡ *$5.* ⊙ *Daily 10–5.*

Mount Bledisloe offers a splendid view across Paihia and the Bay of Islands. The handsome ceramic marker at the top showing the distances to major world cities was made by Doulton in London and presented by Lord Bledisloe in 1934 during his term as governor-general of New Zealand. The mount is 3 kilometers (2 miles) from the Treaty House, on the other side of the Waitangi Golf Course. From a small parking area on the right of Waitangi Road, a short track rises above a pine forest to the summit.

Dining and Lodging

$$ ✕ **Cafe over the Bay.** This bistro-style restaurant serves local seafood, with a sprinkling of Tex-Mex nachos and burritos. The seafood chowder and grilled prawns with chili are recommended. ⊠ *Waterfront, Paihia,* ☎ *09/402–8147. Reservations not accepted. DC, MC, V.*

$$ 🏨 **Austria Motel.** The large, double-bed rooms here are typical of motel accommodations in the area—clean and moderately comfortable but almost totally devoid of charm. Each has a kitchenette. The motel also has a family unit on the ground level of the two-story wing. The shops and waterfront at Paihia are a two-minute walk away. ⊠ *36 Selwyn Rd.,* 🕿 ⅏ *09/402–7480. 7 rooms with bath. AE, DC, MC, V.*

$$ 🏨 **Quality Resort Waitangi.** The biggest hotel north of Auckland and a favorite with coach tour groups, this complex sprawls along a peninsula within walking distance of the Treaty House. Resort-style units face the sea, while garden-facing rooms are deorated in a French provincial style with yellows and blues and wrought iron light fixtures. ⊠ *Waitangi Rd.,* 🕿 *09/402–7411,* ⅏ *09/402–8200. 138 rooms with bath. 3 restaurants, 2 bars, pool, coin laundry. AE, DC, MC, V.*

Outdoor Activities and Sports

BOATING

Moorings Yacht Charters (🕿 09/402–7821) has charter boats for sailors of various abilities. A catamaran operated by **Straycat Day Sailing Charters** (⊠ Doves Bay Rd., Kerikeri, 🕿 09/407–7342 or 025/96–9944) makes one-day sailing trips in the Bay of Islands from Russell and Paihia at $60 per person.

DIVING

The Bay of Islands has some of the finest scuba diving in the country, particularly around Cape Brett, where the marine life includes moray eels, stingrays, and grouper. The wreck of the Greenpeace Vessel, *Rainbow Warrior,* sunk by French agents, is another Bay of Islands underwater highlight. Water temperature at the surface varies from 62°F in July to 71°F in January. From September through November, underwater visibility can be affected by a plankton bloom. **Paihia Dive Hire and Charter** (⊠ Box 210, Paihia, 🕿 09/402–7551) offers complete equipment hire and regular boat trips for accredited divers for about $135 per day.

FISHING

The Bay of Islands is one of the world's premier game-fishing grounds for marlin and several species of shark. **NZ Billfish Charters** (⊠ Box 416, Paihia, 🕿 09/402–8380) goes for the big ones. A far less expensive alternative is to fish for snapper, kingfish, and John Dory in the inshore waters of the bay. **Skipper Jim** (🕿 09/402–7355) and **MV Arline** (🕿 09/402–8511) offer a half day of fishing, including bait and rods, for about $50 per person.

Russell

17 *4 km (2½ mi) east of Paihia by ferry, 13 km (8 mi) by road.*

Russell is regarded as the "second" town in the Bay of Islands, but it is far more interesting than Paihia. Hard as it is to believe these days, sleepy little Russell was once dubbed the Hellhole of the Pacific. Early last century (when it was still known by its Maori name, Kororareka) it was a swashbuckling frontier town, a haven for sealers and for whalers who found the east coast of New Zealand to be one of the richest whaling grounds on earth. Tales of debauchery were probably exaggerated, but British administrators in New South Wales (as Australia was known at the time) were sufficiently concerned to dispatch a British Resident in 1832 to impose law and order. After the Treaty of Waitangi, Russell was the national capital, until in 1844 the Maori chief Hone Heke attacked the British garrison and most of the town burned to the ground. Hone Heke was finally defeated in 1846, but Russell never recovered its former prominence, and the seat of government was shifted first to Auckland, then to Wellington. Today Russell is a delightful town of timber houses and big trees that hang low over the seafront, framing the yachts and game-fishing boats in the harbor. The atmosphere can best be absorbed in a stroll along the Strand, the path along the waterfront.

Pompallier House, at the southern end of the Strand, was named after the first Catholic bishop of the South Pacific. Marist missionaries built the original structure out of rammed earth (mud mixed with dung or straw—a technique known as *pise* in their native France), since they lacked the funds to buy timber. For several years the priests and brothers operated a press here, printing Bibles in the Maori language. The original building forms the core of the elegant timber house that now stands on the site. ⊠ *The Strand, Russell,* ☎ *09/403–7861.* ⌨ *$5.* ⊙ *Daily 9–5.*

The **Russell Museum** houses a collection of Maori tools and weapons and some fine portraits. The pride of its display is a ⅕-scale replica of Captain Cook's ship, HMS *Endeavour,* which entered the bay in 1769. The museum was previously known as the Captain Cook Memorial Museum, and some locals still refer to it by that name. The museum is set back slightly from the waterfront some 50 yards north of Pompallier House. ⊠ *York St., Russell,* ☎ *09/403–7701.* ⌨ *$2.50.* ⊙ *Daily 10–5.*

Christ Church is the oldest church in the country. One of the donors to its erection in 1835 was Charles Darwin, at that time a wealthy but unknown young man making his way around the globe on board HMS *Beagle.* Behind the white picket fence that borders the churchyard, gravestones tell a fascinating and brutal story of life in the early days of the colony. Several graves belong to sailors from HMS *Hazard* who were killed in this churchyard by Hone Heke's warriors in 1845. Another headstone marks the grave of a Nantucket sailor from the whaler *Mohawk.* As you walk around the church, look for the musket holes made when Hone Heke besieged the church. The interior is simple and charming—embroidered cushions on the pews are examples of a folk-art tradition that is still very much alive. ⊠ *Church and Robertson Sts., Russell.* ⊙ *Daily 8–5.*

You can drive between Russell and Paihia, but the quickest and most convenient route is by ferry. Three passenger boats make the crossing between Paihia and Russell, with departures at least every 30 minutes in each direction from 7:30 AM to 11 PM. The one-way adult fare is $1.50. The car ferry is at Opua, about 5 kilometers (3 miles) south of Paihia. This ferry operates from 6:40 AM to 8:50 PM (Friday until 9:50 PM), with departures at approximately 20-minute intervals from either shore. The last boat leaves from Russell at 8:50 (Friday 9:50), from Opua at 9 (Friday 10). The one-way fare is $7 for car and driver plus $1 for each adult passenger.

Dining and Lodging

$$$ ✕ **The Gables.** This trim little waterfront cottage is one of the most sophisticated restaurants in the Bay of Islands. First courses on the mostly seafood menu include terrine of smoked snapper and a warm salad of chicken livers. Panfried snapper fillets with balsamic vinegar, and lamb dishes, are recommended. The lunch menu is limited but less expensive. ⊠ *The Strand, Russell,* ☎ *09/403–7618. AE, DC, MC, V. Closed Mon.; Tues. Mar.–Nov. No lunch.*

$$ ✕ **Bay of Islands Swordfish Club.** Overlooking Kororareka Bay in a pretty cream-and-white timber building, the restaurant of the Swordfish Club is dedicated to fish and fish people, from the decor to the menu to the conversation. First courses are a salad of mussels or fresh

oysters; main courses include fresh scallops and asparagus with oyster sauce. Request a table at the window, and begin the evening with a drink in the friendly bar upstairs—where, in the summer holiday period, you may have to wait for a table anyway. Officially visitors must be signed in by a member of the club, but provided you look sober, neat, and capable of enthusing over marlin fishing, the barman will request a club member to countersign the visitor's book for you (after which it would be diplomatic to stand the member to a drink). ⊠ *The Strand, Russell,* ☎ *09/403–7652. AE, MC, V. No lunch.*

$$ ✕ **The Quarterdeck.** The specialty of this seafront restaurant is fish alfresco—crayfish, lobster, flounder, scallops, and snapper, and chips and salads—and while the prices are rather steep for less than glamorous dining, the outdoor tables overlooking the lively harbor are a pleasant spot on a warm evening. The Quarterdeck is popular with families. ⊠ *The Strand, Russell,* ☎ *09/403–7761. AE, DC, MC, V. BYOB. No lunch weekdays fall–spring.*

$$$$ ✕🔟 **Kimberley Lodge.** The most luxurious accommodation in the Bay
★ of Islands, this splendid white timber mansion occupies a commanding position overlooking Russell and Kororareka Bay. The house has been designed with big windows and sunny verandas to take maximum advantage of its location. Below, terraced gardens fall away down a steep hillside to the sea. The house is opulently furnished in contemporary style, and the en-suite bathrooms are very well equipped. Only one bedroom at the rear of the house—Pompallier—lacks impressive views. The best room in the house is the Kimberley Suite, which costs more than the standard suites. Dinner is available by arrangement. Rates include breakfast. Smoking is not allowed indoors. ⊠ *Pitt St.,* ☎ *09/403–7090,* 🔳 *09/403–7239. 4 rooms with bath. Pool. AE, DC, MC, V.*

$$ 🔟 **Duke of Marlborough Hotel.** This historic hotel is a favorite with the yachting fraternity, for whom ready access to the harbor and the bar downstairs are the most important considerations. Rooms are clean and tidy enough, and all have en-suite facilities, but they have no memorable character despite the hotel's long and colorful history. The front rooms with harbor views are the most expensive but also the ones most likely to be affected by noise from the spirited crowd in the bar, especially on weekends. ⊠ *The Strand,* ☎ *09/403–7829,* 🔳 *09/403–7760. 29 rooms with bath. Restaurant, bar. DC, MC, V.*

$ 🔟 **Russell Lodge.** Surrounded by quiet gardens two streets back from the waterfront, this lodge—owned and operated by the Salvation Army—offers neat, clean rooms in several configurations. It's an especially good value for budget travelers and families. Family units have a separate bedroom with two single beds, and either a double or a single bed in the main room. The largest room is Unit 15, a two-bedroom flat with a kitchen, which will sleep six. Backpacker-style accommodations are also available in rooms for four; towels and sheets are not provided in these rooms but may be rented. All rooms have en-suite bathrooms, and five have kitchen facilities. ⊠ *Chapel and Beresford Sts., Russell,* ☎ *09/403–7640,* 🔳 *09/403–7641. 24 rooms with bath. Pool, coin laundry. AE, MC, V.*

Outdoor Activities and Sports
FISHING

Bay of Islands Sportsfishing (⊠ Box 78, Russell, ☎ 09/403–7008) represents several operators who can meet most sport-fishing requirements. **Dudley Smith** (⊠ Box 203, Russell, ☎ 09/403–7200) and **Nighthawk** (⊠ Russell, ☎ 09/407–8999) are two outfitters.

Opononi

⑱ *85 km (53 mi) west of Paihia.*

Opononi is a small town near the mouth of the Hokianga harbor. It is the place where Opi, a tame dolphin, came to play with swimmers in the mid-1950s, putting the town on the national map for the first and only time in its history. There is a statue in front of the pub commemorating the much-loved creature.

⑲ **Waipoua State Forest** contains the largest remnant of the kauri forests that once covered this part of the country, along with some delicious forest air. A short path leads from the parking area through the forest to **Tane Mahuta,** "Lord of the Forest," standing nearly 173 feet high and measuring 43 feet around its base. The largest tree in New Zealand, it's said to be 1,200 years old. There are other trees of note in the forest, among them the **four sisters,** four trees together in an interesting formation.

Matakohe

95 km (59 mi) south of Opononi.

⑳ The **Matakohe Kauri Museum** is one of the most intriguing museums in the country. Its vast collection of artifacts, tools, photographs, documents, and memorabilia tells the story of the pioneers who settled this part of the country in the second half of the 19th century—a story interwoven with the kauri forests. Here you'll find superb examples of craftsmanship: furniture and a complete kauri house, as well as an early example of an American-built Caterpillar bulldozer, which was used to drag logs from the forest. One of the most fascinating displays is the room of kauri gum, the transparent lumps of resin that form when the sticky sap of the kauri tree hardens. This gum, which was used to make varnish, can be polished to a warm, lustrous finish that looks remarkably like amber—right down to the insects that are sometimes trapped and preserved inside. At one time collecting this gum was an important rural industry. Many of the gum diggers, as they were known, came from Dalmatia, part of present-day Croatia. **Volunteers Hall** contains a huge kauri slab running from one end of the hall to the other, and there is also a "women in the bush" display, a replica of a cabinetmaker's shop, and an exhibition dedicated to fishing in Kaipara Harbour. ⊠ *Matakohe,* ☎ *09/431–7417.* 🎫 *$5.* ⊙ *Daily 9–5.*

Northland and the Bay of Islands A to Z

Arriving and Departing

BY BUS
Northliner Express (☎ 09/307–5873), **InterCity** (☎ 09/358–4085), and **Newmans** (☎ 09/309–9738) run several times daily between Auckland and Paihia.

BY CAR
The main route from Auckland is Highway 1. Leave the city by the Harbour Bridge and follow signs to Whangarei. Driving time for the 250-kilometer (150-mile) journey to Paihia is about four hours.

Contacts and Resources

EMERGENCIES
Dial 111 for **fire, police,** or **ambulance** services.

GUIDED TOURS
Fuller's Northland operates one-, two-, and three-day tours from Auckland to the Bay of Islands. Its three-day Bay Explorer includes a tour of the historic Waitangi Treaty House, a trip to Cape Reinga, a swim

with dolphins, a voyage around the bay aboard a schooner, and accommodations in Russell. ⊠ *Bay of Islands Travel Centre, Shop 2, Downtown Shopping Centre, Customs St., Auckland,* ☎ *09/358–0259.* ⊡ *$459.*

Fuller's Northland runs cruises in the Bay of Islands itself, departing from both Paihia and Russell. The most popular is the half-day catamaran cruise to Cape Brett, at the eastern extremity of the bay. This includes a journey through a large hole in Motukako Island, known naturally enough as "the hole in the rock." The Cream Trip is an enjoyable six-hour cruise that stops in at many of the bay islands. ⊠ *Maritime Bldg., Paihia,* ☎ *09/402–7421.* ⊡ *Cape Brett $52, Cream Trip $65.* ☉ *Cape Brett Cruise departs Paihia daily 9* AM *and 1:30* PM; *Cream Trip departs Paihia Oct.–May, daily 10* AM, *and June–Sept., Mon., Wed., Thurs., and Sat. 10* AM.

Russell Mini Tours offers a one-hour guided tour of the historic sights of Russell. Tours depart from the Fuller's office, opposite the wharf. ⊠ *Box 70, Russell,* ☎ *09/403–7891.* ⊡ *$12.* ☉ *Tour daily at 11, 1, 2, and 3:30.*

VISITOR INFORMATION

Bay of Islands Visitor Information Centre Paihia. ⊠ *Maritime Reserve, Paihia,* ☎ *09/402–7426.* ☉ *Nov.–Mar., daily 7:30–7:30; Apr.–Oct., daily 8–5.*

Bay of Islands Visitor Information Centre Russell. ⊠ *The Strand, Russell,* ☎ *09/403–7866.* ☉ *Daily 8–4:30.*

THE COROMANDEL PENINSULA

New Zealand has countless pockets of beauty that are not included in standard tourist itineraries. One of the most accessible is the Coromandel Peninsula, which juts out like a hitchhiker's thumb east of Auckland. As with so many lands "discovered" by Europeans, the peninsula was looted for its valuable resources: kauri trees, then gum-digging, and finally gold in the 1870s. Relative quiet since the 1930s has allowed the region to recover a little, and without question natural beauty abounds.

The center of the peninsula is dominated by a craggy spine of volcanic peaks that rise sharply to a height of almost 3,000 feet. The west coast cradles the Firth of Thames, while along the east coast the Pacific has carved out a succession of beaches and inlets separated by rearing headlands. Due to its rich volcanic soil, the peninsula has many spectacular gardens, several of which are open to the public. From the town of Thames, the gateway to the region, Highway 25 and the 309 Road circle the lower two-thirds of the peninsula—an exhilarating drive with the sea on one side and great forested peaks on the other. Hiking in the peninsula's lush forest is also exhilarating, and the east coast beaches are spectacular. Especially considering the Coromandel's proximity to Auckland, it would be difficult to find a finer introduction to the wonders of New Zealand.

Thames

㉑ *120 km (75 mi) southeast of Auckland.*

Thames is a historic town in the southwest corner of the peninsula about an hour and a half from Auckland. Since the 1920s, the city has changed from a center for the once active gold-mining industry to one for local agriculture. The mineral history remains, and at the rock lover's **Min-**

The Coromandel Peninsula

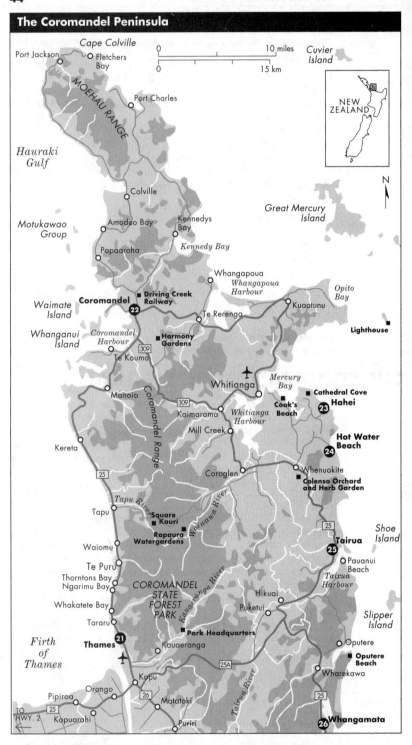

Cape Colville

Port Jackson
Fletchers Bay

MOEHAU RANGE

Port Charles

0   10 miles
0   15 km

Cuvier Island

NEW ZEALAND

Hauraki Gulf

N

Colville

Motukawao Group

Amodeo Bay
Kennedys Bay

Great Mercury Island

Papaaroha

Kennedy Bay

Whangapoua
Whangapoua Harbour

Opito Bay

Coromandel
22

■ **Driving Creek Railway**

Kuaotunu

Waimate Island

Te Rerenga

Lighthouse ■

Coromandel Harbour

■ **Harmony Gardens**

Whanganui Island

309
Te Kouma

Manaia

309

Whitianga ✈

Mercury Bay

■ **Cathedral Cove**
Hahei
23

Kaimarama

Whitianga Harbour

Cook's Beach

Mill Creek

Hot Water Beach
24

Kereta

Coroglen

Whenuakite
■ **Colenso Orchard and Herb Garden**

25

Tapu River

Coromandel Range

25
Tapu

■ **Square Kauri**

Waiwawa River

Tairua
25

■ **Rapaura Watergardens**

Shoe Island

Waiomu

Pauanui Beach

Te Puru
Thorntons Bay
Ngarimu Bay

Tairua Harbour

COROMANDEL STATE FOREST PARK

Kauaeranga River

Hikuai

Slipper Island

Whakatete Bay

Puketui

Tararu

■ **Park Headquarters**

Firth of Thames

Thames
21 ✈

Kauaeranga

Oputere

■ **Oputere Beach**

Kopu

25A

Tairua River

Wharekawa

Pipiroa

Orango

26

25

TO HWY. 2
25

Kopuarahi

Matatoki

Puriri

Whangamata
26

eralogical Museum (✉ Brown and Cochrane Sts.) and the **Historical Museum** (✉ Pollen and Cochrane Sts.) you can look into earlier ways of life in the town. If you want to learn even more about early gold mining efforts in the Coromandel, stop in at the stamper battery and take a brief underground tour of the old Golden Crown Claim, which was first worked in 1868. Five hundred feet below this site, the Caledonia strike was one of the richest in the world. A guide will describe the geological and historical interest of the mine. ✉ *State Hwy. 25, north of Waiotahi Creek Rd.,* ☎ *07/868–7448.* 🔖 *$2 each museum.* ⊙ *Historical Museum daily 1–4, Mineralogical Museum Tues.–Sun. 11–4.*

While in Thames, take a quick look into **St. George's Anglican Church.** The interior is unpainted, and the kauri wood used to build it is gorgeous. ✉ *Willoughby and MacKay Sts.*

Meonstoke is probably the most unusual garden in New Zealand, and nothing can quite prepare you for it. For over 35 years, Pam Gwynne has been working every square inch of her quarter-acre lot. Numerous paths wind through a junglelike space, where the world appears before you as it did in childhood. There are no lookouts or vistas to distract you from closing in on the magic around you. Pam is a collector, not only of top horticultural specimens, but of found objects as well that are incorporated with plants in creative and often humorous ways. On one path, a row of a couple dozen-odd ceramic pitchers hangs from a rod (to collect rainwater?), while a bird-feeder serves two hungry porcelain doves. Tiny winking Chinamen festoon Bonsai plants, and an old black tricycle looks as if a knickered young boy has just left it there. Although the garden is small, allow yourself plenty of time. There are hundreds of delights, many of which you'll miss the first time around. Pam's passion continues indoors, and if you are interested in dolls, ask to see her collection—unbelieveable! Remember that this is a private home, and visitors are welcome only by appointment. The small entry fee goes to local charities. ☎ *07/868–6560 or 07/868–6850.*

Hiking

Coromandel State Forest Park has more than 30 walking trails, which offer anything from a 30-minute stroll to a three-day trek, overnighting in huts equipped with bunks. The most accessible starting point is the delightful Kauaeranga Valley Road, where the Coromandel Forest Park Headquarters provides maps and information (☎ 07/868–6381). The office is open weekdays 8–4. Camping is also available. Keep in mind that the park can be very busy from late December to mid-January. If you're traveling then, plan to visit the park midweek. To reach the Kauaeranga Valley, head south from Thames and on the outskirts of the town turn left on Banks Street, then right on Parawai Road, which becomes Kauaeranga Valley Road.

En Route The Coromandel Ranges drop right down to the seafront Highway 25 as it winds up the west coast of the Peninsula. Turn upon turn makes each view seem more spectacular than the last, and when you top the hills north of Kereta, mountains, pastures, and islands in the Firth of Thames open out before you.

Tapu

25 km (16 mi) north of Thames.

The earthen **Tapu-Coroglen Road** turns off of Highway 25 in the hamlet of Tapu to wind into the mountains. It's another breathtaking route, where 80-foot tree ferns grow out of the roadside hills. About 5 kilometers (3 miles) from Tapu, pull over to climb 178 steps up to the 1,200-year-old **"square kauri,"** so named for the shape that a cross-section of its trunk would have. This elder was spared the ax by a gentlemen's agreement—ironic considering that local forests were otherwise zealously flattened in the 19th century. One hundred thirty-three feet tall and 30 feet around, this is only the 15th-largest kauri in New Zealand. From a platform under the tree there is a splendid view across the valley to Mau Mau Paki, one of the Coromandel Ranges peaks. Continuing east, the road passes **Raparua Watergardens** on its way across the peninsula through forests and sheep paddocks—a mythically beautiful ride in sun or mist.

Raparua Watergardens, full of native and exotic flowering species, has been sculpted from the wilderness in a 65-acre sheltered valley in the Coromandel Ranges. Raparua ("running water") is a wonderful place to witness the role water plays in New Zealand gardens, and the tranquillity that can result. In the garden's various streams, waterfalls, fountains, and 14 ponds, fish and ducks swim among colorful waterlilies and other bog plants while songbirds lilt overhead. Paths wind among the waters through collections of grasses, flax, gunnera, rhododendron, and camellia. Giant tree ferns and remu, rata, and kauri trees form a lush canopy overhead. The combination of delicacy and rugged grandeur may have moved the hardworking gardener to philosophy, which you'll find painted on signs, as in "Keep your values in balance and you will always find happiness." Note that organic gardening practices have fostered all of this beauty. Be sure to take the easy 10-minute walk to the cascading falls known as Seven Steps to Heaven, especially if you aren't planning on spending much time in native forests. Raparua has a tearoom and a crafts shop with work by Coromandel artisans. ⊠ *Tapu-Coroglen Rd., 6 km (4 mi) east of Tapu,* ☎ FAX *07/ 868–4821.* 🎫 *$6.* ⊙ *Daily 10–5.*

Coromandel

㉒ *60 km (38 mi) north of Thames, 29 km (18 mi) northwest of Whitianga.*

Coromandel became the site of New Zealand's first gold strike in 1852 when sawmiller Charles Ring found gold-bearing quartz at Driving Creek, just north of town. The find was important for New Zealand, since the country's manpower had been severely depleted by the gold rushes in California and Australia. Ring hurried to Auckland to claim the reward that had been offered to anyone finding "payable" gold. The town's population soared, but the reef gold could be mined only by heavy and expensive machinery, and within a few months Coromandel resumed its former sleepy existence as a timber town—and Charles Ring was refused the reward.

♻ **Driving Creek Railway** is one man's magnificent folly. Barry Brickell is a local potter who discovered that clay on his land was perfect for his work. The problem was that the deposit lay in a remote area at the top of a steep slope; so he hacked a path through the forest and built his own miniature railroad to haul the stuff. Visitors to his studio began asking if they could go along for a ride, and Brickell now takes passengers on a daily tour aboard his toy train. The route that the diesel-powered, narrow-gauge locomotive follows incorporates a cutting, a double-decker bridge, two tunnels, a spiral, and a switchback. The round-trip takes about 50 minutes. The "station" is about 3 kilometers (2 miles) north of Coromandel township. ⊠ *410 Kennedy's Bay Rd., Coromandel,* ☎ *07/866–8703.* 🎫 *$9.* ⊙ *Late Oct.–Apr., daily at 2, 4, and 10:30.*

Dining and Lodging

$–$$ ✕ **Pepper Tree Restaurant and Bar.** Mussels, mussels, and more New Zealand green-lipped mussels. Eat them steamed or eat them smoked, and eat them here because they're incredibly delicious. Seafood of all kinds is a treat, like local oysters in the half-shell, and don't miss a plate of kumara chips (native sweet potato fries). An after-meal sweet isn't a bad idea either. ⊠ *Kapanga Rd., Coromandel,* ☎ *07/866–8211. AE, MC, V.*

$$ ⊡ **Coromandel Colonial Cottages.** These six immaculate timber cot-
★ tages offer spacious and comfortable self-contained accommodations for about the same price as a standard motel room. Each has two bed-rooms, a lounge room with convertible beds, a large, well-equipped kitchen, and a dining area. Arranged with military precision in two ranks, the cottages face each other across a tailored lawn surrounded by green hills on the northern outskirts of Coromandel. During vacation periods, book several months in advance. ⊠ *Rings Rd., Coromandel,* ☎ *07/866–8857. 6 cottages. Hot tub, croquet, miniature golf, coin laundry. AE, DC, MC, V.*

$$ ⊡ **Karamana.** Mary and Bill Hoyles's historic house provides home-stay accommodations that are exceptional on the peninsula. The kauri house is simply constructed yet embellished with ornamental architraves and a delightful veranda. Guest rooms are furnished with high-qual-ity antiques and scented with potpourri. The location, at the foot of steep, forested peaks, is majestic and serene, as are the Hoyles's gar-dens. Dinner is available by arrangement. Rates include breakfast. ⊠ *Whangapoua Rd., Coromandel,* ☎ ℻ *07/866–7138. 3 rooms, 1 with bath, 2 share 1 bath, 1 shower. MC.*

Colville and Beyond

30 km (19 mi) north of Coromandel.

If you find yourself possessed with the urge to reach land's end on the wilds of the peninsula—with more rugged coastline, beautiful coves, beaches, and pasturelands—follow the sealed road up to Colville. Be-yond that, a gravel road will take you to the Mt. Moehau trail that climbs to the peninsula's highest point (2,923 feet); to the sands at Port Jackson; or all the way to the tip, at Fletcher's Bay (60 kilometers, or 38 miles, from Coromandel). Colville's classic counterculture **General Store** (☎ 07/866–6805) sells foodstuffs, wine, and gasoline, and has a café with vegetarian meals. It is the northernmost supplier on the penin-sula, so don't forget to fill up before you move on.

En Route On your way south from Coromandel, **Harmony Gardens** is delight-ful, tranquil, noted for its rhododendrons, and filled with the sounds of birds and running water. To get there from Coromandel, drive back along Highway 25 for about 4 kilometers (2½ miles) and turn inland where a sign points to WHITIANGA—309 ROAD. After about 2 kilome-ters (1 mile), this road passes the gardens. ☎ 07/866–8487. ⊡ *$4.* ☯ *Spring–fall, daily 10–4.*

Hahei

③ *14 km (9 mi) northeast of Whenuakite on Hahei Beach Rd.*

The beaches and seaside land formations in and around Hahei make for a great day of exploring—or lounging. **Te Pare Historic Reserve** is the site of an old Maori *pa*, a fortified hilltop, though no trace remains of the defensive terraces and wooden spikes that once ringed the hill. A much larger pa was on the hilltop overlooking this site. If you hap-pen to be here at high tide, the blowhole at the foot of the cliffs will add its booming bass note to the crash of the waves and the sighing of the wind in the grass. To reach the pa, follow the red arrow down the hill from the parking area, and after about 50 yards take the right fork, which leads through a grove of giant pohutukawa trees, then through a gate and across a grassy, open hillside. The track is steep in places and becomes increasingly overgrown as you climb, but persist until you reach the summit, and then head toward more pohutukawas off to your right at the southern end of the headland. The reserve itself is past Hahei on Pa Road.

Cathedral Cove is a beautiful white-sand crescent with a great rock arch. It is only accessible at low tide, about a 45-minute walk each way. To get there, travel along Hahei Beach Road, turn right toward town and the sea, and then, just past the shops, turn left into Grange Road and follow the signs. From the parking lot you will get excellent views over Mahurangi Island, a marine reserve.

Cook's Beach lies along Mercury Bay, so named for Captain James Cook's observation of the transit of the planet Mercury in November 1769. The beach is notable because of the captain's landfall here—it was the first by a European, and it is commemorated by a beachside plaque. The beach itself is one of the less attractive in the area.

★ ㉔ The popular **Hot Water Beach** is a delightful thermal oddity. A warm spring seeps beneath the beach, and by scooping a shallow hole in the sand you can create a pool of warm water; the deeper you dig, the hotter the water becomes, but the phenomenon occurs only at low to mid-tide, so time your trip accordingly. For a swim without the spa treatment, there is one of the finest well-protected coves on the coast nearby, with sands tinted pink with crushed shells. It is at the end of Hahei Beach Road. Hot Water Beach is well signposted off of Hahei Beach Road from Whenuakite (fen-oo-ah-kie-tee).

NEED A BREAK?   **Colenso Orchard and Herb Garden,** on Highway 25 just south of the Hahei turnoff, is a relaxed cottage café that you might find yourself wishing would franchise across rural New Zealand. Set in a garden full of lavender and kitchen herbs, Colenso serves fresh juices (from their own orchards), daily soups, focaccia sandwiches, those addictive chocolate fudge biscuits (also called "slices") that are a real Kiwi treat, and Devonshire teas—simple, wholesome fare that goes with the droning of bees and the sound of wind chimes. Before getting back on the road, buy a bag of their freshly harvested fruit at the roadside stand. ⊠ *Main Rd., Whenuakite,* ☎ *07/866-3725.* ◷ *Sept.–July, daily 10–5.*

En Route   Between Tairua and Whangamata you'll pass the mountainous wilderness around the Second Branch of the Tairua River, which is the remarkable domain of Doug Johansen. Over the past 20 years he has cut his own trails in the valley's lush rain forest—but they aren't trails that you'd be able to find yourself, even if you happened to be walking on one. Their minimal invasiveness is uncanny. Heading into the woods with a knowledgeable, and in this case entertaining, guide to point out native plants and their uses can make later hikes on your own even more rewarding. ☞ Kiwi Dundee Adventures *in* Coromandel A to Z, *below.*

Tairua

㉕ *28 km (18 mi) south of Hahei, 37 km (23 mi) north of Whangamata.*

A town that you'll actually notice when you pass through it, Tairua is a harborside center where you can find food stores and a seafood joint or two. The twin volcanic peaks of Paku rise up beside the harbor.

Dining and Lodging

$$$$ ✕⊡ **Puka Park Lodge.** This stylish hillside hideaway, which attracts a largely European clientele, lies immersed in native bushland on Pauanui Beach, at the seaward end of Tairua Harbour on the east coast of the peninsula. Timber chalets are smartly furnished with black cane tables and wooden Venetian blinds, and gauze mosquito nets are draped over the beds for effect rather than practical reasons. Sliding glass doors lead to a balcony perched among the treetops. Bathrooms are well equipped but small. The lodge offers a full range of activities for those who want to take advantage of the splendor of the surrounding beaches and forests. Rates are comparatively low for accommodations of this standard. Food and service in the international restaurant are outstanding. The turnoff from Highway 25 is about 6 kilometers, or 4 miles, south of Tairua. ⊠ *Private Bag, Pauanui Beach,* ☎ *07/864–8088,* ℻ *07/864–8112. 32 rooms with bath. Restaurant, bar, pool, tennis court, bicycles. AE, DC, MC, V.*

$$–$$$ ✕⊡ **Pacific Harbour Motor Lodge.** Clustered between the road and an ocean inlet, the newly built colonial-style cottages here are attractively designed. Peak-ceilinged interiors are trimmed with New Zealand remu pine, and furnishings are pleasant and tasteful. All units have fully equipped kitchenettes. The motor lodge has its own bar and restaurant, with local seafood on the menu, and there is a helpful local activities list available at the front desk. ⊠ *Hwy. 25, Box 5, Tairua,* ☎ ℻ *07/864–8581. 25 suites. Restaurant, bar, hot tub. AE, DC, MC, V.*

En Route   On the road between Tairua and Whangamata, stop at Oputere Beach and the Wharekawa (fah-ray-ka-wa) Wildlife Refuge for a 15-minute stroll through the forest to another great stretch of white sand. The long beach is bounded at either end by headlands, and there are stunning views of Slipper and other ocean islands. An estuary by the car park is a breeding ground for shorebirds. In the late afternoon, waterfowl are often present as the sun slants across the Coromandel Ranges to the west. A handsome bridge arches over the river to the forest walk on the other side.

Whangamata

㉖ *37 km (23 mi) south of Tairua, 60 km (38 mi) east of Thames.*

Whangamata (fahng-a-ma-*ta*) is another harborside village backed by the Coromandel Ranges. The town of 4,000 is a local seat, but the modest houses and main strip won't exactly bowl you over. Its harbor, surf beaches, mangroves, and coastal islands, however, are glorious. It is a great spot for deep-sea fishing, and its bar break brings in some of the best waves in New Zealand. Around the Christmas holidays and into January, it's a favorite for throngs of surfers.

NEED A
BREAK?
     Ginger's Health Shop & Cafe. If you need breakfast or a sandwich to take to the beach, you're sure to find something at this 90% vegetarian haven. The sandwiches, savory and sweet scones (ooh, those date scones), apricot-muesli bars, and other treats here may make Ginger's your favorite local spot for fueling up. ⊠ *601 Port Rd., Whangamata,* ☎ *07/865-7265.* ☉ *Summer, daily 6–5; shorter hrs in winter.*

Dining and Lodging

$$$ ✕⊡ **Brenton Lodge.** Looking out over suburblike Whangamata and
★ the islands in its harbor from your hillside suite, you'll have no trouble settling into an almost luxurious mood. Fresh flowers and a welcoming tray of fruit and muffins greet you on arrival, as do cheerful furnishings: a couch, breakfast table and chairs (for a private break-

fast), a wonderfully comfortable bed, terry cloth robes, and coffee- and tea-making paraphernalia. The lodge's only rooms are two suites on the second floors of attractive, new outbuildings. Stroll around the garden, peep at the birds in the aviary, and in spring breathe in the scent of orange and jasmine blossoms. Restaurants in town aren't abundant, so you may want to tell Jan Preston Campbell in advance that you will join her and Paul for one of her delicious dinners and a little conversation. Breakfast is included in the room rate; dinner is $45. ⊠ *Box 216, Whangamata,* ☎ *07/865–8400. 2 suites. AE, MC, V.*

Coromandel A to Z

Arriving and Departing

BY BUS

Murphy Buses (☎ 07/867–6829) link Whitianga, Thames, and Auckland daily. Bookings can be made through InterCity (☎ 09/358–4085).

The **Coromandel Bus Plan** is the cheapest and most flexible way to travel around the region by bus. It is valid for three months and you can get on and off where you wish. $49 covers the Thames-Coromandel-Whitianga-Tairua-Thames loop, and you can take round-trips to Hahei, Hot Water Beach, and Whangamata. ⊠ *Thames Information Centre,* ☎ *07/868–7284.*

BY CAR

From Auckland, take the Southern Motorway, following signs to Hamilton. Just past the narrowing of the motorway, turn left onto Highway 2 and follow the signs to Thames. Allow 1- to 2½-hours for the 118-kilometer (73-mile) journey.

Contacts and Resources

EMERGENCIES

Dial 111 for **fire, police,** or **ambulance** services.

GUIDED TOURS

Kiwi Dundee Adventures. A trip to New Zealand really wouldn't be complete without a day or more with Doug Johansen and Jan Poole; their humorous tricks along with their enthusiasm for the region inevitably rubs off on anyone who takes a Kiwi Dundee tour. Doug and Jan offer one- to five-day or longer experiences of the majesty of the Coromandel, or all of New Zealand if you'd like. Spectacular coastline, ferny rain forests, mountains, and gorges; glowworm caves, old gold mines, thermal springs, native flora and fauna—natural phenomena that they know intimately and respect deeply—and odd bits of history and bush lore are all rolled into their hikes and walks. They have a great time as conservationists and guides, and you're sure to have one with them in their beautiful neck of the woods. ⊠ *Box 198 Whangamata,* ☎ 𝐅𝐀𝐗 *07/866–8809.*

Mercury Bay Safaris operates a "swim with the dolphins" program, plus a glass bottom boat trip and a journey around islands in the area. Departures from Whitianga Wharf are subject to weather conditions. ⊠ *Whitianga Information Centre, Whitianga,* ☎ *07/866–5555,* 𝐅𝐀𝐗 *07/ 866–2205.* 🎫 *Dolphin Quest $75, glass-bottom boat $30, Seven Island Safari $70.*

VISITOR INFORMATION

Thames Visitor Information Centre. ⊠ *405 Queen St., Thames,* ☎ *07/ 868–7284.* ☉ *Spring–fall, weekdays 9–5, Sat. 9–4, Sun. 10–3; summer, daily 9–5.*

Whitianga Visitor Information Centre. ⊠ *66 Albert St.,* ☎ *07/866–5555.* ☉ *Spring–fall, weekdays 9–5, weekends 10–1; summer, daily 9–5.*

3 Rotorua to Wellington

Sulphuric Rotorua bubbles and oozes with surreal volcanic activity. It is one of the population centers of New Zealand's pre-European inhabitants, the Maori—try dining at a traditional hangi feast. Great hiking abounds in a variety of national parks, glorious gardens grow in the rich soil of the Taranaki province, and charming, Art Deco Napier and the nation's capital in Wellington are friendly counterpoints to the countryside.

NORTH AND SOUTH ISLANDS have different sorts of natural beauty. South Island's best-known heroic landscapes are generally flat or precipitous. North Island's rolling pasturelands have a more human scale—some think of Scotland, not only because of the sheep paddocks. Parts of North Island do break the rhythm of these verdant contours: the majestic Mount Taranaki, also called Mount Egmont, the rugged wilderness areas of Urewera and Tongariro national parks, the rocky forms in the Wairarapa district northeast of Wellington, and the bizarre geological plumbing around Rotorua.

Rotorua is the mid-island's population center, and it has been heavily touristed since Europeans first heard of the healing qualities of local hot springs and pools. All around, nature has crafted a gallery of surreal wonders that includes limestone caverns, volcanic wastelands, steaming geysers, and hissing ponds. From the shores of Lake Taupo—the country's largest lake and the geographic bull's-eye of North Island—Mount Ruapehu, the island's tallest peak, is plainly visible. Site of New Zealand's largest ski area, the mountain is the dominant feature of Tongariro National Park, a haunting landscape of craters, volcanoes, and lava flows that ran with molten rock as recently as 1988, and were throwing up some threatening clouds in 1996.

Southeast of Lake Taupo, on the shores of Hawke Bay, the town of Napier might hit you as an unexpected aggregation of Art Deco architecture. Around Napier, the Hawke's Bay region is one of the country's major wine routes. A diversion to the north will take you to relatively isolated Gisborne and Eastland, which are often overlooked but extremely rewarding. The largely agricultural East Cape juts out above Gisborne, coursing with trout-rich streams and ringed with beaches and coves made even more beautiful by their isolation.

The lush Taranaki region literally sprang from the ocean floor in a series of volcanic blasts, forming that odd hump down the west coast of North Island. The now-dormant cone of Mount Taranaki is the breathtaking symbol of the province. Because of the mountain's proximity to the coast, you can easily climb its sides in the morning and come back down for an afternoon swim on the shores of the Tasman Sea. Agriculture thrives in the area's volcanic soil, and Taranaki's gardens are some of the country's most spectacular, from a massive rhododendron trust to smaller private gardens. It almost goes without saying that the Maori were the province's first settlers, and their local mythology and historical sites deepen any experience of the area.

More and more people are finding their way to Wellington by choice rather than necessity. The city is gaining a reputation for fostering the arts and preserving its culture in a way that the more brash Auckland to the north does not. Because it is perched at the southern tip of North Island, Wellington is the jumping-off point for the ferry south—but don't jump south too quickly. If you delay your departure even for a day, you'll find that Wellington is a charming, sociable city. Small enough to explore easily on foot, it is arguably the country's most cosmopolitan city, with an excellent arts complex, cafés, contemporary clothing designers, and music of all kinds. Also consider taking a side trip to the Wairarapa, another coastal area with a range of outdoor activities and some of the country's finest wineries.

Note: For more information on bicycling, fishing, hiking, and rafting in central North Island, *see* Chapter 6.

Pleasures and Pastimes

Dining

Between Rotorua and Wellington, you'll come across a number of small towns with little more than a country-style pub to satisfy the appetite. Don't avoid these places, as they usually specialize in Kiwi home cooking served with a smile. As you would expect, cities have a much wider variety of restaurants, and don't miss whatever is fresh coming out of the sea.

Rotorua offers a unique New Zealand dining experience: the *hangi,* a Maori feast. Traditionally, meat and vegetables placed in flax baskets were gently steamed in an earth oven lined with heated stones and wet leaves—lamb, pork, and seafood along with pumpkin and *kumara* (sweet potato), a staple of the Maori diet. Almost without exception, hangis in Rotorua are followed by a Maori concert, a performance of traditional songs and dances.

In central North Island, try to arrange a taste of freshly hooked trout. Laws prohibit trout being sold commercially, so you may have to catch it yourself (or know someone who has) and then ask your host or a local chef to cook it for you. Game food is also recommended, especially with a deep red wine from Hawke's Bay or Martinborough. New Zealand cervena venison will be a special treat if you find it on a menu served with tamarillo (tree tomato) sauce.

Fishing

Central North Island is trout country. You can get out on any of the designated lakes and waterways if you have your own gear and a fishing license. It is worthwhile, however, to engage a local guide to take you to the right spots. On the lakes around Rotorua, and perhaps even more on Lake Taupo, few people leave disappointed. For extensive information on central North Island fishing, *see* Chapter 6.

Lodging ✗

New Zealand lodges are often small and exclusive, set in a place of great beauty. Some of the best lodges are in central North Island, the most famous being Huka Lodge just outside of Taupo and Solitaire near Rotorua. They tend to attract people keen on fishing, hunting, or other outdoor activities, and the area's best guides are always nearby. The wine and food available at lodges is another point of appeal, and there is often the opportunity to mix and mingle with other guests over a social hour or two in the lodge's living room. If your budget allows, even one night at one of these lodges will be an experience you won't soon forget.

For most of the year there are many more hotel beds than visitors in Rotorua, and a number of hotels and motels offer significant discounts on their standard rates. The Tourism Rotorua Visitor Centre acts as a clearinghouse for discount accommodations, and you can often save up to half the published rate of a particular hotel by booking through the center on arrival in Rotorua. The exception is school holidays, when you should book in advance.

Tourism Rotorua also has information about bed-and-breakfast accommodations in the area. This alternative will give you a chance to meet area residents and get a little closer to kiwi life. Rates start at about $50. With some hosts, you can arrange to have dinner prepared for an extra charge.

Soaking

In Rotorua and Taupo, thermal springs are literally on tap. You can soak in your own thermal bath in even the cheapest hotels in Rotorua, or take advantage of public facilities such as Polynesian Spa. Many Taupo motels and hotels also have their own thermal baths or pools. Lying on your back and closing your eyes is a great way to relax. After a day's walking about, find a foot pool in Rotorua and join the other people sitting on the edge with their feet in the hot water. You'll be amazed how relaxed you feel afterward.

Walking

Central North Island doesn't have the famous walking tracks of South Island, but it does have plenty of bushwalking just as serious, and plenty easy and walkable. Excellent longer tracks circle around Mount Egmont–Taranaki or climb through the alpine areas in Tongariro National Park. Some of the most rugged bush in the country can be found in Urewera National Park southeast of Rotorua, and hiking opportunities abound around Rotorua, Taupo, and the Wairarapa. Wherever you decide to trek, be prepared if you're going to take on serious wilderness.

Exploring Central North Island and Wellington

You could easily spend a month traveling between Auckland and Wellington and still touch on only the major sights—which brings up the tough part of trip planning in central North Island. Realistically, you're most likely to travel either straight through the middle or down the east or west coasts. The difficulty comes in deciding which coast and which smaller areas to explore. If you're interested in the bizarre thermal activity of Rotorua, start there. If you're a garden lover, starting in Taranaki to the west and stopping at other spots on the way to Wellington is the way to go. If wine routes are more appealing, you can take in three on the east coast: Gisborne, Hawke's Bay, and Wairarapa. If you want to get into some astonishing backcountry, Tongariro and Urewera national parks are unbeatable, as are parts of the Wairarapa. Keep in mind that Wellington is a pleasant city for refreshing yourself for a couple of days before hopping over to South Island.

There are, in other words, a great many activities listed in this chapter. Try not to take on too many. Allow yourself time to get a good sense of where you are by spending three to four days minimum in each area, and allow for more travel time than you might expect—the island is larger than it looks.

Great Itineraries

Numbers in the text correspond to numbers in the margin and on the Central North Island, Napier, and Wellington maps.

IF YOU HAVE 3 DAYS

Three days will only allow you to see one of the major areas covered in the chapter, or scratch the surface of two—especially taking travel time into account. If you do have only three days, spend all of them in **Rotorua,** taking in its sights and smells, popping over to **Waitomo Caves** for the glowworm spectacle, and spending all or part of a day fishing; or **Napier,** with a day in the city and two days in the surrounding wine country and natural beauty; or **Wellington,** taking a day or two in the city and the rest in the **Wairarapa** visiting wineries, hiking, or seeing rare native animals. You would have to fly in and out of New Plymouth for three days in **Taranaki**'s gardens and walking on the slopes of Mount Egmont. If surface treatment will do, you could take a day in Rotorua before dropping down the next morning to Napier for the rest of the time. Fly from there to your next stop.

IF YOU HAVE 6 DAYS

With almost a week to spend covering central and southern North Island, you can put together a more diverse experience of a couple of regions. Pick a path for moving from north to south, and leave a half day or more for travel between Rotorua and Napier or Taranaki, then another half-day plus for the trip down to Wellington if you have a car. Start in **Rotorua,** spending two to three days in the bubble and ooze, fishing, going to a hangi at night, then continue either east to **Napier and Hawke's Bay,** Art Deco city and the surrounding wine country, or west to **Taranaki** for gardens, mountain walks, and beaches for the rest of the time. Or, from Rotorua you could head south to **Lake Taupo** and **Tongariro National Park** for serious outdoor activities: fishing, canoeing, rafting, and hiking. That would combine well with a stop in the **Wairarapa** for more spectacular countryside, including rugged coastal scenery, one of the country's finest wildlife parks, and a wine tour in **Martinborough.** In six days you could also combine Taranaki, the Wairarapa, and Wellington, with one day each in the last two. Or chuck it all and head straight for **Gisborne and Eastland** for six days of New Zealand's finest off-the-beaten-path travel.

IF YOU HAVE 9 DAYS

With so much time, you might think that you can see it all, but try not to get too ambitious. Wherever you are in New Zealand, allowing more time in each place will only give you a better feeling for where you go. Also, the more you take on, the more travel time you'll have between places. One more word of caution: A Napier to Taranaki crossing will run you ragged if you try to take it, so don't. In all cases below, you'll need a day overall for travel time between whatever locations you choose. So then, the two-day-in-each surface treatment options for nine-day stays are **Rotorua–Napier–Wairarapa–Wellington,** or **Rotorua–Taranaki–Wairarapa–Wellington.** To give yourself a better sense of place, each of the five following combinations will provide in-depth experiences of the delights of central and southern North Island: **Taranaki** (4 days)–**Wairarapa** (2 days)–**Wellington** (2 days); or **Eastland** (5 days)–**Napier** (3 days); or **Napier** (3 days)–**Wairarapa** (3 days)–**Wellington** (2 days); or **Rotorua and Taupo** (5 days)–**Wairarapa** (3 days); or **Rotorua and Taupo** (4 days)–**Taranaki** (4 days). Pick one!

When to Tour Central North Island and Wellington

It's easy enough to say that the months of December through mid-April are the best for central and southern North Island. The weather is glorious and everything is open. Outside of the late-spring to early autumn months rainy days can get chilly. Some say that Taranaki's Rhododendron Festival nearly always gets rained on, the answer to which is to skip the festival and go in late November for more than just rhodo blossoms. Of course if you want to do some skiing, August is the month to hit Tongariro National Park and Mount Egmont to put your tips into some white stuff.

ROTORUA, WAITOMO CAVES, AND LAKE TAUPO

It's one of the most extraordinary sights in the country. Everywhere you turn, the earth bubbles, boils, spits, and oozes. Drainpipes steam, flower beds hiss, rings tarnish, and cars corrode. The rotten-egg smell of hydrogen sulphide hangs in the air, and even the local golf course has its own mud-pool hot spots, where a lost ball stays lost forever.

New Zealand's most famous tourist attraction, Rotorua (ro-to-*roo*-ah) sits smack on top of the most violent segment of the Taupo Volcanic Zone, which runs in a broad belt from White Island in the Bay of Plenty to Tongariro National Park, south of Lake Taupo. These spurting geysers and sulphur springs have spawned an unashamedly touristy town—

with a Motel Alley of more than 100 motels—that can be taken in easily in one day. The city has tidied up its act considerably in the past few years, particularly by rerouting sewerage pipes away from the lake and out to the forest. The lakefront, too, has been improved, and is now a pleasant park setting in which to sit and watch the lake activity. Even so, if somebody else's idea of fun and the air in "Sulphur City" sound unappealing, drive outside the city limits and you'll find yourself in magnificent, untamed country, where spring-fed streams sprint through native forests into lakes that are an abundant source of some of the largest rainbow trout on earth. Anglers regularly pull 10-pounders from Lake Tarawera.

Rotorua has a well-established Maori community tracing its ancestry back through the Te Arawa tribe to the great Polynesian migration of the 14th century. Maori culture is stamped indelibly on the town, and for a more intimate contact with their culture, attend a *hangi*—a traditional feast—followed by a Maori concert.

Cambridge

➊ *150 km (94 mi) southeast of Auckland, 85 km (53 mi) northwest of Rotorua.*

A small town in the district of Waikato, Cambridge is a place most visitors drive through in a hurry to get to Rotorua from Auckland, and are left wishing they hadn't. Even a quick glance reveals that this is a charming town, with its historic buildings, tree-lined streets, and rural English atmosphere. If you have a few extra hours, plan to spend them in and around Cambridge. Rotorua is an hour or so away, which gives you plenty of time for a stopover on your way down from the north.

Cambridge has grappled with its image a bit, calling itself variously the town of trees and a center for crafts and antiques. The best way to find both is simply to leave your car and take a walk along Victoria Street. For even more crafts and antiques stores, stroll into Empire and Commerce Streets. Cambridge is also regarded as New Zealand's Kentucky, and, in fact, the thoroughbred industry has become the most prominent local feature.

🐎 **Horse Magic** at Cambridge Thoroughbred Lodge is a must for anyone interested in horse racing or the thoroughbred industry. Thoroughbred tours and shows are held thrice daily. Experienced presenters tailor shows for each audience, easily moving from expert-level information to antics for any kids that might be in the group. A two-year-old thoroughbred is shown off in full racing gear; other horses are led out in costume as well. And if you do come with children, they can go for a short ride while you take a cup of coffee and muffins. Auctions, which are interesting to drop in on if you're in the area, are held in March, May, August, and November. ⊠ *State Hwy. 1, 6 km (4 mi) south of town,* ☎ *07/827–8118,* 🗚 *827–8005.* 🖅 *$9.* ⊙ *Tour daily at 10:30, 2:30, and 3:30.*

Dining
Cambridge has a number of restaurants to choose from. Fran's, a slice of everyday New Zealand, is a good place to stop in for a bite on the way south.

$ Fran's Café and Continental Cake Kitchen. A clutch of tables in the main room, a few on the patio behind—line up inside at an old wooden counter at the back for a hot dish or pick out a sandwich from the self-serve counter on the side, all of it homemade. You might feel yourself slipping back a couple of decades as you sit down with ladies lunching, a

Central North Island

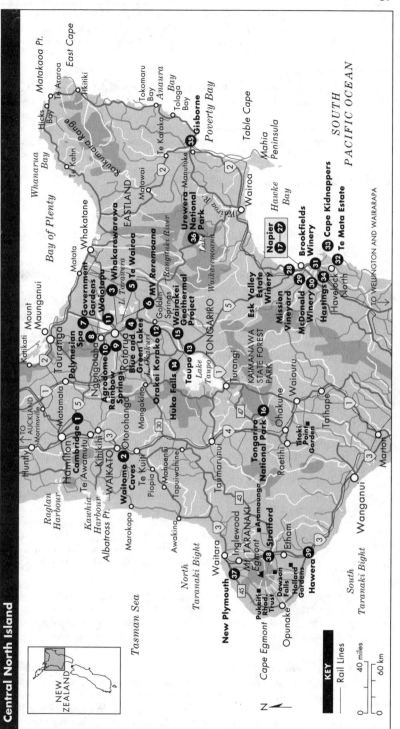

KEY

— Rail Lines

0 ——— 40 miles
0 ——— 60 km

NEW ZEALAND

mother and her children, or a couple of local businesspeople. Don't forget to order a cuppa (Kiwi coffee or tea) and a piece of cake. Food is tasty, and the staff takes obvious pride in it. ✉ *62 Victoria St., Cambridge,* ☎ *07/827–3946.*

Shopping

Cambridge Country Store, in a brightly painted 100-year-old church, is the first building you'll notice as you come into town from the north. The emporium is choc-a-bloc with New Zealand–made goods, everything from wool scarves, throw-rugs, and hand-knitted sweaters, to wine and food products (but not lunch). ✉ *92 Victoria St.,* ☎ *07/827–8715,* FAX *07/827–7247.*

Waitomo Caves

❷ *65 km (41 mi) southwest of Cambridge, 150 km (95 mi) west of Rotorua, 190 km (120 mi) north of New Plymouth.*

Waitomo Caves are parts of an ancient seabed that was lifted and then spectacularly eroded into a surreal landscape of limestone formations and caves, many of them still unexplored. Only two caves are open to the public for guided tours: the Aranui and the Waitomo, or Glowworm Cave. **Waitomo Cave** takes its name from the Maori words *wai* and *tomo,* water and cave, since the Waitomo River vanishes into the hillside here. Visitors are taken through by boat. In **Glowworm Grotto,** the larva of *Arachnocampa luminosa,* measuring between 1 and 2 inches, lives on cave ceilings. It snares its prey by dangling filaments of tiny, sticky beads, which trap insects attracted to the light the worm emits by a chemical oxidation process. Ironically, it is often the adult that is caught and eaten by the infant of the species. A single glowworm produces far less light than any firefly, but when massed in great numbers in the dark, the effect is stunning, a bit like looking at the night sky in miniature.

Aranui Cave, 2 kilometers (1¼ miles) beyond Glowworm Cave, is a very different experience. Eons of dripping water have sculpted a delicate garden in pink and white limestone. The cave is named after a local Maori, Te Rutuku Aranui, who discovered the cave in 1910 when his dog disappeared inside in pursuit of a wild pig. Each cave tour lasts 45 minutes. Glowworm Cave is high on the list of every coach tour, so try to avoid visiting between 11 and 2, when groups arrive from Auckland. ✉ *Te Anga Rd.,* ☎ *07/878–8227.* 🎫 *Waitomo Cave $16.50, both caves $25.* ⏲ *Glowworm Cave tour Nov.–Easter, daily every ½ hr 9–5:30, and Easter–Oct., daily every hr 9–5; Aranui Cave tour daily at 10, 11, 1, 2, and 3.*

In the center of the caves village, the **Museum of Caves** provides an entertaining and informative look at the formation of the caves and the life cycle of the glowworm, with a number of interactive displays designed especially for children. ✉ *Waitomo Caves Village,* ☎ *07/878–7640.* 🎫 *$3.50.* ⏲ *Daily 8–6.*

The **Waitomo Walkway** is a 5-kilometer (3-mile), 2½-hour walk that begins across the road from the Museum of Caves and follows the Waitomo River. The track passes through forests and impressive limestone outcrops, and it may leave you with your fondest memories of Waitomo. It is relatively easy and highly recommended, but you must walk back to Waitomo Caves Village on the same path. If you prefer an alternative to the complete walk, take Te Anga Road from the village, turn left into Tumutumu Road, park at Ruakuri Reserve, and walk the short final section of the track through this delightful reserve.

The **Te Anga–Marokopa Road,** which winds west out of Waitomo toward the coast, makes for a spectacular detour, winding past sheep paddocks and stunning vistas of the hillsides of Waikato and the King Country. Some 26 kilometers (16 miles) out of Waitomo, stop at the **Mangapohue** (mang-ah-po-*hoo*-ay) **Natural Bridge.** From the parking area, there are two approaches to the bridge. One to the right climbs over a hill, dropping into a valley strewn with oyster-fossil rocks that defy description. The natural bridge rises off to the left. The other path follows a stream through a gorge it has carved out. The gorge walls climb ever higher until they meet and form the bridge that closes over the path. The walk takes only 15 to 20 minutes to complete, but you may want to stop a few minutes longer at the bridge to take it all in.

Farther along the road to Marokopa, about 5 kilometers (3 miles) or so, **Piripiri Caves** beckon with their interesting fossil legacy—the marks of giant oysters that resided here during the area's one-time subaqueous existence. The place is fascinating, but the approach and entrance to the caves are steep and slippery, so wear appropriate shoes or boots, and bring a jacket for the cool air and a powerful torch (flashlight) to cut through the gloom if you really want to see the extensive underground network.

A couple of kilometers farther still, the 120-foot **Marokopa Falls** are another local wonder. Look at them from a small roadside platform or walk down a trail to get closer. And a few kilometers beyond the falls, the Maori-run pub at Te Anga is a good place to stop for refreshment before heading back, or onward.

You can continue west on this road to Marokopa, then south on a more difficult stretch if you want a longer, more scenic route to the Taranaki region. If you do, fill up your gas tank before turning off State Highway 1 for Waitomo.

Black-Water Rafting
This is an unusual and entertaining way to see the caves. Participants must first prove themselves with a giant leap into the Huhunoa Stream; the next three hours are spent dressed in wet suits and equipped with cavers' helmets and inflated inner tubes, floating through underground caverns. While the combination of darkness and freezing water might sound like a refined form of torture, the trip is an exhilarating one that will live vividly in your memory long after the goose bumps have disappeared. The cost is $50 per person. Departure times vary, depending on daily demand. ⊠ *Black Water Rafting, Box 13, Waitomo Caves,* ☎ *07/878–7640.*

Rotorua

85 km (53 mi) south of Cambridge, 200 km (125 mi) southeast of Auckland.

❸ **Whakarewarewa** (fa-ka-ree-wa-ree-wa) is one mouthful of a name—locals just call it "Whaka." This is easily the most accessible and popular of Rotorua's thermal areas, and also the most varied, since it provides insight into Maori culture. You are free to wander at your own pace, but you'll gain far more from the experience if you take a guided tour from the Arts and Crafts Institute near the ticket office. The trails winding through the complex pass sinister, steaming pools, spitting mud ponds, and smooth silica terraces that appear to be coated in melted candle wax. **Pohutu** (the big splash) is a rather erratic geyser that from time to time shoots to a height of over 80 feet. You'll also find a reconstructed Maori village with houses, gates, a *marai* (meeting house), and a modern Maori village, where residents cook in the traditional manner by placing meat and vegetables in flax baskets and dunking them in steaming pools at the back of the village. At the village entrance is a graveyard in which the graves are all aboveground, since it's impossible to dig into the earth. A one-hour Maori concert takes place daily at 12:15 in the Arts and Crafts Institute. Whakarewarewa is 3 kilometers (2 miles) along Fenton Street from the Rotorua Visitor Centre, heading toward Taupo. ⊠ *Hemo Rd., Rotorua,* ☎ *07/348–9047.* ⌨ *$10.50, concert $10.50.* ⊙ *Nov.–Easter, daily 8–6; Easter–Oct., daily 8–5.*

❹ Blue and Green lakes are on the road to ☞ Te Wairoa (the buried village) and Lake Tarawera. The Green Lake is off-limits except for its viewing area, but the Blue Lake is a popular picnic and swimming area. To get to them, turn right off of Fenton Street into Amohau Street (at the McDonald's on the left). The road loops through forests and skirts the edge of the lakes.

❺ At the end of the 19th century, **Te Wairoa** (tay why-ro-ah, the buried village) was the starting point for expeditions to the pink and white terraces of Rotomahana, on the slopes of Mount Tarawera. These silica terraces were formed by the mineral-rich water from a geyser. As the water cascaded down the mountainside, it formed a series of baths, which became progressively cooler as they neared the lake. In the latter half of the last century these fabulous terraces were the country's major tourist attraction, but they were completely destroyed when Mount Tarawera erupted in 1886. The explosion, heard as far away as Auckland, killed 153 people and buried the village of Te Wairoa under a sea of mud and hot ash. The village has been excavated, and a path makes a circuit of this fascinating and deceptively tranquil spot, complete with grazing deer. Of special interest is the *whare* (*fah*-ray, hut) of the *tohunga* (priest) Tuhoto Ariki, who predicted the destruction of the village. Eleven days before the eruption, two separate tourist parties saw a Maori war canoe emerge from the mists of Lake Tarawera and disappear again—a vision the tohunga interpreted as a sign of impending disaster. Four days after the eruption, the 100-year-old tohunga was dug out of his buried whare still alive, only to die in the hospital a few days later. The path circles the village, dives down the hill alongside Te Wairoa Falls, then passes through a cave, crosses a bridge, and ascends the moist, fern-covered slope on the far side. The walk is a delight; its lower section is steep and can be slippery in places. ⊠ *Tarawera Rd.,* ☎ *07/362–8287.* ⌨ *$9.* ⊙ *Fall–spring, daily 9–4:30; summer, daily 8:30–5:30.*

❻ From the shores of Lake Tarawera, the **MV *Reremoana,*** a restored lake cruiser, makes regular scenic runs. The two-hour cruise is especially recommended; it departs at 11 AM and stops for 30 minutes at the foot of Mount Tarawera, where you can picnic, swim, or walk across the isthmus to Lake Rotomahana. Forty-five-minute cruises depart from the landing at one-hour intervals from 1:30 to 4:30. Four kilometers (2½ miles) beyond the village, on Spencer Road, a sign points to "Launch Cruises" and the *Reremoana*'s parking lot. ⊠ *Tarawera Launch Cruises,* ☎ *07/362–8595.* ⌨ *$15.*

★ At the northern end of town on the shores of the lake stands **St. Faith's,** the Anglican church for the Maori village of Ohinemutu. Before the present Tudor-style church was built in 1910, one of the ministers was Seymour Spencer Mills, of Hartford, Connecticut, who preached to the Arawa people for 50 years. He is commemorated in a small window above the organ chancel, preaching to a group of Maori as he holds his habitual umbrella. The interior of the church, which is richly decorated with carvings inset with mother-of-pearl, deserves attention at any time, but it's at its best during Sunday services, when the sonorous, melodic voices of the Maori choir rise in hymns. The service at 8 AM is in the Maori language; the 10 AM service is in both Maori and English. ⊠ *Memorial Dr., Rotorua.*

❼ Government Gardens. The Maori call this area *Whangapiro* (fang-ah-pee-ro), "evil-smelling place"—an appropriate name for these bizarre gardens, where sulphur pits bubble and fume behind manicured rose beds. The focus of interest here is the extraordinary neo-Tudor **Bath House.** Built as a spa at the turn of the century, it is now Rotorua's Art and History Museum. One room on the ground floor is devoted to the eruption of Mount Tarawera. A number of artifacts that were unearthed from the debris and a remarkable collection of photographs show the terraces of Rotomahana before the eruption. ⊠ *Arawa St.,* ☎ *07/349–8334.* ☞ *$4.* ◷ *Daily 9:30–5.*

❽ A trip to Rotorua would hardly be complete without a dip in the soothing, naturally heated **Polynesian Spa.** A wide choice of mineral baths is available, from large communal pools to family pools to small, private baths for two. Massage and saunas are also available. The newest addition to the pools is the Lake Spa, set out as four shallow rock pools overlooking Lake Rotorua. There are also two small separate indoor pools for naked bathing and a relaxation lounge with drinks and light snacks available. The pools are close to the Government Gardens. ⊠ *Hinemoa St.,* ☎ *07/348–1328.* ☞ *Family or adult pool $8, private pool $8.50 per ½ hr, lake spa $25.* ◷ *Daily 6:30 AM–11 PM.*

OFF THE BEATEN PATH

Heading north out of Rotorua on Fairy Springs Road, stop in at **Hillside Herbs,** an herb garden that holds demonstrations of various herbal uses: cooking, healing, and making potpourri, among them. Wander around the garden, follow a tour (every half hour), or browse through the shop. ⊠ *166 Fairy Springs Rd.,* ☎ *07/347-9535.* ◷ *Daily 8:30–5:30.*

❾ Leafy **Rainbow Springs** park is home to many species of New Zealand wildlife, including deer, kiwis and other native birds, wild pigs, and most of all, trout. The trout that congregate for feeding sessions at the Rainbow and Fairy springs are the King Kongs of the trout world. On the other side of State Highway 5, Rainbow Farm demonstrates New Zealand farming life. A sheep show Agrodome takes place daily at 10:30, 11:45, 1, and 2:30. ⊠ *Fairy Springs Rd., 5 km (3 mi) northwest of Rotorua,* ☎ *07/347–9301.* ☞ *Rainbow Springs $10, Rainbow Farm $9.50, Springs and Farm $14.50.* ◷ *Daily 8–5.*

❿ The **Agrodome** is a sprawling complex, part of a 320-acre farm, 10 minutes northwest of Rotorua. Most of it is dedicated to the four-footed woolly New Zealander. Shows daily at 9:30, 11, and 2:30 demonstrate the different breeds of sheep, shearing techniques, and sheepdogs at work. Tours lasting 45 minutes are an optional extra after the shows. Children can participate by feeding lambs and milking a cow. ⊠ *Riverdale Park, Western Rd., Ngongotaha,* ☎ *07/357–4350.* ☞ *$10, farm tour $9.* ◷ *Daily 9–4:30.*

⓫ Waiotapu (*why*-oh-*ta*-pu) is a complete thermal wonderland—a freakish, fantastic landscape of deep, sulfur-crusted pits, jade-colored ponds, silica terraces, and a steaming lake edged with red algae and bubbling with tiny beads of carbon dioxide. **Lady Knox Geyser** erupts precisely at 10:15 daily—but not through some miracle of Mother Nature. Five pounds of soap powder poured into the vent of the geyser causes the water to boil, and the vent is then blocked with rags until the pressure builds sufficiently for the geyser to explode. The phenomenon was discovered early this century. Wardens from a nearby prison farm would bring convicts to a pool here to wash their clothes. They found that when the water became soapy the pool would boil fiercely, and one of the wardens built a rock cairn to serve as a nozzle, concentrating the force of the boiling water and making the geyser rise even higher. To get there, leave Rotorua by Fenton Street, which becomes Highway 5, and follow the signs to Taupo. After 30 kilometers (19 miles), turn left where the sign points to Waiotapu. ⊠ *State Hwy. 5,* ☏ *07/366–6333.* ☒ *$9.50.* ☉ *Daily 8:30–5.*

Even if you think you have seen enough bubbling pools and fuming ⑫ craters to last a lifetime, the captivating thermal valley of **Orakei Korako** is likely to change your mind. Geyser-fed streams hiss and steam as they flow into the waters of the lake and you will find an impressive multicolored silica terrace, believed to be the largest in the world since the destruction of the terraces of Rotomahana. At the bottom of Aladdin's Cave, the vent of an ancient volcano, a jade-green pool was once used exclusively by Maori women as a beauty parlor, which is where the name Orakei Korako (a place of adorning) originated. You will find the valley by traveling along Highway 5 toward Taupo. At Kihi Bridge, just past Golden Springs, turn right where the sign points to Orakei Korako, which is reached by jetboat from the shores of Lake Ohakuri. ☏ *07/378–3131.* ☒ *$12.50.* ☉ *Spring–fall, daily 8:30–4:30; winter, daily 8:30–4.*

Dining and Lodging

$$$ **Maori Hangis.** Tamaki Tours' (☏ 07/346–2823) hangi takes place at a Maori *marae,* a meeting house, on the shores of Lake Rotoiti. Hangis at the **Sheraton** (☏ 07/348–7139) and the **Lake Plaza** (☏ 07/348–1174) enjoy long-standing reputations as two of the best in town.

$$$ ✕ **Poppy's Villa Restaurant.** This florid restaurant is Rotorua's big-occasion spot, yet prices are relatively moderate. First courses on the modern, European-style menu include mussels poached in a spicy tomato-and-Parmesan sauce, and sweetbreads in wine and tarragon sauce served with walnut brioche. Baby rack of rosemary-glaze lamb with honey and mustard served in a red-berry sauce is a long-standing favorite main course; or try scallops poached with Thai spices. ⊠ *4 Marguerita St., Rotorua,* ☏ *07/347–1700. AE, DC, MC, V. No lunch.*

$$$ ✕ **You and Me.** With its furry pink-and-black decor, the food at least pays lip service to modern trends with a fashionable Eastern accent. Smoked salmon marinated in lime juice is served with avocado, chicken breast is accompanied with cider and green peppercorn sauce, and cervena venison with zucchini flowers is stuffed with scallops and roasted garlic. This is the only restaurant in Rotorua that can be said to have achieved a notable culinary style. ⊠ *31 Pukuatua St., Rotorua,* ☏ *07/347–6178. AE, DC, MC, V. BYOB. Closed Sun. and Mon. No lunch.*

$$ ✕ **Incas Café.** This casual café caters to most tastes with steamed mussels, vegetable moussaka, spare ribs, beef bourguignon, and coconut lamb curry. You might think from its name that you'd get something south-of-the-border, but the menu doesn't lean in that direction. The restaurant's 1 AM closing time draws the night owls. ⊠ *Pukaki and Fenton Sts., Rotorua,* ☏ *07/348–3831. AE, DC, MC, V. No lunch.*

$$ ✕ **Zanelli's Italian Café.** Rotorua's favorite Italian restaurant offers a predictable range of dishes—spaghetti bolognese, lasagna, cannelloni, and fettuccine with various sauces. The food is well flavored, and the service is efficient. The decor—walls lined with split cane, a stone-tile floor, Formica tables—and up-tempo Italian music create a slightly hectic atmosphere. ⊠ *23 Amohia St., Rotorua,* ☏ *07/348–4908. DC, MC, V. Closed Sun. No lunch.*

$ ✕ **Orchid Gardens Café.** If you are staying close to the city and want an alternative to hotel breakfasts, this is just the place. The breakfast menu lists fruit juice, cereal, toast, eggs, and bacon. Later in the day the menu expands to include soup, quiche, shrimp cocktail, and steak. The café sits at the end of the Government Gardens, and diners are treated to a breakfast surrounded by palm trees and the sound of bird calls and trickling water. It opens at 8 on weekdays, 7 on weekends. ✉ *Government Gardens, Hinemaru St., Rotorua,* ☎ *07/347–6182. MC, V. No dinner.*

$$$$ 🏨 **Muriaroha Lodge.** Although it lacks trout streams and lake views, when it comes to style, facilities, food, and comfort, this handsome lodge on the outskirts of Rotorua evokes the finest traditions of the luxury sporting lodge—at a much lower rate. Guest rooms are paired in bungalows separate from the main building; to ensure privacy, adjoining rooms are not assigned when one of a pair is occupied. The rooms, gardens, lounge, and dining room all have an English country-house flavor. For the duration of your stay, you are extended complimentary membership at the Arikikapaka Golf Course just across the road. ✉ *411 Old Taupo Rd.,* ☎ *07/346–1220,* ℻ *07/346–1338. 8 rooms with bath. Restaurant, pool, bar. AE, DC, MC, V.*

$$$$ 🏨 **Solitaire Lodge.** It would be difficult to imagine a finer backdrop than the lakes, forests, and volcanoes that surround this plush retreat. Set high on a peninsula that juts out into Lake Tarawera, the lodge has been designed as a sophisticated hideaway where a few guests at a time can enjoy the scenery in a relaxed, informal atmosphere. All suites are luxuriously equipped, though the bathrooms in the junior suites are modest in size. The best room is the more expensive Tarawera Suite, which has panoramic views. The surrounding lakes and forests hold many possibilities for hiking, boating, and fishing, and the lodge has boats and fishing gear. Smoking is not permitted indoors. Rates include all meals. ✉ *Ronald Rd., Lake Tarawera,* ☎ *07/362–8208,* ℻ *07/362–8445. 10 rooms with bath. Restaurant, bar, spa, boating, fishing. AE, DC, MC, V.*

$$ 🏨 **Cedar Lodge Motel.** These spacious, modern two-story units, about a half-mile from the city center, are good value, especially for families. All have a kitchen and lounge room on the lower floor, a bedroom on the mezzanine floor above, at least one queen-size and one single bed, while some have a queen-size bed and three singles. Every unit has its own spa pool in the private courtyard at the back. Gray-flecked carpet, smoked-glass tables, and recessed lighting are clean and contemporary. Request a room at the back, away from Fenton Street. ✉ *296 Fenton St.,* ☎ *07/349–0300,* ℻ *07/349–1115. 15 rooms with shower. Coin laundry. AE, DC, MC, V.*

$$ 🏨 **Princes Gate Hotel.** Across the road from the Government Gardens, this ornate timber hotel was built in 1897 on the Coromandel Peninsula. It was brought here in 1917, and efforts have been made to recreate a turn-of-the-century feeling. Rooms are large and comfortable, without the dowdy look they once had. The motel rooms, in a separate wing, are suites with kitchens, a good choice for families. ✉ *1 Arawa St.,* ☎ *07/348–1179,* ℻ *07/348–6215. 28 hotel rooms, 12 motel units. 2 restaurants, bar, spa pool, mineral baths, tennis court. AE, DC, MC, V.*

$ 🏨 **Eaton Hall.** This well-kept, friendly guest house has an outstanding location one street from the heart of Rotorua. Guest rooms are homey and comfortable, maintained to a standard well above that in most guest houses. All rooms have a wash basin, and Room 4, a twin-bedded room with its own shower, is available at no extra charge. A two-course dinner with fresh garden produce is available upon request at an additional charge. Rates include breakfast. ✉ *39 Hinemaru St.,* ☎

07/347–0366, FAX 07/348–6287. 8 rooms share 2 baths. Hot tub. AE, DC, MC, V.

Outdoor Activities and Sports

FISHING

The lakes of the Rotorua and Taupo region are some of the few places where tales of "the big one" can be believed. If you want to keep the trout of a lifetime from becoming just another fish story, it pays to have a boat with some expert advice on board. Expect to pay about $65 per hour for a fishing guide and a 20-foot cruiser that will take up to six passengers. The minimum charter period is two hours, and fishing gear and bait are included in the price. A one-day fishing license costs $11 per person and is available on board the boat. In Rotorua, fishing operators include **Clark Gregor** (☎ 07/347–1730), **Bryan Colman** (☎ 07/348–7766), and **Ray Dodunski** (☎ 07/349–2555). Highly recommended is *Clear Water Pride* (☎ 07/362–8590), a luxury 38-foot launch that operates fishing trips on Lake Tarawera. The cost for up to seven passengers is $95 per hour, including all gear and light refreshments. For 8 to 15 passengers, the cost is $140 per hour and a hostess is provided. ☞ Chapter 6 for fishing information.

RAFTING

The center of North Island has a number of rivers with grade-3 to grade-5 rapids that make excellent white-water rafting. For scenic beauty, the Rangitaki River is recommended. For experienced rafters who want a challenge, the Wairoa River has exhilarating grade-5 rapids. The climax of a rafting trip on the Kaituna River is the drop over a 21-foot waterfall, probably the highest to be rafted by a commercial operator anywhere. With **Kaituna Cascades** (☎ 07/357–5032), transportation, wet suits, and meals are provided. The price of a one-day trip starts at $49 per person, depending on the river. Different rivers are open at different times of year, depending on water levels.

Taupo

⓭   *82 km (51 mi) south of Rotorua, 150 km (94 mi) northwest of Napier, 335 km (210 mi) west of Gisborne.*

The town of Taupo is the base for Lake Taupo, the largest lake in New Zealand. You can take your pick here from a wide range of water sports—sailing, cruising, waterskiing, swimming, but most of all, fishing: Taupo is the rainbow trout capital of the universe. The average Taupo trout weighs in around 4 pounds, and the lake is open year-round. For nonanglers, several sailboats, modern catamarans, and vintage riverboats have sightseeing trips. There are restaurants and lodging in Taupo, if you plan to stay in the area. Otherwise, from Taupo at the top of the lake the drive back to Rotorua takes about 90 minutes.

⓮   At **Huka Falls,** the Waikato River thunders through a narrow chasm and over a 35-foot rock ledge before it pours into Lake Taupo. The view from the footbridge is superb. Turn off to the left just after the Wairakai power station.

Craters of the Moon are just what you'd expect from a place with that name—except that the craters are filled with boiling, bubbling water. The area gets extremely steamy, and is worth the stop if you've missed or avoided the commercially run thermal parks in Rotorua. Entrance is free, and the craters are up Karapiti Road, across from the road from the Huka Falls turnoffs on Highway 5.

⓯   From the junction of routes 1 and 5, the **Wairakei Geothermal Project** is visible in the distance, wreathed in swirling clouds of steam. The steam, tapped through underground shafts, drives generators that provide about 5% of New Zealand's electrical power. There are no guided tours of the plant, but the Geothermal Information Centre close to the highway has a display on the process by which steam is converted into electricity. ⊠ *State Hwy. 1,* ☎ *07/374–8216.* ⊠ *Free.* ☉ *Daily 9–noon and 1–4.*

Dining and Lodging

$$$$ ✕⌂ **Huka Lodge.** Buried in parklike grounds at the edge of the frisky
★   Waikato River, this superb lodge is the standard by which New Zealand's other sporting lodges are judged. The large, lavish guest rooms, decorated in muted grays and whites, are arranged in blocks of two or three. All have sliding glass doors that open to a view across lawns to the river. In the interest of tranquillity, guest rooms are not equipped with telephones, televisions, or radios. The five-course formal dinners are gourmet affairs served at a communal dining table. The wine list is a showcase of the very best New Zealand has to offer—its stores are housed in a wine cellar with over 50,000 bottles of wine from New Zealand and around the world. Breakfasts are superb. Breakfast and dinner are included in the room rate. ⊠ *Huka Falls Rd., Box 95, Taupo,* ☎ *07/378–5791,* FAX *07/378–0427. 17 rooms with bath. Restaurant, bar, spa, tennis court, fishing. AE, DC, MC, V.*

$$$ ⌂ **Cascades Motor Lodge.** Set on the shores of Lake Taupo, these at-
★   tractive brick and timber rooms are large, comfortable, and furnished and decorated in a smart contemporary style. The two-story "luxury" apartments, which sleep up to seven, have a lounge room, bedroom, kitchen, and dining room on the ground floor in an open-plan design, glass doors leading to a large patio, and a second bedroom and bathroom on the upper floor. Studio rooms have only one bedroom. All rooms are equipped with a jet bath. Room 1 is closest to the lake and a small beach. ⊠ *Lake Terr.,* ☎ *07/378–3774,* FAX *07/378–0372. 22 rooms with bath. Pool. AE, DC, MC, V.*

Sports and the Outdoors

FISHING

For great fishing in the Taupo area, contact **Richard Staines** (☎ 07/378–2736) or **Punch Wilson** (☎ 07/378–5596). At the other end of the scale, a luxury cruiser on Lake Taupo costs about $150 per hour; for more information, contact **Chris Jolly Boats** (⊠ Box 1020, Taupo, ☎ 07/378–0623). ☞ Chapter 6 for fishing information.

RAFTING

The grade-5 Wairoa and Mohaka rivers are accessible from Taupo, as are the Rangitaiki and Tongariro. With **Rapid Descents** (☎ 07/377–0419), transportation, wet suits, and meals are provided. The price of a one-day trip is about $75 per person. Different rivers are open at different times of year, depending on water levels.

Tongariro National Park

16 *110 km (69 mi) southwest of Taupo.*

Tongariro is the country's first national park, established on sacred land donated by a Maori chief. Southwest of Lake Taupo, the park is dominated by the peaks of three active volcanoes: Tongariro, Ngauruhoe, and Mount Ruapehu, at 9,175 feet the highest North Island mountain. Ruapehu last erupted in 1996, spewing forth ash and a shower of volcanic rocks. Tongariro's spectacular combination of dense rimu pine forests, crater lakes, barren lava fields, and bird life makes it the most impressive and popular of the island's national parks. It has numerous walking trails, from the 40-minute Ridge Track to the Mount Tongariro Traverse, which crosses the mountain from one side to the other and is one of the finest walks in the country. The longest track in the park is the six-day Round the Mountain track. Wherever you hike, be prepared for rapidly changing weather conditions with warm and waterproof clothing. The Whakapapa ski area, on the north side of Mount Ruapehu, is New Zealand's largest, with about 2,400 feet of vertical drop. On the southern side of the mountain is a second ski area, Turoa, which generally offers a longer ski season than Whakapapa's, from June through October.

Highway 1 skirts the eastern side of the park, but the easiest access is from Highway 47, on the north side. For more information, contact the Department of Conservation Field Centre at Whakapapa Village off Highway 47 (⊠ Whakapapa Visitor Centre, Private Bag, Mount Ruapehu, ☎ 07/892–3729). Accommodations in the village range from the less-appealing-than-it-could-be **THC Tongariro Hotel** (⊠ Mount Ruapehu, ☎ 07/892–3809), in the $$$$ category, to cabins and campsites in motor camps. The park has nine huts for hikers. (At press time, word was out that the hotel was in for an overhaul, so by November 1997 it may be worth looking into.)

Just east of Tongariro National Park, **Kaimanawa Forest Park** is a less visited wilderness. Trails aren't as frequently marked here, so be sure to pick up a Department of Conservation map at the Taupo Information Center (⊠ Tongariro St.). The park has single-day hikes as well as two- to five-day tramps between overnight huts. However far you go, be prepared for rapidly changing weather conditions by taking waterproof and warm clothing at all times of the year. And be aware that the Kaimanawa Ranges are particularly popular with hunters of sika deer in late March and April. At other times, check hunting activities in the area with the Department of Conservation before setting out.

OFF THE
BEATEN PATH
★

Gordon Collier is one of New Zealand's most visible garden diplomats. Having lectured extensively domestically and overseas, he has helped to develop a true New Zealand garden style. His **Titoki Point Garden and Nursery**—carved out of the rolling 5,000-acre Wakarua Sheep Station between Lake Taupo and Wellington—is a highly successful marriage of native New Zealand flora with plants collected from around the world. One highlight is what Collier and his wife Annette refer to as the damp garden, located at the bottom of a gully. One of the best of its kind in the country, it is home to giant gunnera, hosta, bergenia, trillium, native ferns, and primula. Titoki Point also has a towering stand of 70-year-old California redwoods and a lovely avenue of weeping Japanese maples. All of this looks out on the fiesty, nearby Mt. Ruapehu volcano. ⊠ R.D. 1, Bells Junction, 95 km (59 mi) south of bottom of Lake Taupo, 85 km (53 mi) north of State Hwy. 3 in Bulls, ☎ 06/388–0085. ☉ Oct.–May, Wed.–Sun. 10–4.

Rotorua, Waitomo Caves, Lake Taupo A to Z

Arriving and Departing

BY BUS

InterCity (☎ 09/358–4085) has four bus services daily between Auckland and Rotorua. InterCity also operates a daily service between Auckland and Waitomo Caves and between Waitomo Caves and Rotorua. **Newmans** (☎ 09/309–9738) operates twice daily on the Auckland–Rotorua route.

BY CAR

To get to Waitomo Caves from Auckland, take Highway 1 south, following signs to Hamilton, where you will turn south onto Highway 3. For Rotorua, follow Highway 1 south past Hamilton and Cambridge to Tirau, where Highway 5 breaks off to Rotorua. Driving time to both Waitomo and Rotorua is about three hours.

BY PLANE

Air New Zealand (☎ 07/346–1001) and **Ansett New Zealand** (☎ 07/347–0146) have daily flights that link Rotorua with Auckland and Wellington, with further connections throughout New Zealand. Rotorua Airport stands about 10 kilometers (6 miles) from the city center. Taxi fare to the city is $18.

Contacts and Resources

EMERGENCIES

Dial 111 for **fire, police,** and **ambulance** services.

GUIDED TOURS

Gray Line (☎ 09/377–0904) offers two-day tours of the Waitomo Caves and Rotorua from Auckland. Including accommodations, dinner, and breakfast, the tour costs $508 for adults.

Mount Tarawera 4WD Tours offers a sensational half-day, four-wheel-drive trip to the edge of the Mount Tarawera crater. Departures are available at 8:30 AM and 1:30 PM. ⊠ *Box 5157, Rotorua,* ☎ *07/357–4026.* ☜ *$60.*

Tamaki Tours' Volcanic Wilderness Safari is a two-day trip that combines horse trekking in the Rainbow Mountain–Mount Tarawera area, rafting on the Rangitaki River, and an introduction to traditional Maori legends and lifestyle. The tour is only available from November to February. The company is a Maori-owned-and -operated venture. ⊠ *Box 1492, Rotorua,* ☎ *07/346–2823.* ☜ *$320.*

Tarawera Helicopters (☎ 07/348–1223) offers a choice of scenic flights, from a short flight over the city and Whakarewarewa Thermal Reserve ($50 per person) to a longer flight over crater lakes and the Waimangu Valley, with a landing on top of Mount Tarawera ($325 per person).

Tour Magic (☎ 07/345–6080) has a choice of half- and full-day minibus tours of Rotorua's prime attractions, with pickup and drop-off at your accommodations. These tours are recommended for their personal, attentive style. Half-day tours cost $42–$58 per person.

The **Waimangu Round Trip** is probably the most complete tour of Rotorua. It includes an easy 5-kilometer (3-mile) hike through the Waimangu Thermal Valley to Lake Rotomahana, where a cruiser takes visitors past steaming cliffs to the narrow isthmus that divides the lake from Lake Tarawera. After crossing the lake on a second cruiser, the tour visits a village that was buried by a volcanic eruption and ends with a dip in the Polynesian Pools in Rotorua. Lunch is included. ⊠ *Reserve at Rotorua Visitor Information Centre, or* ☎ *07/347–1199.* ☜ *$130.*

The **MV Wairaka** (☎ 07/374–8338) is a vintage riverboat that cruises from Taupo to Huka Falls daily at 10 and 2. The two-hour cruise costs $18 for adults, $8 for children under 12. A barbecue cruise departs at 12:30 and costs $35 for adults.

VISITOR INFORMATION

Taupo Visitor Information Centre. ⊠ *13 Tongariro St., Taupo,* ☎ *07/378–9000.* ☉ *Daily 8:30–5.*

Tourism Rotorua Visitor Information Centre. In addition to an information office, this modern complex houses a café, a film-processing service, a map shop operated by the Department of Conservation, and a lost-luggage facility. ⊠ *67 Fenton St., Rotorua,* ☎ *07/348–5179.* ⊙ *Daily 8–5:30.*

Waitomo Caves Visitor Information Centre. ⊠ *Waitomo Museum of Caves,* ☎ *07/878–7640.* ⊙ *Daily 9–5:30.*

NAPIER AND HAWKE'S BAY

New Zealand prides itself on natural wonders. By that way of thinking, Napier is an exception. This city of 50,000, situated about two-thirds of the way down the east coast of North Island, is best known for its architecture. After an earthquake devastated Napier in 1931, citizens rebuilt it in the fashionable Art Deco style of the day. Its well-kept uniformity of style makes it a pleasant and comfortable sort of period piece. The mild climate and beaches of Hawke Bay make this a popular vacation area for New Zealanders. (*Hawke* Bay is the body of water; *Hawke's* Bay is the region.) Another attraction is wine. The region produces some of New Zealand's best.

Napier

150 km (94 mi) southeast of Taupo, 345 km (215 mi) northeast of Wellington.

The focus of any visit to Napier is its buildings—many of which lie between Emerson, Herchell, Dalton, and Browning streets—and the city is a pleasure to tour on foot. Art Deco was born at the 1925 International Exposition of Modern Decorative and Industrial Arts in Paris. Its influences around the Western world are broad: from skyscrapers and diners to toasters and jewelry. The style is bold and geometrical, often using stainless steel to represent the sleekness of the machine age as it was seen in the 20s, 30s, and beyond. In some cases, Napier's Art Deco heritage has been spoiled by the addition of garish advertising or unsympathetic alterations to shopfronts. The elements that remain are often found above the ground floor, so any walk will involve looking up frequently. After stretching your legs in the morning, relax on a brief wine-tasting tour for the rest of the day. Another point of interest in Hawke's Bay is the gannet colony at Cape Kidnapper—which you can see only between October and March.

⓱ One of Napier's notable buildings is the **ASB Bank,** at the corner of Hastings and Emerson Streets. The Maori theme on the lintels above the main entrance is echoed in the ceiling inside the building.

⓲ The **Criterion Hotel** (⊠ Hastings St.) is typical of the Spanish Mission style, which Napier took on due to its success in Santa Barbara, California, where an earthquake had similarly wreaked havoc just a few
⓳ years before New Zealand's catastrophe. Along **Emerson Street** and its pedestrian mall, **Hannahs,** the **Bowman's Building, McGruers,** and the **Hawke's Bay Chambers** are among the city's finest Art Deco examples.

⓴ **Dalton Street** has its treasures as well. South of the intersection with Emerson Street, the pink **Countrywide Bank Building,** with its balcony, is one of Napier's masterpieces. **Hildebrand's,** at Tennyson Street, has an excellent frieze, which is best viewed from across Dalton. Hildebrand was a German who migrated to New Zealand—hence the German flag at one end, the New Zealand at the other, and the wavy lines in the middle to symbolize the sea passage between the two countries.

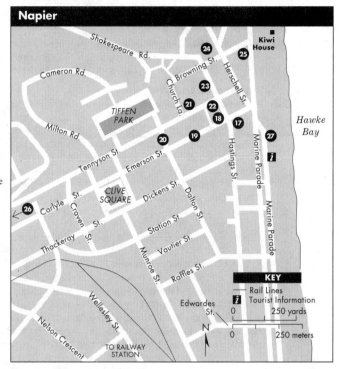

Napier

㉑ The **Daily Telegraph Building** (⊠ Tennyson St. and Church La.) is another Napier classic. If you can turn back the clock in your mind and imagine the city littered with heaps of rubble, you would see the **Market Reserve Building** (⊠ Tennyson and Hastings Sts.) being the first to rise following the earthquake. You would have seen Hartson's Music Shop survive the quake had you lived through it, and you may have lived to see it turn into **Hartson's Bar** (⊠ Hastings St. between Browning and Tennyson Sts.), the facade of which has changed little since its change in ownership replaced songs with suds.

NEED A BREAK? The **Black Market Cafe** is a café-bar with a selection of light meals, salad, rolls, and sandwiches at reasonable prices. ⊠ *53 Hastings St.,* ☎ *06/835-1341.* ⊙ *Daily 11–11.*

㉔ The **Ministry of Works** (⊠ Browning St.), with its decorative lighthouse pillar at the front, takes on the almost Gothic menace that Art Deco architecture (like New York's Chrysler Building) sometimes possesses.

㉕ Using newspaper reports, photographs, and audiovisuals, the **Hawke's Bay Museum** re-creates the suffering caused by the earthquake. It also houses a unique display of artifacts of the Ngati Kahungunu Maori people of the east coast. ⊠ *65 Marine Parade,* ☎ *06/835–9668.* 🎫 *$3.* ⊙ *Daily 10–4:30.*

㉖ Stop in for a natural counterpoint to the city's architecture at the **Botanical Gardens,** about 1½ kilometers, a little over a mile, from Clive Square. Here you can stroll across lawns, among flower beds, over ornamental bridges, and under shady arbors in this delightful haven. Follow Carlyle Street southwest to Chaucer Road. Turn right and continue to Napier Terrace, where the entrance to the gardens is to the left. You may want to visit the adjacent graveyard, where some headstones date to the 19th century. One of them, just inside the gate, belongs to Major-General Sir

George Stoddart Whitmore, who led several campaigns during the Maori wars of the 1860s and '70s. ⊠ *Napier Terrace.* ⊞ *Free.* ⊙ *Daily.*

☺ ㉗ **Napier Aquarium** displays sharks, rays, tropical fish, saltwater crocodiles, turtles, and piranha in a drum-shaped building on the waterfront. ⊠ *Marine Parade, Napier,* ☎ *06/835–7579.* ⊞ *$6.50.* ⊙ *Daily 9–5.*

Dining and Lodging

$$$ ✕ **Bayswater on the Beach.** This bayside restaurant has a long-stand-
★ ing reputation as Napier's finest. Fillet of salmon with scallop mousse, boned quails stuffed with a puree of zucchini and sweet peppers, and pepper-crusted rack of cervena venison are listed on a summer dinner menu that scores high marks for originality. The voguish, white interior has a faintly Art Deco feeling and big doors that open to a sparkling sea view. A moderately priced wine list offers some of the best that Hawke's Bay produces. In warm weather, request a table on the deck outside; otherwise, a table at the window. The restaurant can be hard to spot at night—take Marine Parade out of the city center and it's about a kilometer north of the port just after the playground. ⊠ *Harding Rd., Napier,* ☎ *06/835–8517. AE, DC, MC, V.*

$$$ ✕ **Bucks Great Wall Restaurant.** Housed in a landmark building on Napier's Marine Parade, this opulent and sophisticated restaurant is a real treat for anyone who enjoys Cantonese cooking. The menu lists almost 100 dishes, from Peking duck to crayfish to sautéed prawns with crispy rice, and although it rarely ventures into unfamiliar territory, the food is delicious and beautifully presented. The earthen-pot dishes are particularly good. In addition to the à la carte menu, there are three fixed-price selections, from $30 to $40 per person. The gregarious owner imports her chefs and even installed a laundry on the premises when the local service sent back tablecloths that were not quite whiter than white. ⊠ *Marine Parade and Emerson St., Napier,* ☎ *06/835–0088. AE, DC, MC, V. No lunch weekends.*

$$ ✕ **Pierre sur le quai.** This spare, smart, modern bistro is the backdrop
★ for Pierre Vuilleumier's robust French provincial cooking. Braised lamb shanks with tomato and white wine sauce, baked eel in red wine with rice, and seafood casserole with spring vegetables in champagne sauce are examples from a menu that allows flavor to speak for itself—at outstanding value. A number of simple, light, inexpensive dishes are available at lunch. Combined, the ambience, service, price, and uncluttered cooking should serve as an example to the rest of New Zealand. This waterfront restaurant may take some finding, but make the effort. ⊠ *62 West Quay, Ahuriri,* ☎ *06/834–0189. MC.*

$$ ✕▦ **Mon Logis Hôtel Privé.** The French owner of this seafront house
★ has modeled his accommodations on the *logis* of his homeland—a refined version of traditional bed-and-breakfast accommodations. Rooms are large and prettily decorated in a Continental style with eiderdowns and feather pillows. Although they lack the sea view, the two rooms at the back of the house are quieter: Buttes Chaumont has an en-suite bathroom, while Paris's bathroom is off the hall. But what most sets this place apart from the standard B&B is the food. In the morning guests have complimentary coffee and a basket of freshly baked French breads delivered to their rooms. A four-course dinner at $45 per person, including wine, is available by arrangement. Children are not accommodated. Rates include breakfast. ⊠ *415 Marine Parade, Napier,* ☎ *06/835–2125,* ℻ *06/435–4196. 4 rooms with bath. AE, DC, MC, V.*

$$ ▦ **Anleigh Heights.** Built in 1900 as a town house for a wealthy sheep rancher, this sprawling hilltop guest house is one of Napier's landmark buildings and a fine example of the city's Victorian timber architec-

ture. While the patrician character of the house has not been fully trans-
lated to the interior, the owners are charming and attentive hosts. The
Colenso Suite is recommended. Smoking is not allowed in the house.
Rates include breakfast. ⌧ *115 Chaucer Rd., North Napier,* ☎ 𝖥𝖠𝖷
06/835–1188. 8 rooms, 5 with bath, 3 with shower. MC, V.

$$ 🏠 **Edgewater Motor Lodge.** These motel rooms are about average in
size, facilities, and character, but they offer a central location and sea
views. Rooms on the upper level have balconies, and there are several
room styles to suit couples or families. ⌧ *359 Marine Parade, Napier,*
☎ *06/835–1140,* 𝖥𝖠𝖷 *06/835–6600. 20 rooms with bath. Pool, hot tub,
coin laundry. AE, DC, MC, V.*

Hawke's Bay

Like most parts of New Zealand, the natural world is a part of Hawke's
Bay to appreciate alongside the human factor. The gannet colony on
the coast southeast of the city is a beautiful and fascinating spot. In
the realm of viticulture, Napier's surrounding countryside brings up
highly esteemed grapes, reds being of particular note.

㉘ Esk Valley Estate Winery is terraced on a north-facing hillside, ensur-
ing it full sun and a cherished location for grape growing. Esk Valley
produces Chardonnay, Sauvignon Blanc, Chenin Blanc, Merlot, and a
Cabernet Sauvignon–Merlot–Cabernet Franc blend. Look for reserve
vintages if you want to find out what the winemaker has done with
the best grapes from given years. The winery is 12 kilometers (8 miles)
north of Napier, just north of the town of Bay View before highways
2 and 5 split. ⌧ *Main Rd., Bay View, Napier,* ☎ *06/836–6411.* ☉
Nov.–Mar., daily 9–6; Apr.–Oct., daily 9:45–5; tour by appointment.

㉙ The **Mission Vineyard** at Taradale is the oldest in New Zealand, es-
tablished by Catholic Marist brothers in the late 1850s after an ear-
lier vineyard farther north at Poverty Bay was abandoned. Legend has
it that in 1852 one of the brothers made a barrel of sacramental wine
and shipped it to Napier; the seamen broached the cargo, drank the
wine, and filled the empty cask with seawater. Jewelstone Chardon-
nay is the flagship of the winery, while a range of varietals includes
sauvignon blanc, reisling, and cabernet blends. To reach the vineyard,
leave Napier by Kennedy Road, heading southwest from the city cen-
ter toward Taradale. Just past Anderson Park, turn right into Avenue
Road and continue to its end at Church Road. ⌧ *Church Rd., Taradale,*
☎ *06/844–2259.* ☉ *Mon.–Sat. 8–5, Sun. 1–4.*

㉚ The long-established **McDonald Winery** benefited from an injection of
capital and expertise when the Montana wine-making group bought
it in 1989 in an effort to add a top chardonnay and cabernet sauvi-
gnon to its holdings. And the Church Road Chardonnay and Caber-
net Sauvignon have turned out to excite oenophiles. The winery
operates free tours on weekdays at 11 and 2, weekends at 11, 1, 2,
and 3. ⌧ *200 Church Rd., Taradale,* ☎ *06/844–2053.* ☉ *Summer
(Dec.–Apr.) Mon.–Thurs. 9–5, Fri. and Sat. 10–6, Sun. 11–5; winter
(Mar.–Nov.) Mon.–Sat. 9–5, Sun. 11–4.*

㉛ Brookfields Winery is one of the most attractive wineries in the area,
befitting its status as a premier producer. The Reserve Chardonnay and
Pinot Gris are usually outstanding, but the showpiece is the Cabernet
Merlot, characterized by intense fruit and assertive oak. From Napier,
take Marine Parade toward Hastings and turn right on Awatoto Road.
Follow it to Brookfields Road and turn left; signs will point to the win-
ery. ⌧ *Brookfields Rd., Meeanee,* ☎ *06/834–4615.* ☉ *Daily 11–4.*

㉜ Te Mata Estate is quite simply one of New Zealand's finest wineries, its interesting architectural forms rising out of ground first planted with grapes in the 1890s. Te Mata's Coleraine Cabernet Merlot subtly balances dark fruit and oak flavors, and it will age well into the 2,000s. Other reds show similar restraint and balance, and Chardonnay and Sauvignon Blanc are thoroughly respectable as well. From Napier, head south on Marine Parade through Clive, and turn left at the Mingatere Tree School. Signs from there will lead you to Te Mata Road and the estate. ✉ *Te Mata Rd., Box 8355, Havelock North,* ☎ *06/877–4399.* ⊙ *Weekdays 9:30–5, Sat. 10–5, Sun. 11–4; tour Christmas holidays–Jan., daily at 10:30 or by appointment.*

★ **㉝ Cape Kidnappers** was named by Captain James Cook after local Maoris tried to kidnap the servant of Cook's Tahitian interpreter. The cape is the site of a large **gannet colony.** The gannet is a large white sea bird with black-tipped flight feathers, a golden crown, and wings that can reach a span of up to 6 feet. When the birds find a shoal of fish, they fold their wings and plunge straight into the sea at tremendous speed. Their migratory pattern ranges from western Australia to the Chatham Islands, about 800 kilometers (500 miles) east of Christchurch, but they generally nest only on remote islands. The colony at Cape Kidnappers is believed to be the only mainland gannet sanctuary in existence. Between October and March, about 15,000 gannets build their nests here, hatch their young, and prepare them for their long migratory flight.

You can walk to the sanctuary along the beach from Clifton, which is about 24 kilometers (15 miles) south of Napier, but not at high tide. The 8-kilometer (5-mile) walk must begin no earlier than three hours after the high tide mark, and the return journey must begin no later than four hours before the next high tide. Tidal information is available at Clifton. A rest hut with refreshments is available near the colony.

Because of these tidal restrictions, one easy way to get to the colony is to take a **Gannet Beach Adventures** (☎ 06/875–0898) tractor-trailer, which is pulled along the beach starting from Charlton Road in Te Awanga, 21 kilometers (13 miles) south of Napier. Tractors depart two hours before low tide, and the trip ($18) takes 4–4½ hours. If tides prevent the trip along the beach, the only other access is across private farmland. **Gannet Safaris** (☎ 06/875–0511) runs a four-wheel-drive bus to Cape Kidnappers from Summerlee Station, just past Te Awanga. A minimum of four is required for this tour ($38).

㉞ Hastings is Napier's twin city in Hawke's Bay, and it is well worth a visit if you have an extra day in the area. Some of Hawke's Bay's wineries are actually easier to reach if you are based in Hastings, particularly **Vidals Estate Winery** (✉ 913 St. Aubyn St. E, Hastings, ☎ 06/876–8105), a sister winery of Esk Valley Estate that consistently produces some of New Zealand's finest reds, and **Huthlee Estate Winery** (✉ 84 Montana Rd., Bridge Pa, ☎ FAX 06/879–6234).

If you are traveling with children, spend a couple of hours at **Fantasyland** (☎ 06/876–9856). Disney World it is not, but you'll please the kids with miniature golf, go-cart riding, and a variety of play equipment. The 30-acre park is a fine place for a picnic lunch.

Dining

$$ ✕ **Brookfields Winery Restaurant.** A simple, satisfying menu and an outdoor setting amid the vines make this boutique winery a good choice for sunny-weather lunches. Salads, sandwiches on rye and sourdough bread, pasta, and homemade cakes are particularly tasty alongside a glass of Brookfield's wine. ✉ *Brookfields Rd., Meeanee,* ☎ *06/*

834–4615. *AE, DC, MC, V. No dinner; no lunch Mon.–Thurs. Feb.–Dec.*

Napier and Hawke's Bay A to Z

Arriving and Departing

BY BUS

Newmans (☎ 09/309–9738) and **InterCity** (☎ 09/358–4085) both operate daily bus services between Napier and Auckland, Rotorua, and Wellington. Once in Napier you can book on either operation at the visitor information center.

BY CAR

The main route between Napier and the north is Highway 5. Driving time from Taupo is 2½ hours. Highway 2 is the main route heading south. Driving time to Wellington is five hours.

BY PLANE

Air New Zealand (☎ 06/835–3288) has several flights daily between Napier and Auckland, Wellington, and Christchurch.

BY TRAIN

Bay Express leaves Napier at 2:20 daily for Wellington, arriving in the capital at 7:45. It leaves Wellington for Napier at 8 AM, arriving Napier at 1:20. If you are traveling to South Island, you will probably have to overnight in Wellington before joining the Cook Strait ferry. Bookings can be made for both the train and the ferry at Napier's visitor information center (✉ Marine Parade, ☎ 06/834–4161).

Contacts and Resources

EMERGENCIES

Dial 111 for **fire, police,** and **ambulance** services.

GUIDED TOURS

The Art Deco Trust has an excellent and informative guided walking tour of Napier. The 2-kilometer (1-mile) walk takes 2½ hours and includes slide and video presentations. You can take a self-guided walk any time with the Trust's "Art Deco Walk" guide, available at its shop. ✉ *Art Deco Shop, 163 Tennyson St.* ☞ *$7.* ⊙ *Tour late Dec.–Feb., Wed. and weekends at 2.*

Bay Tours features a four-hour tour of wineries in the area. It offers a chance to sample some of the boutique wines unavailable to independent travelers. ✉ *Napier Visitor Information Centre, Marine Parade,* ☎ *06/843–6953.* ☞ *$25.* ⊙ *Tour daily at 1.*

VISITOR INFORMATION

Napier Visitor Information Centre. ✉ *Marine Parade, Napier,* ☎ *06/834–4161,* 𝔽𝔸𝕏 *06/835–7219.* ⊙ *Weekdays 8:30–5, weekends 9–5.*

GISBORNE AND EASTLAND

Traveling to Eastland takes you well away from the tourist track in North Island. For some people, that is reason enough to make the trip. Once there, you will find rugged coastline, dense forests, and small, predominantly Maori communities. Eastland has a well-established wine industry, accessible beaches, and gentle nature trails. And it provides one of the closest links with the nation's earliest past. Kaiti Beach, near the city of Gisborne, is where the waka (long canoe) Horouta landed, and nearby Titirangi was named by the first Maori settlers in remembrance of their mountain in Hawaiki, their Polynesian island of origin. Kaiti Beach is where Captain Cook set foot in 1769—the first European landing in New Zealand.

Gisborne's warm climate and fertile soil make the region one of New Zealand's most successful wine areas. Often overshadowed by Hawke's Bay (mostly by way of the public relations machine), Gisborne has 7,000 acres under vine, and it is the country's largest supplier of chardonnay grapes. It has in fact been dubbed chardonnay capital of New Zealand, which makes that the variety to concentrate on if you go tasting. If you like sweeter wine, look for local muller thurgau. The red varieties are generally not as well regarded, but there is increasing interest in pinot noir and merlot. Winemaking here dates back to 1921, when Federick Wohnseidler planted the first grapes in Gisborne. His original winery is now owned by the sizeable Montana company, which also makes wine in Hawke's Bay and initiated the Marlborough boom on South Island.

Gisborne

③⑤ *210 km (130 mi) northeast of Napier, 500 km (310 mi) southeast of Auckland.*

Gisborne is the easternmost city in New Zealand, and it is the first in the world to see the new day's sunrise. The Maori name for the Gisborne district is Tairawhiti (tie-ra-fee-tee)—the coast upon which the sun shines across the water. Although the city (population 30,000) is hardly large, you will need a day or so to get around town properly. Most of the historical sights and other attractions are too spread out to explore them all by foot, and you'll need a car to get into the spectacular countryside nearby.

The **Museum and Arts Centre,** with its Maori and Pakeha artifacts and an extensive photographic collection, provides a good introduction to the region's Maori and colonial history. It also has changing exhibits of local and national artists' work. ⊠ *18 Stout St.,* ☎ *06/867–3832.* ⊙ *Weekdays 10–4, weekends 1:30–4.*

Cook Landing Site National Historic Reserve has deep historical significance for New Zealanders, but not so much to keep an international visitor amused. At Kaiti Beach, across the river southeast of the city center, it is marked by a statue of Captain James Cook, who first set foot on New Zealand soil here on October 9, 1769. The beach itself, at low tide, attracts interteresting bird life. ⊠ *Esplanade on south end of Turanganui River.*

The **Titirangi Domain** on Kaiti Hill has excellent views of Gisborne, Poverty Bay, and the surrounding rural areas. Titirangi was the site of an extensive pa (fortified village), the origins of which can be traced back at least 24 Maori generations. The **Titirangi Recreational Reserve,** part of the domain, is a pleasant place for a picnic or a relaxed walk among native trees. The domain is south of Turanganui River. Pass the harbor and turn right into Esplanade, then turn left into Crawford Road, right into Queens Drive and follow it to several lookout points in the Domain.

Te Poho o Rawiri Meeting House is one of the largest Maori marae in New Zealand, and the interior has excellent carving in traditional Maori patterns. On the side of the hill stands the Toko Toro Tapu Church. Request permission to explore both of these sites from the ☞ **Visitor Information Centre** in town. ⊠ *Kaiti Hill,* ☎ *06/867–2835.*

Matawhero Wines is among the most highly regarded in the region. Chardonnay is a high pint, but you can also taste gewurztraminer, chenin blanc, carbernet–merlot, and pinot noir. The vineyard is southwest of Gisborne; follow State Highway 35 out of town. ⊠ *Riverpoint Rd.,*

Gisborne, ☎ 06/868–8366, ℻ 06/867–9856. ☾ *Spring–fall, weekdays 11–4, weekends 11–5; winter, weekdays 11–4.*

Milton Vineyard has an attractive garden area, making it a logical place to sit with a picnic lunch and sip some barrel-fermented chardonnay. The Te Arai River Sauvignon Blanc is also recommended. Milton grows its grapes organically. The vineyard is a little farther out of town than Matawhero Wines off of Highway 35. ⊠ *Papatu Rd., Gisborne,* ☎ 06/862–8680, ℻ 06/862–8869. ☾ *Summer, daily 10–5; winter, by appointment.*

<table>
<tr><td>OFF THE
BEATEN PATH</td><td>

Eastwoodhill Arboretum found its inspiration not in the native trees of New Zealand but in English gardens. After a trip to England, William Douglas Cook returned to New Zealand in 1910 and began planting 160 acres. Only first-rate material was collected for the plantings, and the result today is a stunning collection of over 500 genera of trees from around the world. Eastwoodhill is a place of seasonal change seldom seen in New Zealand. In spring and summer daffodils mass yellow, magnolia bloom in clouds of pink and white, and cherries, crab apples, wisteria, and azalea all add to the spectacle. In autumn and winter leaves of yellow, rust, and scarlet cover the ground. As in other New Zealand gardens, the rapid growth of non-native trees make them outstanding features, well worth a few hours' enjoyment. The main tracks in the park can be walked in about 45 minutes. Maps and self-guided tour booklets are available. Eastwoodhill can be reached by driving west from Gisborne center on Highway 2 toward Napier, and turning at the rotary into the Ngatapa-Rere Road before leaving town. Follow it 35 kilometers (22 miles) to the arboretum. ⊠ *Ngatapa-Rere Rd.,* ☎ 06/863-9800, ℻ 06/863-9081. ☾ *Daily 10-4.*

</td></tr>
</table>

Dining and Lodging

$$$$ ✕ **Pinehurst Manor.** A century-old house and parklike surroundings add to the atmosphere of this local favorite, but it is entrées like prawns, avocado, and brie in phyllo, baked and then served on a chilli plum sauce, or scallops and prawns grilled and served in a homemade pastry case with a basil and white wine hollandaise that really impress. Main dishes include Oriental Snapper, a whole fish steamed with soy sauce, fresh ginger, and spring onions, served on a bed of rice, and char-grilled venison placed on kumara (sweet potato) purée and topped with cranberry and port sauce. ⊠ *4 Clifford St., Gisborne,* ☎ *06/868–6771. AE, DC, MC, V.*

$$$ ✕ **Marina Restaurant.** Occupying the ballroom of a turn-of-the-century house built for the 21st birthday of the original owner's daughter, the Marina concentrates on preparing seasonal menus using local produce, which is paired with the wine of the region. Dishes like deep-fried squid stuffed with spicy moonfish or scallops and fish dumplings in coconut broth lead well into game pie with local white truffle or grilled duck breast with a fruit vinegar glaze. The Marina has excellent views as well, being at the junction of three rivers. On a summer evening, enjoy dinner on the terrace overlooking the rivers. ⊠ *Marina Park, Vogel St., Gisborne,* ☎ *06/868–5919,* ℻ *06/868–5613. AE, DC, MC, V.*

$$ 🏨 **Gisborne Hotel.** The price and quality of the rooms here are very much on the Gisborne local standard, and it just crosses the motel-hotel line because it has a bar and restaurant. Rooms are slightly larger than usual, the furniture and beds are comfortable, and service is friendly. ⊠ *Tyndall and Huxley Rds., Gisborne,* ☎ *06/868–4109,* ℻ *06/867– 8344. 28 rooms with shower. Restaurant, bar, pool. AE, DC, MC, V.*

$$ ☒ **Tudor Park Motel.** The distinctive Tudor exterior is mostly a cover for standard but comfortable motel rooms, which is the prevalent type of accommodation around Gisborne. There are cooking facilities in the rooms, which allows you to keep costs down a little, and four larger units for families. The biggest plus may be its proximity to the beach. ☒ *365 Ormond Rd., Gisborne,* ☎ *06/867–9830,* ☒ *06/867–9074. 8 rooms with shower. MC, V.*

Outdoor Activities and Sports

FISHING

Target albacore, yellowfin tuna, mako sharks, and marlin are all prized catches off the East Cape from January to April. Fishing operators include Tolaga **Bay East Cape Charters** (☎ 06/862–6715) whose skipper Bert Lee has had more than 35 years experience in recreational fishing, and **Coastline Charters** (☎ 06/863–9801).

JET BOATING

Motu River Jet Boat Tours combines the thrills and spills of speeding along the river with the opportunity to learn about the ecology and history of the region. The trip lasts about two hours and costs $60 adults, $30 children. (☎ 07/315–8107).

MOUNTAIN BIKING

Mountain Bike Adventures (☎ 07/315–5577) has an escorted day tour on the Old Motu Coach Road, including two hours of downhill riding through the MereMere Scenic Reserve and Urutawa State Forest. The $70 price tag includes bikes and lunch, and a support vehicle follows riders. The company also has "single track" tours on narrow, winding trails through dense bush.

Gisborne–Opotiki Loop

The beauty and remoteness of Eastland is nowhere more evident than on the loop between Opotiki at the northern entrance to the East Cape and Gisborne. Rolling green hills drop into wide crescent beaches or rock-strewn coves. Small towns appear here and there along the route, only to fade into the surrounding landscape. It is one of the country's ultimate roads less-traveled, one that most New Zealanders haven't even discovered. Some scenic highlights are **Anaura Bay,** with rocky headlands, a long beach, and coastal islands; it is between **Tolaga Bay** and **Tokomaru Bay,** two former shipping towns. Tolaga Bay has an incredibly long wharf stretching over a beach into the sea, and Cooks Cove Walkway, a pleasant walk through the countryside past an interesting rock arch. In **Tikitiki** farther up the coast, an Anglican Church is full of wonderfully carved Maori panels and beams. Tikitiki has a gas station.

East of the small town of **Te Araroa,** which has the oldest pohutukawa (po-hoo-too-ka-wa) tree in the country, the coast is about as remote as you could imagine. At the tip of the cape (21 kilometers, or 13 miles, from Te Araroa), the **East Cape Lighthouse** and fantastic views are a long steep climb from the beach. **Hicks Bay** has another long beach. Back toward Opotiki, **Whanarua** (fahn-ah-roo-ah) **Bay** is one of the most beautiful on the East Cape, with isolated beaches ideal for a picnic and a swim. Farther on, there is an intricately carved Maori marae (meeting house) called Tukaki in **Te Kaha.**

If you plan to take your time along the way, inquire at the ☞ **Gisborne–Eastland Visitor Information Centre** about lodging. There are motel accommodations at various points on the cape. Driving time alone between Opotiki and Gisborne (about 330 kilometers, or 205 miles) is about five hours without stops.

Urewera National Park

36 *125 km (78 mi) west of Gisborne.*

Urewera National Park is a vast, remote region of forests and lakes straddling the Huiarau Range. The park's outstanding feature is the glorious **Lake Waikaremoana** (sea of rippling waters), a forest-girded lake with good swimming, boating, fishing, and walks. The lake is circled by a 50-kilometer (31-mile) walking track; the three- to four-day walk is popular, and in the summer months the lakeside tramping huts are often heavily used. There are many other short walks nearby. The one-hour Lake Waikareiti Track is especially recommended. For information, contact the Department of Conservation Field Centre at Aniwaniwa, on the eastern arm of Lake Waikaremoana (⊠ Aniwaniwa, Private Bag, Wairoa, ☎ 06/837–3803). The motor camp on the lakeshore has cabins, chalets, and motel units. In summer a launch operates sightseeing and fishing trips from the motor camp.

Gisborne and Eastland A to Z

Arriving and Departing

BY CAR

Gisborne is a long way from almost anywhere, though the coastal and bush scenery along the way makes the drive wholly worthwhile. The most direct route from the north is to follow State Highway 2 around coastal Bay of Plenty, then from Opotiki, Eastland's northern gateway, through the Waioeka Gorge Scenic Reserve. The trip from Auckland to Gisborne takes seven hours. South from Gisborne, you will pass through Wairoa, about 90 minutes away, before passing Hawke's Bay and Wairarapa on the way to Wellington, about seven and a half hours by car.

BY PLANE

Air New Zealand Link (☎ 06/867–9490) operates daily flights into Gisborne from Auckland and Wellington.

Contacts and Resources

GUIDED TOURS

Country Helicopters Gisborne has a number of unusual tours, including one in which the guide points out the area's top surfing spots. The company also runs heli-fishing excursions, wine tours, and a "white knuckle" trip. Shorter trips include a tour around Gisborne and its beaches for $60. ☎ *06/868–8911.*

Nomad Off-Road Tours gives new meaning to getting off the beaten track. The company operates four-wheel-drive trips on the Tarndale Slip, formed by the largest movement of earth in the southern hemisphere. The trips involve a lot of river crossings and sometimes incorporate working activities on farms and logging sites. Hosts Roy and Lesley Cranswick are happy to arrange tours specifically suited to your interests. ⊠ *6 Hunter St., Gisborne,* ☎ *06/868–4187.*

VISITOR INFORMATION

The **Gisborne–Eastland Visitor Information Centre** is easily identifiable by the Canadian totem pole next door. ⊠ *209 Grey St., Gisborne,* ☎ *06/868–6139,* FAX *06/868–6138.* ☽ *Daily 9–5.30.*

NEW PLYMOUTH AND TARANAKI

On a clear winter day, with a cover of snow, Mount Taranaki (also called Mount Egmont) towers above its flat rural surroundings and seems to draw the sky right down to the sea. No less astonishing in other seasons, the solitary peak is similar in appearance to Japan's Mount Fuji. It is the icon of the Taranaki region, and the province has shaped itself around the mountain. To the north, the provincial seat of New Plymouth huddles between the monolith and a rugged coastline, while smaller towns dot the road that circles the mountain's base. For visitors, Mount Taranaki (its Maori name, Egmont being its English title) is often the center of attention. You can hike up it and around it, ski on it (for a short period), stay the night on it, and dine at restaurants on its flanks.

The Taranaki region is one of the most successful agricultural areas in the country because of layers of volcanic ash that have created superb free-draining topsoil, and a mountainous coastal position that insures abundant rainfall. What serves farmers serves gardeners as well. Some of the country's most magnificent gardens grow in the rich local soil, and the annual rhododendron festival held late in the year celebrates the area's horticultural excellence.

Taranaki has plenty of other ground-level delights, too. By the water's edge you can surf, swim, and fish, and several excellent museums delve into Taranaki history, which is particularly rich on the subject of the Maori. You could take in most of the area in a couple of days, but that will keep you on the run. Just getting around the mountain from place to place takes time. Most people use New Plymouth as a base, though Stratford and Hawera also have comfortable, if basic, accommodations.

The weather is constantly in flux—locals say that if you can't see Egmont it's raining and if you can it's going to rain. Day in and day out, this meteorological mix makes for stunning contrasts of sun and cloud on and around the mountain. The changing aspects of the volcano, combined with the Maori legends of Mount Taranaki—how as a lover he had fought with other mountains for a woman who didn't learn of his affection until too late, after he retired with his wounds to where he stands today—can lead a traveler to wax poetical:

This fondness of heart—
Will you come back tomorrow,
my Taranaki?

New Plymouth

37 *375 km (235 mi) south of Auckland, 190 km (120 mi) southwest of Waitomo.*

New Plymouth is a center both for one of New Zealand's most productive dairy regions and the nation's gas and oil industries. This natural wealth means that even when New Zealand's economy is in hard times, the people of New Plymouth retain a sense of optimism. Prior to the arrival of Europeans, several Maori pa villages were in the vicinity. In the mid-1800s, Maori-European land disputes racked Taranaki, and open war broke out in New Plymouth in 1860. Formal peace between the government and Maori was made in 1881, after which New Plymouth began to form its current identity.

While you're in New Plymouth, you will always have the impression that nature is beckoning—either the looming mountain or the nearby sea. The city itself doesn't have as much to offer as the surrounding countryside, but take time to explore its serene parkland, and the museum if you have a rainy morning.

If you're driving to Taranaki from the north, the Awakino Gorge on Highway 3 between Mahoenui and the coast is breathtaking. Sheep have worn out trails that seem to hang on the sides of precipitous green hills that are broken here and there with marvelous limestone outcrops. The other thing to look for coming this way is the view of Mount Egmont as soon as you hit the coast—it is nothing short of awe-inspiring.

Pukekura Park and the connected **Brooklands** park are the main reasons to stay in New Plymouth proper. You could easily spend half a day in the parks, especially if you're botanically inclined. Pukekura has water running throughout, and the view from the park's tea house across the boating lake, with Mount Egmont as a backdrop, is one of New Zealand's finest. You can hire rowboats to explore the small islands and nooks and crannies of the main lake. Pukekura Park also has a fernery and botanical display houses—caverns that were carved out of the hillside that connect through fern-cloaked tunnels. The fern and flowering plant collections are some of the most extensive in the country.

Brooklands was once a great estate. During the land wars of the 1860s, local Maori burned down the manor house, and the brick fireplace is all that remains of it, standing alone in the sweeping lawns among trees. Planted in the second half of the 19th century, giant copper beeches, pines, walnuts, and oaks will amaze you with their great presence. The monterey pine, magnolia soulangeana, ginko, and native karaka and kohekohe are all the largest of their kind in New Zealand. Take a walk along the outskirts of the park on tracks leading through native, subtropical bush that are popular with local runners. This area has been relatively untouched for the last few thousand years, and 1,500-year-old trees are not uncommon. A puriri tree near the Somerset Street entrance is believed to be over 2,000 years old.

Other features of Brooklands are **the Gables,** a colonial hospital built in 1847, which now serves as an art gallery and medical museum. The adjacent zoo is an old-fashioned example of how to keep birds and animals, but it is still a favorite of children. Brooklands has a rhododendron dell and a bowl used for a variety of entertainment throughout the year. ⊠ *Liardet St., Brooklands Rd.,* ☎ *06/759–6060.* ☺ *Daily dawn–dusk; teahouse July–May, Wed.–Mon. dawn–dusk; display houses daily 10–noon and 1–4; tour by appointment.*

Taranaki Museum is the second oldest in New Zealand, having first been formed in 1847. The museum cares for a large number of Taonga (Maori treasures) that are associated with various Iwi (tribes). Also of interest is a diverse collection of colonial items, many of which date back to the earliest years of European settlement. ⊠ *Ariki and Egmont Sts.,* ⊟ *Free.* ☺ *Tues.–Fri. 10:30–4:30, weekends 1–5.*

The Queen Elizabeth II National Trust is a publicly funded organization established to conserve privately held native landscapes. The only two New Zealand gardens in the Trust are in Taranaki: in New Plymouth, **Tupare,** and south of the mountain in Kaponga, ☞ **Hollard Gardens.**

Complete with Tudor-style houses, Tupare is truly an English-style garden. Built in 1927, the estate of Sir Russell and Lady Matthews sits on a steep hillside that plunges down to the rushing Waiwhakaiho (why-fah-kie-ho) River. Russell Matthews, a roading contractor, cleverly enlisted his crew during the off-season to build the impressive terraces, garden walls, and pools that define Tupare. Many varieties of maple trees have been planted, along with a grand tulip tree, cherries and magnolias, and a stand of native remu pine. There are numerous rhododendrons and azaleas, to be expected in Taranaki, with under-plantings of helebores, daffodils, and bluebells, creating a glorious floral vision in spring. Tupare is also noted for its autumnal foliage display. ⊠ *487*

Manorei Rd., New Plymouth, ☎ 06/758–6480. ☞ $5. ⊙ Daily 9–5; some paths may be closed in winter for maintenance.

Stately **Mount Egmont** rises 8,309 feet right out of the sea, and if you spend any more than a few hours in the vicinity it is difficult not to be drawn toward it. The lower reaches are cloaked in magical subtropical forests; above the tree line lower vegetation allows you to look out over the paddocks and seascape below. The three main roads to the mountain turn off of State Highway 3 and are all well signposted. The first as you drive south from New Plymouth leads to the **North Egmont Visitor Centre.** Displays at the center are looking tired and outdated, but it's still worth dropping in to learn something about the mountain and its lush vegetation. North Egmont is the starting point for several walks, and it has a cafeteria if you need to get your strength up. The second turnoff to the mountain takes you to the **Mountain House** and, a little farther on **Stratford Plateau,** the mountain's ski field. Here you will find more walks of various durations. The third turnoff takes you to the southernmost **Dawson Falls Visitor Centre,** which also has displays about the mountain and five popular walks of varying difficulty taking from one to two-and-a-half hours.

If you are serious about getting out and striding, consider taking three to five days to walk around the entire mountain. The circuit is well signposted and there are accommodation huts along the way, the cost for which is usually $8 for adults per night. You can also ascend the summit of Mount Egmont quite easily in summer, and a variety of other intermediate options are available.

To get a shadowy feeling for part of the Maori past in New Plymouth, pay a visit to **Koru Pa,** the former stronghold of the Nga Mahanga a Tairi hapu of the Taranaki tribe. The bush has taken it back in large measure, but you can still make out the main defensive ditch and stonewalled terraces that drop a considerable way from the highest part of the pa where chiefs lived down to the Oakura River. Part of the reserve has a picnic site. Take Route 45 out of New Plymouth and turn left onto Wairau Road. Take it to Surrey Hills Road, where another left will take you to the pa site. ⊠ *Surrey Hills Rd.*

On the western outskirts of New Plymouth, the world-renowned
★ **Pukeiti Rhododendron Trust** scenically spreads over 900 acres of lush native rain forest adjacent to Egmont National Park on the northwest slope of the mountain. The Pukeiti (poo-kay-*ee*-tee) collection of 2,500 species and hybrid rhododendrons is the largest in New Zealand. Many of these varieties were first grown here, like the giant winter-blooming *R. protistum var. giganteum* "Pukeiti," collected from seed in 1953 and now standing 15 feet tall; or the beautiful "Lemon Lodge" and "Spring Honey" hybrids that bloom in spring. "Kyawi," a large red rhodie, is the very last to bloom in April (autumn).

Rhododendrons aside, there are many other rare and special plants to be enjoyed at Pukeiti. All winter long the Himalayan daphnes (*D. bholua*) fragrance the pathways. Spring to summer growing *candelabra primula* (primrose) can reach up to four feet, and for a month around Christmas spectacular eight-foot Himalayan *cardiocrinum* lilies sport heavenly scented 12-inch white trumpet flowers. If you're not an avid gardener, walking the paths that wind throughout the vast gardens and surrounding native bush is also a delight. Pukeiti is a wonderful bird habitat, so keep your eyes and ears open for birds, too. ⊠ *Carrington Rd., 20 km (12½ mi) southwest of New Plymouth center, ☎ FAX 06/752–4141; restaurant, ☎ 06/752–4143. ☞ $6. ⊙ Daily dawn–dusk. Closed Dec. 25.*

Dining and Lodging

$$$ ✕ **The Orangery.** The decor and surroundings here have been modeled on a 16th-century Tuscan landscape, complete with citrus trees and a fountain. Start with squid and scallops marinated in chili oil and lime juice then seared in a wok, before looking to main courses such as market-fresh baby snapper manuka- (pungent New Zealand honey) smoked and finished with lime butter and mango vinaigrette, or grilled venison served over a pumpkin and kumara (sweet-potato) galette with blackberry port and pepper sauce. ✉ *Courtney and Leach Sts., New Plymouth,* ☎ *06/758–0589. AE, DC, MC, V.*

$$–$$$ ✕ **L'Escargot Restaurant and Bar.** Arguably the finest restaurant in New Plymouth, L'Escargot focuses on classic southern French preparations, serving lighter world-beat dishes as well. Dine inside New Plymouth's oldest commercial building on such delights as Provençale aïoli soup, Camarguais beef stew slow-cooked with red wine, or more alternative head-turners like crumbed fish and seafood with chili-garlic sauce, or Singaporean chicken satay. Desserts return to Europe for inspiration. ✉ *37-43 Brougham St., New Plymouth,* ☎ *06/758–4812. AE, DC, MC, V.*

$$ ✕ **Devon Seafood Smorgasbord.** Jump into the everyday New Plymouth scene, and back in time a couple of decades in format, for plenty to eat from a buffet where you can have as many helpings as you like. There is a great selection of seafood, meat, vegetarian, and Oriental dishes, and desserts as well. Friday, Saturday, and Sunday nights, costumed characters sing, dance, and generally fool around while you eat. This isn't exactly the place for a romantic dinner, but it is a fun alternative to the average vacation-night-out. ✉ *390 Devon St. East, New Plymouth,* ☎ *06/759–9099,* ℻ *06/758–2229. AE, DC, MC, V.*

$–$$ ✕ **Macfarlane's Caffe.** One of the new generation of New Zealand restaurants—friendly, ambitious, casual, and looking to the rest of the Western world for influences—Macfarlane's does its share to liven up the dining scene in the town of Inglewood, midway between New Plymouth and Stratford. Yogurt and granola or traditional farm-stlye breakfasts, lunches of Caesar salad or attractively assembled sandwiches, and at dinner calamari, chicken focaccia, blackened fish, pasta, pizza, or just a burger are persuasively prepared and pleasantly delivered. A good variety of New Zealand wine is sold by the glass; New Zealand beer is in abundance as well. ✉ *Kelly and Matai Sts., Inglewood,* ☎ *06/756–6665. AE, MC, V. No dinner Sun.–Wed.*

$ ✕ **Steps Restaurant.** The food, the prices, and the old-house homey
★ atmosphere here are sure to get you out of the travel-meal rut while you're in Taranaki. At lunch, earthy broccoli and feta pie or cold salads are welcome feel-good bargains, filling up your plate in a wholesome way. At dinner, nut- and herb-encrusted fish or a Cajun dish might appear on the menu. Bread at The Steps is delicious, as are desserts like pecan pie or puff pastry filled with fruit and topped with whipped cream. Vegetarian meals are available. ✉ *37 Gover St.,* ☎ *06/758–3393. MC, V. BYOB. No dinner Sun. or Mon.*

$$ ⌂ **Devon Hotel.** This hotel has standard, comfortable rooms, and enough flexibility to cater to families. It's easy to find, close to the city, and has a friendly atmosphere to match its family-managed status. Hotel guests may use facilities at a nearby health club. ✉ *390 Devon St. East, New Plymouth,* ☎ *06/759–9099,* ℻ *06/758—2229. 100 rooms with bath and shower. Restaurant, bar, pool. AE, DC, MC, V.*

$$ ⌂ **Henwood House.** This century-plus-old B&B occupies a homestead that has been completely refurbished and refined by architect Graeme Axten and his wife Lynne. The two play the role of charming hosts to the likes of the British High Commissioner in New Zealand (who recommends the place, if you're curious), but the rates make Henwood House accessible not only to heads of state. There is a variety of rooms, including one with a balcony and fireplace. The property is only 6 kilometers (4 miles) from town, but it is extremely peaceful. Breakfast is served in the country-style kitchen each morning, and you'll find it pleasantly easy to relax in the rather grand guest lounge evenings. ⊠ *122 Henwood House, New Plymouth,* ☎ *06/755–1212. 5 rooms, 3 with shower, 2 with shared bath. MC, V.*

Outdoor Activities and Sports

BEACHES

Some of the coast can be wild with waves, so it pays to play it safe and swim at patrolled beaches. **Fitzroy Beach** and **East End Beach** both have lifeguards in summer and are easily accessible from New Plymouth. **Ngamotu Beach,** along Ocean View Parade, is calm and suitable for young children. Fitzroy and East End are both popular with surfers, as is **Back Beach.**

BOATING

★ **Happy Chaddy's Charters** offers a unique blend of cruising, fishing, sightseeing, and jokes—all in an old English lifeboat. Perhaps no other cruise in the world starts with the guide announcing "hold on to your knickers, because we're about to take off," and then justifying himself when the lifeboat rocks back and forth in its shed (with passengers onboard), slides down its rails, and hits the sea with a spray of water. The trip lasts an hour, during which time you can hang a line off the back and try for a kohwhai (*koh*-fie) or two. You'll see seals and get a close-up view of the Sugar Loaf Islands just offshore from New Plymouth. ⊠ *Ocean View Parade, New Plymouth,* ☎ *06/758–9133.* ⌑ *$20, chartered fishing trip $10 per person (minimum 8 people).*

Stratford

38   *41 km (27 mi) southeast of New Plymouth.*

The town of Stratford itself is remarkable for its ordinariness. A stroll down its main drag—with its local shops and food stores—will give you a sense of New Zealand's agricultural life. Above town on the mountain there are excellent hiking trails, and in the valley to the east are some of the country's most interesting private gardens.

Of all the gardens in New Zealand, the one you'll most likely want to
★ return to is **Aramaunga,** whether to see the garden itself or Gwyn Masters, its presiding sage and sprightly creator. A garden is surely a reflection of its maker, and Mrs. Masters has over the last 50 years transformed a farm paddock into a garden with a personality to match her own. At Aramaunga, which means the path between the mountains, you'll witness her enthusiasm, intelligence, and generosity of spirit everywhere. Most visitors comment on the wisteria, from the century-old specimen on the front of the cottage to others cleverly grown as standards or encouraged to climb into the treetops along with various clematis species to throw bursts of color where it is least expected.

The very act of walking through the garden is a delight—through discreet passageways, onto open lawns, around bends, always following the contours of the land. The garden constantly changes as you progress, heightening your sense of anticipation. Beds are filled with masses of color and form that mix beautifully: rhododendrons (ask to see the true red "Gwynneth Masters" hybrid that she developed from seed), azalea mollis, magnolias, cherries, and Japanese maples, along with interesting pottery and herbaceous plants that include lots of self-seeded columbine (she can't bring herself to pull out any of these charmers).

Eventually, the path arrives in front of a stream, which was dammed years ago to form a pond that reflects along its edges golden bog primula, white libertia, purple iris, and lavender wisteria shrubs. Bridges crossing the pond connect with woodland on the opposite shore where a glorious view back across the water, gardens, and cottage bring to mind Gwyn Masters's affinity for Claude Monet's garden at Giverny: his passion for color and the relaxed form. Like Monet, Mrs. Masters is always creating things in her garden, creating beauty just like a painter. Aramaunga is open to the public by appointment; there is a small entry fee. ☎ 06/765–7600.

Dining and Lodging

$$–$$$ ✕🏠 **Mountain House Motor Lodge.** From the restaurant where some of New Zealand's most unique meals are carefully prepared to motel-style rooms that have little more to recommend them than their cleanliness and their location on the eastern flank of Mount Egmont, the Mountain House simply is what it is. (Keith and Bertha Anderson originally created the Swiss-chalet–style Dawson Falls Lodge, then moved here to be closer to town.) Dinner is a marriage of Bertha ("*ber*-ta") Anderson's Swiss upbringing and delicious New Zealand produce. From the sea, creamed local paua (abalone), or delicately smoked freshwater eel that may be the best you've ever tasted, or seasonal whitebait fritters make great starters—especially appropriate with a Marlborough riesling. Moving to heartier main courses as Kiwis do, lamb or lean cervena venison call for pinot noir, or cabernet-merlot for the very hungry. Apple strudel and cream is a wonderful way to wrap up the alpine meal. If you do stay at the motor lodge—trails from the building make it a fine spot from which to ascend or walk the lower reaches of the mountain, and the staff can provide you with maps and suggestions—rooms 4 through 8 stand apart from the main building and are a bit more spacious. In winter, a t-bar lift from the lodge takes you to the base of the snowfields. ⊠ *Pembroke Rd., Box 303, Stratford,* ☎ 🖷 *06/765–6100, 0800/657–100. Restaurant, bar. AE, DC, MC, V.*

Kaponga

18 km (11 mi) west of Stratford.

The reasons to come to Kaponga, unless you're just driving through on your way around the mountain, are Dawson Falls, which is the southern entrance to Mount Egmont National Park, and the magnificent Hollard Gardens. The view of Mount Taranaki from Opunaki Road in the long light of a sunny afternoon is stunning.

★ Surrounded by dairy farms, **Hollard Gardens** was conceived in 1927 when Bernard and Rose Hollard sectioned off a piece of their land and started building the impressive collection of plants now under the care of the Queen Elizabeth II National Trust. The 14-acre garden was created in two stages: The old garden, dating from 1927, is a woodland area with narrow, winding paths, intensely planted with rhododendrons, azaleas, camellias, and other related plants. It is an intimate area with great character. The new garden was established in 1982. Its broad lawns, paths, and large mixed borders contain a comprehensive blend of exotics and natives. Pick up a brochure at the information shelter detailing two self-guided walking tours. It will help you locate some of the treasures.

Look in the Moon Bed for the rare epaulette tree and the native, yellow-flowering kawhai (*kah*-fie), which attracts tuneful bellbirds and tuis. The grand, golden totara foliage on Rabbit Ridge is stunning in winter, and the 70-year-old passion vine draped on tawa trees has bright

orange fruit in autumn. Both are on the Bush Walk. The main season
for flowering is September through March. ⊠ *Upper Manaia Rd., off
Opunake Rd., Kaponga,* ☎ *06/764–6544.* ☞ *$5.* ☉ *Daily 9–5.
Closed Dec. 25.*

Dining and Lodging

$$$ ✕☷ **Dawson Falls Lodge.** The most delightful accommodation in the
region, with a touch of eccentricity, Dawson Falls has been styled on
a Swiss alpine lodge. All rooms have Swiss decor, each with its own
character and touches. It lies about halfway up Mount Egmont, so the
air is very fresh, and the loudest noises you'll hear are those of the local
bird population. Request a room with a view up the mountain. The
restaurant is good, but the lodge itself is the star. ⊠ *Manaia Rd., off
Opunake Rd. from Stratford,* ☎ *06/765–5457. 11 rooms, 2 with
bath, all with shower. Restaurant, bar, lounge. AE, DC, MC, V.*

Hawera

㊴   *29 km (18 mi) south of Stratford.*

Tawhiti Museum is a labor of love for Nigel Ogle, who bought a 70-
year-old cheese factory in 1976 and proceeded to fill it up with life-
size figures from Taranaki's past. The figures are created from molds
of real people—Nigel's friends, relatives, and locals—giving them a far
more lifelike look than those in other museums. You may get a chance
to watch Nigel at work, or discuss the history of the region with him.
On the first Sunday of each month and Sundays during school holi-
days, the Tawhiti Bush Railway takes runs as an extension of the mu-
seum. The railway takes you back to historical logging operations in
Taranaki, where other figures are used to illustrate the life of the times.
Take Onhangai Road southeast out of Normanby, or Tawhiti Road
northeast out of Hawera, and continue 4 kilometers (2.5 miles) to the
museum. ⊠ *7 Ohangai Rd., Hawera,* ☎ *06/278–6837.* ☞ *$5.* ☉
Sept.–May, Fri.–Mon. 10–4; June–Aug., Sun. 10–4.

Just up the road from Tawhiti Museum, **Turuturumokai Pa** is one of
the most impressive Maori citadels in the province. Defense ditches and
walls ring the former village, and the top is pocked with storage pits.
This pa is an astonishing piece of earthwork. ⊠ *Turuturu Rd. near On-
hangai Rd., Hawera.*

Taranaki A to Z

Arriving and Departing

BY BUS

New Plymouth is served daily by both **Newmans** (☎ 09/309–9738) and
InterCity (☎ 09/358–4085) from Auckland, Wellington, and other cities.

BY CAR

New Plymouth looks well out of the way on the map, but it is only four
and a half hours from Auckland, a little longer to Wellington. From the
north, head to Te Kuiti near Waitomo caves, then simply continue on
State Highway 3. To leave Taranaki, take State Highway 3 south to the
next main center, Wanganui. Staying on Highway 3, keep traveling to
Sanson, where you have the option of following State Highway 1 down
the west coast to Wellington, or heading east through Palmerston North,
the Manawatu Gorge, and onto the Wairarapa region.

BY PLANE

Air New Zealand (☎ 09/379–0861) operates flights seven times daily
between Auckland and New Plymouth, and five times daily into
Wellington.

Contacts and Resources

CAR RENTALS
AA Host Southern Cross Rental Cars. ⊠ *49–55 Powderham St., New Plymouth,* ☎ *06/758–1955.*

GUIDED TOURS
'C' Tours has half- and full-day sightseeing tours that will give you a quick sample of what Taranaki has to offer. The company will accommodate any special interests you have, and prices vary accordingly. ⊠ *55 Egmont St., New Plymouth,* ☎ *06/758–4171.*

Taranaki Scenic Flights has a number of tours, the most popular of which is a climb to the snowcapped summit of Mount Egmont–Taranaki. You can also take a trip along the coastline, around the city, or out to the Maui offshore gas field. ⊠ *New Plymouth Airport,* ☎ *06/755–0500,* FAX *06/755–1478.*

LATE-NIGHT PHARMACY
Bruce Laird Pharmacy is open daily 8:30–8:30. ⊠ *68 Vivian St.,* ☎ *06/ 758–8263.*

VISITOR INFORMATION
New Plymouth Information Centre. ⊠ *Leach and Liardet Sts., New Plymouth,* ☎ *06/758–6086,* FAX *06/758-1395.* ⊙ *Weekdays 8:30—5, weekends 10–3.*

Stratford Information Centre. ⊠ *Broadway and Miranda Sts., Stratford,* ☎ *06/765–6708,* FAX *06/765–7500.* ⊙ *Oct.–Mar., weekends 10–3, Mon. 10–2; Apr.–Sept., Sat. 10–3, Mon. 10–2.*

WELLINGTON

New Zealand's capital city was named after the Duke of Wellington, the ultimate conqueror of Napoléon, at Waterloo. It was settled by English pioneers who purchased land from the New Zealand Company. Shortly after the signing of the Treaty of Waitangi in 1840, Auckland was chosen as the site for the national capital. Prosperous and influential gold miners of South Island waged a campaign for a more central capital, however, and in 1865 the seat of government was shifted to Wellington.

This city of 407,000 sits in a glorious location on the western shores of Port Nicholson, squeezed against the sea by peaks rearing up almost 3,000 feet. Behind it, suburbs full of quaint timber houses spill down precipitous slopes. The air currents funneled through Cook Strait, the 17-kilometer (11-mile) channel separating North and South islands, give the city a feisty climate. "Windy Wellington" is a nickname that springs readily to the lips of most New Zealanders who don't live here. Although the city's reputation for climatic vigor is exaggerated, it's no accident that one of its landmarks is an experimental, wind-powered generator that overlooks the suburb of Brooklyn.

Exploring Wellington

A Good Walk
Wellington is an easy city to explore by foot, although some of its tangles of streets can get confusing. The following walking tour includes city views, formal gardens, literary history, some fine examples of 19th-century architecture, and the seat of government. Allow about three hours. The tour starts at the cable car terminal. Much of the city's best shopping lies south of there in Victoria Street and in the Manners and Cuba street pedestrian malls.

Begin at the **Kelburn Cable Car** ⑩ terminus in Cable Car Lane off Lambton Quay, opposite Grey Street. It's a good way to get up and see the city's layout—and end up walking down many of the hills instead of up them.

Leave the Kelburn Terminal and take the Northern Walkway, following the arrow that points to St. Mary Street. This path skirts the edge of the **Wellington Botanic Garden** ⑪ with city views on one side and the domes of the Dominion Observatory on the other. As you round this hilltop, you'll see an immense green hill with transmission towers on top; this is Tinakori Hill, known to the Maoris as Ahumairangi— "sloping down from the sky." Continue along the path, which becomes quite steep as it plunges toward the **Lady Norwood Rose Garden** ⑫, with more than 100 rose cultivars spilling out their blossoms and fragrance between November and the end of April.

Turn from the roses and walk to the right around the enclosed Anderson Park, following the sign to Bolton Street Memorial Park. At the end of this short road, make a detour to the monument on the right. The **John Seddon Memorial** ⑬ is dedicated to the remarkable turn-of-the-century prime minister. Close to the memorial a track zigzags down the hill beneath a stand of pohutukawa trees. At the bottom, cross Bowen Street, walk downhill, take the path to your left, and climb narrow old **Ascot Street** ⑭, with its wonderful old city cottages. At the top of the rise, stop for breath on a bench that has been thoughtfully provided in the shady courtyard.

Turn right into **Tinakori Road** ⑮. Another fact of early life in Wellington is illustrated by **No. 306,** the pasta shop. Pressed for want of level ground, the citizens of early Wellington tended to build tall, narrow houses. This example—one room wide and five stories high—took things to extremes. Just below the house, make a short detour to see the three superbly kept timber houses side by side in Upton Terrace. Behind a green fence a few steps farther down Tinakori Road is **Premier House,** the official residence of the prime minister until 1935, when the new Labour government, caught up in the reforming zeal of socialism, turned it into a dental clinic.

Continue down a relatively drab part of Tinakori Road to No. 25, just beyond the Hobson Street bridge. This is the **Katherine Mansfield House** ⑯, where the celebrated writer was born (as Kathleen Beauchamp) and lived the first five years of her life.

The next section of the walk passes architecture of a more public ilk. Turning back along Tinakori Road to the Hobson Street overpass, and on the far side of the motorway, turn right to walk through the elms of Katherine Mansfield Memorial Park. Turn left around the rather stern compound of the U.S. Embassy, and walk down Murphy Street, which becomes Mulgrave Street, to **Old St. Paul's Cathedral** ⑰, one of the country's wooden Gothic Revival gems. Continue down Mulgrave Street and turn right at Archives House into Aitken Street. The modern building on the right is the **National Library** ⑱, which houses the nation's largest collection of books. Cross Molesworth Street and walk through the gate to the various **Parliament Buildings** ⑲ on the far side. To the left of Parliament House, the **Executive Office Building** ⑳, alias "The Beehive," is the strange-looking office space for government officials.

Walk down the hill from the Beehive to the **Cenotaph** ㉑, the memorial to New Zealanders killed in battle—these were soldiers who oftentimes fought for the British Commonwealth when no immediate threat was posed to the safety of the New Zealand islands themselves. Across

It helps to be pushy in airports.

Introducing the revolutionary new TransPorter™ from American Tourister® It's the first suitcase you can push around without a fight. TransPorter's™ exclusive four-wheel design lets you push it in front of you with almost no effort—the wheels take the weight. Or pull it on two wheels if you choose. You can even stack on other bags and use it like a luggage cart.

Stable 4-wheel design.

TransPorter™ is designed like a dresser, with built-in shelves to organize your belongings. Or collapse the shelves and pack it like a traditional suitcase. Inside, there's a suiter feature to help keep suits and dresses from wrinkling. When push comes to shove, you can't beat a TransPorter™ For more information on how you can be this pushy, call 1-800-542-1300.

Shelves collapse on command.

American Tourister®

Making travel less primitive®

Your passport around the world.

- Worldwide access
- Operators who speak your language
- Monthly itemized billing

MCI Calling Card

415 555 1234 2244
J.D. SMITH

Use your MCI Card® and these access numbers for an easy way to call when traveling worldwide.

Bahrain†	800-002
Brunei	800-011
China (CC)†	108-12
(Available from most major cities)	
For a Mandarin-speaking operator	108-17
Cyprus ♦†	080-90000
Egypt (CC) ♦†	355-5770
Federated States of Micronesia	624
Fiji	004-890-1002
Guam (CC)†	950-1022
Hong Kong (CC)†	800-1121
India (CC)†	000-127
(Available from most major cities)	
Indonesia (CC) ♦†	001-801-11
Iran ✣	(Special Phones Only)
Israel (CC) ♦†	177-150-2727
Japan (CC) ♦†	
To call U.S. using KDD ■	0039-121
To call U.S. using IDC ■	0066-55-121
Jordan	18-800-001
Korea (CC)†	
To call using KT ■	009-14
To call using DACOM ■	0039-12

Phone Booths ✣	Press Red Button 03, then *
Military Bases	550-2255
Kuwait†	800-MCI (800-624)
Lebanon (CC) ✣	600-624
Macao†	0800-131
Malaysia (CC) ♦†	800-0012
Philippines (CC) ♦†	
To call using PLDT ■	105-14
To call using PHILCOM ■	1026-12
For a Tagalog-speaking operator	105-15
Qatar ★	0800-012-77
Saipan (CC) ✣†	950-1022
Saudi Arabia (CC)†	1-800-11
Singapore†	8000-112-112
Sri Lanka	(within Colombo) 440100
	(outside of Colombo) 01-440100
Syria	0800
Taiwan (CC) ♦†	0080-13-4567
Thailand ★†	001-999-1-2001
United Arab Emirates ♦	800-111
Vietnam ●	1201-1022

To sign up for the MCI Card, dial the access number of the country you are in and ask to speak with a customer service representative.

http://www.mci.com

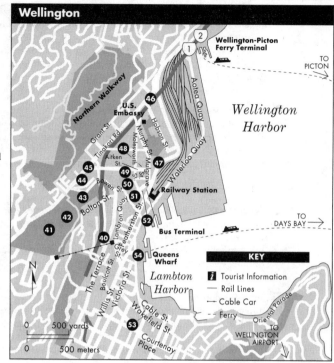

the road from the Cenotaph are the tremendous wooden **Original Government Buildings** ⑤②.

The wide street curving behind the bronze lions is Lambton Quay. As its name suggests, this was once Wellington's waterfront. All the land between your feet and the present-day shoreline has been reclaimed. From this point, the shops of the city center are within easy walking distance along Lambton Quay.

Sights to See

④④ **Ascot Street.** The tiny, doll-like cottages along Ascot were built in the 1870s, and this remains the finest example of a 19th-century streetscape in Wellington. There is a bench at the top end of the street that has been thoughtfully provided in the shady courtyard if you need to catch your breath. ⊠ *Off Glenmore–Tinakori Sts. north of Wellington Botanic Garden.*

⑤① **Cenotaph.** This memorial honors New Zealanders killed in battle, and New Zealand has a proud and distinguished military record. "Few Americans appreciate the tremendous sacrifices made by New Zealanders in the last two world wars," James A. Michener wrote in *Return to Paradise.* "Among the allies, she had the highest percentage of men in arms—much higher than the United States—the greatest percentage overseas, and the largest percentage killed." ⊠ *Bowen St. and Lambton Quay.*

★ **City Gallery.** Whether it's the latest exhibition of New Zealand's avant-garde artists, an international collection visiting the gallery, the Open City film series, or just the gallery's café, there are plenty of reasons to plan to put Wellington's eyes-and-ears-on-the-arts into your schedule. It is an excellent representation of New Zealand's thoughtful, contemporary cultural set—something that you won't see much of in the countryside. The gallery has no permanent collection, so everything here is transitory. You may be in town when a show of local painters is on the walls, or a Max Ernst exhibition; and the film series plays everything from John Huston to New Zealand documentaries scored with music played by the National Symphony Orchestra. ⊠ *Civic Sq., Wakefield St., Box 2199,* ☏ *04/801–3952,* ☏ *04/801–3950.* ⊙ *Fri.–Wed. 11–5, Thurs. 11–8.*

⑤③ Civic Square. Wellington's newish Civic Square is one symbol of the cultural vitality of Wellington, and the interest currently invested in it. Reminiscent of an Italian piazza, it is a delightful sanctuary from the traffic and wind, with its outdoor cafés. The **City Gallery,** perhaps the nation's finest art space, the Library, and the concert venue Town Hall all just steps apart. Architect Ian Athfield's steel nikau palms are a marvel. ⊠ *Wakefield, Victoria, and Harris Sts.*

⑤⓪ Executive Office Building. It would be difficult to imagine a more complete contrast in architectural styles than that of Parliament House and the Executive Office Building. Known for obvious reasons as the Beehive—though the people of Wellington will tell you that it produces nothing sweet—it contains the offices of government ministers and their staffs. ⊠ *Molesworth St.*

④③ John Seddon Memorial. This monument is dedicated to the colorful and popular liberal politician who served as prime minister from 1893 to 1906. Under Seddon's leadership, New Zealand became the first country to give women voting rights and to pay its citizens an old-age pension. ⊠ *Bolton Street Memorial Park, northeast end of Wellington Botanic Garden.*

④⑥ Katherine Mansfield House. This is where the writer was born (as Kathleen Beauchamp) and lived the first five years of her life. Mansfield left to pursue her career in Europe when she was only 20, but many of her short stories are set in Wellington. A year before her death in 1923, she wrote, "New Zealand is in my very bones. What wouldn't I give to have a look at it!" The house, which has been restored as a typical Victorian family home, contains furnishings, photographs, videos, and tapes that elucidate Mansfield's life and times. ⊠ *25 Tinakori Rd., Thorndon,* ☏ ☏ *04/473–7268.* ▣ *$4.* ⊙ *Mon. 10–2:30, Tues.–Sun. 10–4.*

④⓪ Kelburn Cable Car. The Swiss-built funicular railway makes a short but sharp climb to Kelburn Terminal, from which there are great views across parks and city buildings to Port Nicholson. Sit on the left side during the six-minute journey for the best scenery. ⊠ *Lambton Quay at Grey St.,* ☏ *04/472–2199.* ▣ *$1.50.* ⊙ *Departures about every 10 min, weekdays 7 AM–10 PM, Sat. 9:20–6, Sun. 10:30–6.*

★ ④② Lady Norwood Rose Garden. On a fine November day, you couldn't find a better place to go for a sniff and a smile. The rose garden is in fact the most popular area of the ☞ **Wellington Botanic Garden.** Situated on a plateau, the formal circular layout consists of 106 beds, each planted with a single variety of modern and traditional shrubs. Climbing roses cover a brick and timber colonnade on the perimeter. Adjacent to the rose beds, the Begonia House conservatory is filled with tender plants and has a tea house serving light meals. ⊠ *North end of Wellington Botanic Garden, Tinakori Rd. (for carpark),* ☏ *04/472–8167.* ▣ *Small charge.* ⊙ *Weekdays 9–4, weekends 10–4. Closed Dec. 25.*

⑤④ Maritime Museum. Housed in the handsome Harbour Board Building, this museum has paintings, figureheads, various nautical apparatuses, and some fine scale models of ships, including the *Wahine,* which sank in Cook Strait in 1968 with the loss of 51 lives. Most of the displays belong to the old-fashioned, glass-cabinet school of museum design. ⊠ *Queens Wharf,* ☎ *04/472–8904.* ⌑ *$2.* ⊙ *Weekdays 9:30–4, weekends 1–4:30.*

48 **National Library.** This modern building houses the nation's largest collection of books, as well as the remarkable Alexander Turnbull Library. The latter, named after the noted bibliophile who founded it, contains an extensive Pacific history section, including accounts of every important European voyage of discovery since Magellan. A collection of sketches of New Zealand made by early visitors is displayed in changing exhibitions. ⊠ *Molesworth and Aitken Sts.,* ☎ *04/474–3000.* ⊙ *Weekdays 9–5, Sat. 9–1.*

47 **Old St. Paul's Cathedral.** Consecrated in 1866, the church is a splendid example of the English Gothic Revival style executed in wood. Even the trusses supporting the roof transcend their mundane function with splendid craftsmanship. The hexagonal oak pulpit was a gift from the widow of Prime Minister Richard Seddon, in memory of her husband. ⊠ *Mulgrave St., Thorndon,* ☎ *04/473–6722.* ⊙ *Mon.–Sat. 10–4:30, Sun. 1–4:30.*

52 **Original Government Buildings.** This second largest wooden structure in the world is now home to Victoria University's law faculty. You can explore the inside of the building between 9 and 5. ⊠ *Lambton Quay.*

NEED A BREAK?

Reds Espresso Café. Using a little trend-appeal to lure you in from the street, coffee culture and tasty morning and afternoon fare will make you want to linger here awhile, snacking on savory muffins or an avocado and brie roll or turkey if you'd rather. But these are merely appetizers for apple cake, dark rich chocolate cake, croissant cake bread pudding, and fantastic espresso. Stop at Reds to pick up a bite for the ferry to Picton, if you're heading south. ⊠ *49 Willis St.,* ☎ *04/473-3558. MC, V.*

49 **Parliament Buildings.** At a cost of more than $150 million over four years, Parliament Buildings have been painstakingly restored. The pink Gothic Revival structure on the right is the General Assembly Library, a soaring, graceful building compared with the ponderous gray bulk of the Parliament House next door. The layout of the House of Representatives, where legislation is presented, debated, and either passed or rejected by majority vote, is a copy of the British Houses of Parliament at Westminster, right down to the Speaker's mace and the despatch boxes. Tours of the building explain the parliamentary process in detail. ⊠ *Molesworth St.,* ☎ *04/471–9999.* ⌑ *Free.* ⊙ *Tours depart weekdays at varying times.*

45 **Tinakori Road.** The lack of suitable local stone combined with the collapse of most of Wellington's brick buildings in the earthquake of 1848 ensured the almost exclusive use of timber for building here in the second half of the 19th century. Most of the carpenters of the period had learned their skills as cabinetmakers and shipwrights in Europe, and the sturdy houses in this street are a tribute to their craftsmanship. Two notable houses are the tall and narrow number 306 and Premier House just up the road from 306. From the Botanic Garden, follow Glenmore Road northeast until it turns into Tinakori around ☞ **Ascot Street.**

★ **41** **Wellington Botanic Garden.** In the hills overlooking downtown, this urban delight offers scenery as varied as its terrain. Woodland gardens under native and exotic trees fill the valleys, water-loving plants line mountain streams and a pond, dry craggy slopes are studded with succulents and rock-loving plants, and lawns spread over flatter sections with beds of bright seasonal bulbs and annuals. The lovely ☞ **Lady Norwood Rose Garden** is in the northeast part of the garden. **Cater Observatory,** the only one of its kind in New Zealand, has public displays and programs, among which "Public Nights" is a great opportunity for Northern Hemisphereans to learn about the southern night sky. Also at the north end of the garden, the **Bolton Street Memorial Park** is one of the earliest cemeteries in the country, dating from 1840. It's a pleasant place to admire mature trees and antique roses. If you don't want to walk the hill up to the garden, the ☞ **Kelburn Cable Car** can take you. ⊠ *Tinakori Rd. (for carpark), many entrances surround gardens,* ☏ *04/472–8167.* 🖼 *Small charge.* ☉ *Weekdays 9–4, weekends 10–4; Public Nights mid-Dec.–Jan., Tues. and Sat. at 7, and Feb.–early Dec., Tues. and Sat. at 6.*

Around Wellington

★ **Moss Green Garden.** Set in the steep, bush-clad hills along the Akatarawa River, Moss Green makes for a superb day trip from the capital for serious gardeners and off-the-beaten-path finders. Some nine feet of rain fall here annually, and the land and vegetation have evolved to flourish under these conditions, as have Bob and Jo Munro. With great horticultural skill and intelligence, they plant accordingly, boldly using indigenous plants and unusual exotics from the Himalayas, North America, and Europe. Where possible, Jo has planted broad perennial borders (both Munros are English born, and styles of their native land do appear), and Bob has built bridges and ponds and is completing a fern walk through a section of their 40 acres of unspoiled bush. The Munros have also placed copper sentinels, stone tables and chairs, and large ceramic vessels throughout the garden—pieces that they created in their other lives as non-horticultural artists. These are every bit as intriguing as the garden itself.

There are two approaches to the garden, both on Akatarawa Road an hour north of Wellington: from the east, follow Highway 2 from the city to Upper Hutt, where Akatarawa Road climbs into the valley to Moss Green. There are wonderful old trestle bridges as you near the garden. From the west, take Akatarawa Road from Highway 1 in Waikanae. You'll climb it over the pass, dropping down to the garden from above. This approach is not for the faint of heart, as it may be the narrowest, most precipitous road on North Island. Whichever way you come, the reward of a trip to Moss Green is a unique garden in a natural setting where the gardeners after more than 25 years are still amazed by so many shades of green. Visitors are welcome to picnic on the grounds. ⊠ *2420 Akatarawa Rd., Upper Hutt,* ☏ *04/526–7531,* FAX *04/526–7507.* 🖼 *$5.* ☉ *Aug.–May, Wed.–Mon. 10–5; June and July, by appointment.*

Otari Native Botanic Garden. Anyone with even the slightest interest in native New Zealand flora should pick up picnic provisions and spend an afternoon at Otari, just outside the city. Devoted to gathering and preserving indigenous plants, Otari's collection is the largest of its kind. With clearly marked bush walks and landscape demonstration gardens, it aims to educate and thereby ensure the survival of New Zealand's unique and diverse plant life. While in the garden, you'll learn to dissect the forest, from the various *blechnum* ferns underfoot to the tallest emerent trees towering overhead—the rimu, kahikatea (ka-hee-ka-tee-ah), and northern rata—and everything in between. Look and listen for the native birds that flock to this haven: the bellbird (korimako), gray duck (parera), fantail (piwakawaka), New Zealand wood pigeon (kereru), silvereye (tauhou), and tui, among others. Cultivated borders highlight everything from Wellington Coast plants to hebe cultivars to grasses and alpine rock garden plants. ⊠ *Wilton Rd., Wilton; take the #14 Wilton bus from downtown (20 mins.).* ☎ *04/475–3245.* ⊙ *Daily dawn–dusk.*

Southward Museum. This is in fact the largest collection of vintage and veteran cars in the Southern Hemisphere, with more than 250 vehicles: among them Bugattis, a Hispano-Suiza, one of only 17 Davis three-wheelers ever made, a De Lorean, a gull-wing 1955 Mercedes 300SL, gangster Micky Cohen's armor-plated 1950 Cadillac, and another Cadillac once owned by Marlene Dietrich. The motorcycle collection, which has a number of early Harley-Davidsons and Indians, a Brough Superior, and a Vincent V-twin, is almost as impressive. The museum is just off Highway 1, about a 45-minute drive north of Wellington. ⊠ *Otaihanga Rd., Paraparaumu,* ☎ *04/297–1221.* ⊠ *$4.* ⊙ *Daily 9–4:30.*

Dining

Courtenay Place is Wellington's restaurant row. Apart from the restaurants mentioned below, Turkish, Indian, French, and Italian restaurants jostle for attention, along with several bar-brasseries that make this a favorite nightspot for the city's sophisticates.

City Center

$$$$ ✕ **Le Petit Lyon.** The anonymous brick wall at the front hides what many
★ regard as the finest epicurean restaurant in the country. Classical French cuisine is presented with silver, crystal, plush surroundings, and solicitous service. The *menu dégustation* (tasting menu), at $125 per person including wine, is recommended if you would like to indulge completely. ⊠ *8 Courtenay Pl.,* ☎ *04/364–9402. Reservations essential. Jacket required. AE, DC, MC, V. Closed Sun. No lunch Sat.*

$$ ✕ **Brasserie Flipp.** Highly fashionable with Wellington's sophisticates,
★ the innovative international menu makes this restaurant a good choice for lunch or dinner. Main courses include smoked pork kassler sausage with red cabbage, grilled scallops with wild rice and Thai spices, and grilled lamb steak with a green pea purée. The decor is smart and stylish: polished timber floors, dazzling white napery, and subdued lighting. The wine list has a good selection of New Zealand wine and token bottles from just about everywhere else. ⊠ *RSA Bldg., 103 Ghuznee St., Wellington,* ☎ *04/385–9493. AE, DC, MC, V.*

$$ ✕ **Café Paradiso.** A place to see and be seen, this corner site in Courtney Place has long been a favorite of the in-crowd. French, American, and Pacific Rim influences are evident. Main courses include roast duck stuffed with wild mushroom risotto, and beef (yes) Wellington. Large windows look out into the street. ⊠ *20 Courtenay Pl.,* ☎ *04/384–2675. AE, DC, MC, V. No lunch weekends.*

$$ ✕ **Chevy's.** With a name like that and a flashing neon cowboy out front, the burgers, nachos, chicken wings, BLTs, and barbecue spareribs come as little surprise. The salads are crisp, the fries are crunchy, the service is prompt, the quasi-American decor is bright and attractive, and the restaurant stays open until at least 10:30. ⊠ *97 Dixon St., Wellington,* ☎ *04/384–2724. AE, DC, MC, V. BYOB.*

$$ ✕ **Dockside.** Part of the redeveloped warehouse complex on the waterfront, this new, informal restaurant has a nautical theme, a reasonably priced menu, and a choice of casual dining in either the bar or the upstairs restaurant. *Moules marinières* (mussels with pasta in a tomato and chili sauce), salad *niçoise,* smoked chicken salad, and a salad of warm vegetables and cervena venison appear on a menu that is particularly strong on seafood. ⊠ *Shed 3, Queens Wharf, Jervois Quay,* ☎ *04/499–9900. AE, DC, MC, V.*

$$ ✕ **Paris.** Popular with the public servant set, who make up a significant part of the Wellington population, this restaurant has a café–bar on the ground floor that spills out into the sidewalk and a restaurant upstairs. Dishes include avocado and crayfish garnished with ginger and pink grapefruit, and peppered char-grilled wild venison with caramelized shallots and horseradish cream. ✉ *132 Lambton Quay,* ☎ *04/472–4732. AE, DC, MC, V.*

$ ✕ **Dixon Street Gourmet Deli.** This city-center delicatessen stocks a fine
★ range of taste treats. There are home-baked breads and bagels, an international choice of meats, cheeses, pickles, and preserves, plus local smoked fish and oysters—everything you need for a superior picnic. ✉ *45–47 Dixon St.,* ☎ *04/384–2436. MC, V.*

$ ✕ **The Lido.** This popular, bustling corner café across from the tourist information center is a pleasant, funky, place that turns out inspired savory and sweet muffins, pasta dishes, vegetarian food, and yummy desserts—at breakfast, lunch, and dinner (until 10). The café remains open past midnight; and you can sit indoors or out when weather permits. ✉ *Victoria and Wakefield Sts.,* ☎ *04/499–6666. Reservations not accepted. No credit cards.*

Wellington Suburbs

$$$ ✕ **Tinakori Bistro.** Set in a miniature Thorndon shopfront, this popular bistro has a modern, French-influenced menu and a long-standing reputation for reliability. Main courses include char-grilled Scotch fillet with sour cream and horseradish dressing, and grilled cervena venison medallions with a blackberry and port sauce. ✉ *328 Tinakori Rd., Thorndon,* ☎ *04/499–0567. AE, MC, V. BYOB. Closed Sun. No lunch Sat.*

Lodging

Lodging in Wellington is peculiarly polarized, with elegant and expensive hotels on one end, homestays on the other, and nothing in between.

City Center

$$$$ 🏨 **Parkroyal Wellington.** If you are looking for the luxury, facilities,
★ and glamour that only a large international hotel can deliver, this is the best in town—possibly the best in the country. Guest rooms are decorated in sea greens and blues with blond wood furnishings, and bathrooms are comfortably appointed. The bureau rooms, which have a desk and a queen-size bed instead of two doubles, are tailored especially for traveling executives. Request a room with ocean views. Service by the young staff is excellent throughout the hotel. The Parkroyal is in the city center, within walking distance of shops, restaurants, and the central business district. The Panama Street Brasserie is a favorite breakfast spot for the city's power brokers, and the refined upstairs **Kimble Bent's** restaurant is superb. ✉ *Featherston and Grey Sts., Wellington,* ☎ *04/72–2722,* ℻ *04/472–4724. 232 rooms with bath. 2 restaurants, 2 bars, indoor pool, pool, sauna, exercise room, laundry. AE, DC, MC, V.*

$ 🏨 **Halswell Lodge.** Rooms at this hotel on the edge of the city center are compact and functional, but each has en-suite facilities and a reasonable standard of comfort. The surroundings offer a wide choice of restaurants. Rooms at the front are affected by street noise during the daytime. ✉ *21 Kent Terr., Wellington,* ☎ *04/385–0196,* ℻ *04/385–0503. 19 rooms with bath. AE, DC, MC, V.*

$ 🏨 **Homestay.** A five-minute drive from the city center, this timber house offers comfort, style, and good value for those looking for homestay accommodations. The ground-level guest room is rather small and does not have an en-suite bathroom, but the apartment on the floor below has a separate kitchen, bathroom, lounge, and room for four. Throughout, the owners (one is an Austrian, one a New Zealander) have decorated their house simply but stylishly with bunches of dried wildflowers, rustic wooden furniture, Oriental rugs, and polished timber floors. The house has marvelous views across timber houses and gardens that spill down to the harbor in the distance. Rates include breakfast. ⊠ *33 Mortimer Terr., ☎ 04/385–3667. 1 room, 1 apartment with bath. No credit cards.*

Wellington Suburbs

$ 🏠 **Tinakori Lodge.** Situated in a historic suburb overlooking the city, this lodge offers atmospheric bed-and-breakfast accommodations in tranquil surroundings at a reasonable price. The rooms, which can sleep up to three, are simply furnished but comfortable. The city center is a 10-minute walk away, and there are several restaurants in the vicinity. The owners are extremely friendly and helpful. Children are accommodated by arrangement. Rates include breakfast. ⊠ *182 Tinakori Rd., Thorndon, ☎ 04/473–3478, FAX 04/472–5554. 10 rooms share 3 baths. AE, DC, MC, V.*

Nightlife and the Arts

For a current listing of cultural events in Wellington, check the *Capital Times, City Voice,* or *Wellington Evening Post.*

The Arts

Wellington is the home of the **New Zealand Ballet Company** and the **New Zealand Symphony Orchestra.** The main venues for the performing arts are the **Michael Fowler Centre** and **Town Hall** (⊠ Civic Sq., Wakefield St., ☎ 04/801–4242) for theater and music both classical and contemporary, and the **St. James Theatre** (⊠ Manners St.) and the **State Opera House** (⊠ Courtenay Pl.) for drama, ballet, and opera. Tiketek (☎ 04/385–0832) sells tickets for local performances.

The **Downstage Theatre** holds frequent performances of stage classics. ⊠ *Hannah Playhouse, Courtenay Pl. and Cambridge Terr., ☎ 04/384–9639.*

Nightlife

The most vigorous sign of life after dark in Wellington is found in bars. On the ground floor of the Parkroyal Hotel at the corner of Grey and Featherstone streets, the **Arizona Bar** (☎ 04/495–7867) is packed on Friday and Saturday nights, as is the nearby **Malthouse** at 47 Willis Street (☎ 04/499–4355). The best place to catch rock music is **Bar Bodega** (⊠ 286 Willis St., ☎ 04/384–8212), or **St John's Bar** at 5–9 Cable Street (☎ 04/384–3700). However, the main action is on Courtenay Place, where the bar scene operates at fever pitch on Friday and Saturday nights.

Wellington A to Z

Arriving and Departing

BY BUS

InterCity buses (☎ 04/495–2443) arrive and depart from Wellington Railway Station. The terminal for **Newmans** buses (☎ 04/499–3261) is the InterIslander Ferry Terminal, 3 kilometers (2 miles) from the city center.

BY CAR

The main access to the city is via the Wellington Urban Motorway, an extension of National Highway 1, which links the city center with all towns and cities to the north.

The **InterIsland Line** (☎ 0800/802–802) operates vehicle and passenger ferries between Wellington and Picton, at the northern tip of South Island. The one-way adult fare is $38 during school holidays, $30 at other times. Children ages 4–14 who are with their parents and in a vehicle travel free of charge; otherwise, they pay half price. The fare for a medium-size sedan is $150 during school holidays, $114 at other times. The crossing takes about three hours and can be very rough, although the slightly more expensive fast ferry *The Lynx* does the journey in half the time when it runs from November until April. There are at least two departures in each direction every day, and bookings should be made in advance, particularly during holiday periods. The ferry terminal is about 3 kilometers (2 miles) from the city. A free bus leaves Platform 9 at the Wellington Railway Station for the ferry terminal 35 minutes before sailings.

BY PLANE

Wellington International Airport lies about 8 kilometers (5 miles) from the city. **Super Shuttle** (☎ 04/387–8787) operates a 10-seater bus between the airport and any address in the city ($8 for one person, $10 for two). The bus meets all incoming flights; tickets are available from the driver.

BY TRAIN

The **Wellington Railway Station** (☎ 04/498–3000) is on Bunny Street, 1½ kilometers (½ mile) from the city center.

Getting Around
BY BICYCLE

If the sun is shining and the wind is still, a bicycle is an ideal way to explore the city and its surrounding bays. **Penny Farthing Cycles** (✉ 89 Courtenay Pl., ☎ 04/385–2772) hires out mountain bikes for $25 per day or $140 per week, including helmet.

BY BUS

Wellington's public bus network is known as **Ridewell.** For trips around the inner city, the fare is $1 for adults and 50¢ for children 4–14. **Daytripper** tickets ($5), allowing unlimited travel for one adult and two children, are available from bus drivers after 9 AM. For maps and timetables, contact the information center (✉ 142–146 Wakefield St., ☎ 04/801–7000).

Contacts and Resources
EMBASSIES AND HIGH COMMISSIONS

Australian High Commission. ✉ *72–78 Hobson St., Thorndon,* ☎ *04/473–6411.* ⊙ *Weekdays 8:45–12:15.*

British High Commission. ✉ *44 Hill St.,* ☎ *04/472–6049.* ⊙ *Weekdays 9:30–noon and 2–3:30.*

Canadian High Commission. ✉ *61 Molesworth St., Thorndon,* ☎ *04/473–9577.* ⊙ *Weekdays 8:30–4:30.*

United States Embassy. ✉ *29 Fitzherbert Terr., Thorndon,* ☎ *04/472–2068.* ⊙ *Weekdays 10–noon and 2–4.*

GUIDED TOURS

Harbour Capital Bus Tours' Coastline Tour takes in attractions in the city center as well as along the Miramar Peninsula to the east. The 2¾-hour tour departs at 1:30 PM from the Visitor Information Centre at the corner of Victoria and Wakefield streets. ☎ *04/499–1282.* ☜ *$21.*

Trust Bank Ferry, a commuter service between the city and Days Bay, on the eastern side of Port Nicholson, is one of the best-value tours in the city. Weekdays the catamaran departs from Queens Wharf at 7:10, 8:20, noon, 2, 4:15, and 5:30; weekends, at 10:30, noon, 2, and 4:15. The trip takes about 25 minutes. ⊠ *Queens Wharf,* ☎ *04/499–1273.* ▭ *Round-trip $13.*

Wally Hammond, a tour operator with a great anecdotal knowledge and a fund of stories about the city, offers a 2½-hour minibus tour of the city and Marine Drive. This can be combined with a half-day Kapiti Coast Tour, during which Southward Car Museum is visited. Tours depart from Travel World, Mercer and Victoria streets, at 10 and 2. Passengers can be picked up at their city hotels at no extra cost. ☎ *04/472–0869.* ▭ *City tour $20, combined tour $70.*

EMERGENCIES

Dial 111 for **fire, police,** or **ambulance** services.

Wellington Hospital. ⊠ *Riddiford St., Newtown,* ☎ *04/385–5999.*

The After-Hours Pharmacy. ⊠ *17 Adelaide Rd., Newtown,* ☎ *04/385–8810.* ⊙ *Weekdays 5 AM–11 PM, Sat. 9 AM–11 PM, Sun. 10–10.*

TRAVEL AGENCIES

American Express Travel Service. ⊠ *203 Lambton Quay,* ☎ *04/473–1221.*

Thomas Cook. ⊠ *108 Lambton Quay,* ☎ *04/473–5167.*

VISITOR INFORMATION

Wellington Visitor Information Centre. ⊠ *Civic Administration Bldg., Victoria and Wakefield Sts.,* ☎ *04/801–4000.* ⊙ *Daily 8:30–5:30.*

THE WAIRARAPA

Wellington residents call the Rimutaka Range to the north of the city "the Hill," and for years it has been both a physical and psychological barrier that has allowed the Wairarapa region to develop at its own pace, in its own style. The hill has also kept tour buses away, and as a result landscapes such as the Pinnacles—cliff faces carved by the wind into shapes reminiscent of a cathedral—are uncrowded and easy to reach. There are great hikes and walks in the area. Times are changing quickly, however. An expanding wine trail in the southern Wairarapa is drawing visitors in increasing numbers, as well as city dwellers who want to move into the region for a lifestyle change. Meanwhile, the Wairarapa is still a place to discover—yet another delightful corner of New Zealand that can make you agonize over where to spend your time in the countryside.

Martinborough

70 km (44 mi) north of Wellington.

Martinborough is the hub of the Wairarapa's wine industry, and as a result this small town is attracting interest from developers keen to cash in on growing tourist numbers. So far changes have been tasteful, with people refurbishing historic places and opening their homes as B&Bs. The town gets its name from founder John Martin, who planned the streets in a Union Jack pattern stretching out from a square that remains the center of activity. Most restaurants and shops are on or close to the square.

Local records indicate that grapes have been raised in the region since the turn of the century. The present industry only dates back to 1979, and the popularity of **Martinborough wine** has grown tremendously since the mid- to late 1980s. That said, many local producers have small outputs, which means that some local varieties can be scarce everywhere but here, and prices tend to be higher than in other New Zealand wine regions. A number of the wineries are within a 10-minute walk of town, and there is a wine-trail horse-carriage tour as well. As in Hawke's Bay, red grape varieties seem to have the best go in the area's soil, with pinot noir being the most exceptional. Keep in mind that from year to year, any given winery's varieties may change depending on grape quality. Here is a short list of the best of the region's wineries:

Dry River (⌨ Puruatanga Rd., ☎ 06/306–9388) is possibly the country's hottest producer, whose ultra-selectively produced vintages sell out immediately on release. Bringing home a bottle of its Gewürztraminer or Pinot Noir would be a coup. Call ahead for an appointment. **Ata Rangi Vineyard** (⌨ Puruatanga Rd., ☎ 06/306–9570) makes exceptional Chardonnay, Pinot Noir, and Célèbre (a cabernet-merlot-shiraz blend), again in small quantities. Tastings are held October–April, daily 11–5. **Martinborough Vineyard** (⌨ Princess St., ☎ 06/306–9955), open daily 11–5, is a larger but equally superior regional winery—actually the first to convince the world of the Wairarapa's pinot noir potential. Martinborough's Chardonnay is also very fine. **Palliser Estate** (⌨ Kitchener St., ☎ 06/306–9019) has come out with some of the best local whites. Its straight Sauvignon Blanc and Late-Harvest Riesling are distinguished wines. The winery is open daily 10–6.

OFF THE BEATEN PATH	For an excursion that definitely isn't in tourist brochures, visit **Ruakoko-patuna Glow Worm Caves.** You'll walk right through a cave following a freshwater stream, so expect to get wet feet and take a torch (flashlight). The glowworm display here is not quite as impressive as the one at Waitomo in the King Country, but the sense of adventure is much greater—nobody will tell you to duck when you're approaching a low-hanging rock, so be careful. Once you have found a cluster of glowworms, turn your torch off for the best display, then switch it on again to walk as you walk deeper into the cave. And keep in mind that as you stay in the cave longer, your eyes will adjust to the darkness, allowing you to see more lights. Take Lake Ferry Road south from Martinborough 7 kilometers (4 miles), turn left on Dyerville Road and drive another 8 kilometers to a sign for the caves. Entrance is free, and it is best to seek permission before you go. ☎ 06/306–9393.

★ The **Putangirua Pinnacles Scenic Reserve** near the bottom of North Island at Cape Palliser is protected from the hordes by its relative isolation. The big attractions are the spectacular rocks, which have been carved in the cliffs along a stony riverbank by badlands-type erosion. An hour-long walk from the carpark will take you to incredible views. If you're feeling adventurous, there is a bushwalk involving some steep climbs and wonderful vistas of the coast, as far off as South Island on a clear day. The Pinnacles are an hour's drive from Martinborough on good roads. Take Lake Ferry Road south out of town for 25 kilometers (16 miles), turn left at the sign for Cape Palliser and drive 15 kilometers (9 miles) to Te Kopi, from which signs point to the reserve.

Dining and Lodging

$$$ ✕🏨 **Martinborough Hotel.** This restored 1890s hotel is right in Martinborough's town square. The attractive Martinborough Bistrot on site has a garden bar serving local wine, where you can enjoy a game of petanque with other guests while sipping a glass of chardonnay. At dinner, duck terrine with mango and mint salsa or crab cakes with spicy gazpacho sauce make good starters, after which *moules à la marinière*, green-lipped mussels in herbed white wine and cream

sauce, or cervena venison with garlic bean purée and red wine sauce sound very appealing. Rooms have historic atmosphere, each decorated uniquely with area rugs and a mix of antique and contemporary furnishings, such as four-poster beds and writing tables. Some bathrooms have claw-footed tubs, and upstairs rooms open onto a veranda. Room rates include a full country breakfast. ⊠ *33 Strassbourg St.,* ☏ *06/306–9350. 10 rooms with bath. Restaurant, 2 bars. AE, DC, MC, V.*

Masterton

40 km (25 mi) north of Martinborough, 230 km (144 mi) south of Napier.

Masterton is Wairarapa's major population center, but you will find little of interest beyond its suitability as an exploring base. If you're traveling with children, **Queen Elizabeth Park** has a large playground, a rather outdated aviary, mini golf, a minature railway, and a small aquarium.

There are enjoyable bushwalks in beautiful forests laced with streams at **Tararua National Park,** which also has picnic facilities. The Mount Holdsworth area at the east end of the park is particularly popular for tramping. To get there, turn off State Highway 2 onto Norfolk Road, 2 kilometers (1½ miles) south of Masterton.

For nature lovers, **Mount Bruce National Wildlife Centre** is a unique, well-managed wildlife park. The center provides rare glimpses of New Zealand's endangered species, including the takahe, a flightless bird thought to be extinct until it was rediscovered in 1948. The Campbell Island teal, shore plover, saddleback, stitchbird, kokako, and kiwi are all remarkable species, and you can take a look at New Zealand's living dinosaur, the tuatara. There are also trails to walk through native bush, and a tearoom. ⊠ *State Hwy. 2, 30 km (19 mi) north of Masterton,* ☏ *06/375–8004.* 🎫 *$4.* ☉ *Daily 9:30–4. Closed Dec. 25.*

Dining and Lodging

$$$ ✕🏨 **Solway Park Travelodge.** Masterton's largest hotel, the Travelodge is popular with both conference groups and families because of the range of on-site extras, such as tennis and squash facilities, children's play equipment, and indoor games. Rooms are standard but comfortable. There is a choice of restaurants, and the regular buffet meal provides reliable New Zealand–style fare. ⊠ *High St. S, Masterton,* ☏ *06/377–5129,* 🅵🅰🅇 *06/378–2913. 102 hotel rooms, 5 motel units. 2 restaurants, bar, pool. AE, DC, MC, V.*

Wairarapa A to Z

Arriving and Departing

BY CAR

Having a car will allow you the most flexibility in the Wairarapa. State Highway 2 runs through the region from north and south, between Napier and Wellington. From Wellington, you'll drive through Upper Hutt, over the Rimutaka range, then into the gateway town of Featherston. Highway 53 will take you to Martinborough; Masterton is farther north along State Highway 2. The journey from Wellington to Martinborough takes one-and-a-half hours; Masterton is another half hour. From Napier, Masterton is about three hours.

Contacts and Resources

GUIDED TOURS

The Horse and Carriage Establishment runs tours around the vineyards. The company also has twilight carriage drives, mystery tours, and horse and carriage hire for any specific journey. ⊠ *Martinborough,* ☎ *025/477–852.*

VISITOR INFORMATION

Tourism Wairarapa. ⊠ *5 Dixon St., Masterton,* ☎ *06/378–7373,* FAX *06/378–7042.* ☉ *Weekdays 8:30—5:30, weekends 9–4.*

4 Upper South Island

Natural wonders never cease—not on South Island. Nor do the opportunities for adventure: sea kayaking, glacier hiking, trekking, fishing, mountain biking, rafting, and rock climbing. If you'd rather have an easier feast for your senses, fly over brilliant glaciers and snowy peaks, watch whales from on deck, and taste some of Marlborough's delicious wine. Add New Zealand hospitality to that and you can't go wrong.

NORTH AND SOUTH ISLANDS are narrowly separated by Cook Strait, yet the difference between them is far greater than the distance suggests. Whether you first glimpse South Island from the deck of a ferry as it noses through the rocky entrance to Marlborough Sounds or through the window of a plane bound for Christchurch, the immediate impression is that the landscape has turned feral: The mellow, green beauty of North Island has given way to jagged snowcapped mountains and rivers that charge down from the heights and sprawl across vast, rocky shingle beds. South Island has been carved by ice and water, a process still rapidly occurring. Locals will tell you that you haven't seen rain until you've been drenched by a storm on the West Coast—one of the wettest places on earth, where annual precipitation is ambitiously measured in meters.

The top half of South Island is a fair introduction to the contrasts of New Zealand's less-populated island. The Marlborough province occupies the northeast corner, where the inlets of Marlborough Sounds flow around verdant peninsulas and sandy coves. Inland from the sounds is the country's newest land under vine, where since the mid-70s a burgeoning wine culture has developed. An abundance of other fruit is grown in the area as well. Marlborough is relatively dry, beautifully sunny, and in summer the inland plains look something like the American West, with mountains rising out of grassy flats. Throughout upper South Island, you'll notice commercial foresting of the hills—Californian *pinus radiata* (monterey pine) mature rapidly in New Zealand soil. Their 25-year harvest cycle is one of the shortest in the world, a fact duly noted by Japanese lumber concerns.

The northwest corner of the island, the Nelson Lakes province, is a sporting paradise with a mild climate that allows a year-round array of outdoor activities. Sun-drenched Nelson is the area's gateway, a comfortable town with wholesome restaurants, an interesting flock of local craftspeople, and an abundance of their wares. To the west of the city, Abel Tasman National Park, like the Marlborough Sounds across the island, is ringed with spectacular coastal waters—of a nearly indescribable blue—studded with rock outcrops guarding coves and sands that are sea-kayakers', trekkers', beachcombers', and sunbathers' dreams.

After the gentler climate of Marlborough and Nelson, the wild grandeur of the West Coast comes as a surprise. This is Mother Nature with hair down, flaying the coastline with huge seas and drenching rains and littering its beaches with bleached driftwood sculpture. When it rains you'll feel like you're inside a fish bowl; then the sun bursts out you might swear you're in paradise. It is a country that has created a special breed of people, and the rough-hewn and powerfully independent locals—known to the rest of the country as coasters—occupy a special place in New Zealand folklore.

These three regions, which ring the northern and western coasts of South Island, offer an immense variety of scenery, from the siren seascapes of Marlborough Sounds and rocky Kaikoura, to the mellow river valleys of the north coast, to the West Coast's colliding rain forests and glaciers, where the Southern Alps soar to 12,000 feet within 32 kilometers (20 miles) of the shore.

Note: For more information on bicycling, fishing, hiking, and sea-kayaking in uppper South Island, *see* Chapter 6.

Pleasures and Pastimes

Dining

For seafood, game, and fresh fruit and vegetables, the top of the South Island is hard to beat. In Marlborough, dine at at least one winery restaurant. There is no better place to ensure that your meal suits what you're drinking. Salmon is a particular delicacy from the Marlborough Sounds. You'll find it on menus at all meals. In Kaikoura, try crayfish (clawless lobster). The region is in fact named after the delicacy, and you'll find it in restaurants or in makeshift caravans and roadside sheds. Restaurants and cafés around the glaciers can be quick to close their doors at night. Be there by 8:30 or you may go hungry.

Lodging

North Islanders might disagree, but you may find New Zealand's friendliest people in the rural areas of South Island. And the best way to get to know them is to stay with them. Bed and breakfasts, farmstays, and homestays, all a variation on the same theme, can be found throughout upper South Island in some spectacular coastal or mountain settings. Your hosts will feed you great breakfasts and help with advice on where to eat and what to do locally. Other choices include luxury lodges and standard, inexpensive motel rooms—the latter of which there are plenty.

Mountains and Glaciers

South Island is a land of mountains. A massive mountain chain, the Southern Alps, virtually slices the island lengthwise, and many outlying ranges spring up farther north. Most of the mountains are easily accessible. You can walk on and around them, ski, or catch a helicopter to land on a glacier and tramp around. Much of the skiing in the upper half of the South Island is reasonably challenging for intermediate skiers—the more advanced should look farther south.

Trekking and climbing is as challenging as you care to make it. Department of Conservation tracks and huts are spread around the region, and details on hundreds of hikes can be obtained from department offices or information centers. If you just want to take a casual, scenic walk, the opportunities are endless. In many cases, you can just pull over at the side of the road and begin a signposted walk taking anything from five minutes to a few hours.

Wilderness and Wildlife

South Island's West Coast has a rugged beauty that can be inviting in one instance and almost threatening the next. You can wake up to the sun shining off of tall, snowcapped mountains, then a couple of hours later the mist and rain can swirl around the peaks and give them an entirely different complexion. The changing conditions send out a stark warning for anyone wishing to penetrate this wilderness. However, if you take care there is no reason not to get into some of the world's most dramatic mountain, bush, and coastal scenery.

The West Coast is the habitat for some very interesting creatures. South by Lake Moeraki, fiordland crested penguins and seals are abundant, and birdlife up and down the coast is fascinating. On the other side of the island, the Kaikoura Coast is still a sleepy and uncrowded region where you can get as close to whales, dolphins, and seals as possible in their environment.

Wine

In a little over 20 years, Marlborough has made quite a reputation for itself. Because of the region's unique growing conditions, grapes come off of the vines bursting with flavor. It's an exciting feistiness that many

American connoisseurs consider too unbridled—but the wine is delicious, and you should seriously consider bringing a few bottles back with you that you won't be able to buy at your local vintner. If you follow the wine route, focus on a few vineyards rather than rushing from one to another.

Exploring Upper South Island

Most people come to Marlborough and Nelson on the ferry to Picton, the northern entrance to South Island. From here the choices open up before you. In four days you can see much of the northernmost part of the island. To undertake a walk on the Queen Charlotte or the Abel Tasman tracks, you'll need more time. To see the West Coast, three days is a bare minimum—it takes a half-day or more just to get there.

Great Itineraries

Numbers in the text correspond to numbers in the margin and on the Upper South Island map.

IF YOU HAVE 2 DAYS

Spend a day touring the wineries in and around ☒ **Blenheim** ③. On the second day head down to ☒ **Kaikoura** ④, stopping at the **Awatare Valley Gardens** or **Winterhome** on the way to crayfish town before continuing south to Christchurch. You could alternatively head straight from the ferry to ☒ **Nelson** ⑤, taking the first day in town and the second around Nelson before moving to your next area.

IF YOU HAVE 4 DAYS

Big decisions: See the top of the island—the wineries of ☒ **Blenheim** ③, relaxing ☒ **Nelson** ⑤, the beautiful beaches and forests of ☒ **Abel Tasman National Park** ⑩, perhaps all four days hiking one of Abel Tasman's tracks or the **Queen Charlotte Walkway** in the Marlborough Sounds—or head straight for the coastal rock formations, glaciers, and wildlife of the **West Coast.** This is the kind of either/or conundrum that makes trip planning for South Island difficult.

IF YOU HAVE 7 DAYS

You *could* try to cover three of the major areas covered in this chapter—Marlborough, Nelson, and the West Coast, or Marlborough, Nelson, and Kaikoura, but being selective and allowing at least three days each for two areas is a better plan. Spend a day or two at the wineries, a day or two on the Marlborough Sounds sea-kayaking or walking, then head to ☒ **Nelson** ⑤ or the **West Coast.** You could, alternatively, spend the first three days in and around Nelson, looking at arts and crafts, tasting wine, and taking in ☒ **Abel Tasman National Park** ⑩ and **Golden Bay** ⑪, then head to the West Coast. On the way down, stop at the town of Punakaiki for **Pancake Rocks** ⑫. You could overnight at ☒ **Greymouth** ⑬ or ☒ **Hokitika** ⑮ before continuing to Westland National Park to explore ☒ **Franz Josef Glacier** ⑯ or ☒ **Fox Glacier** ⑰. The wildlife around ☒ **Lake Moeraki** ⑲, on the other hand, may be what lures you to the West Coast, in which case you should take as many days there as you'd like. From there, leave the West Coast by heading south to Haast, which also has great beaches, and onto Wanaka or Queenstown via the Haast Pass.

When to Tour Upper South Island

Nelson and Marlborough are pleasant year-round, but beach activities are best December to mid-April. December to early February is the busiest time on walking tracks, with New Zealanders setting out on their holidays. Snow covers the mountains June through October, which is a beautiful sight from seaside Kaikoura. The pleasures of win-

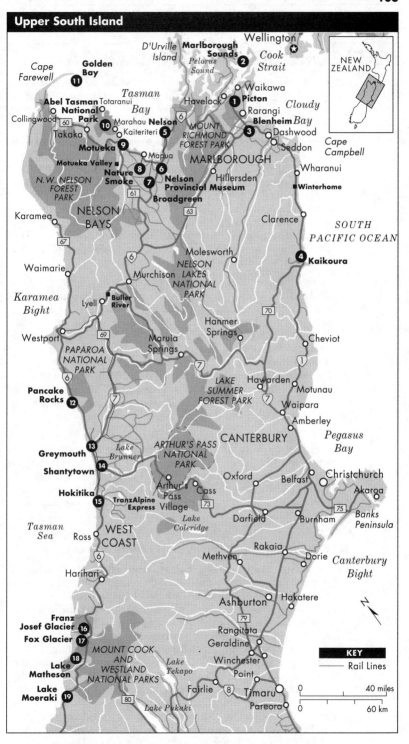

Upper South Island

Wellington

Cook Strait

D'Urville Island

Marlborough Sounds ②

Pelorus Sound

Tasman Bay

Cape Farewell

Golden Bay ⑪

Abel Tasman National Park

Totaranui

Collingwood

Takaka

60

⑩ Marahau
Kaiteriteri

Nelson ⑤

Motueka ⑨

Mapua

Motueka Valley ■

Nature Smoke ⑧ ⑥

⑦

N.W. NELSON FOREST PARK

Nelson Provincial Museum

Broadgreen

61

Karamea

NELSON BAYS

67

Waimarie

Karamea Bight

Lyell ■ Buller River

Westport

69

PAPAROA NATIONAL PARK

6

Pancake Rocks ⑫

Greymouth ⑬

Lake Brunner

Shantytown ⑭

Hokitika ⑮

TranzAlpine Express

Tasman Sea

Ross

WEST COAST

6

Harihari

Franz Josef Glacier ⑯

Fox Glacier ⑰

Lake Matheson ⑱

MOUNT COOK AND WESTLAND NATIONAL PARKS

Lake Moeraki ⑲

80

Lake Pukaki

Waikawa

Havelock

Picton ①

Rarangi

Blenheim ③

Dashwood

Seddon

MOUNT RICHMOND FOREST PARK

MARLBOROUGH

Hillersden

Cloudy Bay

Cape Campbell

Wharanui

■ Winterhome

63

Clarence

Molesworth

NELSON LAKES NATIONAL PARK

Murchison

6

Hanmer Springs

Maruia Springs

7

LAKE SUMMER FOREST PARK

Hawarden

Motunau

7

Waipara

Amberley

ARTHUR'S PASS NATIONAL PARK

CANTERBURY

Oxford

Belfast

Arthur's Pass Village

Cass

73

Lake Coleridge

Darfield

Burnham

Rakaia

Methven

Dorie

Ashburton

Hakatere

79

Rangitata

Geraldine

Lake Tekapo

Winchester

Point

Fairlie

8

Timaru

Pareora

SOUTH PACIFIC OCEAN

Kaikoura ④

70

Cheviot

1

Pegasus Bay

Christchurch

Akaroa

75

Banks Peninsula

Canterbury Bight

NEW ZEALAND

KEY

— Rail Lines

0   40 miles

0   60 km

ter weather around the glaciers—clear skies and no snow at sea level—
are so far a well-kept local secret.

MARLBOROUGH AND KAIKOURA

By Stu Freeman
and Stephen
Wolf

The Marlborough Sounds were originally settled by seafaring Maori
people, who in their day kept to the coastal areas, living off the abundant fruits of the sea. It's no wonder that they didn't venture inland,
because these coastal areas are spectacular.

Captain James Cook met the Maori settlers around 1770, when he
stopped in the sounds to repair his ships and take on fresh provisions.
Whalers later set up shop in Queen Charlotte Sound, but it wasn't until
the 1840s that Pakeha (Europeans) came to the Wairau and Awatere
valleys around Blenheim. Thirty years later, the unwittingly prescient
Charles Empson and David Herd began planting red muscatel grapes
among local sheep and grain farms. Their modest viticultural torch was
rekindled in the next century by the Freeth family, and by the 1940s,
Marlborough wineries were producing constancia, port, sherry, and
Madeira most successfully.

At the same time, commercial wineries were growing up around Auckland and Hawke's Bay. But the volume of their grape production didn't
exactly meet their needs. In the mid-1970s, it occurred to one of the
founders of the North Island Montana company to plant vines in Marlborough to increase the overall supply of New Zealand grapes. The sizeable Penfolds, Corbans, and smaller vintners followed suit, and within
a decade today's major players—like Hunters, whose founder, Ernie
Hunter, almost singlehandedly launched the Marlborough name—had
established the region's international reputation. There are now 25 resident wineries, which is New Zealand's single largest area under vine,
and outside concerns source local grapes for their wines.

Down the coast from Blenheim, Kaikoura is another area that the Maori
settled, and, true to their seafaring heritage, they are active in today's
whale-watching interests. The town's name in fact spells its original
significance for the Maori—"to eat crayfish." These clean-tasting,
clawless lobsters are a delight, and there isn't a better reason to come
to Kaikoura than *kaikoura,* and to take in the refreshing ocean air.

Picton

➊ *29 km (18 mi) north of Blenheim, 110 km (69 mi) east of Nelson.*

➋ Picton is the base for cruising in the **Marlborough Sounds,** the labyrinth
of waterways that was formed when the rising sea invaded a series of
river valleys at the northern tip of the South Island. Backed by forested
hills that at times rise almost vertically from the water, the Sounds are
a wild, majestic place edged with tiny beaches and rocky coves and
studded with islands where such native wildlife as gannets and the primitive tuatara lizard have remained undisturbed by introduced species.
These waterways are the country's second favorite for boating after
the Bay of Islands, but for their isolation and rugged grandeur they
are in a class of their own. Much of the area is a national park, and it
has changed little since Captain Cook found refuge here in the 1770s.
There are rudimentary roads on the long fingers of land jutting into
the Sounds, but the most convenient access is invariably by water. One
of the best ways to discover the area is hitching a ride in Havelock aboard
the launch *Glenmore,* which delivers mail and supplies to outlying settlements scattered around Pelorus Sound (☞ Marlborough and Kaikoura A to Z, *below*).

If you want to get your feet on the ground in and around the Sounds, you can take any number of hikes on the **Queen Charlotte Walkway.** Starting northwest of Picton, the trail stretches 67 kilometers (42 miles) south to north, playing hide and seek with the sound along the way. Tramp through lush native forests filled with interesting birdlife and stop here and there for a swim or to pick up interesting shells on the shore. There are lodges and huts to stay in at a few points on the track, and boats can drop you off at various places for one- to four-day guided or unguided walks, so you can go it on your own or opt for a comfortable bunk-and-hot-shower trek. For information and bookings, contact the **Picton Information Centre** (⌧ The Station, Picton, ☎ 03/573–8838, ℻ 03/573–8858). ☞ Marlborough and Kaikoura A to Z, *below.*

Port Underwood Road is another unbelievably scenic road in a country full of unbelievably scenic roads. There are picnic areas north of Waikawa before you reach the eastern coastal bays, and a couple more near Rarangi. To reach Port Underwood Road, take Waikawa Road north out of Picton, continuing through the town of Waikawa, then turning south at Opihi Bay. You could also pick up the road driving north out of Rarangi.

Heading west out of Picton, **Queen Charlotte Drive** rises spectacularly along the edge of Queen Charlotte Sound. It cuts across the base of the peninsula that separates this from Pelorus Sound, then drops into a coastal plain before entering the town of Havelock. Beyond Havelock the road winds through forested river valleys before it rounds the eastern side of Tasman Bay and reaches Nelson. To reach the start of the drive from the InterIslander ferry terminal in Picton, turn right and follow the signs.

About a third of the way to Havelock, **Governor's Bay** is a gorgeous spot for a picnic, a stroll along the forested shore, or a swim in season. Watch for seabirds, and, if the the sun is dipping in and out of the clouds, the changes in the colors of the bay.

Blenheim

❸ *29 km (18 mi) south of Picton, 120 km (73 mi) southeast of Nelson, 129 km (80 mi) north of Kaikoura.*

Locals pronounce it *blennum,* and most people come to Blenheim for one reason—wine. Marlborough vies with the city of Nelson for the highest total sunshine hours in New Zealand, and this plentiful, yet not intense, sun affords local grapes a long, slow ripening period. That combined with gravelly soil and relatively low rainfall is the key to the audacious flavors of the area's grapes. Some call this abundance of flavor unbalanced, which is why New Zealand reds haven't seen much distribution in the States. Now it's your turn to judge.

In 1973, The Montana company sent two Californian wine authorities to investigate local grape-growing potential. Both were impressed with what they found, though they disagreed on whether the region was best for white or red varieties. It is an argument that persists, because although Marlborough has become best known for its sauvignon blancs and chardonnays, its reds are also beginning to find their place in the world.

While you're in the area, there is no reason to race around to all of the wineries here—if you do, chances are good that your tastebuds won't serve you very well by the time you get to the 17th tasting room. Those mentioned below are among the country's notables, but you won't go wrong if you stop at any of the vineyards around Blenheim. More than half of the wine bottled here is exported to the U.K. and Australia, so it's the rest of us who have the most to discover about all of what Marlborough produces.

The streets where most wineries are located are arranged more or less in a grid, which makes getting around relatively straightforward. Pick up a map of the Marlborough Wine Region at the **Blenheim Information Centre** (☎ 03/578–9904, ☒ 03/577–8084) on Main Street in the east end of town.

Hunter's Wines. As mentioned above, the marketing efforts of Ernie Hunter thrust Marlborough into the international spotlight, and Hunter's continues to be a leader. Tragically, he died in a car accident at the age of 37. Energetic Jane Hunter, his wife, took the reins and has masterfully shaped Hunter's reputation—which should be no surprise, since she has a long family history of winemaking. Varieties change from year to year depending on what grapes are outstanding, but you can expect consistently strong Sauvignon Blanc, tangy and delightfully herbal. Chardonnay will have very subtle oak flavors and intense fruit. There is usually an Estate White and an Estate Red, sometimes a vivacious Gewurztraminer, a cabernet or cabernet blend, maybe even a Rosé. The winery also has a worthy restaurant (☞ Dining, *below*). ✉ *Rapaura Rd., Blenheim,* ☎ *03/572–8489,* ☒ *03/572–8457.* ⊙ *Daily 10–4:30.*

Cloudy Bay Vineyards. From the very start, Kevin Judd has produced first-class sauvignon blanc and chardonnay. That was the intention of Australia's Cape Mentelle Vineyards when they got Cloudy Bay up and running in 1985. The winery's Sauvignon Blanc is one of New Zealand's best, with crisp, well-balanced fruit. Drink it young. Chardonnay is more complex and better suited to a few years in the cellar, and to drinking with more flavorful food—smoked salmon, for example—without being too oakey. The star, however, may be Cloudy Bay's Pelorus sparkling wine, a wonderfully creamy, savory, almost mushroom-tasting méthode champagnoise wine. Very intriguing. ✉ *Jackson's Rd., Blenheim,* ☎ *03/572–8914,* ☒ *03/572–8065.* ⊙ *Daily 10–4:30; tour by appointment.*

Corbans Marlborough Vineyard. The Stoneleigh name is the one to look for at Corbans; it is one of the best known names in stores overseas these days. So you may have already tasted Stoneleigh's Sauvignon Blanc at home, but it's likely that you haven't tried the Riesling, which is strikingly clear, full, and smooth. Corbans also produces a sparkling wine that you may want to try, especially to compare it with Cloudy Bay or Cellier Le Brun's efforts with the méthode champagnoise. ✉ *Jackson's Rd., Blenheim,* ☎ *03/572–8198,* ☒ *03/572–8199.* ⊙ *Daily 10–4:30; tour by appointment.*

Vavasour Wines. Another almost instant hit among Marlborough's mid-80s start-ups, the small, extremely conscientious winemaking operations at Vavasour produce sensitively balanced whites and reds. Based on the quality of a given year's harvest, grapes will be used either for reserve vintages available in limited quantities, among which the 1994 Pinot Noir is a fine example, or the medium price-range Dashwood label. Vavasour is in its own microclimate south of Blenheim, where the viticulturist and winemaker focus on the finesse of smaller grape yields. You won't taste as many varieties here, but what you taste will be interesting and very well crafted. ✉ *Redwood Pass Rd., Awatere Valley, 20 km (12 mi) south of Blenheim,* ☎ *03/575–7481,* ☒ *03/575–7240.* ⊙ *Oct.–Mar., daily 10–4; Apr.–Sept., Mon.–Sat. 10–4; tour by appointment.*

Awatere Valley Gardens. Spend an afternoon strolling in three delightful gardens a short drive south of Blenheim. All have splendid herbaceous borders, as well as their own individual characteristics. At **Alton Downs,** take in the results of Alistair and Gaye Elliot's love of old roses and their 200-foot oak walk. **Richmond Brook** has belonged to one family since 1848, so Yvonne Richmond's garden has many mighty trees, among them a magnificent sequoia standing next to the equally impressive homestead. A newly planted orchard with antique fruit trees is underplanted with a carpet of daffodils in spring. Carolyn and Joe Ferraby's **Barewood** has beautiful terraced borders blooming pink, blue, apricot, and white surrounding their century-old cottage. A sizeable potager filled with ornamental vegetables and herbs is hedged with hornbeam and pathed with old bricks. A 100-year-old cob house on the property was the original home of Mr. Ferraby's ancestors. ⊠ *Alton Downs, Molesworth Rd., north of the Awatare River, 5 km (3 mi) west of State Hwy. 1,* ☏ *03/575–7414.* ⊠ *Richmond Brook, Marama Rd., outside Seddon, 10 km (6 mi) west of State Hwy. 1,* ☏ *03/575–7506.* ⊠ *Barewood, Marama Rd., outside Seddon, 18 km (11 mi) west of State Hwy. 1,* ☏ *03/575–7432.* ☞ *$3 per person per garden.* ☉ *By appointment.*

Dining and Lodging

$$$ ✕ **d'Urville Wine Bar and Brasserie.** On the ground floor of Hotel d'Urville, in the old Public Trust Building, this restaurant serves everything from a cup of coffee to a delightful dinner. The setting is unusual and tasteful, and the food is great as well. Best of all are the Marlborough mussels steamed in white wine served with black bean chili. ⊠ *52 Queen St., Blenheim,* ☏ *03/577–9944,* FAX *03/577–9946. AE, DC, MC, V.*

$$ ✕ **Hunter's Vineyard Restaurant.** Dining at a vineyard is a great way
★ to appreciate just how seriously New Zealand winemakers consider food when creating their wine. Start with focaccia, perhaps, and a seafood trio of local salmon, mussels, and scallops with watercress sauce—good companions for sauvignon blanc or rosé—or salmon wrapped in phyllo pastry served with mustard-dill cream sauce—better with chardonnay. Local venison with wild berry sauce, beef fillet with poached scallops and marsala sauce, and grilled lamb rump served with bacon and a pumpkin mousse may tempt you to try Hunter's Cabernet-Merlot. You may find it hard to look past the frozen pecan chocolate cake when it comes to dessert. Sit at barbecue tables outside, or inside in more elegant surroundings. ⊠ *Raupara Rd., Blenheim,* ☏ *03/572–8803. AE, DC, MC, V.*

$ ✕ **Paddy Barry's Bar and Restaurant.** Locals come here for a chat and a beer, and the menu revolves largely around potato wedges. In other words, it's a good place to come down from traveler's stomach and local gourmandise. A plate of battered and fried seafood is very reasonable, a pleasure even alongside a well-poured Guinness. ⊠ *51 Scott St., Blenheim,* ☏ *03/578–7470. DC, MC, V.*

$ ✕ **Peppercorn's Delicatessen Café.** If you're looking for the ultimate Kiwi picnic lunch, stop here for a salmon pâté-avocado-sprouts club, a redcurrant jelly-roast pork-tomato sandwich on rye, and dessert treats like chocolate-mint slices or chocolate florentines topped with nuts and dried fruit. ⊠ *73 Queen St., Blenheim,* ☏ *03/577–8886.*

$$$$ ✕▦ **Timara Lodge.** Taking a relaxing stroll around the gardens or a
★ dip in the garden pool, rowing about the pond adjacent to the lodge, enjoying a drink inside in the library, or tasting some of the finest meals in the country along with appropriate, well-tended glasses of local wine in a dignified, paneled dining room—Timara Lodge may offer the most luxurious experience on South Island. Built in 1923 as a rural getaway, the lodge is a marvel of craftsmanship and the use of native

timber. Downstairs, beautifully constructed rooms and furnishings speak of the quiet elegance of times past. In rooms, bedsteads swollen with comfortable linens stand alongside interesting antiques. Deborah and Grant Baxter preside over the lodge, with Deborah turning out masterful dishes that focus on the unique freshness of local ingredients: fruits and greens, scallops (with roe in season), salmon, venison, and her own skillfully aged beef. Wine tours, trout fishing, sea-kayaking, golf, and skiing can be arranged for you. The per-person price includes breakfast and dinner. ⊠ *R.D. 2, Dog Point Rd., Blenheim,* ☎ *03/572–8276,* FAX *03/572–9191. 4 rooms. AE, MC, V.*

$$$$ 🏨 **Hotel d'Urville.** Every room is indeed unique in this modern bou-
  ★   tique hotel in the old Public Trust building. In the Raja Room, silk saris are draped over the main bed, a variety of brass ornaments, and a Javanese carved day bed. You could choose an African theme, take in the soft colors of the Angel Room, or have your visual senses tripped up in the Colour Room. One room matches the overall theme of the hotel, and is based on the exploits of Dumont d'Urville, who made voyages to the Pacific and the Antarctic in the 1820s and 1830s. In search of a suitable site for a French penal colony, he surveyed New Zealand and although beaten to the claiming of New Zealand for France by Britain he gave his name to the rugged island in the Tasman Sea to the north of Marlborough. The hotel is built around the Public Trust's original vault, which now serves as a public area for guests. ⊠ *52 Queen St., Blenheim,* ☎ *03/577–9945,* FAX *03/577–9946. 9 rooms, 3 with bath, 6 with shower only. Restaurant, bar. AE, DC, MC, V.*

Fishing

For information on stream fishing in the Nelson Lakes district and deep-sea fishing out of Picton, *see* Chapter 6.

En Route Susan Macfarlane is on the mark when she says that there is no other garden in New Zealand quite like her **Winterhome.** There is the dry limestone soil and an abundance of sunshine that lend a Mediterranean air to this place. But it is with a strong sense of design and drama that Susan and her husband Richard have used to move beyond the cottage garden phenomenon so popular today. Winterhome is virtually a study in the rules of traditional garden design and its emphasis on structure. Straight lines and geometric patterns provide clear boundaries for the plantings. The palette is restrained, and the effect is unified and rhythmic. A large, sunken garden is hedged with dwarf boxwood and filled solely with the fragrant, white "Margaret Merril" roses. A broad pathway takes you past sweeps of lavender boldly punctuated by evergreen spires. High brick walls enclose spaces and provide a sense of intimacy and safety. Benches are exactly where you want them: in a cool spot at the end of a long pathway or overlooking the Pacific. Views are always considered at Winterhome, and somehow made more enticing for having been framed with aesthetic control, be it by greenery or perhaps the span of an arched gateway. Winterhome is near the coast, midway between Blenheim and Kaikoura. ⊠ *State Hwy. 1, Kekerengu,* ☎ *03/575–8674,* FAX *03/575–8620.* 🎫 *Small entry fee.* ☉ *Late Oct.–Easter, daily 10–4.*

Kaikoura

  ❹ *129 km (81 mi) south of Blenheim, 182 km (114 mi) north of Christchurch.*

The town of Kaikoura sits on a rocky protrusion on the east coast, backed by an impressive mountainous upthrust. There is plenty of local crayfish to be had at roadside stalls, which is an excellent reason to come here, but an even better one is sighting the sperm whales that frequent the coast in greater numbers than anywhere else on earth. The sperm whale, the largest toothed mammal, can reach a length of 60 feet and a weight of 70 tons. The reason for the whales' concentration in this area is the abundance of squid—among other species the giant squid of seafaring lore—which is their main food. Scientists speculate that the whales use a form of sonar to find the squid, which they then bombard with deep, powerful sound waves generated in the massive cavities in the fronts of their heads. Their hunting is all the more remarkable considering that much of it is done at great depths, in darkness. The whales' food sources swim in the trench just off the continental shelf, barely a half mile off Kaikoura. You are most likely to see the whales between October and August.

Fyffe House is Kaikoura's oldest surviving building, built soon after Robert Fyffe's whaling station was established in 1842. Built on a pile of whale bones, the house provides a look at what life was like in Kaikoura when whales were aimed at by harpoons, rather than cameras. ⊠ *62 Avoca St., Kaikoura,* ☎ *03/319–5835.* ☞ *$3.50.* ☉ *Daily 10–5.*

The Kaikoura Peninsula has two **walks** that are particularly worthwhile, considering the town's spectacular coastal scenery: the clifftop walk, from which you can look over seal colonies, and the longer shoreline walk that takes you much closer to the colonies and requires some advance planning because of tides. ⊠ *Walks start at the end of Fyffe Quay.*

Dining and Lodging

$$$ ✕ **White Morph Restaurant.** Set in what was once the first bank of Kaikoura, White Morph has a feeling of historic elegance. Locally made gilded mirrors and marine art adorn the walls, but the best scenes are the seaside views from the front windows. Crayfish and crayfish mornay are obvious highlights, but you'll also find fish of the day, cervena venison, and rack of lamb on the menu. ⊠ *92–94 the Esplanade,* ☎ *03/319–5676,* ℻ *03/319–5015. AE, DC, MC, V.*

$$ ✕ **The Craypot.** As the name suggests, this casual and modern café relies strongly on the local delicacy. As with all restaurants in the region, crayfish will cost more than anything else on the menu, but it's worth the money. Steaks, chicken, salads, and homemade desserts are all available, too. During summer there is outdoor dining, and in winter an open fire roars at night. ⊠ *70 West End Rd.,* ☎ *03/319–6027. AE, DC, MC, V.*

$ ✕ **Hislops Café.** Homey and wholesome Hislops is a few minutes' drive north of town and well worth the trip for breakfast, especially when the sun streams in its windows. You'll find tasty eggs and bacon, and a real treat in the freshly baked wholemeal bread served with marmalade or honey. There are also tasty muffins both sweet and savory. Salads are available at lunch, you can sit outside on a veranda on fine days, and the café is open for dinner on Thursday, Friday, and Saturday. ⊠ *Main Hwy.,* ☎ *03/319–5557,* ℻ *03/319–5556. MC, V.*

$$ ▦ **Beachfront Bed and Breakfast.** The big attraction here is the beachside location and the sea views—which are best in upstairs rooms. Sit on the balcony and enjoy a crayfish tail and a bottle of wine while you take in the sea air. The owners are friendly and know the area very well. This is always the first bed and breakfast in town to sell out, so phone well ahead to book a room. ⊠ *78 the Esplanade,* ☎ *03/319–5890. 4 rooms with shower. MC, V.*

$$ ▦ **White Morph Motor Inn.** Standard motel rooms, just across the road from the beach—this used to be the Kaikoura standard. Each unit has a double and single bed, plus cooking facilities. Upstairs rooms have decks, and downstairs units have courtyards. ⊠ *92–94 the Esplanade, Kaikoura,* ☏ *03/319–5014,* ℻ *03/319–5015. 16 rooms with shower. AE, DC, MC, V.*

$ 🖬 **Old Convent.** Don't expect luxury, and you'll enjoy the musty atmosphere of this converted convent school with friendly hosts and a diverse mix of guests. The old convent chapel is now a lounge, and the one-time refectory has become the breakfast room. Somewhere between a bed and breakfast and a backpackers' lodge, the convent is a few minutes' drive out of town. ⊠ *Mt. Fyffe Rd.,* ☏ *03/319–6603. 3 rooms with shower, 4 rooms with shared bath. MC, V.*

Outdoor Activities and Sports

Whale-watching and swimming with dolphins are both extremely popular in December and January, so either avoid Kaikoura at those times or book well in advance.

Whale Watch Kaikoura Ltd. (☏ 0800/655–121) has three-hour whale-spotting trips, depending on weather ($95). Take motion sickness pills if you suspect you'll need them—even in calm weather, the sea around Kaikoura often has a sizeable swell.

Swimming with dolphins and/or seals is a growing attraction in Kaikoura, though it is usually regarded as a secondary activity to whale-watching. **Top Spot Seal Swims** (☏ 03/319–5540) has two trips daily ($25 per person). **Dolphin Mary Charters** (☏ 03/319–6777) has dolphin swims at 6 AM, 9 AM, and 12:30 PM from October to April. The cost is $80 per person.

Marlborough and Kaikoura A to Z

Arriving and Departing

BY BUS

InterCity (☏ 03/72–8297) and **Mount Cook Landline** (☏ 03/79–0690) operate daily buses between Christchurch and Kaikoura.

BY FERRY

InterIsland Line (☏ 0800/802–802) runs vehicle and passenger ferries between Wellington and Picton. The one-way adult fare is $38 during school holidays, $30 at other times. The fare for a medium-size sedan is $150 during school holidays, $114 at other times. The crossing takes about three hours and can be very rough, although InterIsland's slightly more expensive fast ferry *The Lynx* does the journey in half the time when it runs from November until April. There are at least two departures in each direction every day, and bookings should be made in advance, particularly during holiday periods. The ferry docks in Picton at the town wharf.

BY PLANE

Air New Zealand Link (☏ 09/366–2400) has 10 departures to and from Wellington daily. **Soundsair** (☏ 0800/505–005) also operates between the two centers.

Getting Around

BY BOAT

☞ Guided Tours, *below.*

BY CAR

Blenheim is a 25-minute drive from the ferry terminal in Picton, and a two-hour drive from Nelson to the west and Kaikoura to the south.

Contacts and Resources

CAR RENTAL

Most rental agencies have an easy North to South Island transfer program for their vehicles: Leave one car off in Wellington and pick another one up in Picton on the same contract. It is common practice, quickly and easily done. If you initiate a rental in Picton the following agencies are represented at the ferry terminal: **Avis** (☎ 03/573–6363), **Budget** (☎ 03/573–6009), and **Hertz** (☎ 03/573–7224).

EMERGENCIES

Dial 111 for **fire, police,** or **ambulance** services.

GUIDED TOURS

Beachcomber Cruises (✉ Beachcomber Pier, Town Wharf, Box 12, Picton, ☎ 03/573–6175, FAX 03/573–6176) can take you to and from any point on the Queen Charlotte Walkway if you want to freedom walk (unguided) for a day or more.

The *Glenmore,* a small launch that makes a daylong trip ferrying mail and supplies around the reaches of Pelorus Sound, offers one of the best ways to discover this waterway and meet the people who live there. The boat departs from Havelock, west of Picton, Tuesday to Thursday at 9:30 and returns about 5:30. On Friday from mid-December to Easter, passengers can combine the cruise with a four-hour bushwalk along the Nydia Track. ✉ *Glenmore Cruises, 73 Main Rd., Havelock,* ☎ *03/574–2276.* 🖭 *$45.*

Marlborough Sounds Adventure Company offers one- and four-day guided kayak tours of the Sounds, as well as kayak rentals for experienced paddlers. The cost is $60 for a one-day guided tour, $450 for a four-day guided tour. A kayak rental costs $35 per day. The company also guides trampers on the Queen Charlotte Walkway on one- to four-day trips. ✉ *Boat Shed, London Quay, Picton,* ☎ *03/573–6078,* FAX *03/573–8827.*

Secrets of Marlborough (✉ Awatere Valley, Blenheim, ☎ 03/575–7525) has a selection of tours that focus on gardens, wine, local scenery, and other local interests.

VISITOR INFORMATION

Blenheim Visitor Information Centre. ✉ *Forum, Queen St., Blenheim,* ☎ *03/573–7477,* FAX *03/573–8362.*

Kaikoura Information and Tourism. ✉ *West End,* ☎ *03/319–5641,* FAX *03/319–6819.*

NELSON AND THE NORTHWEST

Set on the broad curve of its bay with views of the Tasman Mountains on the far side, with a sunny and agreeable climate, Nelson makes a strong case for itself as one of the top areas in New Zealand for year-round adventure. To the west, the sandy crescents of the Abel Tasman National Park and Golden Bay beckon with their seaside charms. To the south, mellow river valleys and the peaks and glacial lakes of Nelson Lakes National Park are a pristine wonderland for hikers, mountaineers, and cross-country skiers. Beyond those geographic splendors, Nelson has more hours of sunlight than any major city in the country. New Zealanders are well aware of these attractions, and in December and January the city is swamped with vacationers. Apart from this brief burst of activity, you can expect to have the roads and beaches almost to yourself.

Nelson

⑤ *116 km (73 mi) west of Blenheim.*

Relaxed, hospitable, and easy to explore on foot, Nelson is one of the country's most pleasant cities. Local craftspeople weave wool into clothing and blankets and make pots and jewelry that fill up shops throughout the area. You can make your way around town in a day, poking into shops and stopping at cafés, but you may want to stay in the city longer if you need to get yourself back together in the midst of a busy itinerary. Use Nelson as a base for a variety of activities within an hour's drive of the town itself.

Nelson's iffy architectural contribution is **Christ Church Cathedral,** which sits on a hilltop surrounded by gardens. Work on the church began in 1925 and dragged on for the next 40 years. During construction the design was altered to withstand earthquakes, and despite its promising location, it looks like a building designed by a committee.

Suter Art Gallery exhibits both historical and contemporary art. It is the easiest way to see work from an area that has long attracted painters, potters, woodworkers, and other artists. Many of them come for the scenery, the lifestyle, and the clay, with Nelson considered the ceramics center of New Zealand as a result. In recent years, the gallery has increased its emphasis on painting and sculpture. Exhibits change every three or four weeks. ⊠ *Queens Gardens, Bridge St.,* ☎ *03/548–4699,* ⅢⅩ *03/548–1236.* ☑ *$2.* ⊙ *Daily 10:30–4:30.*

Seifrieds Vineyard is a 15-minute drive from Nelson's main center, on the way to Motueka, and is the best known winery in the region. While Nelson's wine industry is well overshadowed by that of nearby Marlborough, the wines here are well worth a try. Hermann Seifried is credited as one of the vineyard pioneers in the region, having established his vineyard in 1974. Dry red wine had been produced at a small vineyard in the area from 1918, but it was hardly what you'll find today. Seifrieds produces fine sauvignon blanc, chardonnay, and riesling, plus red varietals such as pinot noir and cabernet sauvignon. ⊠ *State Hwy. 60 and Redwood Rd., Appleby,* ☎ *03/544–1555,* ⅢⅩ *03/544–1700.* ⊙ *Daily 9–5.*

Dining and Lodging

$$ ✕ **Appleman's.** Long established as one of Nelson's best restaurants,
★ Appleman's was named the Taste of Nelson Gourmet Restaurant of 1995. Because of the city's seafood harvest, anything from the sea is recommended, although the trio of spring lamb, filled with cumin seed, gouda-and-tamarillo (tree tomato) chutney, roasted, then served on lemon thyme and roasted garlic cloves glaze is also a fine dish. ⊠ *38 Bridge St., Nelson,* ☎ *03/546–8105. AE, DC, MC, V. No lunch.*

$$ ✕ **Broccoli Row.** This friendly, self-styled fish and vegetarian restau-
★ rant is highly regarded in Nelson for its presentation and innovative cooking. The menu is small, but it caters to varied appetites with dishes such as grilled scallops with rosemary, salmon fillet stuffed with ratatouille, asparagus and Brie tart with tomato-basil sauce, a tapas platter, Caesar salad, and seafood chowder with garlic focaccia. The cheerful, Mediterranean-style courtyard is the place to eat when the sun is shining. ⊠ *5 Buxton Sq., Nelson,* ☎ *03/548–9621. AE, DC, MC, V. Closed Sun.*

$$ ✕ **Chez Eelco Coffee House.** The menu, with an array of steaks, burgers, seafood, and salads, may not try too hard, but it's impossible to ignore this cheerful sidewalk café at the foot of the cathedral on Nelson's main street. Decor includes huge copper sculptures of insects and some scattered antiques and curios. In warm weather, the outside tables are recommended, otherwise, there's a magazine rack if you have time to kill on a rainy day. ⊠ *296 Trafalgar St., Nelson,* ☎ *03/548–7595. No credit cards. BYOB.*

$$ ✕ **Pomeroy's.** This smart, popular bistro brings a modern European selection and a touch of class to Nelson's dining scene. The menu offers croissants, focaccia, bagels, and more substantial fare, such as lamb stuffed with sun-dried tomatoes and served with a spinach salad. ⊠ *276 Trafalgar St., Nelson,* ☎ *03/548–7524. AE, DC, MC, V. BYOB. Closed Sun. No dinner Mon.–Wed.*

$$$ 🏨 **California Guest House.** Set at the end of a garden brimming with
★ flowers, Shelley and Neil Johnston have made this country charmer in the city a bed-and-breakfast with character, though it is looking a bit worn. Guest rooms are moderately large, comfortable, and furnished with antiques. The best rooms are the slightly more expensive Victorian Rose and Everett. Breakfasts include muffins, filter coffee, ham-and-sour-cream omelets, fresh fruit, and pancakes with strawberries and cream. Shelley has collected quite a bit of information on the town and assembled it into a very useful notebook. Children are not accommodated, and smoking is not permitted indoors. Rates include breakfast. ⊠ *29 Collingwood St., Nelson,* ☎ *03/548–4173. 4 rooms with bath. MC, V.*

$$$ 🏨 **Cambria House.** Built for a sea captain, this 1860 house has been
★ sympathetically modernized to offer B&B accommodations with personality and a dash of luxury. The furnishings mix antiques and floral-print fabrics, and the rooms are very comfortable. Each has an en-suite bathroom. The house is in a quiet street within easy walking distance of the center of Nelson. Children are not accommodated. Rates include breakfast. ⊠ *7 Cambria St., Nelson,* ☎ *03/548–4681,* 𝖥𝖠𝖷 *03/546–6649. 5 rooms with bath. MC, V.*

$$$ 🏨 **Mapledurham.** This Victorian ranch house, presided over by Deborah and Giles Grigg, is as friendly and comfortable a place as you'll find around Nelson. The hosts are ever-ready with suggestions about local activities and restaurants, and the garden around the house and fresh flowers in your room make it a pleasant place to come to at the end of the day. Incredible full breakfasts make for a lavish start in the morning. ⊠ *8 Edward St., Richmond,* ☎ 𝖥𝖠𝖷 *03/544–4210. 3 rooms, 1 with bath. MC, V.*

Outdoor Activities and Sports

There is hiking and sea-kayaking aplenty in the glorious forest-and-coastal Abel Tasman National Park west of Nelson (☞ Abel Tasman National Park, *below*). For information on stream fishing in the Nelson Lakes district, *see* Chapter 6.

Shopping

There are crafts shops in various parts of town, and a stroll will take you past many of them. There is also a Saturday morning flea market. If you are going to be in town in August or September, call ahead to find out when the Wearable Arts Awards will be held—entries from around the world are eye-opening; some are quite inspired.

Handweavers and Fibre Artists. The work of numerous craftswomen is well represented here—everything from sweaters, wraps, hats, throws, and rugs to interesting baskets woven with twigs. ⊠ *280 Trafalgar St.,* ☎ *03/548–1939 or 03/546–7738. AE, MC, V.*

Jens Hansen Workshop. Hansen's skilled craftspeople create thoughtfully designed, well-made jewelry. Contemporary pieces are handmade at the workshop-showroom, many are set with local stones and shells. ⊠ *320 Trafalgar Sq.,* ☎ *03/548–0640.*

Around Nelson

6 The **Nelson Provincial Museum** is on the grounds of Isel Park and has a small but outstanding collection of Maori carvings. The museum also has a number of artifacts relating to the "Maungatapu murders," a grisly goldfields killing committed near Nelson in 1866. **Isel House** was built for Thomas Marsden, one of the region's prosperous pioneers. The Marsden family's impressive collection of porcelain and furniture is displayed inside. It was Marsden who laid out the magnificent gardens surrounding the house, which include a towering California redwood and a 140-foot Monterey pine. The house is near the Nelson Provincial Museum. To get to the park from Nelson, follow Rutherford Street out of town; the street was named for the eminent nuclear physicist Ernest Rutherford, who was born nearby and educated at school here. On the outskirts of the city, take the right fork onto Waimea Road and continue as it becomes Main Road. Turn left into Marsden Road, where a sign points to the park. ⊠ *Isel Park, Stoke, 7 km (4 mi) south of Nelson,* ☎ *03/547–9740.* ⌨ *Isel Park $2, Isel House $2.50.* ☼ *Isel Park Tues.–Fri. 10–4, weekends 2–5; Isel House Sept.–May, weekends 2–4.*

7 **Broadgreen** is a fine example of a Victorian "cob" house. Cob houses, made from straw and horsehair bonded together with mud and clay, are commonly found in the southern English county of Devon, where many of Nelson's pioneers originated. The house is furnished as it might have been in the 1850s, with patchwork quilts and kauri furniture. ⊠ *276 Nayland Rd., Stoke,* ☎ *03/546–0283.* ⌨ *$2.* ☼ *Nov.–Apr., Tues.–Fri. 10:30–4:30, weekends 1:30–4:30; May–Oct., Wed. and weekends 2–4:30.*

★ **8** It might be hard to resist stopping at **Nature Smoke,** operated by Dennis Crawford, who buys his fish right off local boats, fillets it, marinates it according to a secret recipe, and smokes it. The result is delicious, and Crawford will happily offer samples. Especially if you're headed south, you won't find a better lunch along the way than a slab of smoked snapper or albacore tuna with a loaf of crusty bread from the bakery in Motueka and apples from one of the roadside orchard stalls. Nature Smoke is in Mapua Port on the wharf in a blue corrugated iron building. ⊠ *Mapua Wharf,* ☎ *03/540–2280.* ☼ *Daily 9–5:30; extended hrs in summer.*

En Route West of Mapua, on the way to Motueka, Highway 60 loops around quiet little sea coves that, for all but the warmest months of the year, mirror the snow-frosted peaks on the far shore. The tall vines along the roadside are hops, used in the making of beer.

Motueka

9 *50 km (31 mi) west of Nelson.*

Motueka (mo-too-*eh*-ka) is an agricultural center—tobacco, hops, kiwifruit, and apples are among its staples. South of town, the Motueka River valley is known for trout fishing, rafting, and its sporting lodges. About 15 kilometers (9 miles) northeast of town on the edge of the national park, **Kaiteriteri Beach** is one of the most scenic and popular in the area—great for a swim.

....
NEED A   Next door to the Motueka Museum, **Annabelles Café** serves snacks and
BREAK?   light, inexpensive meals: scones, muffins, salads, sandwiches, and great
              espresso. The café has a choice of indoor or outdoor tables. ⊠ *140
              High St., Motueka,* ☎ *03/528-8696.* ☼ *Daily 11-3.*
....

Boating and Rafting

Nelson Raft Company has various trips along the Motueka and Buller Rivers, from $35 for two hours to $95 for a full day. Transport to and from Nelson is included. ⊠ *Lodder La., R.D. 3, Motueka,* ☎ *03/546–6212.*

Dining and Lodging

$$$$ ✕🏠 **Motueka River Lodge.** A recent addition to New Zealand's list of exclusive fishing retreats, this lodge offers tranquillity, marvelous scenery, and a superb standard of comfort. Owned and operated by a former Auckland adman, the lodge is set on a hillside with views across a deer farm to the valley of the Motueka River. Inside, the rustic flavor of the house is accented with folk art collected around the world. Guest rooms are luxuriously equipped but do not have telephones or TVs. The lodge offers a range of activities—tramping, river rafting, golf, tennis—but its specialty is fishing, especially dry-fly fishing for brown trout in the wild river country, which can be reached only by helicopter. The activities are restricted outside the October–April fishing season. Rates include all meals. ⊠ *Hwy. 61, Ngatimoti, Motueka,* ☎ *and* ☎ *03/526–8668. 4 rooms with bath. Tennis court, fishing. AE, DC, MC, V.*

$$$ ✕🏠 **Doone Cottage.** This serene, homey farmstay is set in a pretty part of the Motueka River valley, within easy reach of five trout streams and a 40-minute drive from Nelson. The hosts are a relaxed, hospitable couple who have lived in this valley for many years. Guest accommodations are comfortable and crowded with family memorabilia. Dinners are likely to feature organically grown vegetables, local meat, and fish fresh from the rivers. Children are not accommodated. ⊠ *R.D. 1, Motueka,* ☎ *03/526–8740. 2 rooms with bath. V.*

Abel Tasman National Park and Golden Bay

77 km (48 mi) northwest of Motueka, 110 km (69 mi) northwest of Nelson.

❿ Beyond the town of Motueka, Highway 60 passes close to Kaiteriteri Beach, then turns inland to skirt **Abel Tasman National Park,** the smallest of New Zealand's national parks. Its coastline is a succession of idyllic beaches backed by a rugged hinterland of native beech forests, granite gorges, and waterfalls. The cove and inlets at **Anchorage,** to mention one part of the park, are spectacular.

Abel Tasman has a number of walking trails, from both Totaranui at its northern end and Marahau in the south. The most popular is the two- to three-day **Coastal Track,** open year-round. Launches of **Abel Tasman National Park Enterprises** (☞ Hiking, *below*) will drop off and pick up hikers from several points along the track. A popular way to explore the clear waters and rock-strewn coastline is by sea kayak (☞ Outdoor Activities and Sports, *below*). The main accommodations base for the national park is ☞ **Motueka.**

⓫ The sweep of sand north of Highway 60 and the town of Takaha is known, deservedly, as **Golden Bay,** but it once had a very different name. The Dutch navigator Abel Tasman anchored here briefly just a few days before Christmas 1642; his visit ended tragically when four of his crew were killed by Maoris. Bitterly disappointed, Tasman named the place Moordenaers, or Murderers' Bay, and sailed away without ever setting foot on New Zealand soil. If you have time to explore it, Golden Bay is a delight—a sunny 40-kilometer (25-mile) crescent of rocks and sand with a supremely relaxed crew of locals who firmly believe they live in paradise.

Outdoor Activities and Sports

FISHING

For information on deep-sea fishing out of Takaka in Golden Bay, *see* Chapter 6.

HIKING

Bushwalk on your own—it's called freedom walking—or opt for a guided walk. The **Department of Conservation Field Centre** (⊠ 1 Commercial St., Takaka, ☎ 03/525–9136) provides trail maps.

Abel Tasman National Park Enterprises guides two-, three-, and four-day treks along the southern half of the Abel Tasman Track. This is one of the most popular trails in the country, particularly in summer. Spend nights in comfortable lodges; during the day explore the coastline and forests of the national park. One day of the four-day trip is spent sea-kayaking. Walkers carry only a light day pack, and all meals are provided. The guided walks, which have an "easy" grading, depart each Tuesday and Friday. ⊠ *Old Cedarman House, Main Rd., Riwaka,* ☎ *03/528–7801.* ☞ *$250–$680.*

SEA-KAYAKING

Abel Tasman Kayaks has one- and two-person kayaks for hire at Marahau, at the southern end of Abel Tasman National Park, which gives paddlers ready access to beaches and campsites that are often inaccessible to hikers. The company does not rent to solo kayakers, and a minimum two-day rental is required. The cost is $90 for two days. Guided kayak tours cost $80 for one day, $260 for three days. ⊠ *Marahau, R.D. 2, Motueka,* ☎ *03/527–8022.*

En Route   At the Rothmans Clock Tower in Motueka, turn south onto Highway 61, following the sign to Murchison. The road snakes through **Motueka Valley** alongside the Motueka River, which is edged with poplars and yellow gorse, with the green valley walls pressing close alongside. If this river could talk, it would probably scream "Trout!" There are many deer farms in the area, easily identified by their high fences. After the town of Tapawera, turn south on State Highway 6 and continue to the West Coast.

Nelson and the Northwest A to Z

Arriving and Departing

BY BUS

InterCity buses are readily available to Nelson from the ferry terminal in Picton. From Nelson, InterCity runs the length of both the west and east coasts daily (reservations from Nelson, ☎ 03/548–1539; Greymouth, ☎ 03/768–1435; Franz Josef, ☎ 03/752–0780).

BY CAR

Nelson is about a two-hour drive from the ferry in Picton. The distance is 145 kilometers (90 miles), but the winding roads don't allow for fast open-road driving.

From Nelson, Highway 6 runs southwest to the West Coast, down the coast to the glaciers, then over the Haast Pass to Wanaka and Queenstown. If you're going to the West Coast, allow at least seven hours for the 458-kilometer (284-mile) journey from Nelson to Franz Josef. The same applies if you plan to drive from Nelson to Christchurch, 424 kilometers (265 miles) to the southeast, whether you drive through the mountains of Nelson Lakes National Park or through Blenheim and Kaikoura down the coast.

Air New Zealand (☎ 03/546–9300) and **Ansett New Zealand** (☎ 04/471–1044) link Nelson with Christchurch, Queenstown, Dunedin, the west-coast town of Hokitika, and all major cities on North Island. **Nelson Airport** is 10 kilometers (6 miles) south of the city. **Super Shuttle** (☎ 03/547–5782) operates buses that meet all incoming flights and charges $7 to the city for one passenger, $5 each for two. Taxi fare to the city center is about $14.

Contacts and Resources

CAR RENTAL
Avis (✉ Airport, ☎ 03/547–2727), **Budget** (✉ 74 Trafalgar St., ☎ 03/546–9255), and **Hertz** (✉ Trent Dr., ☎ 03/547–2299).

EMERGENCIES
Dial 111 for **fire, police,** or **ambulance** services.

GUIDED TOURS
The **Scenic Mail Run** is a five-hour tour aboard the bus that delivers the mail and supplies to isolated farming communities around Cape Farewell, at the northwestern tip of Golden Bay. The tour includes lunch on a 2,500-acre grazing property. The eight-seater bus departs from the Collingwood post office on Golden Bay. ✉ *Collingwood Bus Services, Collingwood,* ☎ *03/524–8188.* ▱ *$30.* ☉ *Tour weekdays at 9:30.*

Abel Tasman National Park Enterprises runs boats along the majestic shoreline of the park. A popular option is to leave the boat at Bark Bay on the outward voyage, take a two-hour walk through forests, and reboard the boat at Torrent Bay. The 6½-hour cruise departs daily from Kaiteriteri, a one-hour drive northwest of Nelson, at 9 AM. A bus connection from Nelson leaves the Visitor Information Centre at 7:35 AM. A cruise/flight option is also available. Passengers should buy a take-out lunch at Motueka—supplies on board are basic. ✉ *Old Cedarman House, Main Rd., Riwaka,* ☎ *03/528–7801.* ▱ *Cruise from Kaiteriteri $42, cruise-flight from Nelson $112, Nelson–Kaiteriteri round-trip bus $17.*

Nelson Day Tours has trips around the city and its immediate district, as well as going farther afield to Motueka and Kaiteriteri Beach, and south to Nelson Lakes National Park. ✉ *258 Rutherford St., Nelson,* ☎ *03/545–1055,* FAX *03/546–9170.*

VISITOR INFORMATION
Nelson Visitor Information Centre. ✉ *Trafalgar and Halifax Sts.,* ☎ *03/548–2304.* ☉ *Daily 9–5.*

THE WEST COAST

Southwest of Nelson, the wild West Coast region is virtually a land unto itself. The mystical Pancake Rocks and blowholes around Punakaiki (poon-ah-*kie*-kee) set the scene for the rugged, sometimes forlorn landscape to the south. Early Pakeha (European) settlers lived a hardscrabble life, digging for gold and farming where they could, constantly washed by the "Wet Coast" rains. The towns along the way don't have much of interest in their own right, but they can be used as bases from which to explore the coast, mountains, lakes, and forests of the region.

At the glacier towns of Franz Josef and Fox, the unique combination of soaring mountains and voluminous precipitation mean that the massive valleys of ice descend straight into rain forests—interestingly enough a combination also found on the southwest coast of South America. South of the glaciers, the road follows the seacoast, where fur seals and fiordland crested penguins inhabit fantastic beaches and forests. On sunny days, the Tasman Sea along the stretch between Lake Moeraki and Haast takes on a shade of transcendent, nearly unbelievable blue.

For all of its beauty, this is not the most hospitable of New Zealand's provinces. The people are friendly and welcoming, but the landscape and weather can make things difficult if you don't have an adventurous streak. Locals pride themselves on their ability to coexist with the wild, primeval landscape on their doorstep. Be prepared for rain, fog, and cold nights, all of which can get your spirits down. The meteorological mix can, unfortunately, mean that the glacier flight that you planned at Franz Josef or Fox won't fly the day that you're there. If you do end up here on a rainy "wet coast" day, keep in mind that you might be lucky enough to wake up the next morning to have brilliant sunshine lighting up the region's glorious scenery.

En Route   If you're driving to the West Coast from Nelson or Motueka, the road beyond Murchison parallels the broad **Buller River** as it carves a deep gorge from the jagged mountain peaks. Nineteen kilometers (12 miles) south of Murchison, the **Newtown Hotel,** no longer licensed, teeters on the brink of the gorge, surrounded by a fantastic junkyard of obsolete farm machinery. The Buller once carried a fabulous cargo of gold, but you'll have to use your imagination to reconstruct the days when places such as Lyell, 34 kilometers (21 miles) past Murchison, were bustling mining towns. **Hawk's Crag,** where the highway passes beneath a rock overhang with the river wheeling alongside, is the scenic climax of the trip along the Buller. Before the town of Westport, turn left to continue along Highway 6. You are now entering the West Coast region.

Punakaiki

269 km (168 mi) southeast of Nelson.

Punakaiki is just a small collection of shops at first glance. In fact, the big attraction is not the town. From the visitor center, an easy 10-minute walk leads to a fantastic maze of limestone rocks stacked high above ⑫ the sea. These are the fantastic **Pancake Rocks,** the outstanding feature of the surrounding **Paparoa National Park** (☎ 03/731–1895). At high tide, a blowhole spouts a thundering geyser of spray. Mount Cook is sometimes visible to the south.

Greymouth

⑬ *44 km (28 mi) south of Punakaiki.*

The town of Greymouth (said like the anatomical feature) is aptly named—it's a pretty dispirited strip of motels and timber mills. But the **Jade Boulder Gallery** is a great place to pick up a distinctive souvenir. The gallery exhibits the work of Ian Boustridge, one of the country's most accomplished sculptors of greenstone, the jade that is highly prized by the Maori. Earrings start at about $35, and sculpture can cost anything up to $1,000. ✉ *1 Guiness St., Greymouth,* ☎ *03/768–0700.* ☉ *Daily 8–5.*

⑭ On the southern outskirts of Greymouth, **Shantytown** is a lively reenactment of a gold-mining town of the 1880s. Except for the church and the town hall, most of the buildings are replicas, but the gold diggings are authentic and fascinating. Displays include a water jet for blasting the gold-bearing quartz from the hillside, water sluices, and a stamper battery powered by a 30-foot water wheel for crushing the ore. You can pan for gold, and because the creek is peppered with gold

In case you want to be welcomed there.

We're here to see that you're always welcomed at establishments everywhere. That's why millions of people carry the American Express® Card – for peace of mind, confidence, and security, around the world or just around the corner.

do more®

Cards

In case you're
running low.

We're here to help with more than 118,000 Express Cash
locations around the world. In order to enroll, just call
American Express before you start your vacation.

do more

Express
Cash

And just in case.

We're here with American Express® Travelers Cheques
and Cheques *for Two*® They're the safest way to carry
money on your vacation and the surest way to get a
refund, practically anywhere, anytime.

Another way we help you...

do more ®

**Travelers
Cheques**

dust, there is a good chance of striking "color." ✉ *Rutherglen, Greymouth,* ☎ *03/762–6634.* 🎫 *$7.* ⊙ *Daily 8:30–5.*

Dining and Lodging

$$$$ ✕🏨 **Lake Brunner Sporting Lodge.** Set on the southern shore of Lake
★ Brunner, a 40-minute drive southeast of Greymouth, this sprawling lodge offers excellent fishing, a variety of activities, and a high level of comfort at a price that is relatively low by the standards of New Zealand's elite lodges. Rooms are large and well equipped, with the emphasis on comfort rather than opulence. The best rooms are at the front of the house, overlooking the lake. The lodge is known for its "clear water stalking," since brown trout can be easily seen in the clear waters of the surrounding rivers. Hunting, hiking, boating, mountain biking, and bird-watching are also available. Children are welcome, a rare concession at sporting lodges. Rates include all meals. ✉ *Mitchells, R.D. 1, Kumara, Westland,* ☎ *03/738–0163,* 📠 *03/738–0163. 12 rooms with bath. Fishing, mountain bikes, nature tours, hunting, library. AE, DC, MC, V. Closed July–Sept.*

$$ 🏨 **Ashley Motor Inn.** This motor inn has modern, comfortable rooms, though Greymouth and its surroundings, compared with other parts of the west coast, have little to justify an overnight stop. ✉ *70 Tasman St., Greymouth,* ☎ *03/768–5135,* 📠 *03/768–0319. 60 rooms with bath. Restaurant, bar, pool, spa, coin laundry. AE, DC, MC, V.*

Hokitika

⑮ *41 km (26 mi) south of Greymouth.*

Hokitika may not wow you, but if you're finding the drive down to the glaciers a bit long, it is a convenient stopover for the night. There are crafts shops in town if you have time for browsing or a few local bushwalks, and the beach is littered with some very interesting driftwood. If you happen to get into town in the middle of a rainstorm, it might seem a little bleak.

Lodging

$–$$ 🏨 **Teichelmann's Central Bed & Breakfast.** Named for the surgeon-mountaineer-conservationist who built the original part of the house, this is the most comfortable place in town. Rooms are in the old house, decorated in a stylistic variety of furnishings. Teichelmann's is, as its name suggests, centrally located in town, and hosts Russell Wenn and Judie Collier are happy to make suggestions for local activities and dining. Rates include breakfast. ✉ *20 Hamilton St.,* ☎ 📠 *03/755–8232. 6 rooms, 4 with bath. AE, MC, V.*

Franz Josef and Fox Glaciers

⑯ ⑰ *Franz Josef is 146 km (91 mi) south of Hokitika, Fox is 24 km (15 mi) south of Franz Josef.*

The northern end of Westland National Park begins at the Franz Josef glacier field—New Zealanders say "glassy-ur." The glaciers are formed by the massive rainfall of the west coast—up to 300 inches per annum—which descends as snow on the névé, or head, of the glacier. The snow is compressed into ice, which actually flows downhill under its own weight. There are more than 60 glaciers in the park; the most famous and accessible are at **Franz Josef** and **Fox.** Both glaciers have parking areas from which you can walk about 30 minutes to reach their terminal faces. Both parking lots can be terrorized by keas—mountain parrots—which specialize in destroying the rubber molding around car windows. Keas are harmless to humans, and a coating of insect repellent around the window frames should safeguard your vehicle.

Trails from the parking lots wind across the valley floor to the glacier faces, where a tormented vocabulary of squeaks, creaks, groans, and gurgles can be heard as the glacier creeps down the mountainside at an average rate of up to 3 feet per day. Care must be taken here, since rocks and chunks of ice frequently drop from the melting face. These being New Zealand glaciers, there is much to do besides admire them. You can fly over them and land on their névé, or walk on them. If you have a yearning to walk on the ice, go with guides. Remember that these structures are dynamic and always changing—an ice cave that was there yesterday may not be there today. Ice is pushed and pulled so that some of the fascinating formations that you see on the top of the glacier were fairly recently at the very bottom of it higher up in the valley. It pays not to be in or on anything that is about to collapse. Flights are often best made early in the morning, when visibility tends to be better. Fox Glacier is slightly larger and longer than Franz Josef, but you'll miss nothing important if you see only one. Both glaciers have separate townships, and if you are spending the night, Franz Josef is marginally preferable.

Seasons around the glaciers are an interesting thing. Summer is of course warmer, and by far the busiest season. But there is a lot more rain and fog that can nix flightseeing and hiking plans. In winter, snow doesn't fall at sea level in Franz Josef or Fox. Winter is in fact a well-kept secret. Skies are clearer, which means fewer cancelled flights and glacier hikes, and more of the dazzling sunshine that makes views of the mountains so spectacular both from the towns and at elevations.

⑱ Outside the town of Fox Glacier, **Lake Matheson** has one of the country's most famous views. A walking trail winds along the lakeshore, and the snowcapped peaks of Mount Cook and Mount Tasman are reflected in the water. Allow at least an hour for the complete walk to the "View of Views." The best time is early morning, before the mirrorlike reflections are fractured by the wind. From town, turn toward the sea where a sign points to Gillespies Beach, then turn right again to reach the lake.

Dining and Lodging

$$ ✕ **Blue Ice Pizza.** This newish face in Franz Josef introduces an alternative both in cuisine and in decor to the usual "steak and chips" joints so common on the West Coast. Along with pizza and a light menu of salads, lasagna, and the like, you'll find green lip mussels, pork ribs, rack of lamb, and cervena venison. Coffee and desserts such as hot kumara (sweet potato) custard pudding or fudge cake are delicious. Blue ice has a bar, but some things never change—the place closes down at 9 PM with the rest of the town, even on Friday and Saturday nights. ⊠ *South end of Main Rd., Franz Josef,* ☎ *03/752–0707. MC, V.*

$$ ✕▥ **Westland Motor Inn.** The largest motel in the glacier region, this complex at the north end of Franz Josef village offers rooms a cut above the average in size and furnishings. Be sure to ask for a room with glacier views that are particularly stunning as the sun rises from the Tasman Sea to the east. Larger suites with upgraded facilities are also available, and the motor lodge has a choice of dining facilities and a piano bar that's by far the liveliest thing in town. ⊠ *State Hwy. 6, Franz Josef,* ☎ FAX *03/752–0709. 100 rooms with bath. Restaurant, bar, 2 spa pools, coin laundry. AE, DC, MC, V.*

Outdoor Activities and Sports

FISHING

For information on stream fishing around Franz Josef and Fox, *see* Chapter 6.

ON AND ABOVE THE GLACIERS

The walks to the glacier heads mentioned above are the easiest and most basic ways to experience the glaciers. There are walks below that are the most reasonable of all guided glacier trips—and by all means getting out onto the ice to see the formations created by movement and streams of water is unforgettable. Flying over the glaciers is also utterly thrilling, and the thrill comes at considerable expense. The ultimate combination is to fly by helicopter or fixed-wing plane to the middle or top of the glacier and get out on it. Heli-hikes give you the most time on the ice, two to three hours of snaking up and down right in the middle of a stable part of the glacier. Fixed-wing landings on the snow atop the ice fields are another sensation, but you will only have 10 minutes out of the plane.

Alpine Guides offers a choice of half- or full-day guided walks on Fox Glacier, the only way to safely experience the ethereal beauty of the ice caves, pinnacles, and crevasses on top of the glaciers. The three-hour walks travel about 2 kilometers (1 mile) up the glacier. The climb is quite strenuous and extremely slippery, despite the metal-pointed staves and spiked boots supplied to hikers. ⊠ *Box 38, Fox Glacier,* ☎ *03/751–0825.* ▨ *½-day $34, full-day $43.* ☉ *Tour daily at 9:30 and 2.*

Franz Josef Glacier Guides have half- and full-day hikes from the lower reaches of the glacier to the first icefall. You will learn a fair amount about the ice masses from guides, which is one advantage of using them. ⊠ *Main Rd., Franz Josef,* ☎ *03/752–0763,* ☏ *03/752–0102.* ▨ *½-day $35, full-day $70.* ☉ *Tours daily at 9:15 and 2.*

The **Helicopter Line** operates several scenic flights over the glaciers from heliports at Franz Josef and Fox. The shortest is the 20-minute flight over the Franz Josef Glacier ($40 per person); the longest is the Mountain Scenic Spectacular, a one-hour flight that includes a landing on the head of the glacier and a circuit of Mount Cook and Mount Tasman ($130 per person). Two- to three-hour heli-hikes are yet another option ($175 per person). If you've never flown in a helicopter, the experience can be nearly heart-stopping. It is exactly what you'd imagine flying on a magic carpet would be like—the pull of the rotors lifts you right up over the glacial valleys. There are times when the pilot banks the copter so that the only things between you and the mass of ice below you are a sheet of glass and centrifugal force. It's a wild ride. ⊠ *Main St., Box 45, Franz Josef,* ☎ *02/883–1767.*

Mount Cook Airline has fixed-wing skiplanes that fly over the glaciers. Landings amid craggy peaks in the high-altitude snowfields are otherworldly. Prices range from $60 to $180 per person, depending on the route and whether or not you land atop the glacier. *Franz Josef,* ☎ *03/752–0714; Fox,* ☎ *03/751–0812; 0800/800–737.*

Lake Moeraki

⑲ *90 km (56 mi) south of Fox Glacier, 30 km (19 mi) north of Haast.*

Lake Moeraki sits in the midst of Westland National Park. It isn't a town, it's the site of a thoughtfully designed wilderness lodge (☞ *below*). The immediate area's public access is **Monro Beach.** The forty-five-minute walk to the beach takes you through spectacular, fern-filled native forest to a truly remarkable beach: rock clusters jut out of waters incredibly blue, and rivers and streams flow over the sand into the Tasman Sea. You might arrive at a time when spunky little Fiordland crested penguins are in transit from the sea to their stream- or hill-side nests. Early morning and late afternoon are good but not sure bets.

A mile or more south on the beach is a seal colony, which you will smell before you see it. If you venture that way, be sure to keep 5 meters (16½ feet) away from the seals (the legal distance), and don't block their path to the sea. A spooked seal will bowl you right over, and may even bite, so be extremely respectful of their space. Sculpted dark gray rocks also litter the beach to the south, and seals like to lie behind and among them, so look carefully before you cross in front of these rocks.

Monro beach is an utter dream, not least if you collect driftwood or rocks. On the road a kilometer or two south of it, there is a lookout over the rock stacks at **Knights Point.** Farther south still, between Moeraki and Haast, the walkways and beach at **Ship Creek** are another stop for ferny forests and rugged coastline. Sandflies here can be voracious. Bring insect repellent and hope for a windy day!

En Route   Beyond Lake Moeraki, Highway 6 continues along the south coast to Haast, where it turns inland to Wanaka and Queenstown. The driving time between Moeraki and Wanaka is about five hours.

Dining and Lodging

$$$ ✕▥ **Wilderness Lodge Lake Moeraki.** The natural splendor of the sur-
★   roundings at Lake Moeraki is the equal of any on the West Coast. The lodge lies along a river flowing out of the lake, north of the town of Haast. Fiordland crested penguins—the rarest on earth—nest along streams and on hills above the beach. Guides will take you to see fur seals and, if he's around, the giant elephant seal whom they call Humphrey. They will also take you along while they feed local eels in the morning. Canoes and kayaks are available for paddling the lake, and forest trails from the lodge, some of which lead to the beach, echo with the sound of rushing streams and birdcalls. After a day outdoors, you'll eat local produce and drink New Zealand wine at dinner. There are also glowworm and night sky walks, on which guides point out the enchanting constellations of the southern hemisphere. The lodge is owned and operated by Dr. Gerry McSweeney and his family. Dr. McSweeney is a leading voice in New Zealand's conservation movement, and he took over the lodge with the intention of demonstrating that tourism was an economic alternative to logging in the forests of South Westland. His knowledge of and feeling for the area, along with that of naturalists on staff, contribute much to any visit. Rates include full breakfast and dinner, short guided nature activities, and the use of canoes and mountain bikes. Longer guided hikes, fishing guides, lunch, and dinner drinks are available for an extra charge. ✉ *Private Bag, Hokitika,* ☎ ℻ *03/750–0881. 20 rooms with bath. AE, DC, MC, V.*

Fishing
For information on deep-sea fishing out of Haast, *see* Chapter 6.

West Coast A to Z

Arriving and Departing

BY BUS

InterCity buses run the length of the West Coast daily (reservations from Nelson, ☎ 03/548–1539; Greymouth, ☎ 03/768–1435; Franz Josef, ☎ 03/752–0780).

BY CAR
BY CAR
The northern end of the West Coast is roughly a four-hour drive from Nelson, or a five- to six-hour drive over Arthur's Pass from Christchurch, the very top of which is harrowing to say the least (Hokitika and Greymouth are about 256 kilometers, or 166 miles, from Christchurch).

BY TRAIN
The West Coast in general is poorly served by the rail network, but one glowing exception is the **TranzAlpine Express,** which ranks as one of the world's great rail journeys. This passenger train crosses the Southern Alps between Christchurch and Greymouth, winding through beech forests and mountains that are covered by snow for most of the year. The bridges and tunnels along this line, including the 8-kilometer (5-mile) Otira Tunnel, represent a prodigious feat of engineering. The train is modern and comfortable, with panoramic windows as well as dining and bar service. Smoking is not permitted on board. The train departs Christchurch daily at 9:15 AM and arrives in Greymouth at 1:25 PM; the return train departs Greymouth at 2:35 PM and arrives at Christchurch at 6:40 PM. The one-way fare is $69 (☎ 800/802–802).

Contacts and Resources

EMERGENCIES
Dial 111 for **fire, police,** or **ambulance** services.

VISITOR INFORMATION
Franz Josef Glacier Visitor Information Centre. ⊠ *State Hwy. 6, Franz Josef,* ☎ *03/752–0796.* ⊙ *Daily 8–4:30.*

Greymouth Visitor Information Centre. ⊠ *Regent Theatre Bldg., McKay and Herbert Sts.,* ☎ *03/768–5101.* ⊙ *Weekdays 9–5.*

5 Christchurch and Lower South Island

This is it—picture postcard New Zealand, where the country's tallest mountains are reflected in crystal clear lakes and sheer rock faces tower above the fjords. The choice of activity is yours. You can enjoy some of the world's most dramatic views in complete peace and quiet, or leap— literally, if you'd like—from one adrenaline rush to the next.

A **S THE KEA FLIES,** it's only 130 kilometers (80 miles) from the eastern shores of South Island to its highest peak, the 12,283-foot Mt. Cook. As many as sixty glaciers of varying size are locked in the Southern Alps, slowly grinding their way down to lower altitudes where they melt into running rivers of uncanny blue-green hues. Mount Cook National Park is a World Heritage Area, and the alpine region around it contains the Tasman Glacier, New Zealand's longest.

The wide open Canterbury Plains separate the mountains from the ocean. This is some of New Zealand's finest pastureland, and the higher reaches of the Canterbury are sheep station country, where life and lore mingle in South Island's cowboy country. This is the territory where young Samuel Butler dreamed up the satirical *Erewhon*—the word is an anagram for "nowhere." The station he lived on is now on a horse trekking route.

Trekking is one of the things that Southland does best. The southwest corner of the island, where glaciers over millennia have cut the alps into stone walls dropping sheer into fjords, is laced with walking tracks that take you into the heart of wild Fiordland National Park. The Milford Track is the best known—it has been called the finest walk in the world since a headline to that effect appeared in the London *Spectator* in 1908. If you're not keen on walking all the way to the Milford Sound, drive in and hop on a boat and take in the sights and sounds from on deck.

Christchurch was built on the fortunes made from the Canterbury region's sheep runs. People call it the most English city outside of England, which may owe something to the grand, but unworkable, settlement scheme of devout Tory John Robert Godley. His fears of the collapse of religion and civility in the mid-nineteenth century may have had something to do with establishing the earthy gentility that makes the city such a pleasant foil for the wilds of South Island.

Gold, on the other hand, fueled Dunedin's glory days. Following the Central Otago strike of 1861 thousands of tons of gold were shipped out of the city's port, not before some of it went into building some of New Zealand's finest buildings in the city. Southwest of Dunedin, hanging off the bottom of South Island, Stewart Island is virtually a study in remoteness. Commercial fishing settlements give way to bushland that the kiwi so rare elsewhere in the country still haunts. Expansive views across the Foveaux Strait from time to time alight with the *aurora australis,* the spectacular southern hemisphere equivalent of the northern lights.

South Island is without doubt the wilder of the country's two largest islands. Beyond the well-defined tourist routes, its beech forests, lakes, trout streams, and mountain trails are a paradise for hikers, anglers, and anyone who enjoys a good dose of fresh air.

Note: For more information on bicycling, cross-country skiing, fishing, hiking, horse trekking, rafting, and sailing in lower South Island, *see* Chapter 6.

Pleasures and Pastimes

Dining

Christchurch has a fairly wide range of eateries, from cosmopolitan restaurants to earthy vegetarian cafés. The small fishing town of Bluff is known for two reasons in New Zealand—it is the southernmost tip of the South Island and it gives its name to an oyster. The Bluff oyster is one of the country's great delicacies, so pick up a dozen fresh ones from a fish shop if you can, or try them in a restaurant. You'll find plenty of variety in Dunedin because of its student population, and Queenstown, which caters to visitors from around the world.

Hiking

Not to detract from the rest of New Zealand, but lower South Island is the land of legendary tramping. The Milford Track, the Kepler, the Routeburn, the Hollyford—it doesn't get any better than these. Mountains, fjords, waterfalls, rain forests, you'll see it all.

Jumping

Don't worry, New Zealanders aren't going to pressure you into jumping off a bridge with an elastic cord tied to your ankles. But if you have an overwhelming desire to bungee, this is the place to do it. The cost of the jump usually includes a "been there–done that" T-shirt and even a video of your daredevil act.

Lodging

No matter where you stay in Christchurch, you're sure to find some of the best lodging in New Zealand, from luxury hotels to very fine B&Bs. The rest of lower South Island is blessed with great views, and you will always be able to find a place to stay overlooking a lake, river, or mountainous landscape. If you can forego luxury, basic but comfortable cabins can often be found in the most beautiful of places. And farmstays are often set on lush green grasslands with snowcapped mountains as a backdrop.

Skiing

South Island's best known ski areas are here—use Wanaka as a base for Treble Cone and Cadrona, and Queenstown serves Coronet Peak and the Remarkables. For the biggest thrill, go heli-skiing and cover areas otherwise unreachable.

Exploring Christchurch and Lower South Island

Great Itineraries

Touring the lower half of South Island requires making difficult choices. Do you want to walk the Milford Track, or does the remote Stewart Island appeal more? Will you go away disappointed if you miss Queenstown, the adventure capital, or would you just as soon station yourself in the snowy reaches of Mt. Cook? The Otago Peninsula has its own spectacular scenery, interesting wildlife, and the charming city of Dunedin. And then there is Christchurch and side trips from the city to the Banks Peninsula.

To literally see it all would take a good three weeks, if you want to do it all justice and stay sane. Short of that, treat each of these areas as two- to three-day segments, mix them up to suit your fancy, and take into account travel time of three to five hours between each.

Numbers in the text correspond to points of interest on the Canterbury Region and the Southern Alps; Christchurch; and Southland, Otago, and Stewart Island maps.

IF YOU HAVE 3 DAYS

Spend the first or last day in Christchurch, strolling through the beautiful **Botanic Gardens** ⑤, poking around the **Arts Centre** ⑧, perhaps heading out to **Mona Vale** ⑫ for afternoon tea. Then choose whether to fly to **Mt. Cook** ㉒ or to **Queenstown** ㉕, or **Stewart Island** for two days. If you pick Mt. Cook, explore some of South Canterbury one day, making sure to stop at **Lake Tekapo** ⑲ and marvel at the view from inside the **Church of the Good Shepherd** ⑳. You could spend the night there or on Mt. Cook. On the next day take a flight over the mountain or onto the **Tasman Glacier** ㉓, followed by a walk into the Hooker Valley or up Mt. Sebastopol.

IF YOU HAVE 5 DAYS

Spend two days in Christchurch, using the second to see the **International Antarctic Centre** ⑩ or ride the **Christchurch Gondola** ⑭. You could otherwise take the whole day and go to the town of **Akaroa** ⑮ on the Banks Peninsula, drive up the summit of the volcanic dome, then take a road down to one of the bays on the other side of the peninsula. On the third day fly to Queenstown. Depending on how active you are, you could easily spend three days here throwing yourself off a bridge, heli-skiing, jetboat riding, white-water rafting, and taking a steamer trip on Lake Wakatipu. Leave some time to relax and take in the stunning views from the **Skyline Gondola** ㉖ as well. On the fourth day, head to **Milford Sound** ㉙ to take in the amazing spectacle of sheer cliffs, deep water, and dense native bush. You could spend a day in Wanaka, stopping in at **Stuart Landsborough's Puzzle Museum** and/or taking a half- or full-day hike in the area. From here you could easily tack on a trip to the stunning West Coast (covered *in* Chapter 4), driving over the scenic Haast Pass to get there.

IF YOU HAVE 8 DAYS

With eight days, you have the luxury of taking your time. You could spend four of them on the **Milford** or the **Kepler** track, a couple more in **Queenstown,** and a couple more in **Christchurch** or **Dunedin.** Or feel like your skirting the edge of the earth by driving to **Dunedin** ㉚ to explore the fascinating Otago Peninsula and view its wildlife, **Larnach Castle** ㉛, and **Taiaroa Head** ㉜, then continuing to the southernmost **Stewart Island,** where you can spend four days doing some serious bush walking and looking for kiwi birds in the wild. You could easily enough combine two or three days in Christchurch with two or three in Dunedin and the same on Stewart Island. Or just go alpine and spend all of your time around Mt. Cook, Wanaka, and Queenstown.

When to Tour Christchurch and Lower South Island

Not surprisingly because of the alps, this is the part of New Zealand that gets cold with a capital C in winter, so if you're coming for a warm-weather holiday stay away between May and September. For skiing, snowboarding, etc., this is the time to come. From July through September you can be assured of snow around Queenstown and Wanaka, and the ski scene is pretty lively in both towns. In the height of summer, in December, January, and into February, popular towns can get so crowded that they lose the relaxed, laid-back atmosphere New Zealand is famous for. This is true in spades in Queenstown. If you hold off until April or May, leaves turn yellow and red, and the nearby mountains have a smattering of early season snow. You'll have more room to yourself, and some lodgings offer bargains.

CHRISTCHURCH

Christchurch is something of a paradox—a city under the grand delusion that it is somewhere in southern England. The drive from the airport into town takes you through pristine suburbs of houses lapped by seas of flowers and past playing fields where children flail at one another's legs with hockey sticks. The heart of this pancake-flat city is dominated by church spires, its streets are named Durham, Gloucester, and Hereford, and instead of the usual boulder-leaping New Zealand torrents, there bubbles, between banks lined with willows and

The Canterbury Region and the Southern Alps

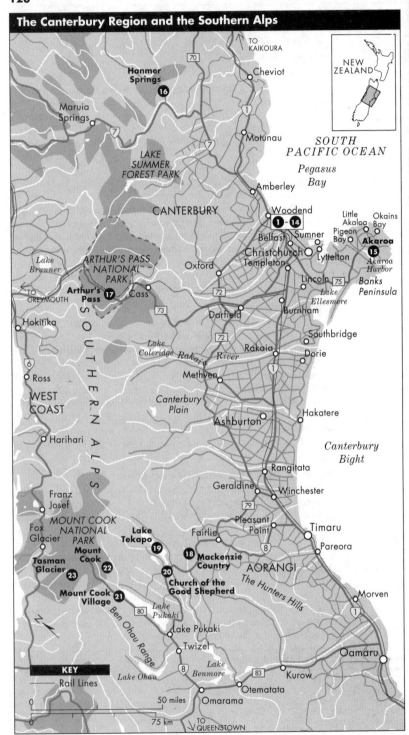

oaks, the serene River Avon, suitable only for punting. The inner city is compact and so easy to explore by foot that there is little need to follow a pre-set walking tour. Just pick a sight or two and set out—it won't be far away. Outside of the city boundaries, there are a number of special-interest museums and activities about 20 minutes away by car. There are also side trips from Christchurch into the Canterbury Plains countryside and to the Akaroa Peninsula, the remnant of an ancient volcanic dome whose steep, grassy walls drop to the sea.

With a population approaching 300,000, Christchurch is the largest South Island city, and the only one with an international airport. It is also the forward supply depot for the main U.S. Antarctic base at Mc-Murdo Sound, and if you come in by plane you are likely to see the giant U.S. Air Force transport planes of Operation Deep Freeze parked on the tarmac at Christchurch International Airport.

Exploring Christchurch

❹ Antigua Boatshed. Built for the Christchurch Boating Club, this is the only boat shed that remains of the half dozen that once stood along the Avon. Canoes may be rented for short river trips. ⊠ *Rolleston Ave.,* ☎ *03/366–5885.* 🎫 *Single canoe $5 per hr, double canoe $10 per hr.* ☉ *Daily 9:30–4:30.*

❽ Arts Centre. Why Canterbury University gave up its former quarters seems a mystery. The collection of Gothic Revival stone buildings it used to inhabit represents some of New Zealand's finest architecture. In the college days of Ernest Rutherford (1871–1937), the university's most illustrious pupil, classes were of course held in what is now the Arts Centre. Just past the information desk inside is "Rutherford's Den," the modest stone chamber where the eminent physicist conducted experiments in what was at the time a new field, radioactivity. It was Rutherford who first succeeded in splitting the atom, a crucial step in the harnessing of atomic power. In 1908 Rutherford's work earned him the Nobel prize—not for physics but for chemistry.

The Arts Centre houses diverse galleries, shops, theaters, and crafts studios. It is also an excellent place to stop for food, coffee, or a glass of wine if you are walking from the Cathedral Square to the Canterbury Museum—there are three cafés and a wine bar. And there is a **Saturday Market,** where you'll find handmade items of clothing and crafts that you may want to bring home with you. ⊠ *Worcester St. between Montreal St. and Rolleston Ave.,* ☎ *03/366–0989.* ☉ *Shops and galleries weekdays 8:30–5, weekends 10–4.*

NEED A BREAK?
The Arts Centre has four eateries in its stone buildings and quadrangles. Housed in a mock-Tudor building, **Dux de Lux** is an upbeat, popular cafeteria-style restaurant. The blackboard menu offers vegetarian items and seafood: quiches, crepes, sandwiches, pies, fresh vegetable juices, and a range of crisp salads and breads. The courtyard is a great spot on a sunny day, especially with a beer from the brewery next door. And at night, the brewery bustles with twenty- and thirty-somethings. The **Boulevard Bakehouse** is another spot, great for coffee and a sweet, there is a café half a block down from the Bakehouse, and the **Wine Bar** is the most refined of the four, a very pleasant place to taste New Zealand wine alongside bistro fare. All but the wine bar have outdoor seating in season. ⊠ *41 Hereford St., near Montreal St.,* ☎ *03/366–6919. No credit cards.*

❷ Bridge of Remembrance. Arching over the Avon, this bridge was built in memory of the soldiers who crossed the river here from King Ed-

130

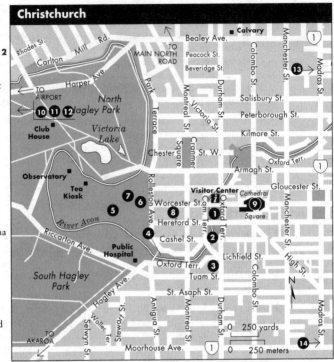

Christchurch

ward Barracks, just down Cashel Street, on their way to the battlefields of Europe during the First World War. ⊠ *Avon River at Cashel St.*

6 **Canterbury Museum.** If you're used to sophisticated international museums, this one, like many in New Zealand, won't exactly twirl your buttons. In case you do come, expect to see a reconstruction of an early Christchurch streetscape and the display of Maori artifacts. The Hall of Antarctic Discovery charts the links between the city and the U.S. bases on the frozen continent from the days of Captain Scott; Christchurch is still used as a forward supply depot for U.S. Antarctic bases. The museum lies on the eastern end of the Botanic Gardens. ⊠ *Rolleston Ave. and Worcester St.,* ☎ *03/366–8379.* 🖾 *Donation requested.* ☉ *Daily 9:30–4:30.*

1 **Captain Robert Falcon Scott statue.** "Scott of the Antarctic" (1868–1912), who visited Christchurch on his two Antarctic expeditions, is just across Worcester Street from the information center. The statue was sculpted by his widow, Kathleen Lady Kennett, and inscribed with his last words, written as he and his party lay dying in a blizzard on their return journey from the South Pole. ⊠ *Worcester St. and Oxford Terr.*

5 **Christchurch Botanic Gardens.** Your introduction to the garden will probably begin just beyond the ☞ **Robert McDougal Gallery** at the remarkable 310-foot herbaceous border, which should clue you in to the scale of things to come. These superb gardens are well known for the magnificent trees that were planted in the 19th century. Many are the largest specimens found in the country—or even in their native lands. Pick up the Historic Tree Walk brochure for a self-guided who's who tour of the tree world. There are a number of specialty gardens to visit, as well. In spring, spend time in the woodlands, carpeted in daffodils, in the rock garden, or at the primula (primrose) garden. In summer, the rose garden is a demonstration of every conceivable way to grow these beauties. The annual plantings call out for attention now as well, and the water garden provides a cool spot to explore. In autumn, that magnificent perennial border and the herb garden continue to amaze. And as the weather cools, the hips of species roses begin to redden, putting on yet another display. There is also a heather garden. Spend time in the conservatories on days when you'd rather not be outside and discover tropical plants, cacti, and ferns. Any time of the year, be sure to go to the New Zealand plants area, because seeing plant life that you won't find in other countries is one of the best reasons to come here. A small information center has displays, books, and plant information. ⊠ *Rolleston Ave.,* ☎ *03/366–1701.* ⊙ *Daily 7 AM–dusk, conservatories daily 10:15–4.*

❾ Christchurch Cathedral. The city's dominating landmark was begun in 1864, 14 years after the arrival of the Canterbury Pilgrims, but it wasn't consecrated until 1904. Carvings inside commemorate the work of the Anglican missionaries, including Tamihana Te Rauparaha, the son of a fierce and, for the settlers, troublesome Maori chief. Free guided tours begin daily at 11 and 2. For a view across the city to the Southern Alps, climb the 133 steps to the top of the bell tower. The cathedral is known for its boys choir, which can be heard singing evensong at 4:30 Friday, except during school holidays. It is in **Cathedral Square,** the city's focal point, which functions as a bus terminal and a venue for an arts-and-crafts market, food stalls, and street musicians, as well as a hangout for the city's unemployed youth.

If it's close to 1 PM when you emerge from the cathedral, look for the bearded gentleman with long hair, who's easy to spot because of the crowd that instantly forms around him. This is the **Wizard,** who offers funny and irreverent dissertations on just about any controversial subject—especially religion, politics, sex, and women's issues. Originally a freelance soapbox orator, the Wizard (whose real name is Ian Channel) became so popular that he is now employed by the city council—one of his frequent targets. Don't be too disappointed if he's not around; his appearances have become less frequent in recent years, and he doesn't come out in winter, between May and October. ⊠ *Cathedral Sq.* ☲ *Tower $2.50.* ⊙ *Daily 8:30 AM–9 PM.*

❶❹ Christchurch Gondola. East of the city in the Port Hills, the gondola is the best vantage point from which to overlook Christchurch, the Canterbury Plains, and Lyttelton Harbour. At the top, you can wander through the **Time Tunnel,** which gives a brief history of the region and finishes with an audiovisual about present-day Canterbury. Best of all, sit with a drink at the Red Rock Cafe and watch the sunset. Remember to ride the tram with your back to the mountain for the best views. If you don't have a car, free shuttles leave regularly from the visitor center. ⊠ *10 Bridle Path Rd., Heathcote,* ☎ *03/384–4914.* ☲ *$12; $9 after 5 PM.* ⊙ *Mon.–Sat. 10 AM–12:45 AM, Sun. 10 AM–11:45 PM.*

❶❶ International Antarctic Centre. Ever since Scott wintered his dogs at nearby Quail Island in preparation for his ill-fated South Pole expedition of 1912, Christchurch has maintained a close connection with the frozen continent. Dedicated to the past, present, and future of Antarctic exploration, this complex includes intriguing historic artifacts and photographs, as well as displays showing the sophisticated clothing and hardware that modern-day scientists use to carry out their work at the Antarctic bases. The audiovisual show is superb. The exhibition is within walking distance of the airport, and about a 20-minute drive from central Christchurch. ⊠ *Orchard Rd.,* ☎ *03/358–9896.* ☲ *$10.* ⊙ *Oct.–Mar., daily 9:30–8:30; Apr.–Sept., daily 9:30–5:30.*

⑫ **Mona Vale.** One of Christchurch's great historic homesteads, the turn-of-the-century, riverside Mona Vale makes for a lovely outing from the city. Come for lunch or Devonshire tea, and make believe that your estate lies along the Avon as you stroll under the stately trees and through the well-tended fucshia, dahlia, herb, and iris gardens. Stop to smell the many roses, then move on to the fernery and lily pond. If the mood really takes you, go for a punt ride and contemplate your travels from the water. ⊠ *63 Fendalton Rd., 1 ⁷⁄₁₀ km (1½ mi) from city center,* ☎ *03/348–9659 or 03/348–9666.* ⊘ *Grounds Oct.–Mar., daily 8–7:30, and Apr.–Sept., daily 8:30–5:30; morning and afternoon tea Sun.–Fri.; smorgasbord lunch Sun.*

⑬ **Nga Hau E Wha National Marae.** This Maori culture center provides a rare chance to gain insight into South Island Maori culture. Its name means "marae (meeting house) of the four winds," where people from all points of the compass meet and are welcome. Guides explain elements of Maori culture, history, and protocol. If you visit by night you are challenged in a traditional, fearsome, Maori way, before pressing noses as part of the welcoming ceremony. You also eat a hangi (traditional Maori feast) and view Maori action songs. Bookings are essential for the evening meal and performance, and the price includes round-trip transport from the city. ⊠ *250 Pages Rd.,* ☎ *03/388–7685.* ⊡ *Tour $5.50, hangi meal and cultural performance $55.* ⊘ *Tour daily at 11 and 2, hangi and performance daily at 7.*

☙ ⑪ **Orana Park Wildlife Trust.** This slice of the African plains in Canterbury is home to endangered species such as cheetah and white rhino. Animals have plenty of room to roam, which happily doesn't leave you with those feelings of pity that traditional zoos sometimes inflict. Orana also has native reptiles and birds and is a particularly good place to see the elusive tuatara, a reptilian relic of prehistoric New Zealand. The park also offers a twilight safari experience (reservations essential) from early October to mid-March. Orana is 25 minutes from the city center, in the same general direction as the International Antarctic Centre. ⊠ *McLeans Island Rd., Harewood,* ☎ *03/359–7109.* ⊡ *$12, twilight safari (including barbecue) $35.* ⊘ *Daily 10–5:30, last admission 4:30; twilight safari begins 5:45.*

⑦ **Robert McDougal Art Gallery.** You're likely to see some of the city's more innovative shows here, along with works by 19th-century New Zealand artists and an international collection of painting and sculpture, including two Rodins. It is behind the Christchurch Museum next to the Botanic Gardens. ⊠ *Rolleston Ave.,* ☎ *03/365–0915.* ⊡ *Free.* ⊘ *Daily 10–4:30.*

③ **St. Michael and All Saints Anglican Church.** St. Michael's dates from the city's earliest days. Christchurch was founded in 1850 by the Canterbury Association, a group of leading British churchmen, politicians, and peers who envisioned a settlement that would serve as a model of industry and ideals, governed by the principles of the Anglican faith. The first settlers the association sent out were known as the Canterbury Pilgrims, and their churches were focal points for the whole community. Built in 1872, the white timber St. Michael's is an outstanding building. One of the bells in the wooden belfry came from England aboard one of four ships that carried the Canterbury Pilgrims. ⊠ *Oxford Terr. and Durham St.* ⊘ *Daily noon–2.*

OFF THE
BEATEN PATH
⋯⋯⋯⋯⋯⋯ **GETHSEMANE GARDENS –** Set high overlooking Pegasus Bay in suburban Sumner, Gethsemane isn't quite like your local garden center back home. It is, as you might guess from the name, a born-again Christian garden, and the benefit the plants receive from the tonic of spirituality is

clear. The nursery, with its extensive display gardens, has the largest, most colorful, disease- and pest-free plants going. As you approach, take note of the 90-foot-long fencework that spells GETHSEMANE. Inside, four meticulous knot gardens form a Star of David, Star of Bethlehem, and two parallel Jerusalem crosses. The "Rosery" is filled with fragrant old-fashioned roses and more lettering: The pathwork spells Jesus. The potager, an ornamental vegetable garden, has as its centerpiece a life-size *pietà* covered by a trellised structure supporting a forbidding crown of thorns plant. The plant people among you may be too amazed by the lushness of the gardens to notice any symbolism. Perhaps, then, you should end your visit to Gethsemane at the small chapel, where you can pray for plants like these of your own. The garden is a 20-minute drive east of central Christchurch. ⊠ *33 Revelation Dr., at top of Clifton Terr., Sumner,* ☎ *03/326–5848.* ⊡ *$2.* ⊙ *Daily 9–5.*

Dining

$$$$ ✕ **Canterbury Tales.** The fine dining room of the Parkroyal Hotel has
★ won New Zealand's Hotel Restaurant of the Year award so many times it's become embarrassing. This is the finest restaurant in the city, specializing in the lamb, seafood, and venison of the Canterbury region. The surroundings are hushed and sophisticated, and presentation and service are outstanding. ⊠ *Kilmore and Durham Sts.,* ☎ *03/365–7799. Jacket and tie. AE, DC, MC, V. No lunch.*

$$$$ ✕ **Sign of the Takahe.** Set in a splendid baronial castle that overlooks the city and the Southern Alps from the heights of the Cashmere Hills, this mock Gothic restaurant is well known for its game and lobster, the house specialty. The buffet lunch is a less expensive option, but it lacks the stiff white napery, silver service, and candlelit tables that make dinners magic. The restaurant is a 20-minute drive from the city center. Dinners can be heavily booked by large Japanese tour groups, and other diners may face long delays, so call ahead to ask about the evening's prospects. ⊠ *Dyers Pass and Hackthorne Rds., Cashmere Hills,* ☎ *03/332–4052. Reservations essential. Jacket and tie. AE, DC, MC, V.*

$$ ✕ **Azure.** Tasty food and a casual atmosphere attracts both the local business set and visitors to town to this relatively new café-style restaurant. Apart from blackboard specials—often the best dishes of the day—look for the salmon and vegetable lasagna with squid ink pasta. Wide floors, large windows, and a choice of indoor and outdoor dining give Azure a light and breezy feeling and make it a great place for lunch. ⊠ *128 Oxford Terr.,* ☎ *03/365–6088. AE, DC, MC, V.*

$$ ✕ **Bardellis.** The name says it all—a bar, a deli, and an Italian accent. Stylish and medium loud, this bar-brasserie is where Christchurch's chic crowd comes for marinated octopus salad and fine New Zealand wine, some of which is available by the glass. The international menu, which changes frequently, is heavy on seafood, salads, pizza, and pasta. Typical dishes are fresh pasta with mussels in a tomato and chili sauce, and grilled chicken focaccia. Steaks and the standard New Zealand rack of lamb also make an appearance. This is a good choice for casual outdoor eating on a warm summer evening. ⊠ *98 Cashel Mall,* ☎ *03/353–0001. AE, DC, MC, V.*

$$ ✕ **Espresso 124.** This smart, modern restaurant is a good bet for mid-
★ morning coffee or midnight snacks. Simplicity is the key on a menu that features char-grilled steaks, lamb, and seafood, and salads dressed with olive oil and balsamic vinegar. The restaurant has a high-energy atmosphere generated by the fashionable crowd that frequents it. The river and the heart of the city are both close. Next door to the restaurant is a lunch deli with inexpensive sandwiches, focaccia, pasta, and

savory pies, and a choice of indoor or outdoor dining. ⊠ *124 Oxford Terr.,* ☎ *03/365–0547. AE, DC, MC, V.*

$ ✕ **Main Street Café and Bar.** If you lived in Christchurch and liked hearty
★ vegetarian cooking, you'd probably end up at this home-style store-
front haunt once a week with a good friend. Pumpkin and kumara (native sweet potato) balls with peanut sauce are rich and yummy, and
daily soups or the choice of three mixed salads with a piece of homemade bread will help you get out of a vacation-food rut. Espresso is
great, and desserts are phenomenally delicious. Main Street is open for
all meals (counter service only), and there's plenty of seating at old
wooden tables in a few rooms downstairs, upstairs, and outside. The
bar next door has good beer. ⊠ *840 Colombo St., at Salisbury St.,* ☎
03/365–0421. ☉ *Daily 10 AM–10:30 PM.*

Lodging

$$$$ ⊞ **Millennium.** The Millennium is the most stylish of a new crop of
Christchurch hotels, with an interesting mix of European and Asian
touches in the public areas. In rooms Italian lamps stand beside Oriental ginger jars, and the designer has chosen strong classical colors
instead of pastels, with sophisticated results. The primary advantage
that the Millennium has is its location, right on Cathedral Square. ⊠
14 Cathedral Sq., ☎ *03/365–1111,* ℻ *03/365–7676. 179 rooms with
bath. Restaurant, bar, health club, sauna, business services, valet parking. AE, DC, MC, V.*

$$$$ ⊞ **Parkroyal Christchurch.** This plush hotel, in a prime location over-
★ looking Victoria Square and the river, added a touch of glamour to the
city's accommodations scene when it opened in 1988. The rooms are
large and luxurious, and the soft furnishings were all upgraded in
1996 to overcome a slightly faded '80s look. In summer the best views
are from rooms overlooking Victoria Square, but in the winter popularity switches to those with views of the snowcapped alps to the west.
The hotel is especially well equipped with restaurants and bars. The
☞ **Canterbury Tales** dining room and the Japanese restaurant, Yam-
agen, are among the city's finest. ⊠ *Kilmore and Durham Sts.,* ☎
03/365–7799, ℻ *03/365–0082. 297 rooms with bath. 4 restaurants,
3 bars, sauna, exercise room, bicycles. AE, DC, MC, V.*

$$$ ⊞ **Cashmere House.** From their perch above the city in the Cashmere
★ Hills 15 minutes from central Christchurch, Monty and Birgit Clax-
ton graciously preside over their palatial manor house. Rich wood pan-
eling clad downstairs rooms, and lead light doors and windows speak
of the artisanship that went into building the house. Upstairs, one room
has a bed from Kilkenny Castle in Ireland, and another is incredibly
spacious, with a porch room and a bay window overlooking the city
and the Southern Alps. Breakfasts are generous and delicious—muesli
and yogurt fortified with tasty muffins and hot dishes. There is a piano
in the conservatory room, and the billiard room has an exquisite full-
size, 2-inch slate billiard table (with infuriatingly small pockets) man-
ufactured in London around 1880. Step outside and enjoy Birgit's
gardens around the house as well. ⊠ *141 Hackthorne Rd.,* ☎ *03/332–
7864. 5 rooms with bath. AE, MC, V.*

$$$ ⊞ **Centra.** A hotel with the business traveler at heart, the Centra has
some of the most interesting rooms in town. A converted bank build-
ing, guests stay in what once were offices—rooms' shapes and sizes are
anything but standard. The hotel is in the central business district, just
a minute or two's walk from Cathedral Square and close to Victoria
Square. The Streetside Bar is arguably the best place in Christchurch
to have a gin and tonic, to watch Christchurch's working population
go by on a weekday, or to mix with them in the evening. ⊠ *Cashel*

and High Sts., ☎ *03/365–8888,* FAX *03/365–8822. 201 rooms with bath. Restaurant, bar, health club, business services. AE, DC, MC, V.*

$$ 🏨 **Autolodge.** This attractive, colonial-style hotel is close to Hagley Park and the Avon, about 1½ kilometers (1 mile) from the city center. Rooms are large, modern, and well equipped, and rates are often discounted on weekends. Larger suites with a separate lounge are also available. ✉ *72 Papanui Rd.,* ☎ *03/355–6109,* FAX *03/355–3543. 74 rooms with bath. Restaurant, bar, exercise room. AE, DC, MC, V.*

$$ 🏨 **Riverview Lodge.** This grand Edwardian manor overlooking the
★ Avon is one of the finest bed-and-breakfasts in Christchurch. Completely restored in 1991—there is interesting native timber in details throughout the house—it offers superbly comfortable, historic accommodations and a cooked breakfast at about the same price as for a motel room. Upstairs, the Turret Room is spacious and interesting, but the large room on the side is also bright, with interesting woodwork and its own bathroom. Ernst Wipperfuerth is an amiable, offbeat host, and don't hesitate to ask him about dining or exploring suggestions. Children are accommodated by prior arrangement. The city center is a pleasant (and safe at night) 15-minute walk along the river, which allows you to leave the car behind. Rates include a very nice breakfast. ✉ *361 Cambridge Terr.,* ☎ FAX *03/365–2860. 4 rooms with bath. Boating, bicycles. MC, V.*

$$ 🏨 **Turret House.** This century-old lodge has comfortable, well-maintained rooms and a friendly atmosphere that makes it another standout among Christchurch's bed-and-breakfast accommodations. All rooms are different, and prices vary accordingly. The largest, the Apartment, has a lounge room, a separate bedroom, and a kitchen, and it could easily sleep four. For a couple, the medium-size rooms offer a good combination of space and value. Despite its location close to a major intersection, noise is not a problem. Rates include breakfast. ✉ *435 Durham St.,* ☎ *03/365–3900. 8 rooms with bath. AE, DC, MC, V.*

Nightlife

Christchurch's after-dark action doesn't match the range of activities available during the day, but that doesn't mean you have to tuck into bed as soon as the sun goes down. A recent addition to the city is the **Christchurch Casino,** which has blackjack, roulette, baccarat, gaming machines, and other ways to try your luck. It is the only casino on South Island. Dress is smart casual or better, and you will be turned away at the door if you arrive in jeans. ✉ *30 Victoria St.,* ☎ *03/365–9999.* ☉ *Mon.–Wed. 11 AM–3 AM, Thurs. 11 AM–Mon. 3 AM.*

For a dance into the wee hours, your best bet is **The Ministry,** modeled on the concept of the European club, The Ministry of Sound. The club attracts a fairly young crowd, so if you're feeling a bit gray it does have a front bar where the music is not so loud. ✉ *90 Lichfield St.,* ☎ *03/379–2910.* 🎟 *$6.* ☉ *Wed.–Sun. 9 PM–7 AM.*

Outdoor Activities and Sports

Bicycling
Southern Cycle Adventures offers a 10-day escorted bicycle tour from Christchurch to Picton via Hanmer Springs and Lewis Pass. All meals and accommodation in basic lodges or cabins are provided, but bicycle rental costs an additional $12.50 per day. A backup bus is available for weary riders. ✉ *Box 10–180, Christchurch,* ☎ *03/366–4318.* 🎟 *$1,553.*

Fishing

For information on trout and salmon fishing in Rakaia in the Canterbury region, *see* Chapter 6.

Horse Trekking

Around Christchurch, the dramatic contrast of the Canterbury Plains and mountain ranges encircling the area provides a remarkable setting for riding. Two outfitters, **Alpine Horse Safaris** (⊠ Waitohi Downs, Hawarden, North Canterbury, ☎ FAX 03/314–4293) and **Wild Country Equine Adventures** (⊠ Flock Hill, North Canterbury, ☎ 03/337–3872, FAX 03/332–8363), have treks of varying lengths in many types of terrain for differing interests, from half-day trips with afternoon tea to 10-day backcountry journeys staying in overnight huts.

Shopping

The best **Arts Centre** shopping is at the **Saturday morning craft market** that has various Kiwi goods, including handmade sweaters and woolens, that you might want to take home with you. Inside Arts Centre buildings, the **Galleria** consists of a dozen shops and studios for artisans and craftworkers, from potters to weavers to some very good jewelery makers. The quality of work varies considerably from shop to shop, but this is one of the few places where many craftworkers are represented under one roof. Most shops, including a bookstore, are open 10 to 4; some are closed weekends. Most do not take credit cards. ⊠ *Worcester St.,* ☎ *03/379–7573.*

Bivouac sells a complete range of outdoor gear and maps. ⊠ *76 Cashel St.,* ☎ *03/366–3197.*

Johnson Grocer–Leight & Co. If you happen to spot this old-time grocer on Colombo Street on your own, good for you. If not, stop in at tiny number 787 between Kilmore and Peterborough, which is choc-a-bloc with food products from the world over, with a British emphasis, of course. Toffee, fudge, bread and cheese for a picnic, canned goods—Leight & Co. has been in the hands of only two owners since 1911, and the current one has been here since 1950. ⊠ *787 Colombo St.*

Christchurch A to Z

Arriving and Departing

BY BUS AND TRAIN

Mount Cook Landline (☎ 03/343–8085) and **InterCity** (☎ 03/377–0951) operate daily bus services between Christchurch and Dunedin, Mt. Cook, Nelson, and Queenstown. InterCity also operates a daily **TranzAlpine Express** train to Arthur's Pass Village and Greymouth. The **Super Shuttle** (☎ 03/365–5655) also goes to Arthur's Pass Village and Greymouth from Christchurch.

BY CAR

Highway 1 links Christchurch with Kaikoura and Blenheim in the north and Dunedin in the south. Driving time for the 330-kilometer (205-mile) journey between Christchurch and Mount Cook Village is 5 hours; between Christchurch and Dunedin, 5½ hours.

BY PLANE

Ansett New Zealand (☎ 03/371–1146) and **Air New Zealand** (☎ 03/379–5200) link Christchurch with cities on both North and South islands. **Mount Cook Airlines** (☎ 03/379–0690) flies from Christchurch to Queenstown, Mt. Cook, and Te Anau. **Christchurch Airport** is 10 kilometers (6 miles) northwest of the city. **Super Shuttle** buses (☎ 03/361–5655) meet all incoming flights and charge $7 per passenger to city hotels. **CANRIDE** buses operate between the airport and Cathedral Square from 6 AM to 11 PM daily. The fare is $2.70. A **taxi** to the city costs about $15.

Getting Around

The city of Christchurch is flat and compact, and the best way to explore it is on two legs.

BY BICYCLE

Trailblazers (⊠ 96 Worcester St., ☎ 03/366–6033) hires out mountain bikes for $25 per day. The shop is open weekdays 9–5:30 and weekends 10–4.

BY BUS OR TRAM

The historical **Christchurch Tramway** (☎ 03/366–7830) serves as an attraction in its own right and doubles as a way to get around when those legs tire. A city circuit takes in Cathedral Square, Worcester Boulevard, Rolleston Avenue, Armagh Street, and New Regent Street. It stops close to all major attractions, including the Arts Centre, Botanic Gardens, and Canterbury Museum. A one-hour ticket costs $5 for adults; a full-day pass costs $10. You'll have no need to use the confusing bus system unless you are actually heading out of town.

Contacts and Resources

EMERGENCIES

Dial 111 for **fire, police,** or **ambulance** services.

GUIDED TOURS

Guided walking tours ($8) of the city depart daily at 10 and 2 from the red-and-black booth in Cathedral Square and last two hours.

Punting on the Avon is perfectly suited to the languid motion of Christchurch. Punts with expert boatmen may be hired from the Worcester Street bridge, near the corner of Oxford Terrace, from 10 to 6 in summer and 10 to 4 the rest of the year. The price of a 20-minute trip is $8.

The **Gray Line** (☎ 03/343–3874) runs a half-day Morning Sights tour ($26) and a full-day tour of Akaroa ($54). All tours leave from the Christchurch Visitor Information Centre daily at 9 AM.

VISITOR INFORMATION

Christchurch Visitor Information Centre. ⊠ *Worcester St. and Oxford Terr., Christchurch,* ☎ *03/379–9629.* ☉ *Weekdays 8:30–5, weekends 8:30–4.*

SIDE TRIPS FROM CHRISTCHURCH

Akaroa and the Banks Peninsula

⑮ *82 km (50 mi) east of Christchurch.*

Dominated by tall volcanic peaks, the Banks Peninsula—that nub that juts into the Pacific southeast of Christchurch—has a wonderful coastline indented with small bays where sheep graze almost to the water's edge. Its main source of fame is the town of Akaroa, which was chosen as the site for a French colony in 1838. The first French settlers arrived in 1840 only to find that the British had already established sovereignty over New Zealand by the Treaty of Waitangi. Less than 10 years later, the French abandoned their attempt at colonization, but the settlers remained and gradually intermarried with the local English community. Apart from the street names and a few surnames, there is little sign of a French connection anymore, but the village has a splendid setting, and on a sunny day it makes a marvelous trip from Christchurch. A half day will get you to and from Akaroa, including a drive up to the edge of the former volcanic dome, but take a full day if you want to do other exploring of the peninsula.

The best way to get the feel of Akaroa is to stroll along the waterfront from the lighthouse to Jubilee Park. The focus of historic interest is the **Akaroa Museum,** which has a display of Maori greenstone and embroidery and dolls dating from the days of the French settlement. The museum includes Langlois-Eteveneaux House, the two-room cottage of an early French settler, which bears the imprint of his homeland in its architecture. ⊠ *Rues Lavaud and Balguerie,* ☎ *03/304–7614.* 🖃 *$2.50.* ⊙ *Daily 10:30–4:30.*

The picture-book **Church of St. Patrick,** near the museum, was built in 1864 to replace two previous Catholic churches—the first destroyed by fire, the second by tempest. ⊠ *Rue Pompallier.* ⊙ *Daily 8–5.*

The contrast of the rim of the old volcanic cone and the coves below is striking, and an afternoon driving to the summit, around it, then dropping into one of the coves leaves you with a feeling like you've found your own corner of the world. **Okains Bay** is one of five bays on the peninsula to go to for that. A small settlement lies at the bottom of a road winding down from the summit to a beach sheltered by tall headlands. There's a cave in the rocks on the right and a path above it that leads to the remnants of a pier, now just a cluster of tilting pilings in the water. A stream lets out into the bay on the left side of the beach. Sheep paddocks rise a couple of hundred feet on either side of the sand, cradling it in green. There's a small general store in the village that doubles as a post office, and a tiny old church to poke your head into if you're curious.

Another way to get to the feel of the peninsula is by stopping for a cold one with locals afternoons at the **Hilltop Tavern.** ⊠ *Hwy. 75 and Summit Rd.*

Hiking

The 35-kilometer (22-mile) **Banks Peninsula Track** crosses beautiful coastal terrain. From Akaroa you hike over headlands, past several bays, waterfalls, seal and penguin colonies, and you might see Hector's dolphins at sea. Two-day ($60) and four-day ($100) tramps are available between October 15 and May 15. Overnight in cabins with fully equipped kitchens, which you might share with other hikers. Rates include lodging, transport from Akaroa to the first hut, landowners' fees, and a booklet describing the features of the track. ⊠ *Box 50, Akaroa,* ☎ *03//304–7612.*

Lodging

$$$ 🏨 **Oinako Lodge.** Surrounded by a garden and greenery a five-minute walk from the town and harbor of Akaroa, this charming Victorian still has its original ornamented plaster ceilings and marble fireplaces. You'll find fresh flowers in the spacious and pleasantly decorated rooms; some have balconies. There are books, music, and a piano in the guest lounge. Children are accommodated by prior arrangement. Rates include breakfast. ⊠ *99 Beach Rd., Akaroa,* ☎ *03/304–8787. 5 rooms with bath. AE, MC, V.*

Arriving and Departing

BY CAR

The main route to Akaroa is Highway 75, which leaves the southwest corner of Christchurch as Lincoln Road. The 82-kilometer (50-mile) drive takes about 90 minutes.

Guided Tours

Akaroa Tours (☎ 03/379–9629) operates a shuttle service between the Christchurch Visitor Information Centre and Akaroa; buses depart Christchurch weekdays at 10:30 and 4, Saturday at noon, and Sunday at noon and 6:45; buses depart Akaroa weekdays at 8:20 and 2:20, weekends at 10:30 (round-trip $30).

Hanmer Springs

16 *120 km (75 mi) north of Christchurch.*

Long before Europeans arrived in New Zealand, Maori travelers knew the Hanmer Springs area as Waitapu (sacred water). Early settlers didn't take long to discover these thermal springs, which bubble out into serene alpine environment, just a two-hour drive from Christchurch. More than 100 years ago, the European visitors would "take the water" for medicinal purposes, but nowadays you will find it far more pleasant to lie back and relax in the water than to drink the stuff. The **Hanmer Springs Thermal Reserve** remains the number one reason to visit the area and now consists of seven thermal pools, a freshwater 25-meter pool, and a toddler's pool. The reserve also has a sauna and steam room, a therapeutic massage service, a health and fitness center, and a fully licensed restaurant. Unfortunately, the facility, nicely built though it is, looks more like a town pool than a scenic spa. It's a functional, not an aesthetic, retreat. ⊠ *Amuri Ave., Hanmer Springs,* ☎ *03/315–7511.* ⌨ *$6, private pool $10 per person (minimum 2 people), sauna $6 per ½-hr.* ☉ *Daily 10–9.*

If you have time to spare before or after your soak in Hanmer Springs, take a walk. The forest around the town was planted by convict labor in the early 1900s and has a distinctly European look to it. You'll find European larch, Austrian pine, European alder, and other varieties. The information center has maps and fact sheets detailing several walks.

This excursion from Christchurch up the coast and then inland to Hanmer Springs requires the best part of a day.

Arriving and Departing

BY CAR

From Christchurch, follow Highway 1 north to Highway 7 at Waipara, 57 kilometers (35 miles) from the city. The drive then continues through the small town of Culverden, where Highway 7A turns toward Hanmer Springs, which is well signposted.

Visitor Information

Hurunui Visitor Information Centre. ⊠ *Off Amuri Rd. next to Hanmer Springs Thermal Reserve,* ☎ *03/315–7128.*

THE SOUTHERN ALPS

The Canterbury Plains, which ring Christchurch and act as a brief transition between the South Pacific and the soaring New Zealand Alps, are the country's finest sheep pastures, as well as its largest area of flat land. But although this may be sheep—and horse-trekking—heaven, the drive south along the plain is mundane by New Zealand standards until you leave Highway 1 and head toward the Southern Alps. By contrast, the drive to Arthur's Pass quickly takes you up into the hills, and Route 73 is a good way to get to Westland and the glaciers at Fox and Franz Josef, but it would be the long way to Queenstown.

Arthur's Pass

🔟 *153 km (96 mi) northwest of Christchurch.*

Arthur's Pass National Park is another of New Zealand's spectacular alpine regions, and hiking opportunities abound. On the way to the pass, the **Castle Hill Conservation Area** is littered with interesting rock formations. There is a parking area on the left several miles past Lake Lyndon. The national park has plenty of half- and full-day hikes and 11 backcountry tracks with overnight huts for backpacking amid local natural wonders: waterfalls, gorges, alpine wildflowers and higher-altitude grasslands, and stunning snowcapped peaks.

The Pass is the major mid-island transit to the West Coast. The west side of the pass is unbelievably steep—be aware that this may be the most hair-raising paved road you'll ever drive. The village of Arthur's Pass itself isn't much to speak of, and in foul weather it looks rather forlorn. There is a restaurant and a store for basic food supplies.

Mt. Cook

330 km (205 mi) southwest of Christchurch.

🔟 You will know you have reached the **Mackenzie Country** after you travel through Burkes Pass and the woodland is suddenly replaced by high-country tussock grassland, which is dotted with lupines in the summer months. The area is named for James ("Jock") Mckenzie (the man is Mckenzie, but the region that took his name is *Mackenzie*), one of the most intriguing and enigmatic figures in New Zealand history. Mckenzie was a Scot who may or may not have stolen the thousand sheep that were found with him in these secluded upland pastures in 1855. Arrested, tried, and convicted, he made several escapes from jail before he was granted a free pardon nine months after his trial—and disappeared from the pages of history. Regardless of his innocence or guilt, there can be no doubt that Mckenzie was a master bushman and herdsman.

🔟 Cradled by snowy mountain peaks, the long, narrow expanse of **Lake Tekapo** is one of the most photographed sights in New Zealand. Its extraordinary milky-turquoise color comes from rock-flour—rock ground by glacial action and held in a soupy suspension. On the eastern side of the lakeside power station is the tiny **Church of the Good Shepherd,** which strikes a dignified note of piety in these majestic surroundings. A nearby memorial commemorates the sheepdogs of the area. Before fences were erected around their runs, shepherds would tether dogs at strategic points to stop their sheep from straying. Now, as you drive into the small town you'll notice a knot of glitzy Asian restaurants with tour buses parked outside. It's rather an off-putting image if you've come for peace and quiet, but it's relatively easy to keep the township at your back and your eyes turned on the lake and mountains. Of course, it does mean that you can always find a tasty meal when you'd like one.

🔟 **Mount Cook Village** consists of a visitor center, a grocery store, and a couple of hotels. The national park surrounds the village. Mt. Cook National Park includes 22 peaks that top the 10,000-foot mark, the tallest of which is **Mt. Cook**—at approximately 12,283 feet, it is the highest peak between Papua New Guinea and the Andes. The mountain was dramatically first scaled in 1894 by three New Zealanders, Fyfe, Graham, and Clarke, just after it was announced that an English climber and an Italian mountain guide were to attempt the summit. In a frantic surge of national pride, the New Zealand trio resolved to beat them to it, which they did on Christmas Day. Mt. Cook is still considered a difficult ascent. In the summer of 1991 a chunk of it broke away, but fortunately there were no climbers in the path of the massive avalanches. High Peak, the summit of the mountain, is now about 66 feet lower, as a result providing a much more difficult ascent. If the sun is shining, the views are spectacular and the walks are inspiring. If the cloud ceiling is low, however, you may wonder why you came—and the mountain weather is notoriously changeable. Because a lengthy detour is required to reach Mount Cook Village, it is advisable to contact the **Visitor Information Centre** (☎ 03/435–1818) to check weather conditions. The center is open daily 8–5.

Radiating from the Mt. Cook visitor center is a network of **hiking trails** offering walks of varying difficulty, from the 10-minute Bowen Track to the 5½-hour climb to the 4,818-foot summit of Mt. Sebastapol. Particularly recommended is the walk along the Hooker Valley, a two- to four-hour round-trip. There are frequent ranger-guided walks from the visitor center, with informative talks on flora, fauna, and geology along the way.

The other main activity at Mt. Cook is **flightseeing.** From the airfield at Mount Cook Village, helicopters and fixed-wing aircraft make spectacular scenic flights across the Southern Alps. One of the most exciting is the one-hour trip aboard the ski planes that touch down on the ❷❸ **Tasman Glacier** after a dazzling scenic flight. The 10-minute stop on the glacier doesn't allow time for much more than a snapshot, but the sensation is tremendous. The moving tongue of ice beneath your feet—one of the largest glaciers outside the Himalayas—is 29 kilometers (18 miles) long and up to 2,000 feet thick in places. The intensity of light on the glacier can be dazzling, and sunglasses are a must. Generally, the best time for flights is early morning. During winter the planes drop skiers on the glacier at 10,000 feet, and they ski down through 13 kilometers (8 miles) of powder snow and fantastic ice formations. With guides, this run is suitable even for intermediate skiers. Skiplane flights cost about $195 for adults; helicopter flights range from $140 to $270. Ski-plane flights are operated by **Mount Cook Line** (☎ 03/435–1848), helicopters by the **Helicopter Line** (☎ 03/435–1801). **Alpine Guides Ltd.** (✉ Box 20, Mount Cook, ☎ 03/435–1834) can assist with guides for all treks and ski trips in the national park.

Dining

$$$ ✕ **Panorama Room.** It's the view rather than the food that dazzles at the dining room of the Hermitage Hotel (☞ Lodging, *below*). The service is efficient and the food well presented, but the meals are vastly more expensive than in the neighboring Alpine Restaurant. Choices from the menu include fillet of sole stuffed with spinach, crayfish thermidor, and venison liver flamed in whiskey with shallots. ✉ *Mount Cook Village,* ☎ *03/435–1809. Reservations essential. Jacket required. AE, DC, MC, V. Closed Apr.–Sept. No lunch.*

Lodging

Lodging at Mount Cook Village is controlled by a single company that operates four hotels there. There is also a YHA Hostel in town. And one option below is in the town of Fairlee in the mountains on the way to Mt. Cook.

$$$$ 🏨 **The Hermitage.** Famed for its stupendous mountain views, this rambling hotel is the luxury option at Mount Cook Village. Most rooms have been redecorated since 1993; however, the layout and ambience of the hotel do not match its surroundings, and you're likely to find it disappointing. Rooms that have not been renovated are dowdy and

should be avoided. ⌧ *Mount Cook Village,* ☎ *03/435–1809,* FAX *03/435–1879. 104 rooms with bath. 3 restaurants, bar, sauna. AE, DC, MC, V.*

$$$ ⊡ **Kimbell Colonial Cottages.** These neat, self-contained cottages are in the Mackenzie Country north of Fairlie, about midway between Christchurch and Mt. Cook. Prettiest of the three is Laurel, a simple timber cottage in the midst of flower beds and sheep pastures. Furnishings in each are simple and appropriately rustic. The surroundings offer trout fishing and deer hunting, and the Kimbell pub is a great source of local color. Rates include breakfast. ⌧ *R.D. 17, Fairlie, South Canterbury,* ☎ *03/658–8170,* FAX *03/685–8170. 3 cottages. Pub. AE, MC, V.*

$$$ ⊡ **Mount Cook Travelodge.** The views here are similar to those at the Hermitage, but the drop in the quality of rooms and facilities is far greater than the drop in price. Rates include breakfast. ⌧ *Mount Cook Village,* ☎ *03/627–1809,* FAX *03/435–1879. 57 rooms with bath. Restaurant. AE, DC, MC, V. Closed early May–Oct. (dates vary).*

$$ ⊡ **Mount Cook Chalets.** These metal-roof A-frames with cooking facilities are the budget option at Mount Cook Village, although in terms of comfort and facilities they are vastly overpriced. Each has two small bedrooms plus a fold-down couch and can sleep up to six. ⌧ *Mount Cook Village,* ☎ *03/627–1809,* FAX *03/435–1879. 18 chalets. AE, DC, MC, V.*

$ **Mount Cook YHA Hostel.** This friendly, well-equipped, well-located alternative is open all day and has facilities for guests with disabilities. Call ahead to reserve space; it fills up in summer. ⊡ *Bowen at Kitchener Dr.,* ☎ *03/435–1820. 59 beds in 14 rooms with shared showers. Sauna.*

Outdoor Activities and Sports

BICYCLING

Exploring South Island on a bicycle is the only way to see it all up close—the range of scenery may be unmatched in all of the world. A great variety of tours, as well as individual rentals, are available from **Adventure Center** (⌧ 1311 63rd St., No. 200, Emeryville, CA 94608, ☎ 510/654–1879, FAX 510/654–4200); **New Zealand Backroad Cycle Tours** (⌧ Box 33–153, Christchurch, ☎ 03/332–1222, FAX 03/332–4030); and **New Zealand Pedaltours** (⌧ Box 37–575, Parnell, Auckland, ☎ 09/377–0761, FAX 09/302–0967).

CLIMBING

Hikes among the mountains of Mt. Cook National Park are spectacular, and the area is also ideal for rock climbing. Experienced climbers and beginners alike can sign up for the appropriate level of **Alpine Guides'** 7- to 10-day mountaineering courses (⌧ Box 20, Mount Cook, ☎ 03/345–1834).

Southern Alps A to Z

Arriving and Departing

BY BUS AND TRAIN

Buses and the TranzAlpine Express train can also take you there from Christchurch (☞ Arriving and Departing, *below*), and the village of Arthur's Pass has a couple of eateries if you don't bring a picnic. The **Park Visitor Centre** in the village (☎ 03/318–9211) has exceptional information and natural history displays on the park. The center is open daily 8–5.

BY CAR

Arthur's Pass is a 2½- to 3-hour drive from Christchurch.

The 330-kilometer (205-mile) drive from Christchurch straight through to Mount Cook Village takes five hours.

BY PLANE

Mount Cook Airlines (☎ 03/379–0690) flies from Christchurch to Mt. Cook.

Visitor Information

Mount Cook Visitor Information Centre. ✉ *Mount Cook Village,* ☎ *03/435–1818.* ☉ *Daily 8–5.*

SOUTHLAND

Most of Southland, the western lobe of lower South Island, is taken up by two giant national parks, Fiordland and Mt. Aspiring. Fiordland, the name generally given to the southwest coast, is a majestic wilderness of rocks, ice, and beech forest, where glaciers have carved deep notches into the coast. The scenic climax of this area—and perhaps of the whole country—is Milford Sound. A cruise on the sound is a must, but anyone who wants to experience the raw grandeur of Fiordland should hike along one of the many trails in the area, among them the famous four-day Milford Track, what some call the finest walk in the world. The accommodations base and adventure center for the region is Queenstown.

Wanaka

🏵 *70 km (44 mi) northeast of Queenstown, 87 km (54 mi) south of Haast Pass.*

Set on the southern shore of Lake Wanaka, with some of New Zealand's most impressive mountains stretched out behind it, Wanaka is the welcome mat for Mount Aspiring National Park. It is a favorite of Kiwis on holiday, an alternative of sorts to Queenstown. The region has numerous trekking opportunities, a choice of ski areas, and a diverse selection of other outdoor activities. The town has a couple of unusual man-made attractions as well if you arrive on a rainy day.

Without the well-established publicity machine of Queenstown, Wanaka has tended to be overlooked by many people in the past. For that reason it has managed to retain an almost sleepy-village atmosphere for most of the year. This changes during the December–January summer holidays, and some of the favorite bars and restaurants get lively in the middle of the ski season as well. At those times, it certainly pays to book accommodations ahead.

On your way into town you'll pass the **New Zealand Fighter Pilots Museum**—a good place to start a joyride flightseeing the region in a Tiger Moth, de Havilland Dominie, or even a World War II P-51 Mustang, though the latter, at a cost of $2,000, is a little steeper than the $40 Dominie ride. The museum is a tribute to New Zealand fighter pilots, of whom the country contributed more per capita than any other nation in World Wars I and II. Biographies of New Zealand's 95 fighter aces hang on the walls of the museum. Remember to visit both the main museum building and the nearby annex. The rarest aircraft in the museum is the Japanese Oscar MkI, which is displayed complete with bullet holes from the war. ✉ *Hwy. 6,* ☎ *03/443–7010,* FAX *03/443–7011.* 🎫 *$6.* ☉ *Daily 9:30–4.*

Don't make **Stuart Landsborough's Puzzling World** your first stop in Wanaka—you may get hooked trying to solve one of the myriad of brainteasers and not leave until closing. The complex includes the amazing

Southland, Otago, and Stewart Island

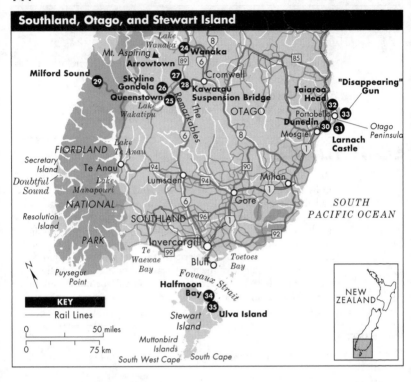

Tumbling Towers and Tilted House, which is on a 15-degree angle. In that environment everything seems somehow unreal. Is the water really running uphill? The maze can be as demanding as you want to make it by setting individual challenges. Most people spend about 30 minutes in the maze. The place in which to dwell is a section called the puzzle center, which has dozens of people hooked at any given time of day. You're free to take on the puzzle of your choice, order a cup of coffee, and proceed to get worked up. The place is 2 kilometers (1½ miles) east of town—just look for the cartoonlike houses on funny angles. ⊠ *Hwy. 89,* ☎ *03/443–7489.* ⊠ *Puzzle center free; Tilted House and Hologram Hall $3; Tilted House, Hologram Hall, and Maze $6.* ☉ *Daily 8:30–4:30, extended hrs in summer.*

Dining and Lodging

$$ ✕ **Relishes Café.** On winter nights an open fire roars in this casual café, with its hints of colonial architecture. The daytime menu is of the burger-quiche-and-salad variety, but by night it switches to more ambitious fare, such as marinated venison on plum chutney, and blackened cod on Cajun red beans and rice. Relishes sits across a road from the lake; it's a friendly place, consistent and reliable if not exceptional. ⊠ *1/99 Ardmore St.,* ☎ *03/443–9018. AE, DC, MC, V.*

$$ ✕ **White House.** You'll almost always find something with a Morrocan–North African influence on the international menu at this aptly named eatery. The Magreb Special is a tasty combination of dahl, basmati rice, yogurt and cucumber, and dried figs. The atmosphere is casual, with outdoor seating in the summer. Come for lunch or dinner, or just sit with a cuppa—coffee, that is. The homemade ice cream is also a treat. ⊠ *Dunmore and Dungarvon Sts.,* ☎ *03/443–9595. AE, DC, MC, V.*

$ ✕ **Tuatara Pizza Bar.** A favorite with backpackers in summer, and with snowboarders and skiers in winter, Tuatara has plenty of atmosphere and wholesome food to go around. The place has a relaxed, friendly feeling, and there is always good background music playing. ⊠ *Ardmore St.,* ☎ *03/443–8186. MC, V.*

$$ ✕⌂ **Wanaka Motor Inn.** Close to the lake and 2 kilometers (1½ miles) from town, this family-run motor inn has a friendly and casual atmosphere. The rooms have a natural color scheme—with timber walls and green carpets—which work well with their views. Upstairs rooms have private terraces from which you can enjoy the scenery. Its restaurant and bar areas are particularly cozy. ⊠ *Mt. Aspiring Rd., Wanaka,* ☎ *03/443–8216,* ⌷ *03/443–9108. 36 rooms with bath. Restaurant, bar. AE, DC, MC, V.*

$$$ ⌂ **Willow Cottage.** Built from stone and cob (a commonly used mixture
★ of mud, straw, and horse manure) in the 1870s, this charming white cottage is set on a farm five minutes' drive from Wanaka amid mountains and farmlands. The cottage has been caringly restored by hosts Kate and Roy Summers, who have filled it with period furnishings. One treat is sitting out on the cottage's veranda with a glass of wine or coffee, another is having breakfast with the Summerses in their farmhouse. There is also an antiques shop on the property. ⊠ *Maxwell Rd., Mt. Barker,* ☎ *03/443–8856. 2 rooms share bath. Coin laundry. AE, DC, MC, V.*

Outdoor Activities and Sports

FISHING

Locals will tell you that fishing on Lake Wanaka and nearby Lake Hawea is better than the more famed Taupo area. You won't want to enter that argument, but chances are good that you'll catch fish with the right guide. **Harry Urquhart** (☎ 03/443–1535) has trolling excursions for rainbow trout, brown trout, and quinnat salmon on Lake Hawea, and he has fly fishing trips as well. **Gerald Telford** (☎ 03/443–9257) will take you fly fishing, including night fishing. For information on trout fishing around Wanaka, *see* Chapter 6.

WALKING AND TREKKING

You could stay for a week in Wanaka, take a different walk into the bush and mountains each day, and still come nowhere near exhausting all options. If you have time for only one walk, **Mt. Iron** is relatively short and rewarding. A rocky hump carved by glaciers, its summit provides panoramic views of Lakes Wanaka and Hawea, plus the peaks of the Harris Mountains and Mt. Aspiring National Park. The access track begins 2 kilometers (1½ miles) from Wanaka, and the walk to the top takes 45 minutes. To avoid going over old ground, descend on the alternative route down the steep eastern face—another 45-minute walk.

Mt. Roy is a daylong commitment. A track starts at the base of the mountain, 6 kilometers (4 miles) from Wanaka on the road to Glendhu Bay. The return journey takes about 6 hours. The track is closed from early October to mid-November.

For information on other local walks, contact the **Department of Conservation** (⊠ Ardmore St., ☎ 03/477–0677).

Queenstown

㉕ *70 km (44 mi) southeast of Wanaka, 530 km (330 mi) southwest of Christchurch.*

Set on the edge of a glacial lake beneath the sawtooth peaks of the Remarkables, Queenstown is the most popular tourist destination on South Island. Once prized by the Maori as a source of greenstone, the town boomed when gold was discovered in the Shotover, which quickly became famous as "the richest river in the world." Queenstown could easily have become a ghost town when gold gave out—except for its location. With ready access to mountains, lakes, rivers, ski fields, and the glacier-carved coastline of Fiordland National Park, the town has become the adventure capital of New Zealand. Its shop windows are crammed with skis, polar tech, Asolo walking boots, and Marin mountain bikes. Along Shotover Street, travel agents offer white-water rafting, jet boating, caving, trekking, heli-skiing, parachuting, and parapenting (rappeling). New Zealanders' penchant for bizarre adventure sports reaches a climax in Queenstown, and it was here that the sport of leaping off a bridge with a giant rubber band wrapped around the ankles—bungee jumping—took root as a commercial enterprise. Taking its marvelous location for granted, Queenstown is mostly a comfortable, cosmopolitan base for the outdoor activities around it.

Some of the best views of the town and the mountains all around are from the **Queenstown Gardens,** on the peninsula that encloses Queenstown Bay. The **Skyline Gondola** whisks passengers to the heights of Bob's Peak, 1,425 feet above the lake, for a panoramic view of the town and the Remarkables. The summit terminal has a cafeteria, a buffet restaurant, and "Kiwi Magic," a 25-minute aerial film tour of the country with stunning effects. ⊠ *Brecon St., Queenstown,* ☎ *03/442–7540.* ✉ *Gondola $12, Kiwi Magic $6.* ☉ *Daily 10–10; Kiwi Magic screens every hr on the hr, 11–9.*

NEED A BREAK?   **The Remarkable Naff Café.** A 40-year-old Faema coffeemaker takes pride of place on the counter of this coffee shop, placing the emphasis squarely on coffee. The locals say that you don't need to eat after a cup of strong from this place. A cuppa alone may not be *quite* that satisfying, but if you take a piece of banana cake as well, you almost certainly won't feel like lunch for a few hours. Choose from a dozen or more coffees, a few teas, or a hot chocolate, and a small range of cakes and cookies. ⊠ *1/62 Shotover St., Queenstown,* ☎ *03/442–8211. No credit cards.*

Dining and Lodging

$$ ✕ **Avanti.** This restaurant at the heart of Queenstown serves better-than-average Italian dishes at a far lower price than most in this resort area. Pasta and pizza are prominent on an extensive menu, but so are more substantial meals such as venison goulash and several veal dishes. Servings are designed for appetites honed on the mountain slopes. ⊠ *The Mall, Queenstown,* ☎ *03/442–8503. AE, DC, MC, V. BYOB.*

$$ ✕ **The Boardwalk.** You might want to eat there just for the view. On ★   the second floor of the steamer wharf building, the restaurant looks over Lake Wakatipu toward The Remarkables. Nothing can quite beat that, but the menu makes a good attempt, and this restaurant has become a favorite with both locals and visitors. Seafood is the specialty, including dishes such as creamy smoked salmon soup, steamed prawn dim sum, lightly poached New Zealand sole fillets in a chardonnay, avocado, and shrimp sauce, and lamb with pumpkin ratatouille, spinach leaves, and mint oil. ⊠ *Steamer Wharf, Queenstown,* ☎ *03/442–3630. AE, DC, MC, V.*

$$ ✕ **The Cow.** The pizza and pasta at this tiny, stone-wall restaurant are some of the best-value meals in town, but the place is immensely popular, so be prepared to wait for a table. A roaring fire provides a cozy

atmosphere on chilly evenings, but patrons aren't encouraged to linger over dinner, and you may be asked to share your table. ⊠ *Cow La., Queenstown,* ☎ *03/442–8588. MC, V. BYOB. No lunch.*

$ ✕ **Gourmet Express.** The food may not reach gourmet standards, but the service is certainly express. A popular breakfast spot, this casual diner at the front of a shopping arcade serves pancakes with maple syrup, eggs any way you want, and heart-starting coffee. A variety of inexpensive grills and burgers is available for lunch and dinner. ⊠ *Bay Centre, Shotover St., Queenstown,* ☎ *03/442–9619. AE, DC, MC, V. BYOB.*

$ ✕ **Stonewall Café.** There is nothing remarkable about the sandwiches, salads, soups, and pasta at this center-of-town café, but the outdoor tables are a good choice for lunch on a sunny day. ⊠ *The Mall, Queenstown,* ☎ *03/442–6429. AE, MC, V. Closed weekends.*

$$$$ 🏠 **Millbrook Resort.** A 20-minute drive from Queenstown, this glamorous resort offers luxurious, self-contained accommodations with ★ special appeal for golfers. Millbrook is an elevated cluster of big, comfortable, two-story villas surrounded by an 18-hole golf course that was designed by New Zealand professional Bob Charles. The villas are decorated in country style: pine tables, textured walls, shuttered windows, and a cream-and-cornflower-blue color scheme. Each has a fully equipped kitchen, laundry facilities, a large lounge–dining room, ski closet, and two bedrooms, each with an en-suite bathroom, and the price, all things considered, is a bargain. ⊠ *Malaghans Rd., Arrowtown,* ☎ *03/442–1563,* ℻ *03/442–1145. 56 villas with bath. Restaurant, bar, 18-hole golf course, tennis court. AE, DC, MC, V.*

$$$$ 🏠 **Millennium Queenstown.** The most luxurious accommodation close ★ to town, the Millennium is built at the point where American scientists sighted Venus in 1870. One of the conditions of building the hotel was that the rock from which the planet was sighted be left intact. Of more tangible importance are the comfortable, well-equipped rooms, and the Observatory Restaurant, which adds an international touch to New Zealand fare. ⊠ *Franklin Rd. and Stanley St., Queenstown,* ☎ *03/441–8888,* ℻ *03/441–8889. 220 rooms with bath. Restaurant, bar, sauna, excercise room, baby-sitting. AE, DC, MC, V.*

$$$$ 🏠 **Nugget Point.** Poised high above the Shotover River, this modern, ★ stylish retreat offers the finest accommodations in the Queenstown area. Rooms are cozy and luxuriously large, and each has a balcony, a kitchenette, and a bedroom separate from the lounge area. The lodge is a 10-minute drive from Queenstown on the road to Coronet Peak, one of the top ski areas in the country. ⊠ *Arthurs Point Rd., Queenstown,* ☎ *03/442–7630,* ℻ *03/442–7308. 35 rooms with bath. Restaurant, bar, pool, sauna, spa, tennis court, squash. AE, DC, MC, V.*

$$$ 🏠 **Stone House.** On the hillside overlooking Queenstown and the lake, this handsome, historic cottage has been brought back to life by its enthusiastic owners and is nicely decorated in a charming, country style. Breakfasts are large and magnificent. Smoking is not permitted inside the house, and children are not accommodated. Rates include breakfast. ⊠ *47 Hallenstein St., Queenstown,* ☎ ℻ *03/442–9812. 1 room with bath, 2 with shower. MC, V.*

$$ 🏠 **Trelawn Place.** Perched on the brink of the Shotover Gorge 3 kilometers (1½ miles) from Queenstown, this stone-and-timber colonial-style house has homey comforts and million-dollar views. The most popular of the three spacious guest rooms is the blue room, on the ground floor. If you want more privacy and the option of making your own meals, reserve the two-bedroom cottage for a few extra dollars. Rates include breakfast. ⊠ *Box 117, Queenstown,* ☎ *03/442–9160. 4 rooms with bath, 1 cottage with bath. Hot tub. MC, V.*

Outdoor Activities and Sports

BUNGEE JUMPING

AJ Hackett Bungy, the pioneer in the sport, offers two jumps in the area. Kawarau Bridge is the original jump site, 23 kilometers (14 miles) from Queenstown on State Highway 6. Daredevils who graduate from the 143-foot plunge might like to test themselves on the 230-foot Skippers Canyon Bridge. The price is $129 for the Kawarau jump including video and T-shirt, $100 for Skippers Canyon, including T-shirt and transport. ⊠ *Box 488, Queenstown,* ☎ *03/442–1177.* ☉ *Winter, daily 8:30–5; summer, daily 9–7.*

FISHING

For information on trout fishing around Queenstown, *see* Chapter 6.

HIKING

For information on taking guided multi-day hikes on the Milford, Routeburn, and Hollyford Tracks, *see* Hiking–Tramping *in* Chapter 6.

HORSE TREKKING

Moonlight Stables has a choice of full- or half-day rides with spectacular views of the mountains and rivers around the Wakatipu–Arrow Basin. Ride across some of the 800 acres of rolling land that make up Doonholme deer farm. Both novice and experienced riders are welcome. Transportation from Queenstown is provided. ⊠ *Box 784, Queenstown,* ☎ *03/442–1229.* 🖅 *½-day trip $50 per person.*

JET-BOAT RIDES

The **Dart River Jet Boat Safari** is a 2½-hour journey 32 kilometers (20 miles) upstream into the ranges of the Mt. Aspiring National Park. This rugged area is one of the most spectacular parts of South Island, and the trip is highly recommended. Buses depart Queenstown daily at 8, 11, and 2 for the 45-minute ride to the boats. ⊠ *Box 76, Queenstown,* ☎ *03/442–9992.* 🖅 *$99.*

The **Shotover Jet** is the most famous jet-boat ride in the country (and one of the most exciting): a high-speed, heart-stopping adventure on which the boat pirouettes within inches of canyon walls. If you want to stay relatively dry, sit beside the driver. The boats are based at the Shotover Bridge, a 10-minute drive from Queenstown, and depart frequently between 7 AM and 9 PM from December through April, 9:30–4:30 the rest of the year. ⊠ *Shotover River Canyon, Queenstown,* ☎ *03/442–8570.* 🖅 *$65.*

RAFTING

Kawarau Raft Expeditions runs various half-, full-, and two-day whitewater rafting trips in the Queenstown area. The most popular is the grade-3½ to grade-5 ride along the Shotover River, an unforgettable journey that ends with the rafts shooting through the 560-foot Oxenbridge Tunnel. ⊠ *35 Shotover St., Queenstown,* ☎ *03/442–9792.* 🖅 *$95–$239 per person.*

Arrowtown

㉗ *22 km (14 mi) northeast of Queenstown, 105 km (66 mi) south of Wanaka.*

Another gold-mining town, Arrowtown lies 20 kilometers (13 miles) to the northeast. It had long been suspected that there was gold along the Arrow River, and when Edward Fox, an American, was seen selling large quantities of the precious metal in nearby Clyde, the hunt was on. Others attempted to follow the wily Fox back to his diggings, but he kept giving his pursuers the slip, on one occasion even abandoning his tent and provisions in the middle of the night. Eventually a large party of prospectors stumbled on Fox and his team of 40 miners. The secret was out, miners rushed to stake their claims, and Arrowtown was born.

After the gold rush ended, the place was just another sleepy rural town until tourism created a new boom. Lodged at the foot of the steep Crown Range, this atmospheric little village of weathered-timber shop fronts and white stone churches shaded by ancient sycamores was simply too gorgeous to escape the attention of the tour buses. These days it has become a tourist trap, but a highly photogenic one, especially when autumn gilds the hillsides.

In a less visited part of the town is the former **Chinese settlement.** Chinese miners were common on the goldfields in the late 1860s, but local prejudice forced them to live in their own separate enclave. A number of their huts and Ah Lum's Store, one of the few Chinese goldfield buildings to survive intact, have been preserved. ⊠ *Bush Creek (western end of town).* ⊙ *Daily 9–5.*

㉘ Kawarau Suspension Bridge is where the bungee jumpers make their leaps—a spectacle well worth the short detour. As a promotional stunt, the AJ Hackett company once offered a free jump to anyone who would jump nude, but there were so many takers that the scheme had to be abandoned. The bridge is on Highway 6, not far from Arrowtown.

Gibbston Valley Wines is in the Kawarau Gorge and is the best known winery in Central Otago—the world's southernmost wine-producing region. The vineyards in this area are also the highest and farthest from the sea in New Zealand. The Gibbston property was bought by a television journalist in the 1970s, and the winery, cellar, and restaurant were opened to the public in 1990. In 1995, Gibbston added a *cave* (cellar), which was blasted out from the side of the hill the property is on. Wine tasting tours are held in the cave regularly and are now one of the most interesting aspects of a visit to Gibbston. The showcase wine here is Pinot Noir, which suits the hot days, cold nights, and the lack of coastal influence. Also available is riesling, chardonnay, and that almost classic New Zealand white, sauvignon blanc. ⊠ *Gibbston R.D. 1,* ☎ *03/442–6910,* 𝔽𝔸𝕏 *03/442–6909.* ▦ *Wine cave tour and tasting $8.50.* ⊙ *Daily 9:30–5:30.*

Milford Sound

㉙ *290 km (180 mi) west of Queenstown.*

From Queenstown, the road to Milford Sound passes through the town of Te Anau, then winds through deep, stony valleys where waterfalls cascade into mossy beech forests as it enters **Fiordland National Park.** Fiordland, the largest national park in New Zealand, takes its name from the deep sea inlets, or sounds, on its western flank. This is the most rugged part of the country. Parts of the park are so remote that they have never been explored, and visitor activities are mostly confined to a few of the sounds and the walking trails. The nearest services base is the town of Te Anau, which offers a choice of motel, hotel, or motor camp accommodations. Allow at least 2½ hours for the 119-kilometer (74-mile) journey from Te Anau to Milford Sound.

For most visitors, Fiordland's greatest attraction is **Milford Sound,** the sort of overpowering place where poets run out of words, and photographers out of film. Hemmed in by walls of rock that rise from the sea almost sheer up to 4,000 feet, the 16-kilometer-long (10-mile-long) inlet was carved by a succession of glaciers as they gouged a track to the sea. Its dominant feature is the 5,560-foot pinnacle of Mitre Peak, which is capped with snow for all but the warmest months of the year. Opposite the peak, Bowen Falls tumbles 520 feet before exploding into the sea. Milford Sound is also spectacularly wet: The average annual rainfall is around 20 feet. An inch an hour for 12 hours straight isn't uncommon, and two days without rain is reckoned to be a drought. In addition to a raincoat you'll need insect repellent—the sound is renowned for its voracious sandflies.

From the road end, a number of **cruise boats** depart frequently, from about 11 AM to 3 PM, for trips around the sound; expect to pay about $40 for the ride. During the summer holiday period it's essential to book ahead. ⊠ *Fiordland Travel, Steamer Wharf, Queenstown,* ☎ *03/442–7500.*

There isn't any lodging at Milford Sound, just transportation to and fro. You need to stay in Queenstown or Te Anau and make the trek in the day you plan to come. It is a long drive in and out, so consider letting someone else do it for you. For information on buses and flights to Milford Sound, *see* Southland A to Z, *below.*

Hiking

If you plan to walk the **Milford Track**—a wholly rewarding, four-day, 54-kilometer (34-mile) bushwalk through Fiordland National Park—understand that it is one of New Zealand's most popular hikes. The track is strictly one-way, and because park authorities control access, you can feel as though you have the wilderness more or less to yourself. Independent and guided groups stay in different overnight huts. Be prepared for rain and snow but also for what many call the finest walk in the world, through a geological wonderland of lush vegetation and fascinating wildlife, past waterfalls, glowworm caves, and burgeoning trout streams. If you plan to hike independent of a tour group, call the **Fiordland National Park Visitor Centre** (⊠ Box 29, Te Anau, ☎ 03/249–8514, ✆ 03/249–8515) well in advance—up to a year if you plan to go in December or January. Freedom walking without a guide requires you to bring your own food, utensils, and bedding. You can fish along the way for trout if you have a license. Going with a guide requires deep pockets (the service costs $1,489) and stamina to carry your pack over the passes, and provides comfortable beds and someone else who does the cooking. Freedom and guided walks begin at Glade Wharf on Lake Te Anau (tay ahn-o) and end with a ferry taking you from Sandfly Point over to the Milford Sound dock. You'll need to take a bus or plane from there to where you'll stay next. For information on guided walks, *see* Hiking *in* Chapter 6, *below.*

The 67-kilometer (42-mile) **Kepler Track** forms a loop beginning and ending at the south end of Lake Te Anau. It skirts the lakeshore, climbs up to the bush line, passes limestone bluffs, the Luxmore Caves, and has incredible alpine views and overlooks of South Fiord. There is wonderful bird life along the track, as well. You can camp overnight in huts or use a tent on this three- to four-day tramp, and you'll need to bring food, utensils, and bedding. For information and bookings, call the **Fiordland National Park Visitor Centre** (⊠ Box 29, Te Anau, ☎ 03/249–8514, ✆ 03/249–8515).

Southland A to Z

Arriving and Departing

BY BUS

From Queenstown, **Mount Cook Landline** (☎ 03/442–7650) runs into Milford Sound. **InterCity** (☎ 03/442–8238) buses go to Nelson via the west-coast glaciers. Both run daily to Christchurch, Mt. Cook, and Dunedin.

BY CAR

Highway 6 enters Queenstown from the west coast; driving time for the 350-kilometer (220-mile) journey from Franz Josef is eight hours. From Queenstown, Highway 6 continues south to Invercargill—a 190-kilometer (120-mile) distance that takes about three hours to drive. The fastest route from Queenstown to Dunedin is via Highway 6 to Cromwell, south on Highway 8 to Milton, then north along Highway 1, a distance of 280 kilometers (175 miles), which can be covered in five hours.

BY PLANE

Queenstown is linked with Auckland, Christchurch, Rotorua, and Wellington by both **Ansett New Zealand** (☎ 03/442–6161) and **Mount Cook Airlines** (☎ 03/442–7650), which also flies several times daily to Mt. Cook. Mount Cook Airlines also flies into Milford Sound, which is a beautiful flight, weather permitting. Queenstown Airport is 9 kilometers (6 miles) east of town. The **Johnston's Shuttle Express** (☎ 03/442–3639) meets all incoming flights and charges $6 per person to hotels in town. The taxi fare is about $15.

Contacts and Resources

EMERGENCIES

Dial 111 for **fire, police,** and **ambulance** services.

GUIDED TOURS

The **Double Decker** (☎ 03/442–6067) is an original London bus that makes a 2½-hour circuit from Queenstown to Arrowtown and the bungee-jumping platform on the Karawau River. Tours ($25) depart Queenstown daily at 10 and 2 from the Mall and the Earnslaw wharf.

Fiordland Travel has a wide choice of fly-drive tour options to Milford and Doubtful sounds from Queenstown. The cost of a one-day bus tour and cruise on Milford Sound is $132. ⊠ *Steamer Wharf, Queenstown,* ☎ *03/442–7500.*

Milford Sound Adventure Tours offers a bus-cruise trip to Milford Sound from Te Anau ($80) that includes a cycling option. From the Homer Tunnel, passengers can leave the bus and coast 13 kilometers (8 miles) down to the sound on mountain bikes. These tours are smaller and more personal than many others. ⊠ *Box 134, Te Anau,* ☎ *03/249–7227 or 0800/80–7227.* ☉ *Tour departs Te Anau daily at 7:30 AM.*

The **TSS *Earnslaw*** is a vintage lake steamer that has been restored to brassy, wood-paneled splendor and put to work cruising Lake Wakatipu from Queenstown. A lunch cruise, an afternoon cruise across the lake to a sheep station, and a dinner cruise are available from July through May. ⊠ *Steamer Wharf, Queenstown,* ☎ *03/442–7500.*

VISITOR INFORMATION

Fiordland National Park Visitor Centre. ⊠ *Box 29, Te Anau,* ☎ *03/249–7921.*

Queenstown Visitor Information Centre. ⊠ *Clocktower Centre, Shotover and Camp Sts.,* ☎ *03/442–4100.* ☉ *Daily 7–7.*

DUNEDIN AND OTAGO

The province of Otago stretches southeast of Queenstown to the Pacific. Flatter than Southland—most of the world is—it may look like parts of North Island. Its capital, Dunedin (dun-*ee*-din), is one of the unexpected treasures of New Zealand: a harbor city of steep streets and prim Victorian architecture, with a royal albatross colony on its doorstep. Invercargill is the southern anchor of the province, essentially a farm service community that few travelers will find any reason to visit unless continuing to remote Stewart Island (☞ *below*).

Dunedin

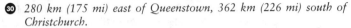 *280 km (175 mi) east of Queenstown, 362 km (226 mi) south of Christchurch.*

Clinging to the walls of the natural amphitheater at the western end of Otago Harbour, South Island's second-largest city, Dunedin, combines wildlife, inspiring seascapes, and a handsome Victorian townscape. It also has a large number of university students, who give the city a vitality far greater than its population of 120,000 might suggest.

Dunedin is the Gaelic name for Edinburgh, and the city's Scottish roots are evident. It was founded in 1848 by settlers of the Free Church of Scotland, a breakaway group from the Presbyterian Church; today it has the only kilt shop in the country and the only whiskey distillery. The city prospered mightily during the gold rush of the 1860s. For a while it was the largest city in the country, and the riches of the Otago goldfields are reflected in the bricks and mortar of Dunedin, most notably in the Italianate Municipal Chambers building. A great statue of Robert Burns presides over the heart of the city. The most compelling attraction for visitors is probably the royal albatross colony at Taiaroa Head, the only place on earth where these majestic seabirds can be seen with relative ease. Dunedin is also noted for its rhododendrons, which are at their best in October. Its size makes it easy to explore on foot.

The **Octagon** is at the center of town, a sort of city's navel. The **statue of Robert Burns** sits in front of the cathedral "with his back to the kirk and his face to the pub," a telling sign to say the least. On Stuart Street at the corner of Dunbar, take notice of the late-Victorian **Law Courts.** Above the Stuart Street entrance stands the figure of Justice, scales in hand but without her customary blindfold (though the low helmet she wears probably has the same effect).

The **Dunedin Railway Station,** a cathedral to the power of steam, is a massive bluestone structure in Flemish Renaissance style, lavishly decorated with heraldic beasts, coats of arms, nymphs, scrolls, a mosaic floor, and even stained-glass windows portraying steaming locomotives. This extravagant building earned its architect, George Troup, the nickname Gingerbread George from the people of Dunedin and a knighthood from the king. The station has far outlived the steam engine, and for all its magnificence receives few trains these days. ⊠ *Anzac Ave. at Stuart St.* ⊙ *Daily 7–6.*

The **First Presbyterian Church** on the south side of Moray Place is perhaps the finest example of a Norman Gothic building in the country. The **Early Settlers Museum** preserves an impressive collection of artifacts, from the years when this was a whaling station to the days of the early Scottish settlers to the prosperous gold-rush era of the late-19th century. ⊠ *220 Cumberland St.,* ☎ *03/477–5052.* ▧ *$4.* ⊙ *Weekdays 10–5, weekends 1–5.*

The 35-room Jacobean-style **Olveston** mansion was built between 1904 and 1906 for David Theomin, a wealthy businessman and patron of the arts, who amassed a handsome collection of antiques and contemporary furnishings. The house and its furnishings are undoubtedly a treasure from an elegant age, but apart from some paintings collected by Theomin's daughter there is very little in it to suggest that it's in New Zealand. Even the oak staircase and balustrade were prefabricated in England. The one-hour guided tour is recommended. ⊠ *42 Royal Terr.,* ☎ *03/477–3320.* 🖃 *$10.* ☉ *Daily 9–5; tour daily at 9:30, 10:45, noon, 1:30, 2:45, and 4.*

Dining and Lodging

$$$$ ✕ **Bellpepper Blues.** One of the country's most respected chefs, Michael Clydesdale, combines esoteric ingredients with recipes drawn from both the Pacific and the Mediterranean to produce food with flair. Blue cod comes baked in a parcel of rice paper, venison is roasted with an onion and orange bourbon *jus,* and steak tournedos comes with wasabi and sesame-seed butter. The setting, inside a converted pub, is casual and attractive. ⊠ *474 Princes St., Dunedin,* ☎ *03/474–0973. AE, DC, MC, V. Closed Sun. No lunch Mon., Tues., or Sat.*

$$$ ✕ **Harbour Lights.** Poised on the shores of the Otago Peninsula over-
  ★ looking the harbor, this restaurant is an exception to the rule that good food and good views don't usually coincide. Fish and game dishes are prominent on a menu that features such main courses as smoked South Island salmon with fresh herbs, wild boar schnitzel, and grilled grouper steak with béarnaise sauce. The balcony is a favorite spot for summer dining. ⊠ *494 Portobello Rd., MacAndrew Bay,* ☎ *03/476–1604. AE, DC, MC, V. No lunch Mon.–Sat.*

$$ ✕ **Palms Cafe.** Vegetarians are especially well served at this casual, popular restaurant. The menu sometimes includes a casserole of olives, feta cheese, mushrooms, and tomatoes, and a Greek pastry roll filled with spinach and feta. Nonvegetarian mains may include lamb kebabs with peanut sauce, a whole sole with garlic sauce, and fillet of lamb with a green peppercorn glaze. The restaurant has a no-smoking policy. ⊠ *84 Lower High St., Dunedin,* ☎ *03/477–6534. AE, DC, MC, V. BYOB. No lunch.*

$$ 🏨 **Cargills Motor Inn.** In a convenient location close to the city center, this motor inn offers superior motel-style rooms as well as two-bedroom family suites. Reduced rates apply Friday to Sunday night. ⊠ *678 George St., Dunedin,* ☎ *03/477–7983,* 🖷 *03/477–8098. 50 rooms with bath. Restaurant, bar. AE, DC, MC, V.*

$ 🏨 **Magnolia House.** Overlooking the city of Dunedin in a prestige suburb, this gracious B&B offers atmospheric accommodations. The spacious guest rooms are furnished with antiques, and the house is surrounded by a pretty garden that includes native bushland. The house has a no-smoking policy. Dinner is available by arrangement, and children are welcome. Rates include breakfast. ⊠ *18 Grendon St., Maori Hill, Dunedin,* ☎ *03/467–5999. 3 rooms share bath. No credit cards.*

Fishing

For information on deep-sea fishing out of Dunedin, *see* Chapter 6.

En Route If you're driving in or out of Dunedin up the coast, the **Moeraki Boulders** are good to stop and gawk at for a while. These giant spherical rocks are concretions, formed by a gradual build-up of minerals around a central core. Some boulders have sprung open, revealing—no, not alien life forms—interesting calcite crystals. The boulders populate the beach north of the town of Moeraki and south as well at Katiki Beach off Highway 1, about 60 kilometers (37 miles) above Dunedin, or 40 kilometers (25 miles) below Oamaru.

Otago Peninsula

The main areas of interest on the claw-shape peninsula that extends northeast from Dunedin are the albatross colony and Larnach Castle.

On the return journey to Dunedin, the Highcliff Road, which turns inland at the village of Portobello, is a scenic alternative to the coastal Portobello Road.

㉛ Set high on a hilltop with commanding views from its battlements, **Larnach Castle** is the grand baronial fantasy of William Larnach, an Australian-born businessman and politician. The castle was a vast extravagance even in the free-spending atmosphere of the gold rush. Larnach imported an English craftsman to carve the ceilings, which took 12 years to complete, and the solid marble bath, marble fireplaces, tiles, glass, and even much of the wood came from Europe. The mosaic in the foyer depicts Larnach's family crest and the modest name he gave to his stately pile: the Camp. Larnach rose to a prominent position in the New Zealand government of the late 1800s, but in 1898, beset by a series of financial disasters and possible marital problems, he committed suicide in Parliament House. (According to one romantic version, Larnach's third wife, whom he married at an advanced age, ran off with his eldest son; devastated, Larnach shot himself.) A café in the castle ballroom serves Devonshire teas and light snacks. ⊠ *Camp Rd.,* ☎ *03/476–1302.* ⊡ *$10.* ⊙ *Daily 9–5.*

㉜ **Taiaroa Head,** the eastern tip of the Otago Peninsula, is the site of a breeding colony of royal albatrosses. Among the largest birds in the world, with a wingspan of up to 10 feet, they can take off only from steep slopes with the help of a strong breeze. Outside of Taiaroa Head and the Chatham Islands to the east, they are found only on windswept islands deep in southern latitudes, remote from human habitation. The colony is open for viewing from October through August, with the greatest number of birds present shortly after the young hatch around the end of January. Between March and September parents leave the fledglings in their nests while they gather food for them. In September the young birds fly away, returning about eight years later to start their own breeding cycle. From the visitor center, groups follow a steep trail up to the Albatross Observatory, from which the birds may be seen through narrow windows. They are only rarely seen in flight. Access to the colony is strictly controlled, and visitors must book in advance. ⊠ *Taiaroa Head, Dunedin,* ☎ *03/478–0499.* ⊡ *1½-hr tour (including fort) $25, 1-hr tour (excluding fort) $20.* ⊙ *Mid-Nov.–Aug., daily 10:30–4.*

㉝ In the same area as the colony is the **"Disappearing" Gun,** a 6-inch artillery piece installed during the Russian Scare of 1888. When the gun was fired, the recoil would propel it back into its pit, where it could be reloaded out of the line of enemy fire. The gun has been used in anger only once, when it was fired across the bow of a fishing boat that had failed to observe correct procedures before entering the harbor during World War II. ⊡ *$8.*

Lodging

$ 🏨 **Larnach Lodge.** A modern timber building on the grounds of Larnach Castle, 19 kilometers (12 miles) from Dunedin, the lodge offers comfortable motel suites with marvelous views. Dinners are available in the castle by arrangement; otherwise the nearest restaurant is a 10-minute drive away. Budget rooms with shared facilities are available in the converted coach house. ⊠ *Camp Rd., Otago Peninsula, Dunedin,* ☎ *03/476–1616. 27 rooms with bath. AE, DC, MC, V.*

Dunedin and Otago A to Z

Arriving and Departing

BY BUS

Dunedin is served by **Mount Cook Landline** (☎ 0800/800–287 or 03/474–0677) and **InterCity** buses (☎ 0800/664–545 or 03/477–8860).

BY CAR

Driving time along the 280 kilometers (175 miles) between Queenstown and Dunedin (via Highway 6 and Highway 1) is four hours. The main route between Dunedin and Invercargill is Highway 1—a 3½-hour drive. A slower, scenic alternative is along the coast, which adds another 90 minutes to the journey.

BY PLANE

Dunedin is linked with all other New Zealand cities by **Ansett New Zealand** (☎ 0800/800–146 or 03/477–4146) and **Air New Zealand** (☎ 03/477–5769). **Dunedin Airport** lies 20 kilometers (13 miles) south of the city. **Johnston's Shuttle Express** (☎ 03/476–2519), a shuttle service between the airport and the city, meets all incoming flights and charges $10 per person. Taxi fare to the city is about $30.

Contacts and Resources

EMERGENCIES

Dial 111 for **fire, police,** and **ambulance** services.

GUIDED TOURS

Twilight Tours offers various minibus tours of Dunedin and its surroundings, including an afternoon tour that focuses on the albatrosses, penguins, and seals of the Otago Peninsula. The penguin sanctuary is a privately operated venture, and this tour is the only way to see the rare yellow-eyed and little blue penguins. The tour price does not include admission to the albatross colony. Tours depart from the Dunedin Visitor Information Centre. ⊠ *Box 963, Dunedin,* ☎ *03/474–3300.* ☑ *$46.* ☺ *Tour departs Apr.–Oct., daily at 1:30; Nov.–Mar., daily at 2:30.*

VISITOR INFORMATION

Dunedin Visitor Information Centre. ⊠ *48 the Octagon,* ☎ *03/474–3300,* 𝔽𝔸𝕏 *03/474–3311.* ☺ *Weekdays 8:30–5, weekends 9–5; extended hrs in summer.*

STEWART ISLAND

The third and most southerly of New Zealand's main islands, Stewart Island is separated from South Island by the 24-kilometer (15-mile) Foveaux Strait. Even by New Zealand standards, Stewart Island is remote, raw, and untouched. Electricity is a recent innovation, roads total about 20 kilometers (13 miles), and apart from the settlement of **Halfmoon Bay** on Paterson Inlet, the place is practically uninhabited. For most visitors, the attractions are its seclusion, its relaxed way of life, and—despite a once-busy lumber-milling industry—its untouched quality.

The island covers some 1,700 square kilometers (650 square miles). It measures about 64 kilometers (40 miles) from north to south and about the same distance across at its widest point. On the coastline, sharp cliffs rise from a succession of sheltered bays and beaches; in the interior, forested hills rise gradually toward the western side of the island. Seals and penguins frequent the coast, and the island's prolific bird life includes a number of species rarely seen in any other part of the country. In fact, it is one of the surest places to go to see Kiwi birds. One of the best spots for birding is **Ulva Island,** a one-hour launch trip around the coast from Halfmoon Bay (☞ Guided Tours *in* Stewart Island A to Z, *below*).

Dining and Lodging

$$$$ ✕🏠 **Stewart Island Lodge.** The most luxurious accommodations on the island offer comfortable, centrally heated suites with private baths. The focal points of life at the lodge are the guest lounge and the dining room, both of which offer expansive views across the bay. The owners have a game-fishing launch and can arrange scenic tours of the island. Local seafood is a specialty on the dinner menu. Rates include all meals. ⊠ *Halfmoon Bay, Nichol Rd., Stewart Island,* ☎ 🅵🅰🆇 *03/219–1085. 4 rooms with bath. AE, DC, MC, V.*

$ 🏠 **Rakiura Motel.** Within easy walking distance of Halfmoon Bay, the Rakiura offers standard motel units that sleep up to six. ⊠ *Horseshoe Bay Rd., Halfmoon Bay,* ☎ *03/219–1096. 5 rooms with bath. MC.*

Outdoor Activities

FISHING

For information on deep-sea fishing out of Halfmoon Bay, *see* Chapter 6.

HIKING

A network of walking trails has been established on the northern half of the island, leaving the south as a wilderness area. A popular trek is the **Northern Circuit,** a 10-day walk from Halfmoon Bay that circles the north coast and then cuts through the interior to return to its starting point. The island's climate is notoriously changeable, and walkers should be prepared for rain and mud. For information on walks, contact the **Department of Conservation** (⊠ Main Rd., Halfmoon Bay, ☎ 03/219–1218).

Stewart Island A to Z

Arriving and Departing

BY BOAT

Stewart Island Marine (☎ 03/212–7660, 🅵🅰🆇 03/212–8377) operates a ferry service between the island and the port of Bluff, the port for Invercargill. The one-way fare is $37. Ferries depart Bluff weekdays at 9:30 and 4 between May and August (winter) and Monday to Saturday at 9:30 and 5 the rest of the year. On Sunday, there is a 5 PM service only. The crossing takes one hour.

BY PLANE

Southern Air (☎ 03/218–9129, 🅵🅰🆇 03/214–4681) operates several flights daily between Invercargill and Halfmoon Bay. The 20-minute flight costs $118, round-trip. The free baggage allowance is 15 kilograms (33 pounds) per passenger.

Contacts and Resources

EMERGENCIES

Dial 111 for **fire, police,** and **ambulance** services.

GUIDED TOURS

For information on fishing trips, bird-watching trips to Ulva Island, and boat trips around Paterson Inlet, contact **Stewart Island Travel** (⊠ Box 26, Stewart Island, ☎ 03/219–1269).

VISITOR INFORMATION

Stewart Island Visitor Information Centre. ⊠ *Main Rd., Halfmoon Bay,* ☎ *03/219–1218.* ◷ *Weekdays 8–4:30.*

6 Adventure Vacations

Bicycling

Canoeing and Sea-Kayaking

Cross-Country Skiing

Diving

Fishing

Hiking–Tramping

Horse Trekking

Rafting

Sailing

By David
McGonigal,
Doug
Johansen, and
Jan Poole

YOU WILL MISS an important element of New Zealand if you don't explore the magnificent outdoors. The mountains and forests in this clean, green land are made for hiking and climbing, the rivers for rafting, and the low-traffic roads for bicycling. The rugged coastline looks wonderful from the deck of a small vessel or, even closer to the water, a sea kayak. And this is the country that invented jet-boating.

These activities are commonly split into soft and hard adventures. Hard adventure requires a substantial degree of physical participation, although you usually don't have to be perfectly fit; in a few cases, prior experience is a prerequisite. In soft adventures the destination rather than the means of travel is often what makes it an adventure. With most companies, the adventure guides' knowledge of flora and fauna—and love of the bush—is matched by a level of competence that ensures your safety even in dangerous situations. The safety record of adventure operators is very good. Be aware, however, that most adventure-tour operators require you to sign waivers absolving the company of responsibility in the event of an accident or a problem. Courts normally uphold such waivers except in cases of significant negligence.

You can always choose to travel without a guide, and the material in this chapter complements information in the rest of the book on what to do in different parts of the country. The advantage of going out with a guide is often educational. In unfamiliar territory—New Zealand is exotic if you haven't spent time in a rain forest or in the Southern Hemisphere—you'll learn more about what's around you by having a knowledgeable local by your side than you could traveling on your own.

Far more adventure-tour operators exist than can be listed in this chapter. Most are small and receive little publicity outside their local areas, so contact the relevant tourist office if you need more information in a specific area of interest.

Bicycling

Cycling is an excellent way to explore a small region, allowing you to cover more ground than on foot and observe far more than from the window of a car or bus. Riding down quiet country lanes is a great way to relax and get fit at the same time. Cycling rates as hard adventure because of the amount of exercise.

New Zealand's combination of spectacular scenery and quiet roads is ideal for cycling. Traditionally South Island, with its central alpine spine, has been more popular, but Auckland is where most people arrive, and North Island has enough curiosities—the hot mud pools of sulfurous Rotorua, the Waitomo Caves, and the old gold-mining area of the Coromandel Peninsula—to fill days. The average daily riding distance is about 60 kilometers (37 miles), and support vehicles are large enough to accommodate all riders and bikes if circumstances so demand. The rides in South Island extend from the ferry port of Picton to picturesque Queenstown, the center of a thriving adventure day-trip industry. New Zealand Pedaltours operates on both islands, with tours of 9–19 days. New Zealand Backroad Tours has South Island tours of 4–10 days.

Season: October–March.
Locations: Countrywide.
Cost: From $750 for four days to $1775 for eight days and $4,650 for 19 days, including accommodations, meals, and support vehicle. Bikes can be rented for about $17 a day.

Tour Operators: **Adventure Center** (⊠ 1311 63rd St., No. 200, Emeryville, CA 94608, ☎ 510/654–1879, 𝔽𝔸𝕏 510/654–4200); **New Zealand Pedaltours** (⊠ Box 37-575, Parnell, Auckland, ☎ 09/302–0968, 𝔽𝔸𝕏 09/302–0967); **New Zealand Backroad Cycle Tours** (⊠ Box 33–153, Christchurch, ☎ 03/332–1222, 𝔽𝔸𝕏 03/332–4030).

Canoeing and Sea-Kayaking

Unlike rafting, where much of the thrill comes from negotiating white water, commercial canoeing involves paddling down gentle stretches of river. The enjoyment comes from the relaxing pace, the passing scenery, and the constant, comforting murmur of the river. Canoeing is soft adventure, as is sea-kayaking, its oceanic equivalent, which is excellent in Northland, the Coromandel Peninsula, the top of South Island, Kaikoura, and as far south as Stewart Island.

The tour with Ocean River Adventure Company in the sheltered waters of Abel Tasman National Park provides a waterline view of a beautiful coastline. It allows you to explore otherwise inaccessible golden-sand beaches and remote islands and to meet fur seals on their home surf. When wind conditions permit, paddles give way to small sails, and the kayaks are propelled home by an onshore breeze. Southern Sea Ventures' nine-day trip includes seven days of kayaking on Doubtful Sound in the southwestern corner of South Island. This is a dramatic area of steep fjords and cascading waterfalls. Wide river mouths provide forest campsites. The residents of this remote wilderness are bottlenose dolphins and fur seals, which often swim alongside the kayaks.

Season: December–May.
Locations: Northland, the Coromandel Peninsula, Abel Tasman National Park, Marlborough Sounds, Kaikoura, Doubtful Sound, South Island.
Cost: Around $60 for a one-day tour, $450 for four-day tour.
Tour Operators: Bay of Islands Kayak Co. (⊠ Box 217, Russell, ☎ 𝔽𝔸𝕏 09/403–7672); **Fiordland Wilderness Experience** (⊠ 66 Quinton Dr., Te Anau, ☎ 03/249–7700, 𝔽𝔸𝕏 03/249–7700); **Mercury Bay Sea Kayaks** (⊠ 17 Arthur St., Whitianga, Coromandel Peninsula, ☎ 𝔽𝔸𝕏 07/866–2358); **Marlborough Sounds Adventure Company** (⊠ Boat Shed, London Quay, Picton, ☎ 03/573–6078, 𝔽𝔸𝕏 03/573–8827); **Ocean River Adventure Company** (⊠ Main Rd., Marahau Beach, R.D. 2, Motueka, ☎ 03/527–8266, 𝔽𝔸𝕏 03/527–8006); **Stewart Island Kayak Adventures** (⊠ Box 32, Stewart Island, ☎ 𝔽𝔸𝕏 03/219–1080).

Cross-Country Skiing

Cross-country skiing is arguably the best way to appreciate the winter landscape, and New Zealand's is spectacular. While crowds build up on groomed slopes, going cross-country you'll get away from the hordes and feel like you have the mountains to yourself. Cross-country skiing is hard adventure—the joy of leaving the first tracks across new snow and the pleasure afforded by the unique scenery of the snowfields is tempered by the fatigue that your arms and legs feel at the end of the day. Many tours are arranged so that skiers stay in lodges every night.

Mt. Cook and its attendant Murchison and Tasman glaciers offer wonderful ski touring, with terrains to suit all levels of skiers. Tours typically commence with a flight to the alpine hut that becomes your base; from there the group sets out each day for skiing and instruction.

Season: July–September.
Location: Mt. Cook.

Cost: $1,575 for seven days, including guide fees, accommodations, food, transport, and aircraft access.
Tour Operator: Alpine Recreation Canterbury (✉ Box 75, Lake Tekapo, 8770, ☎ 03/680–6736, ℻ 03/680–6765).

Diving

The Bay of Islands is perhaps New Zealand's best diving location. In the waters around Cape Brett, you can encounter moray eels, stingrays, grouper, and other marine life. Surface water temperatures rarely dip below 60° F. One of the highlights of Bay of Islands diving is the wreck of the Greenpeace vessel, *Rainbow Warrior,* which French agents sunk in the '80s. It is about two hours from Paihia by dive boat. From September through November, underwater visibility can be affected by a plankton bloom.

The clear waters around New Zealand make for good diving in other areas as well, such as the Coromandel Peninsula where the Mercury and Aldermen islands have interesting marine life. With Hahei Explorer, dive in the newly created marine reserve or right off the coast. Whangamata, with three islands just off the coast, also has very good diving.

Season: Year-round.
Location: Bay of Islands and the Coromandel Peninsula.
Cost: Around $135 per day.
Tour Operator: Hahei Explorer (✉ Hahei Beach Rd., Hahei, Coromandel Peninsula, ☎ 07/866–3532 or 025/424–306); **Paihia Dive Hire and Charter** (✉ Box 210, Paihia, ☎ 09/402–7551, ℻ 09/402–7110).

Fishing

Fishing means different things to different people. For some it is the simple joy of being away from it all in a remote area, at a stunning beach, or on a beautifully clear river. For others it's the adrenaline rush when a big one strikes and the reel starts screaming. Still others say it's just sitting on a wharf or a rock in the sun with a line in hand. The waters in and around New Zealand being some of the cleanest and clearest in the world only makes fishing here that much better.

Most harbor towns have reasonably priced fishing charters available. They are generally very good at finding fish, and most carry fishing gear you can use if you do not have your own. Inland areas usually have streams, rivers, or lakes with great trout fishing, where guides provide their knowledge of local conditions and techniques. And with the aid of a helicopter, heli-fishing can get you into very remote locations. It's a unique combination of the thrill of a chopper ride along with the great sensation of fishing from a spot that few people have ever seen.

There are a vast number of fishing guides throughout New Zealand, so don't hesitate to ask your innkeeper or the local information bureau about guides in areas not listed below. You'll find that Kiwis are friendly people, always happy to help out, and local recommendations are by rule trustworthy. Fishing in New Zealand is as good as it gets, so don't pass up the opportunity to drop a line in the water.

Saltwater Fishing: No country in the world is better suited than New Zealand for ocean fishing. The coastline has an incredible variety of locations, whether you like fishing off rocks, on reefs, surf beaches, islands, or harbors. Big-game fishing is very popular, and anglers have taken many world records over the years. All the big names are here—black, blue, and striped marlin, both yellowfin and bluefin tuna, and sharks like mako, thresher, hammerhead, and bronze whaler.

The most sought-after fish around North Island are snapper (sea bream), kingfish, grouper or hapuka, tarakihi, John Dory, trevally, mao-mao, and kahawai, to name a few. Many of these also occur around the top of South Island. Otherwise, South Island's main catches are blue cod, butterfish, hake, hoki, ling, moki, parrot fish, pigfish, and trumpeter, which are all excellent eating fish.

Perhaps the most famous angler to fish our waters was adventure novelist Zane Grey, who had his base on Urupukapuka Island in the Bay of Islands. On North Island, the top areas are the Bay of Islands, the nearby Poor Knights Islands, Whangaroa in Northland, the Coromandel Peninsula and its islands, and the Bay of Plenty and White Island off its coast.

Freshwater Fishing: Trout and salmon, natives in the northern hemisphere, were introduced into New Zealand in the 1860s and 1880s. Rainbow and brown trout in particular have thrived in the rivers and lakes, providing arguably the best trout fishing in the world. Salmon do not grow to the size that they do in their native habitat, but they still make for good fishing. New Zealanders have the early European settlers to thank for the right of free access to all water, as well as good commonsense regulation. You may have to cross private land to fish certain areas, but a courteous approach for permission is normally well received. To make it easier for the next angler, always treat a farmer's land and livestock with respect.

The three methods of catching trout allowed in New Zealand are fly fishing, spinning or threadlining, and trolling; in certain parts of South Island using small fish, insects, and worms as bait are also allowed. Deep trolling using leader lines and large capacity reels on short spinning rods is widely done on lakes Rotoma, Okataina, and Tarawera around Rotorua and on Lake Taupo, with the most popular lures being tobies, flatfish, and cobras. Streamer flies used for trolling are normally the smelt patterns: Taupo tiger, green smelt, ginger mick, Jack sprat, Parsons glory, and others. Flies, spoons, or wobblers used in conjunction with monofilament and light fly lines on either glass fly rods or spinning rods are popular on all the other lakes.

The lakes in the Rotorua district—Rotorua, Rotoiti, and Tarawera are the largest—produce some of the biggest, best conditioned rainbow trout in the world, which get to trophy size because of an excellent food supply, the absence of competition, and a careful and selective breeding program. In Lake Tarawera, fish from six to 10 pounds can be taken, especially in the autumn and winter, when bigger trout move into stream mouths before spawning.

The season around Rotorua runs from October 1 to June 30. In the period between April and June, just before the season closes, flies work very well on beautiful Lake Rotoiti. From December to March fly fishing is good around the stream mouths on Lake Rotorua. The two best areas are the Ngongotaha stream and the Kaituna River, using nymph, dry fly, and wet fly. Lake Rotorua remains open for fishing when the streams and rivers surrounding the lake are closed.

Lake Taupo and the surrounding rivers and streams are world renowned for rainbow trout—the lake has the largest yields of trout in New Zealand, an estimated 500 tons. Trolling on Taupo and fishing the rivers flowing into it with a guide are almost surefire ways of catching fish. Wind and weather on the lake, which can change quickly, will determine where you can fish, and going with local knowledge of the conditions on Taupo is essential. The streams and rivers flowing into the lake are open for fly fishing from October 1 to May 31. The lower reaches of the Tongariro, Tauranga-Taupo, and Waitahanui rivers, and the lake itself, remain open year-round.

Lake Waikaremoana in Urewera National Park southeast of Rotorua is arguably North Island's most scenic lake, and its fly fishing and trolling are excellent. River and stream trout fishing in North Island is also very good in the Taranaki, Hawke's Bay, and Manawatu provinces.

South Island has excellent rivers with very clear water. Some of them hardly ever see anglers, and that untouched quality is particularly satisfying. South Island's best areas for trout are Marlborough, Westland, Fiordland, Southland, and Otago.

The Canterbury has some productive waters for trout and salmon—along with the West Coast it is the only part of New Zealand where you can fish for salmon: the quinnat or Pacific chinook salmon introduced from North America. Anglers use large metal spoons and wobblers on long, strong rods with spinning outfits to fish the Waimakariri, Waitaki, Rakaia, Ashburton, and Rangitata rivers around Christchurch, often catching salmon of 20 to 30 pounds.

Trout fishing is normally tougher than in North Island, with trout being a little smaller on average. But occasionally huge browns are caught. You can catch brown and rainbow trout in South Island lakes using flies, or by wading and spinning around lake edges or at stream mouths.

Licenses: There are many different districts in New Zealand for which you need different licenses. For example, Rotorua is not in the same area as nearby Lake Taupo. So it pays to check at the local fish and tackle store to make sure you are fishing legally. Fees are approximately $50 per year, but at most tackle stores you can purchase daily or weekly licenses. They can also advise you about local conditions, lures, and methods.

Publications: *How to Catch Fish and Where,* by Bill Hohepa, and *New Zealand Fishing News Map Guide,* edited by Sam Mossman, both have good information on salt- and freshwater fishing throughout the country.

Season: Generally October through June in streams and rivers; year-round in lakes and at sea.

Location: Countrywide.

Cost: Big-game fishing: $800 to $1,200 per day, depending on location. Saltwater sportfishing: $30 to $50 per half day depending on how many are on the boat. Heli-fishing: $480 per person, per day. Trolling and fly-fishing for lake trout: from $65 per hour; on rivers and streams from $50 per hour.

North Island Saltwater Operators: Bream Bay Charters (Steve and Brenda Martinovich, ✉ 59 Bream Bay Dr., Ruakaka, Northland, ☎ 09/432–7484); **Christina** (Terry Lay, ✉ Hawke's Bay, ☎ 06/835–1222 or 06/835–0888); **Kerikeri Fish Charters** (Steve Butler, ✉ 23 Mission Rd., Kerikeri, Bay of Islands, ☎ 09/407–7165); **Land Based Fishing** (✉ Box 579, Kaitaia, Northland, ☎ 09/409–4592); *Ma Cherie* (John Baker, ✉ Bay of Plenty, ☎ 07/307–0015 or 025/940–324); **Mako Charters** (Graeme McIntosh, ✉ Russell Harbour, ☎ FAX 09/403–7770); **M.V. *Swansong*** (Tom Lovatt, ✉ Hawke's Bay, ☎ 06/836–6893 or 025/426–899); **M.V. *Taranui*** (✉ 17 Pacific Dr., Tairua, Coromandel Peninsula, ☎ 07/864–8511); **NZ Billfish Charters** (✉ Box 416, Paihia, Bay of Islands, ☎ 09/402–8380); **Outrigger Charters** (✉ 45 Williams Rd., Paihia, Bay of Islands, ☎ 09/402–6619, FAX 09/402–8111); *Predator* (Bruce and Ann Martin, ✉ Box 120, Paihia, ☎ FAX 09/405–9883); **Sea Spray Charters (N.Z.) Ltd.** (Daryl Edwards, ✉ Box 13060, Tauranga, Bay of Plenty, ☎ 07/572–4241 or 025/477–187); **Seeker** (Ross

Mossman, ✉ Hawke's Bay, ☎ 06/835–1397 or 025/442–082); **Te Ra–The Sun** (✉ Whangamata Harbor, Whangamata, Coromandel Peninsula, ☎ 07/865–8681); **Waipounamu Sport Fishing** (John Leins, ✉ Ferry Landing, Whitianga, Coromandel Peninsula, ☎ 07/866–2053); **Whangarei Deep Sea Anglers Club** (✉ Box 401, Whangarei, Northland, ☎ 09/434–3818, FAX 09/434–3755).

North Island Freshwater Operators: Mark Aspinall, (✉ Lake Taupo, ☎ 07/378–4453); **Bryan Colman** (✉ Rotorua, ☎ 07/348–7766); **Mark Draper Fishing & Outdoors** (Mark Draper and Diane Chilcott, ✉ Box 445, Opotiki, Bay of Plenty–East Cape, ☎ FAX 07/315–7434); **Clark Gregor** (✉ Rotorua, ☎ 07/347–1730, FAX 07/347–1732); **Belinda Hewiatt** (✉ Lake Taupo, ☎ 07/378–1471, FAX 07/377–2926); **Helicopter Line** (Lance Donnelly and Joanne Spencer, ✉ Box 3271, Auckland, ☎ 09/377–4406, FAX 09/377–4597); **Chris Jolly Fishing** (✉ Box 1020, Taupo, ☎ 07/378–0623, FAX 07/378–9458); **Lindsay Lyons** (✉ Rotorua, ☎ 07/357–4087); **Taupo Commercial Launchman's Association** (✉ Box 1386, Taupo, ☎ 07/378–3444, FAX 07/377–2926); **Dennis Ward** (✉ Rotorua, ☎ 07/357–4974).

South Island Saltwater Operators: The Agency Stewart Island (✉ Nicola Mckay, ✉ Elgin Terr., Halfmoon Bay, ☎ 03/219–1171, FAX 03/219–1151); **Haast Fish and Dive** (✉ Box 58, Haast, West Coast, ☎ 03/750–0004, FAX 03/750–0869); **Kenepuru Tours** (Gary and Ellen Orchard, ✉ Kenepuru Sounds, R.D. 2, Picton, Marlborough Sounds, ☎ FAX 03/573–4203); **Miss Portage Charters** (✉ Picton, Marlborough, ☎ 03/573–7883); **M.V. *Spirit of Golden Bay 2*** (✉ Golden Bay Charters, Box 206, Takaka, Golden Bay, ☎ FAX 03/525–9135); **Samara Gamefishing Company** (Richard Allen, ✉ Box 5589, Dunedin, Otago, ☎ 03/477–8863, FAX 03/447–7558); **Thorfinn Charters** (Bruce Story, ✉ Box 43, Halfmoon Bay, Stewart Island, ☎ FAX 03/219–1210).

South Island Freshwater Operators: Alpine Trophies (Dave Hetherington, ✉ Box 34, Fox Glacier, West Coast, ☎ 03/751–0856, FAX 03/751–0857); **Chris Jackson** (✉ Nelson Lakes district, ☎ 03/545-6416); **Fish Fiordland** (Mike Molineux, ✉ R.D. 1, Te Anau, Fiordland, ☎ 03/249–8070); **Fishing & Hunting Services** (Gerald Telford, ✉ 210 Brownston St., Wanaka, Central Otago, ☎ FAX 03/443–9257); **Kamahi Tours** (Bill Hayward, ✉ Box 59, Franz Josef, West Coast, ☎ 03/752–0793, FAX 03/752–0699); **Scott Murray** (✉ Nelson Lakes district, ☎ 03/545–9070); **Rakaia Salmon Safaris** (Geoff Scott and Ray Watts, ✉ The Cedars, R.D. 14, Rakaia, Canterbury, ☎ 03/302–7444, FAX 03/302–7220); **Southern Lakes Guide Service** (Murry and Margaret Knowles, ✉ Box 84, Te Anau, Fiordland, ☎ 03/249–7565, FAX 03/249–8004); **South Pacific Fishing Safaris** (Barry Neilson, ✉ Box 331, Queenstown, Central Otago, ☎ 03/442–9806); **Western Safaris** (Vern Thompson and Maggie Carlton, ✉ 34 McKerrow St., Te Anau, Fiordland, ☎ 03/249–7226); **Wilderness Fly Fishing N.Z.** (Stephen Couper, ✉ Box 149, Wakatipu, Queenstown, Central Otago, ☎ FAX 03/442–3589).

Hiking and Tramping

There isn't a better place on earth for hiking than New Zealand. Kiwis call it tramping. If you're looking for short hikes, you may want to head off on your own. For long treks, however, it can be a big help to go with a guide. The New Zealand wilderness is full of interesting flora and fauna that you'll glaze over if you're in the country for the first time. Many guides have a humorous streak that can be entertaining as well.

If it seems from the list below that every New Zealand company is involved in trekking, wait till you see the trails. They can be crowded enough to detract from the natural experience, particularly in the peak months of January and February. One advantage of a guided walk is that companies have their own tent camps or huts, with such luxuries as hot showers—and cooks. For the phobic, it's worth mentioning one very positive feature: New Zealand has no snakes or predatory animals, no poison ivy, poison oak, leeches, or ticks. In South island, especially on the West Coast, in Central Otago, and in Fiordland, be prepared for voracious sandflies, known to some as the state "bird." Bring along some New Zealand insect repellent—their repellent repels their insects.

One of the top areas in North Island for hiking and walking is the rugged Coromandel Peninsula, with 3,000-foot volcanic peaks clothed with semitropical rain forest and some of the best stands of the giant kauri tree, some of which are 45 feet around, and giant tree ferns. There is also gold mining history on the peninsula, and today the flicker of miners' lamps has given way to the steady green-blue light of millions of glowworms in the mines and the forest. Kiwi Dundee Adventures, Ltd., has a variety of hiking trips that cover all aspects of the peninsula, as well as New Zealand–wide eco-walking tours away from the usual tourist spots.

Tongariro National Park has hiking with a difference—on and around active volcanoes rising to heights of 10,000 feet, the highest elevation in North Island. It is a beautiful region of contrasts: of deserts, forests, lakes, mountains, and snow. (The 1995 ski season was literally a blast—snowfields were forced to close because of huge eruptions from Mount Ruapehu.) Sir Edmund Hillary Outdoor Pursuits Centre of New Zealand guides hikes and more strenuous tramping around Ruapehu, as well as other activities at Turangi.

The three- to six-day walks on the beaches and in the forests of the Marlborough Sounds' Queen Charlotte Walkway and in Abel Tasman National Park (in northern South Island) are very popular, relatively easy, and well suited to family groups: your pack is carried for you, and you stay in lodges. Karavan Adventure Treks has a series of unusual walks throughout South Island. One of the most appealing is a four-day trip in Nelson Lakes National Park, near the top of the island. For two nights your base is the Angelus Basin Hut, spectacularly located beside a beautiful mountain lake beneath towering crags. Another option is the Alpine Recreation Canterbury 15-day minibus tour of South Island, with two- to six-hour walks daily along the way. It provides an extensive and scenic cross section, visiting three World Heritage areas and six national parks specializing in natural history, but it misses the magic of completing a long single walk.

The most famous New Zealand walk, the Milford Track—a four-day trek through Fiordland National Park—covers a wide variety of terrains, from forests to high passes, lakes, a glowworm grotto, and the spectacle of Milford Sound itself. As the track is strictly one-way (from south to north), you rarely encounter other groups and so have the impression that your group is alone in the wild, despite the number of people along its length. Independent and escorted walkers stay in different huts about a half-day's walk apart. Escorted walkers' huts are serviced and very comfortable; independent walkers' huts are basic, with few facilities. There are other walks in the same area: the Hollyford Track (five days), the Greenstone Valley (three days), and the Routeburn Track (three days). Greenstone and Routeburn together form the Grand Traverse.

If you want to get serious with a mountain, Alpine Guides has a world-renowned seven-day course on the basics of mountain climbing around

Mt. Cook, the highest point in the New Zealand Alps. There is also a 10-day technical course for experienced climbers. New Zealand is the home of Sir Edmund Hillary, who, with Tenzing Norgay, made the first ascent of Mt. Everest. The country has a fine mountaineering tradition, and Alpine Guides is the nation's foremost training school.

Season: October–March for high-altitude walks, year-round for others.
Location: Coromandel Peninsula and Tongariro National Park in North Island, Mt. Cook and Fiordlands National Park in South Island.
Cost: One- to three-day hikes range from $120 to $895; $1,489 for the six-day escorted Milford Track walk; $2,500 for 13 days. The climbing school costs $1,575 for seven days, including aircraft access, meals, accommodations, and transportation.
Tour Operators: Abel Tasman National Park Enterprises (✉ Old Cederman House, Main Rd., Riwaka, Motueka R.D. 3, Nelson, ☎ 03/528–7801, FAX 03/528–6087); **Alpine Guides** (✉ Box 20, Mt. Cook, ☎ 03/435–1834, FAX 03/435–1898); **Alpine Recreation Canterbury** (✉ Box 75, Lake Tekapo, ☎ 03/680–6736, FAX 03/680–6765); **Hollyford Tourist and Travel Company** (✉ Box 94, Wakatipu, Otago, ☎ 03/442–3760, FAX 03/442–3761); **Karavan Adventure Treks** (✉ 117 Harris Crescent, Christchurch, ☎ FAX 03/352–2177); **Kiwi Dundee Adventures, Ltd.** (✉ Box 198, Whangamata, Coromandel Peninsula, ☎ 07/865–8809, FAX 07/865–8809); **Marlborough Sounds Adventure Company** (✉ Boat Shed, London Quay, Picton, ☎ 03/573–6078, FAX 03/573–8827); **Milford Track Office** (✉ Box 185, Te Anau, ☎ 03/249–7411, FAX 03/249–7590); **Routeburn Walk Ltd.** (✉ Box 568, Queenstown, ☎ 03/442–8200, 03/442–6072); **Sir Edmund Hillary Outdoor Pursuits Centre of New Zealand** (✉ Private Bag, Turangi, ☎ 07/386–5511, FAX 07/386–0204); **World Expeditions** (✉ 441 Kent St., 3rd floor, Sydney, NSW 2000, ☎ 02/264–3366, FAX 02/261–1974).

Horse Trekking

Operators all over New Zealand take people horseback riding along beaches, in native forests, on mountains, up rivers through pine plantations to all sorts of scenic delights. In North Island, Pakiri Beach and Horse Rides north of Auckland, Rangihau Ranch in the Coromandel Peninsula, and Taupo Horse Treks at Lake Taupo run trips from several hours to several days.

In South Island, the sweep of the Canterbury Plains around Christchurch—and the surrounding mountain ranges—creates some of New Zealand's most dramatic scenery. One of the best ways to explore the area in some detail is on horseback. Wild Country Equine Adventures has a variety of rides, from a half day with afternoon tea to a three-day excursion including meals and accommodations. Hurunui Horse Treks and Alpine Horse Safaris have similar rides from a couple of hours to a couple of days. They also offer 8- and 10-day horse treks into remote backcountry in groups of six or fewer, on which you'll stay in rustic huts (without electricity, showers, or flush toilets). The feeling of riding in so much open air, on horseback, watching the trail stretch to the distant horizon, is unparalleled. Terrain varies from dense scrub to open meadows and alpine passes. In the Nelson area at the top of South Island contact Stonehurst Farm Treks.

Season: October–March.
Location: Canterbury high country.
Cost: From $90 for a day to $1,200 for 10 days.
Tour Operators: Alpine Horse Safaris (✉ Waitohi Downs, Hawarden, N. Canterbury, ☎ FAX 03/314–4293); **Hurunui Horse Treks** (✉ Taihoa Downs, R.D. Hawarden, ☎ 03/314–4204, FAX 03/314–4204); **Stone-**

hurst Farm Treks (⊠ R.D. 1 Richmond, Nelson, ☎ 03/542−4121, FAX 03/542−3823); **Wild Country Equine Adventures** (⊠ Flock Hill, North Canterbury, ☎ 03/337−3872, FAX 03/332−8363).

Rafting

The exhilaration of sweeping down into the foam-filled jaws of a rapid is always tinged with fear—white-water rafting is, after all, rather like being tossed into a washing machine. While this sort of excitement appeals to many people, the attraction of rafting in New Zealand involves much more. As you drift downriver during the lulls between the white water, it's wonderful to sit back and watch the wilderness unfold, whether it's stately rimu or rata trees overhanging the stream or towering cliffs with rain-forest on the surrounding slopes. Rafting means camping by the river at night, drinking tea brewed over the fire, going to sleep with the sound of the stream in the background, and at dawn listening to the country's wonderful bird music. The juxtaposition of action and serenity gives rafting an enduring appeal that leads most who try it to seek out more rivers with more challenges. Rivers here are smaller and trickier than the ones used for commercial rafting in North America, and rafts usually hold only four to six people. Rafting companies provide all equipment—you only need clothing that won't be damaged by water (cameras are carried in waterproof barrels), a sleeping bag (in some cases), and sunscreen. Rafting qualifies as hard adventure. There are many rafting rivers on both islands of New Zealand.

In North Island, near Rotorua, the Rangitaiki offers exciting grade-4 rapids and some good scenery. Nearby, the Wairoa offers grade 5—the highest before a river becomes unraftable—and the Kaituna River has the highest raftable waterfall in the world: a 21-foot free-fall. The Tongariro River flows from between the active 10,000-foot volcanic peaks of Tongariro National Park into the southern end of Lake Taupo, New Zealand's largest lake. The Tongariro, as well as the mighty Motu River out toward the East Cape, is great for rafting.

In South Island, the great majority of activity centers on Queenstown. The most popular spot here is the upper reaches of the Shotover River beyond tortuous Skippers Canyon. In winter the put-in site for the Shotover is accessible only by helicopter, and wet suits are essential year-round, as the water is very cold. Some of the rapids are grade 5. The Rangitata River south of Christchurch is fed by an enormous catchment basin, and Rangitata Rafts claims that the river offers grade-5 excitement at all water levels.

To combine the thrill of white water with a wilderness experience, take the two-day Danes trip down the Landsborough River, which flows through Mt. Cook National Park past miles of virgin forest into some very exciting rapids.

Season: Mainly October–May.
Location: Rotorua, Taupo, the Canterbury, and Queenstown.
Cost: From $80 for one day to $500 for two days (with helicopter set-down), including all equipment (wet suits, helmets, footwear).
Tour Operators: Danes Shotover Rafts (⊠ Shotover and Camp Sts., Box 230, Queenstown, ☎ 03/442−7318, FAX 03/442−6749); **Kaituna Cascades** (☎ 07/357−5032); **Rangitata Rafts** (⊠ Peel Forest, R.D. 20, South Canterbury, ☎ 03/696−3735, FAX 03/696−3534).

Sailing

Varied coastline and splendid waters have made sailing extremely popular in New Zealand. Although the image of beautiful people sipping gin slings and watching the sunsets in the tropics may be a little ex- aggerated, your role as a passenger on a commercial sailing vessel can hardly be described as strenuous. You are likely to participate in the sailing of the vessel more than you would on a regular cruise line, but for all intents and purposes this is a soft adventure in paradise. The best sailing areas in New Zealand are undoubtedly from the Bay of Is- lands south to the Coromandel Peninsula and the Bay of Plenty. This coastline has many islands and a deeply indented shoreline, which makes for wonderful, sheltered sailing. You can take a piloted launch, or if you have the experience captain a sailboat yourself.

At the bottom of South Island, Southern Heritage Expeditions uses a Finnish-built, 236-foot, 19-cabin, ice-strengthened vessel, the *Akademik Shokalski,* to explore the islands of the Southern Ocean and beyond to Antarctica, with one short voyage each season (November to mid- March) through the deeply indented coastline of Fiordland. In all the areas visited on these programs humans have attempted to occupy the enviroment. At present, nature is winning it back in the presence of congregations of wildlife, such as the royal albatross, Hookers sea lion, elephant seals, and several penguin species (royal, yellow-eyed, king, gentoos, and emperor).

Season: Year-round.
Location: Bay of Islands in North Island, lower South Island.
Cost: Bay of Islands from $415 to $725 per night depending on the craft; Doubtful Sound from $1,300 for 5 days; Fiordland National Park area from $2,100 for 8 days; sub-Antarctic islands of Australia and New Zealand from $4,700 for 16 days.
Tour Operators: Moorings Yacht Charters (mailing address, ⊠ 23B Westhaven Dr., Westhaven, Auckland; mooring address, ⊠ the Jetty, Opua, Bay of Plenty, ☎ 09/402–7821; reservations in the U.S., ☎ 813/530–5424, FAX 813/530–9747); **Southern Heritage Expeditions** (⊠ Box 20-219, Christchurch, ☎ 03/359–7711, FAX 03/359–3311); **Stray- cat Day Sailing Charters** (⊠ Doves Bay Rd., Kerikeri, Bay of Islands, ☎ 09/407–7342 or 025/96–9944).

7 Portraits of New Zealand

New Zealand at a Glance: A Chronology

Flora and Fauna

Books and Videos

NEW ZEALAND AT A GLANCE: A CHRONOLOGY

c. AD 750   The first Polynesians arrive, settling mainly in South Island, where they find the moa, a flightless bird and an important food source, in abundance.

950   Kupe, the Polynesian voyager, names the country Aotearoa, "land of the long white cloud." He returns to his native Hawaiki, believed to be present-day French Polynesia.

1300s   A population explosion in Hawaiki triggers a wave of immigrants who quickly displace the archaic moa hunters.

1642   Abel Tasman of the Dutch East India Company becomes the first European to sight the land—he names his discovery Nieuw Zeeland. But after several of his crew are killed by Maoris, he sails away without landing.

1769   Captain James Cook becomes the first European to set foot on New Zealand. He claims it in the name of the British crown.

1790s   Sealers, whalers, and timber cutters arrive, plundering the natural wealth and introducing the Maoris to the musket, liquor, and influenza.

1814   The Reverend Samuel Marsden establishes the first mission station, but 11 years pass before the first convert is made.

1832   James Busby is appointed British Resident, charged with protecting the Maori people and fostering British trade.

1840   Captain William Hobson, representing the crown, and Maori chiefs sign the Treaty of Waitangi. In return for the peaceful possession of their land and the rights and privileges of British citizens, the chiefs recognize British sovereignty.

1840–1841   The New Zealand Company, an association of British entrepreneurs, establishes settlements at Wanganui, New Plymouth, Nelson, and Wellington.

1852   The British parliament passes the New Zealand Constitution Act, establishing limited self-government. The country's first gold strike occurs in the township of Coromandel in the Coromandel Peninsula.

1861   Gold is discovered in the river valleys of central Otago, west of Dunedin.

1860–1872   Maori grievances over loss of land trigger the Land Wars in North Island. The Maoris win some notable victories, but lack of unity ensures their ultimate defeat. Vast tracts of ancestral land are confiscated from rebel tribes.

1882   The first refrigerated cargo is dispatched to England, giving the country a new source of prosperity—sheep. A century later, there will be 20 sheep for every New Zealander.

1893   Under the Liberal government, New Zealand becomes the first country to give women the vote.

1914   New Zealand enters World War I.

1931   The Hawke's Bay earthquake kills 258 and levels the city of Napier.

1939 New Zealand enters World War II.

1950 New Zealand troops sail for Korea.

1965 Despite public disquiet, troops are sent to Vietnam.

1973 Britain joins the European Economic Community, and New Zealand's loss of this traditional export market is reflected in a crippling balance-of-payments deficit two years later.

1981 Violent antigovernment demonstrations erupt during a tour by a South African rugby team.

1985 The Greenpeace ship *Rainbow Warrior* is sunk by a mine in Auckland Harbour and a crewman is killed. Two of the French secret service agents responsible are arrested, jailed, and, shortly afterward, transferred to French custody—from which they are soon released.

Sir Paul Reeves is sworn in as the first Maori Governor-General. The newly elected Labour goverment of David Lange begins a process of drastic economic reform that includes dismembering the traditional welfare state. The resulting social unrest worsens when unemployment tops 10%.

Relations with the United States sour when the government bans visits by ships carrying nuclear weapons. The U.S. government responds by ejecting New Zealand from the ANZUS alliance.

1989 David Lange resigns as prime minister.

1990 The National Party replaces the Labour Party in government.

1993 The country votes for a major constitutional change, replacing the "first past the post" electoral system inherited from Britain with a "mixed member proportional" (MMP) system. The election sees the National Party clinging to power, beginning a term of forming coalitions to retain its majority.

1995 New Zealand's "Black Magic" boat wins the America's Cup yachting regatta. The country goes into party mode over the win, which signals not only sporting triumph but a "coming of age" technologically.

Mount Ruapehu in North Island's Tongariro National Park bubbles and sputters. Nobody is hurt, and the eruptions attract interested onlookers from around the world.

New Zealanders' abhorrence to all things nuclear comes to the fore again with major floating protests against France's resumed nuclear testing in the South Pacific.

1996 Ruapehu spews debris into the air, covering nearby towns with a few inches of ash and dusting cars with ash as far as 200 miles away.

FLORA AND FAUNA

FOR ALL OF ITS EONS OF isolation in the South Pacific, New Zealand has by no means quietly evolved since it separated from the Gondwanaland supercontinent around 100 million years ago. Parts of the country have retained some of the aspects of a forest that has gone uninterrupted for that long, but geological and climatological disturbances have been fairly regular occurrences. Ice has spread north from Antarctica on a few occasions, the most recent glacial retreat happening 10 to 15 thousand years ago. Those polar intrusions have affected plant life on South Island and much of North Island. Except for northern portions of North Island, which is interestingly enough the extent of the realm of the great kauri trees, much of the country's flora has recolonized areas taken by ice differently after each retreat, altering the character of the forests. Rashes of volcanic activity have also affected North Island, with carpets of ash settling here and there, sometimes in great abundance. The soils in these areas are as a result tremendously rich.

Animals on the islands were, at least until the arrival of humans, positively prehistoric. The only mammal was a tiny bat, and there were no predators—none, other than hunger. The birds that walked and flew included the 12-foot flightless moa, which the Maori hunted to extinction. Again bring to mind that for ages and ages these birds had no need to develop evasive behavior in order to stay alive. The Maori brought dogs and rats, and Europeans brought deer, possums, goats, trout, and other fauna, some of which were used for their pelts, others for sport. In almost all cases, the exotic fauna have done tremendous damage to the landscape. And the human presence itself—the first Maori arrived over 1,000 years ago—has dramatically altered the land. Early Maori farming practices involved burning, which reduced a portion of the forests. When Europeans settled the country, they brought sheep, cattle, and the grasses that their livestock needed to eat. And they cut forests for among other uses ship masts, for which the towering kauri served the purpose better than any other wood in the world and paid in numbers for that virtue.

None of this makes New Zealand forests any less unique, or any less enthralling. Some plants have adapted growth cycles in which the plant completely changes appearance—lancewood is an example—some of them two or three times until they reach maturity. As a result botanists at one time believed there to be two or three species where in fact there was only one. If you have never been in a rain forest, the sheer density of vegetation in various subtropical areas will be dazzling. There are species here that exist nowhere else on earth. And keep in mind that one-fifth of the country is set aside as parkland. In those wild woods, you will still find no predators, and native species are alive and well, in many cases making comebacks very dramatic indeed.

Here is a short list of plants and animals that you might encounter in New Zealand.

Bell bird. The New Zealand forest has a different sound than any other, and it's this bird and one other that make it so unique. It's a welcoming, exotic, chiming song.

It's a lot easier to get into the grips of a **bush lawyer** plant than out of them. It is a thorny, viney thing that grows in dense forest, climbing in and out of whatever it chooses.

The odd plant clumps fastened to the sides of trees throughout forests are **epiphytes,** not parasites. They grow on the trees, but make their own living off of water and other airborne particles. Some are orchids, a marvelous sight if you catch them in bloom.

The abundance of **ferns** may be what you most readily associate with the New Zealand bush. Two of the most magnificent are the mamaku and the ponga. The former also goes by the English name black tree fern, and it is the one that grows up to sixty feet tall and is found countrywide, with the exception of the east coast of South Island. The Maori used to cook and eat parts of the plant that are said to taste a bit like applesauce. The ponga is shorter than the mamaku, reaching a height of thirty feet. Its English name, silver tree fern, comes from the color of the undersides of the fronds. Their silvery whiteness illuminates darker parts of the bush. The ponga is the ferny emblem of New Zealand's international sports teams and Air New Zealand.

The towering **kahikatea** (ka-*hee*-ka-*tee*-ah) is the tallest tree in the country, reaching as high as 200 feet with its slender and elegant profile. A mature tree bears a tremendous amount of berries, which Maori climbers used to ascend 80 branchless feet and more to harvest. These days wood pigeons are the prime consumers of the fruit.

There are still **kauri** trees in Northland and the Coromandel Peninsula that are as many as 1,500 years old, which means that their girth is at least 30 feet, their height upwards of 150 feet. The lower trunks of the trees are branchless, on an old tree branches begin over 50 feet above the ground. Lumberjacks in the 1800s spared some of these giants, and their presence is awesome. These, like so many other native trees, are slow growers—a young 80-year-old will stand only 30 feet tall. Kauri gum was another valuable item. It doesn't rot, so specimens of all ages were usable to make varnish and paint. It is now illegal to cut down a kauri, and as a result the trees are making a solid comeback.

Much is said of the formidable South Island **kea** (kee-ah), a mountain parrot, which, because it has been accused of killing sheep, has in the last century barely escaped extinction. Its numbers are significant today, much to the dismay of campers and anyone who lives under a tin roof. Keas love to play, which means anything from ripping tents to shreds to clattering around on metal roofs at all hours to peeling out the rubber gaskets around car windows. They are smart birds, smart enough, perhaps, to delight in taking revenge on those who tried to wipe them out. Observe their behavior keenly, it may be the only way to maintain a sense of humor if harassed.

Don't bet on seeing a **kiwi** in the wild. These nocturnal, bush-loving birds are scarce and shy, their numbers having dwindled with the felling of forests over the last 150 years. Along with the now-extinct giant moa and other species, the kiwi is one of the remarkable New Zealand na-

tives that live nowhere else on earth. If you're keen on seeing one in the feather, plan a trip to Stewart Island and hire a guide to take you on a search, or stop at a wildlife park.

The **manuka** is a small tree shrub found throughout the country in tough impenetrable thickets. Early settlers made a fair tea from the plant until something tastier came along. The tea tree's white or rosy blossoms attract bees in profusion, and they in turn produce the popular, strong-tasting manuka honey that you can find in stores just about everywhere.

The **nikau palm** is one of the country's most exotic-looking trees, growing to a height of about 30 feet. The Maori used different parts of the leaves both for food and for thatch in shelters.

Phormium tenax, also called New Zealand flax, even though it isn't a true flax, has been useful as cordage in traditional and contemporary weaving. It favors damp areas and hillsides. Its thick, spiky, dark green leaves originate from a central saddle and can grow to six feet. The telltale flower stalk can reach to fifteen feet and bears dark red flowers. A number of varieties are ornamental and are very popular in New Zealand gardens.

The **pohutukawa** (po-*hoo*-too-*ka*-wa) tree is a sight both for its gnarly roots that like watery places and its red blossoms, which burst forth toward the end of December—hence its Kiwi name: New Zealand's Christmas tree.

Possums. Currently about 80 million in number, this introduced species is gobbling up New Zealand forests. Try as they may to get rid of them, Kiwis are having a rough go with the tree-dwellers. Their nickname, squash 'ems, comes from the number you see splayed out on roads throughout the country.

Pukeka (poo-*keh*-ka). Effectively the New Zealand chicken, this bird kicks around on farms and roadsides often enough that you're likely to see plenty of them. They're blue, with a red bill, and they stand about 15 inches tall.

Rangiora (rang-ee-*ohr*-ah). You'll get to know this plant better if you remember it as "bushman's friend"—its soft, silvery underside is the forest's best tissue for your underside.

There are a couple of species of **rata.** The northern rata is a parasite, climbing a host tree and eventually cutting off its light and water supplies. The rata and its host wage a long-term struggle, and the rata doesn't always win. The southern rata is a free-standing tree, yielding beautiful red lumber. Rata flowers are a pretty red themselves, resembling the pohutukawa tree's blooms but coming out about a month earlier in November.

If you're in the country in November, you'll see at first more evidence of the **re-warewa** (*re*-wa-*re*-wa) tree in its fallen blossoms on the ground. They are tightly woven magenta bottle-brushlike flowers, with touches of chartreuse and black, that are some of the most enchanting in the country, if in part for their uniqueness.

One of those ingenious New Zealand plants that goes through three stages of being on its way to maturity, the **rimu** red pine is a valuable source of timber. It spends its first stage in life as a delicate treelet with pale green, weeping branches that look something like an upright moss. It then turns itself into a conical shape before finishing its growth as a soaring, 100-plus-foot wonder with a branchless trunk and a rounded head. Charcoal from rimu was used in traditional Maori tattooing.

Supplejack vines just hang about in the forest, so dense in places that they could make passage next to impossible. You'll often find that their soft, edible tips have been nipped off by the teeth of wild goats that Pakeha (Europeans) introduced. Believe it or not, this is a member of the lily family.

Along with the bell bird, the **tui** is the *chanteuse extraordinaire* that fills Aotearoa's woods with its magically clear melodies. You may have never thought of birds as actually singing, but you certainly will when you hear a tui.

Wekas (weh-kah) are funny birds. They can appear to be oblivious to what's going on around them as they walk about pecking at this or that, looking bemused. They are flightless rails, and they'll steal your food if you're camping, so hide it away. Generally speaking, they're pleasant to have around, particularly if you're looking for some entertainment.

Wood pigeon. You'll have no trouble figuring out that this is a pigeon, but your jaw'll drop at the bird's size. They're beautiful birds.

—Stephen Wolf and Barbara Blechman

BOOKS AND VIDEOS

Books

Because of the limited availability of many first-rate books on New Zealand outside the country, there is only so much that you'll be able to read before you go. So leave room in your suitcase for pickup reading once you arrive, and bring something home to keep your trip lingering longer. One caveat: Because of economies of scale in the New Zealand publishing industry, books tend to be expensive. That's one reason to do some secondhand shopping; the other is the stores' usually knowledgeable staff, who can help with recommendations.

History. *The Oxford Illustrated History of New Zealand,* edited by Keith Sinclair, provides a comprehensive and highly readable account of the country's social, political, cultural, and economic evolution from the earliest Maori settlements and their world view to 1989. *The Colonial New Zealand Wars,* by Tim Ryan and Bill Parham, is a vivid history of the Maori-British battles. Lavishly illustrated with photographs of colonial infantry and drawings of Maori hill forts, flags, and weapons, the book makes far more compelling reading than the dry military history suggested by the title. J. C. Beaglehole's *The Discovery of New Zealand* is an authoritative and scholarly analysis of the voyages of discovery, from the first Polynesians to the Europeans of the late 18th century.

Fiction. New Zealand's best known novelist is **Katherine Mansfield** (1888–1923), whose early stories were set in and around the city of Wellington, her birthplace. Reading her journals will give you a sense of her passionate romantic side, and as much as she disliked the small-minded provincial qualities of New Zealand, she loved the country deeply.

New Zealand's most distinguished living writer is **Janet Frame.** Her works are numerous, from novels such as her successful *The Carpathians* to a three-part autobiography, which is a lyrical evocation of growing up in small-town New Zealand in the 1920s and 1930s, and of the gradual awakening of a writer of great courage. Kiwi filmmaker Jane Campion adapted the middle of it for the screen into *An Angel at My Table.* **Maurice Gee** is another distinguished novelist. His *Plumb* won the James Tait prize for the best novel in Britain when it was published. *Plumb* reaches back to the early 20th century for its story of a renegade parson and his battle with Old-World moral pieties. One particularly compelling scene is set in a mining town, where Plumb happens to be the man to preside over the deathbed of a notorious murderer.

Two of the finest and most exciting writers at work in the country today are **Patricia Grace** and **Witi Ihimaera,** Maori whose story collections and novels are on a par with the best fiction in the U.K. and the States. Grace's stories are beautifully and fluidly related, very much from inside her characters, taking everyday feelings and expanding them into something almost timeless. Ihimaera (ee-hee-may-ra) also uses very clear prose and Maori experience. His early novel *Tangi* opens with the death of a father and moves through the 22-year-old son's experience of loss and innocence to his acceptance of his role as a man. Maori elements of the story are fascinating both culturally and emotionally. The most internationally celebrated work of fiction to come from New Zealand in recent years is **Keri Hulme**'s *The Bone People,* winner of the Booker McConnell Prize in 1985. Set on the isolated west coast of the South Island, this challenging, vital novel weaves Polynesian myth with Christian symbolism and the powerful sense of place that characterizes modern Maori writing. More recently, Alan Duff's *Once Were Warriors* is a frank, uncompromising, and ultimately transcendent look at urban Maori society. Both the novel and the film were real sensations in New Zealand.

Garden Guides. If you are serious about visiting gardens while in New Zealand, any of the books listed below would be helpful. These are not typically stocked in U.S. bookstores, so make a well-supplied store one of your first stops when you arrive. Hundreds of gardens are listed in Alison McRae's *Garden's to Visit in New Zealand* and Beverly Bridge's *Register of New Zealand Private Gardens Open to the*

Public, Vol 2. They both give descriptions of gardens and list addresses, telephone numbers, and visiting times. Two other books are more limited in providing information but offer glossy photographs and make good souvenirs: Julian Matthews and Gil Hanly's *New Zealand Town and Country Gardens* and Premier Books's *Glorious New Zealand Gardens.* A superb monthly magazine, *New Zealand Gardener,* highlights several of the country's gardens in each issue. It is available at newspaper shops and bookstores countrywide.

Specialized Guidebooks. Strictly for wine lovers, *The Wines and Vineyards of New Zealand,* by Michael Cooper, is an exhaustive evaluation in words and pictures of every vineyard in the country. For travelers who plan to make hiking a major component of their vacations, *Tramping in New Zealand,* published by Lonely Planet, is an invaluable guide.

Illustrated Books. *Salute to New Zealand,* edited by Sandra Coney, is a coffee-table book that intersperses lavish photographs with chapters by some of the country's finest contemporary writers. *Wild New Zealand,* published by Reader's Digest, is a pictorial account of the country's landscape, flora, and fauna, supplemented by an informative text with such a wealth of detail that it turns the sensory experience of the landscape into a cerebral one.

Videos

New Zealand's film industry has had a relatively small output, but the quality of its films has been quite high. Jane Campion's *The Piano* (1993) is a prime example, as are her earlier *An Angel at My Table* (1990) and *Sweetie* (1988), made in Australia. Roger Donaldson's 1977 thriller *Sleeping Dogs* was the first New Zealand film released in the United States, followed by the equally worthy *Smash Palace* (1982). The tough, urban portrayal of *Once Were Warriors* (1995) is one of the most recent to make it across the Pacific. Its portrait of urban Maori life, unfortunately, makes New Zealand look a little too much like L.A.

INDEX

NOTES

CNN ✈
Airport Network

Your
Window
To The
World
While You're
On The
Road

Keep in touch when you're traveling. Before you take off, tune in to CNN Airport Network. Now available in major airports across America, CNN Airport Network provides nonstop news, sports, business, weather and lifestyle programming. Both domestic and international. All piloted by the top-flight global resources of CNN. All up-to-the minute reporting. And just for travelers, CNN Airport Network features two daily Fodor's specials. "Travel Fact" provides enlightening, useful travel trivia, while "What's Happening" covers upcoming events in major cities worldwide. So why be bored waiting to board? TIME FLIES WHEN YOU'RE WATCHING THE WORLD THROUGH THE WINDOW OF CNN AIRPORT NETWORK!

WHEREVER YOU TRAVEL, *H*ELP IS NEVER FAR AWAY.

From planning your trip to providing travel assistance along the way, American Express® Travel Service Offices are always there to help.

New Zealand

American Express Travel Service
101 Queen Street
Auckland
9/379-8243

Guthrey Travel (R)
126 Cashel Street
The Guthrey Centre
Christchurch
3/379-3560

Destinations Travel (R)
485 Papanui Road
Papanui (Christchurch)
3/352-2612

Calder and Lawson Travel Ltd. (R)
455 Grey Street
North Island
Hamilton East
71/856-9009

Nelson Holiday Shoppe (R)
Cnr. Haven Rd. and Rutherford St.
Nelson
3/548-9079

Pukekohe Travel (R)
89 King Street
Pukekohe
9/237-1049

Blackmores Galaxy United Travel (R)
411 Tutanekai Street
Rotorua
7/347-9444

Small World Travel (R)
23 Rathbone Street
Whangarei
9/438-2939

http://www.americanexpress.com/travel